THE FRIENDS OF GOD AND THE WORK OF THE SPIRIT

AN ILLUSTRATED BOOK OF THE HOURS FOR THE 21ST CENTURY

BY TIM REEVE

The author of *The Way to the Kingdom*,
a copy of which was given to Pope John-Paul II by the Archbishop of Canterbury in 1992
as the official gift of the Church of England.

ILLUSTRATED BY DIANA CATCHPOLE FROM DESIGNS BY THE AUTHOR

Ferard Reeve Publishing

Greenfields Farmhouse, Kings Barn Lane,
Steyning, W. Sussex BN44 3YG
(01903) 813 581

Copyright © 2005 Ferard Reeve Publishing

Author: Tim Reeve
Editor: Patrick Reeve
Proof Reader: Will Steeds
Publisher: Ferard Reeve Publishing Limited
Illustrator: Diane Catchpole
Designer: Alison Gardner
Production: Robert Paulley

A catalogue record of this book is available from the
British Library

Printed and hand finished in China
by WKT Company Limited

ISBN 0 9517017-2-X

'GIVE THANKS TO GOD'

The Chaplain's badge and motto of the Worshipful Company of Girdlers of the City of London, founded in 1327.
It illustrates St Lawrence, who is the Company's patron saint

The book is dedicated to the Company by kind permission of the Master and Court

CONTENTS

PROLOGUE AND ACKNOWLEDGEMENTS

This is a book that I have long wanted to read myself! Its subject is a quest for evidence of how the Holy Spirit, The Spirit of God, works in the world. However no one has written about this subject in a way that answers the questions that it raises in my mind. I therefore felt compelled to attempt to explore the subject myself and to seek the advice of my clerical friends.

I approach the subject by studying the lives and works of hundreds of Christian heroes and heroines over the past 2,000 years. I call the book *The Friends of God*, a title that I borrowed from *The History of the Franks*, written by Bishop St Gregory of Tours. He called those who had given their lives to God *Amici Domini*, a definition that he may have taken from Christ's words in St John's Gospel: '*You are my friends if you do what I command*' (John 15.14). This has enabled me to cover a broad spectrum of believers, whether Roman Catholic or non-Catholic.

The book is divided into seven parts. Part I is 'An Introduction to the Holy Spirit'. This is an attempt to illustrate the way the Holy Spirit works within all of us. Part II of the book, 'The Spiritual Symbols of the Four Gospels', examines the authorship, authenticity and dating of the gospels and outlines some of the questions they and the other New Testament writings raise. Part III describes the lives of the Apostles and Evangelists. Part IV shows the importance of St Paul's letters which mention the Holy Spirit more than 60 times. Part V is a short historical summary to bridge the period between the Apostolic Age until the year 451. Part VI is 'An Illustrated Calendar of Saints'. This records the lives briefly of 750 saints. Its main purpose is to try and trace how the Holy Spirit had inspired them, how they had interpreted the gospel message and where, if at all, they had erred.

Part VII is called 'The Unquenchable Spirit, 1300–2000'. This covers the work of the Spirit from 1300, when the Papacy began to lose its influence in international affairs, until our own times. This account ends with a short set of Conclusions to sum up the grounds for belief in the Spirit and to consider the future for this faith in a rapidly changing world.

I have had the guidance of the Right Revd Bishop Simon Barrington-Ward, DD. Ever since he was Bishop of Coventry until now, as a Fellow of Magdalene College, Cambridge, he has given me invaluable tutorials and written me many letters on my draft texts, filled with generous advice and encouragement. It is impossible for me to thank him enough for this and also for allowing me to quote some of his words. One of his most helpful sayings – '*The great saints are those who bring about important changes*' – has been my criterion for selecting certain saints at the end of each monthly Calendar for special study. Bishop Simon has also encouraged me to publish the book, saying: '*Nothing could make a greater theme than this attempt to show the Spirit at work; I rejoice in all that this book is going to do for so many*'.

I owe another great debt of gratitude for his advice to my friend General Hervé Burin des Roziers, Legion d'Honneur, Croix de Guerre. He lectures on historical aspects of the faith to scholars and students in Paris. He introduced me to the Abbey of St Robert at La Chaise Dieu about 100km south-east of Clermont-Ferrand. The Abbey is famous for its magnificent set of fourteenth-century Flemish tapestries of '*Le Bible des Pauvres*'. These were designed to show how much that was foretold in the Old Testament was fulfilled in the New. My tours with him in a land where more towns and villages are named after saints or 'Ste

Marie' than in any other country, taught me why France was rightly given the title of *'La Première Fille de l'Église'*. She was given this following the conversion to Christianity of the Frankish King Clovis at the end of the fifth century.

I was fortunate in being introduced to the mystery of the Holy Spirit by my late friend the Revd Roy Boff, former vicar of our parish church of St Andrew's in Steyning, who gave me permission to quote his moving words on his experience on the working of the Spirit during his 38 years' ministry. My understanding of the Holy Spirit was also helped by my friend the late Revd Basil Watson, MA OBE RN, former Naval Chaplain at Greenwich, who became Vicar of St Lawrence Jewry and Chaplain to the Worshipful Company of Girdlers in the City of London, of which I was Master in 1994–95. He told me that *'if you can understand St Paul, you can understand Christianity'*.

I am also grateful for the way Basil's successor at St Lawrence Jewry and as chaplain to the Girdlers, the Revd Prebendary David Burgess, a Chaplain Royal, has allowed me to describe how private talks after his lunchtime services and organ recitals have helped him to relieve many who are suffering from the stress of working in today's busiest financial centre. Thus contrary to the belief of many, the Church today can still, as the great third-century theologian Origen described, *'be the school of souls'*.

Origen, who died in 254 from the effect of the tortures he had suffered during the persecution of the Emperor Decius, was the theologian whose works had inspired the Early Greek Fathers, especially St Basil the Great and his brother St Gregory of Nyssa. They and the Greek Church regarded Origen as a saint, but his sainthood was revoked by the Emperor Justinian I quite unjustly 300 years after his death. Modern theologians now study Origen's work more than that of any other Early Father. I have therefore included a summary of his works at the end of the Calendar for January which includes St Basil's feast-day.

I was enabled to do this and to quote from the works of all the Early Fathers because my son-in-law James' uncle, the late Revd Tom Selwyn-Smith, generously gave me his set of four volumes of *The Dictionary of Christian Biography, Literature, Sects and Doctrines of the First Eight Centuries*, published by John Murray in 1877–87. It was through these that I discovered two important fifth-century saints, St Vincent of Lerins and Saint Isidore of Pelusium, who are quite undeservedly omitted from all popular English dictionaries of saints.

St Victor, as the text at the end of the May Calendar shows, taught the Church in the fifth century how there should be progress in religion as new discoveries were made. The Church failed to remember this for over 1,500 years, during which it tried the great astronomers Giordano Bruno and Galileo for alleged heresy, burning Bruno and forcing Galileo to deny that the earth and planets rotated round the sun.

St Isidore was the tutor of St Cyril of Alexandria who, as will be seen in the February and June Calendars, was a stern critic of Cyril. His words build up a strong case to prove how Cyril's Egyptian nationalist ambitions caused serious and lasting splits in the Eastern Church. Their differences were so great that after studying them during his travels, Muhammad decided to reject Christianity as the faith in the one God for his Arab people. He gave as his reason in the Koran that *'the sects cannot agree on the nature of the God they worship'*. It was through this that Christianity lost all Arabia, Macedonia, Syria, Egypt, North

Africa and most of Asia Minor to Islam. It can be seen from this that my search for evidence of the working of the Spirit in history is far from producing a hagiography. The fact is that until the Reformation, and even until modern times, though there were still many more great saints, the rigid interpretation of the great spiritual mysteries drove the Catholic Church into cul-de-sacs from which there was no exit without admitting that it had erred.

I have tried to preserve the sense of mystery by making 80 rough drawings of the saints and others in action, which Diana Catchpole has converted into designs for altar-pieces or church tapestries in the style used for illustrating Books of Hours in the middle ages. Those books assisted people in private study during the eight canonical hours for holy offices, from Matins and Lauds through to Vespers and Compline. I am grateful to her for her latest work and I am pleased that many who saw her illustrations in my first book and heard that I was working on a new book, have asked me whether she was to illustrate this one.

I have tried in the last quarter of this book to bring the story of the working of the Spirit up to modern times. I am therefore very grateful for the permission I have received to quote the words of the Right Revd Lord Carey on prayer when he was Archbishop of Canterbury and also for his letter to me in which he wrote of my plan for the book: 'What a terrific idea'. The late Right Revd Hugh Montefiore, former Bishop of Birmingham, allowed me to quote the story in his autobiography O God, What Next? of his receiving a vision of Jesus and hearing him say: 'Follow me', when he was a Jewish schoolboy at Rugby and knew nothing about Christ. He was so moved by this that he became a Christian and had himself baptised.

I also describe how the senior Russian Orthodox archbishop in Western Europe, Metropolitan Anthony of Sourozh, had a vision of Jesus when he was still an unbeliever in Paris in 1934 and immediately became converted to Christianity. I quote the description of this in the obituary for him in the Daily Telegraph for 6 August 2003 and I am grateful to the Editor for his permission to do so. I also thank the editor of The Times, and the Trustees of Bernard Levin for allowing me to quote from Mr Levin's interview with the-then Archbishop of Canterbury, Robert Runcie, which was reported in The Times on 30 March 1987.

It was in this article that in answer to the question as to whether the falling numbers in the church pews meant that the Churches had failed, the Archbishop replied that 'Saints have been nurtured in the parishes' and 'Far more people than you may imagine in comparison with the numbers in the pews are motivated by Christian values'. He then gave examples of this, which are included in the full text in section 10 of Part VII of this book, on 'The Unquenchable Spirit'. I must also thank the Editors of The Oxford Companion to Christian Thought for allowing me to quote their article on Origen which says that 'Only St Thomas Aquinas and St Augustine of Hippo are his peers as a theologian'.

Also I must thank the Editor of The Spectator for allowing me to quote in my 'Conclusions' the review in his edition for 11 September 2004 of the latest book The Case for Religion by the last Regius Professor of Divinity at Oxford, Professor Keith Ward. The reviewer, Mary Wakefield, writes that the author had told her that 'religious experience is more common than we realise . . . I've never met a world-class physicist who doesn't think that there's more to the universe than just atoms bumping together. Something mind-like is at work, some *intelligence'*. I also describe how belief in this and in the strengthening power of the Spirit which can be seen in the wartime experiences of two great clergymen, an admiral, two army padres and myself. The Spirit exists in all of us and gives us a capacity to respond.

This belief is the cornerstone on which this book and the whole case for religious belief depends. I am therefore grateful to our much-loved Vicar, Dr Paul Rampton, D. Phil, M. Theo, for agreeing with my words and also for all his help at so many crucial points in my text. I have also been fortunate in having the advice of so many friends, especially the Revd His Honour Christopher Lea, MC, now a non-stipendiary priest at Mortimer in Berkshire, who even quoted one of my stories about St Teresa of Avila in his sermon on All Saints' Day.

Finally I could not have finished this book without the love and support of my artist and sculptress wife Penelope, the encouragement of my children and for the the way my merchant banker son Patrick has edited the text. He has also found the excellent Alison Gardner to do the page design and layout of the book and the patient and experienced Robert Paulley to organise the printing and binding. They have produced a work which, I hope, will be a family treasure and a key that will open many doors through which readers can explore further.

TIM REEVE, Steyning, Sussex, June 2005

PART ONE

AN INTRODUCTION TO THE HOLY SPIRIT

The Pilgrims' badge

Sketches in top two rows of cave-drawings in France and in the bottom row from Australian caves, from 12,000–25,000 years ago

AN INTRODUCTION TO THE HOLY SPIRIT

I began my search for evidence of the human soul and of the existence of a spiritual dimension outside normal human senses, by looking for the earliest-known examples of human creative activity. Before writing was invented, human beings could draw. They could not only draw, but as the sketches on the opposite page show, they could draw exquisitely as early as a 1,000 generations before the birth of Christ.

The top two rows of the animal sketches were copied from wall-paintings in France that were painted as early as 20,000 years ago. They have a grace and liveliness, achieved in a few lines, that remind one of some of the drawings by the twentieth-century artist Picasso (1881–1973). The scenes of dancing figures and rituals depicted below were drawn about 12,000 years ago in the caves in the Bradshaw Hills of Northern Australia. Some of these dancing figures are like the silhouettes painted by Henri Matisse (1887–1985). Cave and rock drawings have also been found in Spain, the Sahara and in Central and Southern Africa.

These drawings are of such high quality that they must have been preceded by a long period of artistic development. Carbon dating has proved that cave paintings of similar subjects and in the same style were painted 3,000 years apart. This suggests that the earliest cave artists could have been at work shortly after Homo Sapiens appeared about 100,000 years, or 1,000 generations ago.

We can only guess at the purpose of these drawings. The animal scenes may have been part of some hunting ritual, while those of the dancing figures suggest some form of worship. They all show that the artists had a well-developed sense of beauty, which is a spiritual dimension. Therefore these earliest ancestors of ours must have had an innate

spiritual sense, a spirit that made them aware of the mysterious powers that seemed to control the movements of the stars, the changing seasons, birth, life and death. The purpose of the pictures may have been religious, in which case the cave artists had something in common with all artists. For example the French artist and humanist Marc Chagall (1887–1985) once wrote that *'Art, painting, is religious by nature, like everything that is creative'*. Chagall's contemporary, the painter Matisse, meanwhile, wrote that it was not landscapes or still-life that interested him, but *'the human figure. It is this which permits me to express my religious awe towards life.'*

This spiritual awareness led our early ancestors to pray and to offer burnt sacrifices to the ultimate reality whom they came to believe in as a divine spirit. It was this sense of beauty that led St Augustine of Hippo (354–430), the great theologian of the West, to exclaim in his *Confessions* after his conversion: *'Late have I loved thee, O Beauty'*. Even today the Greek Orthodox Church refers to God as 'Supreme Beauty'.

I am therefore tempted to claim that this inner spirit was given to our race of Homo Sapiens so that God could communicate with us through his Spirit. However we cannot prove this, though spiritual experiences have been recorded throughout history. These may only be considered as circumstantial evidence, but there are so many of them that they do suggest that the Spirit is at work and therefore that God has a purpose for us.

The slow way that art developed in the caves matches the slowness with which God acts in history to enlighten the human mind. The fourth-century Patriarch of Constantinople, St Gregory of Nazianzus, explained this in a sermon in 381: *'the Spirit guides by enlightening us in proportion to our capacity to understand'*. St Paul also told the Corinthians of the difference between what we can understand on earth and the truth we shall find in heaven: *'Now I know in part; then I shall understand fully, even as I am understood'* (I Corinthians 12.12).

We need also to remember that the Holy Spirit of the New Testament is the same in essence as the Spirit of God in the Old Testament. In the latter the Spirit is variously described as the *'Breath'*, *'Wind'*, *'Will'* and *'Wisdom'* of God. In the New Testament Jesus also described the Spirit as being like the wind. He told Nicodemus: *'The wind blows where it wills, and you hear the sound of it, but you do not know whence it comes or whither it goes'* (John 3.8). Later, at the supper described by St John, Jesus promised that after his death *'the Counsellor, the Holy Spirit, whom the Father will send in my name, he will teach you all things, and bring to your remembrance all that I have said to you'* (John 14.26). Also Jesus said of the Spirit *'He will convince the world concerning sin and righteousness and judgement'* (John 16.7).

Jesus' contemporary, the Alexandrian Jewish theologian Philo (25BC–40AD), taught that the Spirit of God was identical to the *Logos* or 'Word of God' identified by Plato and the Greek philosophers. It was this that caused the philosopher and Christian teacher St Justin Martyr, who was beheaded for his faith in 165, to say that those philosophers and also the Jewish Prophets, were *'Christians before Christ'*. St John records Jesus as saying that *'God is Spirit'* (John 4.4) and St Paul wrote that *'the Lord is Spirit'* (II Corinthians 3.17), thus providing the inspiration for the doctrine that God is a Trinity of Three Persons: Father, Son and Holy Spirit.

The Holy Spirit is the one Person of our Trinitarian God who is always present in the world, yet he cannot be grasped any more than we can hold a handful of running water or catch a capful of wind. St Paul wrote reassuringly to the Romans that *'the Spirit dwells in you'* (Romans 8.9). He also told them that when we pray, *'the Spirit bears witness with our spirit'* (Romans 8.16). It is worth remembering, therefore, that when we pray, we are literally only a whisper away from the Spirit of God, who is God himself.

Examples of the ways in which the Spirit comes to us through prayer and the scriptures will be found in the lives of the saints and other faithful witnesses in the illustrated Calendar in Part VI of this book, but many ordinary people today also have religious experiences. As they read the scriptures in a prayerful mood, they may discover that a verse literally leaps off the page to convert them and change their lives. This type of experience was confirmed in a letter to me by Bishop Simon Barrington-Ward. It has also been described in the series of publications on the Anglican faith by the Doctrine Commission of the Church of England, 1986–88.

In his Second Letter to Timothy, St Paul also expressed this, when he wrote that *'All scripture is God-breathed'* (II Timothy 3.16). The German Protestant theologian Karl Barth (1886–1968) explained this in greater detail in his massive work *Church Dynamics*. He wrote that *'The Word of God is dynamic . . . It is the event of God speaking to man through Jesus Christ. It is his personal revelation of himself to us. The Word of God is not a static object, but a subject that takes control of us . . . It is something that demands a response. Though the words as written in the Bible are fallible human words, they become God's words when he chooses to speak through them.'* Pope Pius XII said that Karl Barth was *'the greatest theologian since St Thomas Aquinas'.* Thomas' definition of the soul will be described in the Calendar for the month of January.

Some liberal clergy and those who have lost their faith sometimes say about prayer that *'there is nobody up there listening to you, but it may do you some good'.* However, as Dr George Carey (now Lord Carey of Clifton) said when he was Archbishop of Canterbury, and as even I once found, *'sometimes when we pray coincidences occur'.* Also, as long ago as the so-called 'Age of Faith' in the middle ages, when derogation of prayer was prevalent in some circles, St Bernard of Clairvaux (1090–1153) wrote against this mistaken view, saying that *'When I pray, the Spirit sends me ideas that I could not possibly have thought of myself'.*

This is also the experience of many who pray deeply and in silence. Ideas then come flooding in as one lets go of the world. One may sometimes also become aware of being involved in a conversation with someone 'other', who is outside and beyond ourselves. That is why St Teresa of Avila wrote in her sixteenth-century autobiography that *'prayer for me is like a conversation with Him Who loves us'.*

St Paul's letters mention the Holy Spirit more than 60 times. He told the Galatians about *'the Fruit of the Spirit'* which is *'joy, peace, patience, kindness, goodness, faithfulness, gentleness, self-control'* (Galatians 5.22–4). He also told the Corinthians that *'to each is given the manifestation of the Spirit for the common good'* (I Corinthians 12.4). Thus every one of us has different qualities and we are called to God's service in different ways.

We can also detect the presence of the Spirit through our own experiences in life. A lovely description of this was given in a letter to me by the late Revd Roy Boff, former vicar of our parish. He wrote to me from his study in answer to a question I had raised: *'One of the most exciting things in my thirty-four years' ministry is the discovery that the numbers of ways God speaks to and uses people to accomplish his purpose are as immense and as different from each other as are the millions of snowflakes that are now falling on the dales around this rectory as I write'.*

Belief in the Spirit of God and experience of him is not confined to one faith. This was perceived by St Basil of Caesarea. In a sermon in the fourth century he said that *'Thou hast visited humanity in many ways. There is no culture or religion that has not received and does not express a "Visitation of the Word."'*

This inspired advice was ignored by the Church for 16 centuries until, at the Second Vatican Council in 1961, Pope John XXIII reminded it that *'the seed of the Spirit can be seen in all the world's faiths today'.* What a U-turn that was for the Church compared with its attitude dating back to long before the Crusades! Belief in the Spirit of God, which even the primitive animists understood, acts as a guide to conduct and is the most important belief shared by all faiths.

The next important question that we need to examine is how do we test the authenticity of the spiritual ideas and inspirations that come through to us? This was the task of the Catholic Inquisition, which sought to distinguish between thoughts that were divinely inspired from those that were blasphemous and which came from the Devil. As so often with difficult questions like this, we can find the answer in

St Paul's Letters. He wrote to the Thessalonians about the promptings of the Spirit: *'Do not quench the Spirit . . . but test everything'* (I Thessalonians 5.19–21). By 'test' he meant testing against the teaching of the gospels, because when we hold these in our hands we are but the thickness of a single page away from the Spirit of God, which is God himself.

The Holy Spirit is a divine mystery that one can go on discussing endlessly. It may help to sum up by quoting another letter to me from Roy Boff in 1993 in answer to some of my questions: *'The Spirit is, as you say, a teacher, but he is more than that, he is a* Comforter *– as in the Greek* Parakaleo, *one who is always alongside more as a companion rather than as a Rabbi, a guide. Think then of your own picture of a pilot, or co-pilot. He is one who can take over. Or think of him as an automatic pilot, when our craft is moving and when we do not seem to be in control and God carries us through in spite of ourselves. After all, our conscious awareness of God is not a continuing awareness, is it? Mine seems to be a "stop-start" pilgrimage and sometimes God seems very distant, yet his Spirit never leaves us. As Jesus said: "I will never leave you or forsake you, lo! I am with you always until the end of the age."'* (Matthew 28.20).

We all have a feeling that there is a spiritual identity within us, the 'I' or the 'You'. According to many of Jesus' statements in the Gospels, this spirit or soul, this 'us', is destined to outlive our bodies. This destiny cannot be proved, but it is the most logical conclusion to reach if one considers the way that God has intervened in history to reveal himself in human form through his Son. Yet no one has been able to explain medically or scientifically the bodily source of this inner spirit.

To the Greek philosophers like Plato, this spirit, which is our 'form' or essence, returns to God after our bodily death. The gospels and St Paul refer to this future life or resurrection as an *Anastasis*, a Greek word meaning the resumption of life in a new form, which is more explicit.

Most of the world's faiths today profess a belief in a future life and in a judgement to come, based upon individual records of conduct in life. General belief in this, however, which was so powerful in Christian missionary activities in previous centuries, is not strong today. Lack of medical or other scientific proof of the existence of a soul within us is a formidable obstacle to this traditional faith. This disenchantment sprang progressively from the way the Church refused to accept the discoveries of science and also from the way, from the late sixteenth century onwards, people's minds were turned from a concern about the spirit to concentration on the self. In the eighteenth century the philosophers denied the existence of a human soul. However today there is a growing belief among mathematicians that, as with the mystery of Quantum Mechanics, there may be a powerful influence that is beyond logic, but which exists within the brain. They are now exploring this possibility, which is suggested by the discovery that the brain generates electromagnetic fields. These appear to stimulate mental activity even if that stimulation comes from outside and it may be that the undiscovered source of this is what we call conscience. Genuine understanding cannot exist without consciousness, which led Cardinal John Henry Newman (1809–89) to believe that conscience is the source of our soul.

The main theme of this book is more concerned with the mystery of how the Spirit guides us than with the soul and its future salvation. If we are honest with ourselves, few of us are worthy of salvation in the sense of living in God's abode, even if our resurrection is to be a much less glorious one than that of his Son. We are all guilty of sins at least in the sense of omission or of not always being strong enough to live up to our ideals as Christians. Salvation is therefore a matter for the grace of God alone. We cannot make ourselves worthy of such grace by ourselves, merely by pulling ourselves up by our own boot-strings as the fourth-century British monk Pelagius claimed. What we can however do in a constructive and more humble way, is to follow Christ's commands, so that we can advance the Kingdom of God, by acting with love to make our families, friends and those around us happy.

I had no idea what was meant by a spiritual experience until I had been accepted by the Royal Air Force in January 1941 at the age of 18 to train as a pilot. I will describe what then happened to me, so that I can at least show that I know what even a minor spiritual experience is like and what effect it can have.

It happened when I and about 20 other trainee pilots were marched to a lecture hall to take the oath of allegiance to King George VI. On the way I realised that this was more than a formality, but was the first major independent step that I was taking in my life. I therefore said a short prayer, asking God to give me strength to do my duty and not to make a mess of it. I also asked God to accept me in the service of his Church, which the Nazis were threatening.

We were each given a Bible on which to swear. During the ceremony something made me put my finger at random into the book to see if there might be a message for me. I had never done such a thing before,

nor have I done so since. At the end of the oath-taking I found that my finger pointed to the first chapter of St Paul's First Letter to Timothy, my namesake. There I read in verse 18 *'Go thou my son Timothy and fight thou a good warfare'*. I was utterly astonished. It seemed that my prayer had been answered. I felt uplifted and filled with joy and inner warmth. Then I said to myself, *'Surely God does not listen to the prayers of the most junior airman in the service?'*, and I decided that what had happened to me was an extraordinary set of coincidences. The first of these was my opening the Bible at the letter to my namesake Timothy. Secondly, this happened at that wartime ceremony, thirdly this took place on that particular day, fourthly that message to Timothy was the perfect one for a young man going off to war.

This story may not mean much to anyone else, but like all spiritual experiences it changed my whole attitude to life. I had, until then, had a simple schoolboy faith in the existence of God, but from that day on my faith became one of knowing for certain that he exists. Yet, though I believed something special had happened to me of great spiritual significance, I still felt the need for someone to interpret it for me.

During the war I always said those words *'Go thou and fight a good warfare'* to myself before taking off in my aircraft on a mission against the enemy. This always put me in the right frame of mind for the task ahead. Then, when peace came, I realised that the 'warfare' that St Paul wrote about was the spiritual warfare that we all have to fight in our lives, the daily battle to choose between the right and difficult ways and the wrong but easiest courses of action.

It was not until 1993, when I was discussing my plans for this book with Bishop Simon Barrington-Ward, who was then Bishop of Coventry, that my experience at the oath-taking ceremony was explained to me. Bishop Simon had asked me to tell him how my spiritual journey had begun and I told him about my experience in 1941. I also asked him what had really happened to me. He looked at me quietly for a few moments and then gave me his answer: '*I believe that what happened to you was that the Holy Spirit spoke to you through the Scriptures*'. I then realised with great excitement that this answer was also the key to what had filled the hearts of the saints I was writing about and which explained how they were converted. Although only relatively few of the 750 saints in my book described their conversion, the important ones who did so were St Antony of Egypt, St Basil of Caesarea, St Francis of Assisi, St Teresa of Avila and St Ignatius of Loyola. I also realised from their experience that such a conversion, as St Anselm wrote in the twelfth century, is but the beginning of a life-long spiritual journey and one of constant discovery.

PART TWO

THE SPIRITUAL SYMBOLS OF THE FOUR GOSPELS

The Spiritual Symbols of the Four Gospels

THE SPIRITUAL SYMBOLS OF THE FOUR GOSPELS

In his book *The Go-Between God*, written in 1978, the Bishop of Winchester, John V. Taylor, wrote that *'The chief actor in the historic mission of the Christian Church is the Holy Spirit. He is the director of the whole enterprise.'* The Bishop then warned that *'this fact, so patent to Christians in the first century, is largely forgotten in our own'.*

This fundamental importance to us of the Holy Spirit was never explained to me in my youth. I never even thought about this Third Person of the Holy Trinity until I visited a sixth-century church on the edge of the hill-town of Tuscania about 50 miles north-west of Rome. I was deeply impressed by the life-sized stone carvings of the four spiritual symbols of the evangelists on the front of the church.

As soon as I could I then researched the origin of the symbols and learned that their purpose was exactly as Bishop Taylor had described. They were to remind the faithful that the Gospels were inspired by the Spirit, as Jesus had promised to his disciples before his betrayal. His words were that the Spirit *'will bring to your remembrance all that I have said to you'* (John 14.26).

This late discovery of mine made me aware in a much more convincing way that the Gospels really are inspired by the Holy Spirit of God. The first thing to appreciate about the symbols is that they were devised to identify the spiritual source of the different Gospels which were all published anonymously.

The Evangelists did not sign their books. Therefore each Gospel was given a symbol to indicate its spiritual themes. These symbols are illustrated on the previous page. Although their attribution between the four evangelists was changed from time to time, the final allocation of them was fixed by the start of the fourth century.

The following are their meanings:

WINGED LION: St Mark's Gospel – which emphasised the Kingship of the Son of Man.

WINGED YOUTH: St Matthew's Gospel – the symbol of Jesus' incarnation through the Spirit.

WINGED OX: St Luke's Gospel – a sacrificial emblem to represent the theme of Jesus' destiny.

WINGED EAGLE: St John's Gospel – to indicate the gift of the Holy Spirit, Christ's image on earth.

These spiritual symbols were derived from the winged messengers of God described in The Book of Ezekiel and also in The Revelation of John. They indicated that the Spirit of God in the Old Testament is identical with the Holy Spirit of God in the New Testament.

In Ezekiel (2.1–3.11) the prophet saw *'a hand stretched before me and a scroll was in it'*. He was then told to speak the words he saw to the Children of Israel. In his 'Revelation' John, after seeing the winged messengers, hears the words: *'Write what you see in a book'* (Revelations 1.9). In each case therefore the command to write came direct from the Almighty.

THE AUTHORSHIP, DATES AND AUTHENTICITY OF THE GOSPELS

The *'Good News'* or Gospel depicting the life and words of Jesus Christ was preached orally by the Apostles and other disciples right from the Day of Pentecost, 50 days after the Passover and Jesus Christ's Resurrection. St Luke describes in his Acts of the Apostles the first public occasion when this took place, as St Peter spoke to the assembled Jews after the Holy Spirit had descended on the gathering in that upper room. We also know from St Luke and St Paul that St Mark and St Barnabas and others were evangelising for at least 25 years before Mark wrote down his Gospel in the year 63, a date which I will explain later.

We also have important information from *The Exposition of the Oracles of Our Lord*, written by Bishop Papias of Hierapolis in Syria in about 135. He wrote that many of Jesus' sayings were recorded in lists (since lost), but that Matthew made his own collection of sayings. Even more important than this, Papias says that St Mark received much of his Gospel direct from St Peter, whose secretary and interpreter he was in Rome in the early 60s. This then became the basis for St Matthew's and St Luke's Gospels. They included 90 per cent and 50 per cent respectively of Mark's Gospel, word for word, in their own much longer versions.

The decision of the Church to include only the gospel writings of the Four Evangelists, Matthew, Mark, Luke and John, in the New Testament Canon in the second century was made on the grounds that only those gospels should be included which were believed to be 'Apostolic'. That is to say, gospels compiled by those who had known Jesus or which were, as in the case of Luke, in accordance with the Apostolic oral tradition and, following Jesus' promise, they were inspired by the Holy Spirit. The authorities behind this choice included St Polycarp, Bishop of Ephesus

(martyred 156) and St Irenaeus of Lyons (c.130–200). Irenaeus wrote that when he was a young man he had heard Polycarp say that in his youth he had actually heard St John preaching.

The dates when the Gospels were written have long been the subject of debate, but it now seems that at least those of St Mark and St Matthew were finalised as early as 63–4, much earlier than it used to be thought. Because of their dependence on Mark's Gospel these first three Gospels are called 'The Synoptic Gospels'. That is to say, *'written from the same point of view'*. Matthew and Luke's Gospels also include the results of their own investigations and information from a now-lost source of Jesus' sayings that they shared. This is known as 'Q', German for 'Quelle' or 'source'. Luke's Gospel is thought to have been written in about 80 and St John's Gospel, which includes about 5 per cent of Mark, may have been written in the 90s or even in about 100. Much of John's Gospel may have been taken down earlier, being dictated to his disciples. This would account for so many duplications of John's definition of Jesus.

A convincing case for the dating of the Gospels of St Mark and St Matthew was published in 1993 by the Swedish papyrologist, the late Professor Revd Peter Carsten Thiede, after he had examined papyrus fragments of St Mark's and St Matthew's Gospels. The St Mark fragment was from his chapter 6, which was in the library of Magdalen College, Oxford. The fragment of papyrus containing words from St Matthew's Gospel, chapter 26, had been found in one of the Qumran caves, which also contained some of the non-Christian 'Dead Sea Scrolls'. It was the evidence gained from these papyri fragments that led Professor Thiede to claim that St Mark's Gospel must have been written in the year 63 and St Matthew's Gospel shortly afterwards, but no later than in 68. Sadly,

Professor Thiede, the greatest biblical scholar of modern times, died in December 2004.

This discovery is important because of the bearing it has on the authenticity of the Gospel stories and of Jesus' sayings in them. Since these two Gospels were written a generation after Jesus' death, their accuracy necessarily depends on memories. Memories are fallible. However St Mark, according to Bishop Papias in 135 in his *Exposition of the Oracles of Our Lord*, acted as St Peter's secretary in Rome in 62–4, and recorded St Peter's own accounts of the words of Jesus. St Peter, and others amongst Jesus' followers, must have heard Jesus repeat the same words of his gospel many times as he preached to different audiences during his journeys round Galilee.

Therefore it is reasonable to suggest that the revolutionary words which Jesus spoke must have become indelible in Peter's memory. I know how true this can be from my own clear memory of words said to me 40 to 60 years ago by people who were important in my life. It is therefore even more likely that the words of the greatest being who ever lived would never have been forgotten by those who had heard him speak.

An interesting attempt to analyse Jesus' sayings and to decide which ones were authentic was made in 1993 at a seminar of 100 leading theologians at Berkeley, the University of California. They concluded by a majority vote that not more than 20 per cent of Jesus' reported words were actually his own. This is a daring and challenging opinion. However if we look at the Gospels we can show that even this view does not devalue the 'Gospel truth' we have inherited. If one lists all Jesus' sayings in each of the first three Gospels and subtracts those that are repeats of Mark in Matthew and Luke, one can see that they provide about 350 different

sayings. This is only a rough estimate, since some of his sayings have to be extracted from long speeches as in St Matthew's Sermon on the Mount. However if this total is accepted as a fair estimate, then it means on the Berkeley 20 per cent estimate that at least 70 different sayings are the authentic words of Jesus.

To these must be added a further 20 original sayings on the same basis from the 100 or so sayings attributed to Jesus in St John's Gospel. This brings the total to at least 90 authentic sayings of Jesus. The 280 others in the Synoptic Gospels and the 80 or so in St John's Gospel, cannot have all been invented; they therefore must at least be echoes of Jesus' words or of what he wanted his hearers to understand. Do we really need any more in order to help us believe what God has spoken to us through the person he sent to reveal himself and his commands to the world?

Those who doubt the authenticity of Jesus' words according to the Gospels, ask too much. The Berkeley figure is perhaps the lowest estimate of true sayings, some of which are so revolutionary that no devout Jew could have said them without authority from above. In short, Jesus can be seen through these sayings to be just what he implied and was to admit to being to the High Priest at his trial: one sent from God.

One set of Jesus' sayings that it is particularly important to consider is the record of the 150 occasions in the Gospels when he referred to the *'kingdom of heaven'* and *'the kingdom of God'*. That is almost three times for every two Gospel pages. Jesus' words about them occupy almost a quarter of the Gospel texts. This proves the importance to Jesus of this part of his teaching. Sometimes his statements on the kingdom seem to apply to its coming through Jesus himself as God's anointed returning to Zion, as had been promised in the Old Testament. This was to be the climax of the story of the Children of Israel, although the Jews would not recognise Jesus' self-sacrifice at Jerusalem as the start of a new era. At other times Jesus' references to the kingdom refer directly to the day of judgement, to a general resurrection and promises of a future life for all who believed.

Not even the Berkeley theologians could invalidate so many sayings as editorial additions designed to embellish Jesus' message. The fact that Jesus referred to a future life so often should therefore be a great comfort to the dying and to their family and friends, even though the form of that spiritual life remains a mystery.

It is today fashionable to believe that a future life means only that we live on through our children and the effect of our deeds which act like stones thrown into water and whose ripples roll on into eternity. That is a very brave and stoical view of how God wants us to behave and also of what is a profound mystery, which can only be answered here through faith. Yet, if we accept the words of the Gospels, that stoical view is not what Jesus taught. Also it is illogical to reject Jesus' words while accepting the accounts of his resurrection and his example of unconditional love in sacrificing himself for us. It was his Resurrection, God's proof of his victory over death, that shows that death is not the end but the beginning of life. That is what inspired and convinced thesaints and other faithful.

None of the stories of the early martyrs and saints in this book will be meaningful unless we remember that they all believed in a future life after death. Nor can the Christian faith mean anything without the belief that Jesus died and was raised again so that we might believe that in spite of our sins, our souls also would be saved for some unknown divine purpose. The evangelists and St Paul actually gave us a guide as to what a future 'Resurrection' meant to them, but which the English translation of that word misses. The Greek word they used for Resurrection was *Anastasis*. This means 'the continuation of life in a new form'. It does not mean some form of physical reconstruction of dead bodies.

No human being can know what happens after death to the unique person we feel within us – the 'I', 'Me', 'You' and 'Us'. It is a matter of faith both as to the fact and to the form it takes. On this question I will quote Bishop Simon Barrington-Ward's words to me: *'I do not believe that we die into nothing'*. Also, since both St John and St Paul wrote that God and the Lord are Spirit (John 4.24 and II Corinthians 3.17), perhaps it does not require too great a stretch of the imagination to believe that our souls also can, as spiritual forms, meet Him in some spiritual way. The arguments to the contrary, however logical, just seem to be implausible in the light of the Gospels.

Nevertheless, the often-fanatical concentration of individuals and the Churches on Salvation – typified in the anxious question *'Are you saved?'* – has often led to neglect of the primary aims and commands of Jesus as expressed in St Matthew's Sermon on the Mount. Disagreements on the validity of claims to salvation have also caused noisy and schismatic battles between different sects within the Churches. Examples of the fatal results of this will be found in the stories about the Greek Church in 'A Calendar of Saints' in Part VI of this book and also on the Reformation in Part VII, 'The Unquenchable Spirit'.

PART THREE

THE APOSTLES AND EVANGELISTS

Jesus spreading his gospel amongst his disciples

THE LIFE AND IMPORTANCE OF ST PETER

The fisherman Simon, whom Jesus called Peter – or *Cephas* in Aramaic, meaning 'the rock' – is the first of the twelve disciples mentioned in all the lists given in the Gospels. He was without question their recognised leader, passionate, impulsive and loyal to a fault. It was he who at Caesarea Philippi was the first to acclaim Jesus as the Messiah, Christ. I therefore begin with this picture of Jesus blessing Peter at Philippi after Peter had said: '*You are the Christ, the Son of the living God*' (Matthew 16.16). Jesus then said: '*Flesh and blood has not revealed this to you, but my Father who is in heaven. And I tell you, you are Peter, and on this rock I will build my Church.*' Only Matthew includes this last sentence about founding the Church, though both Mark and Luke describe the rest of the meeting at Philippi in the same words.

'*You are Peter and upon this rock I will build my Church*'

remarks that '*and Peter also remembers*' (Mark 11.21). This is the strongest evidence in support of Papias' claim. The second piece of evidence is that Mark gives Peter's words on 14 occasions in his Gospel and these are also the only quotations concerning Peter that are given in the other two synoptic Gospels. Indeed they quote Mark's version word for word as he wrote them except on two occasions.

The first occasion when Matthew's account differs slightly from Mark is in his version of the story of how the disciples saw Jesus walking on water. Matthew adds to Mark's account how Peter lost his faith and nearly drowned (Matthew 14.31). Perhaps Peter had preferred to forget this part of the story when dictating his version to Mark. Its inclusion by Matthew does however suggest that he was an actual witness of the scene. The second occasion on which Matthew's account differs from Mark's is when his Gospel is the only one to record Jesus' words at Caesarea Philippi that 'I tell you, you are Peter and upon this rock I will build my Church'. That is a saying of Jesus whose authenticity even some Roman Catholic scholars doubt. All the rest of what we know of Peter comes from his First Letter in the New Testament, from St John's Gospel and from what St Luke tells us of Peter in his Acts of the Apostles.

St Peter was always present when Jesus preached around Galilee, therefore he would have heard him repeat his gospel words many times. These words would therefore have become indelible in his memory. This justifies the claim for the authenticity of the words of Our Lord that are quoted in St Mark's Gospel and which Peter dictated to him in Rome. In other words, the Gospel of Peter is actually enclosed in that of Mark. This claim is supported by two pieces of internal evidence in Mark's Gospel. The first of these is where Mark

St John's Gospel mentions Peter less often than the other evangelists. However St John does quote Jesus as saying of Simon Peter that *'You shall be called Cephas (which means Peter)'*. Also in his chapter 13 John mentions several conversations between Jesus and Peter, which perhaps John alone could have heard. Only John records at the betrayal scene that it was Peter who struck off the ear of the High Priest's servant with a sword. This helps to prove that John was present himself.

In Peter's own First Letter he wrote: *'Blessed be the God and Father of our Lord Jesus Christ! By his great mercy we have been born anew to a living hope through the resurrection of Jesus Christ from the dead, and to an inheritance which is imperishable.'* (I Peter 1.3). The words *'born anew'* seem to have come from Jesus' own lips, as they also appear in John's Gospel, chapter 3, when Jesus tells Nicodemus that we must all be *'born anew'* through the Spirit, if we are to see the kingdom of God. There is no way, other than tradition, that we can attribute the source of Luke's account of the Holy Spirit at Pentecost and of Peter's address to the disciples and the crowds of Jews in which he explained what had happened.

There is no record of Peter's death in Rome as a victim of Nero's persecution in 64, when the Christians were massacred for allegedly setting fire to the city. However the tradition that he was martyred then is too strong to be ignored. Also there is evidence to support the tradition that he was buried on the site of the present Basilica of St Peter's in Rome. About a century ago a ruined tomb was discovered in the foundations. This had the words *'Hic Petrus'* carved upon it. The tomb probably dates from the fourth century, but it may be the remains of one of the shrines that were restored in Rome by the Emperor Constantine I after his victory in 312 over Maxentius.

In support of this is the fact that the tiles on the tomb are of a design that was only used for imperial tombs. Perhaps the emperor wanted to honour St Peter in this special way.

There is a famous apocryphal story about Peter, which must be mentioned. It is recorded in the third-century religious novel *The Acts of Peter*. This tells that Peter fled from Rome to escape Nero's soldiers and then had a vision of Christ walking towards him along the Appian Way. Peter is said to have stopped and ask Jesus: *'Domine, quo vadis?'* – *'Lord, where are you going?'* According to the story Jesus replied that he was on his way to be crucified a second time. Peter, remembering his three denials of Jesus before the cock crowed during Jesus' trial, was mortified at the thought of denying Christ yet again. He turned back to meet his fate in Rome. The story captures perfectly the hasty vigour and also the sudden perceptiveness of Peter as revealed by the evangelists.

ST MARK

I have already suggested that important parts of St Mark's Gospel were dictated to him by St Peter in Rome. Peter would have spoken in Aramaic, the *lingua franca* of the whole region from Egypt through Mesopotamia, Palestine and Syria; it was the language that Jesus himself spoke. Although Mark's Gospel was written in Greek, linguists have shown that his Greek phrases and crude syntax were instant translations of the original Aramaic in which he had received his Gospel. Clearly he wrote them in Greek to appeal to the Roman and Greek audience at whom they were aimed.

We also know from 'Acts' and St Paul's Letters that Mark had been preaching the oral Gospel at least from about 48 to 50, after he and his cousin Barnabas had left St Paul to preach on their own. This was during the intervening years before Paul summoned him to Rome as St Paul's Second Letter to Timothy (II Timothy 4.11) describes. Before going to Rome in about 62 Mark may have already written a draft of all he had learned previously from witnesses who had known and followed Jesus. This is only my assumption, but it helps to explain how he was able to produce his final Gospel so soon after his contact with Peter and Paul in Rome. As will be suggested below, Mark's final version may have been completed in Rome before Peter's death in 64.

St Mark is usually accepted to have been the same person as the 'John Mark' referred to in Luke's Acts of the Apostles, when Peter escaped from prison in Jerusalem and fled to *'the house of Mary, the mother of John whose other name was Mark'* (Acts 12.12). There is also a possible autobiographical reference in Mark's Gospel that suggests he may have been with Jesus in the garden at his betrayal. The text reads: *'And a young man followed him, with nothing but a linen cloth about*

his body; and they seized him, but he left the linen cloth and ran away naked' (Mark 14.31). If this young man was Mark the future evangelist, then he might have been about 15-18 years old. There is also another reason to accept this account as a personal experience, because who else but an actual witness would include such a vivid 'streaking' as the aftermath of that terrible scene of betrayal? We hear of Mark when Barnabas and 'Saul' – or Paul – returned from Jerusalem *'bringing with them John whose other name was Mark'* (Acts 13.13). They took Mark with them to Cyprus, but he left them on the return journey in about 47 or 48. Mark may have left Paul following a disagreement between them, because Paul refused to take him on his second recorded missionary journey (Acts 15.39). Instead Barnabas took his cousin John Mark to evangelise in Cyprus. Mark by then would have been about 33 to 36 years old.

As mentioned in the text in Part II about the dating of the Gospels, convincing evidence in support of an early date of about 64 or 65 for both Mark's and Matthew's Gospels was provided by the Swedish papyrologist Professor the Revd Peter Carsten Thiede in 1993. This recorded the results of his examination of two sets of papyrus fragments. One set with a section of Mark's chapter 6 was found in Egypt and given to Magdalen College, Oxford in 1901. This was for a long time thought to date from the third century. The other set was found in 1947 with some of the Dead Sea Scrolls of the Jewish sect of Essenes and contained a verse of Matthew's chapter 26.

The details of the investigation of these papyrus fragments were published in 1996 in *The Jesus Papyrus* by Professor Thiede and Matthew D'Ancona, the historian and Fellow of All Souls College,

Oxford. They showed that the fragments of Mark from the Qumran caves could not have been deposited there later than 68, when the Roman armies overran the area on their way to destroy the Essene and Qumran community in their fortress of Masada near the Dead Sea. The absence of any coins in the Qumran caves of a date later than 68 supports this view.

Professor Thiede then established that both sets of fragments, those from the cave and those in the Magdalen library, were from two codices. The importance of this discovery is that it was the custom in the first century to write original documents on scrolls and only to transfer them to codices or book form after the original scrolls had become worn out. This means that both sets of the codex fragments must have been copied from older original scrolls dating from some years before 68, i.e. at least from around 63–64 in the case of the Marcan fragment found in the Qumran cave. In reaching their conclusions the authors used the most modern equipment to date the papyri and also to compare the actual scripts, whose style proved them to be contemporary with each other. The research on these two sets of papyri fragments is still going on as it seems possible that the Marcan fragments may imply the existence of an original scroll dating from as early as 48–50. This is a date when some scholars believe St Peter may have paid his first visit to Rome.

I am not going to analyse Mark's or any of the Gospels except to draw attention to some important sayings of Jesus and references to the Holy Spirit. My aim is simply to provide a background for the debates within the Church and involving the saints whose lives will be described in the Calendar. Therefore only eight sayings in Mark's Gospel will be mentioned here. The first statement is Mark's startling and uncompromising proclamation in the opening words of his Gospel – *'The beginning of the Gospel of Jesus Christ, the Son of God'*. That is the shortest 'birth-story', giving the divine origin of Jesus, in all the synoptic Gospels. The title *'Son of God'* indicates that by the time Mark wrote the final version of his Gospel a new understanding of the nature of Jesus had arisen. He was no longer seen just as a Jewish Messiah, but as born after being divinely quickened by the Holy Spirit. The limitations of language then meant that the faithful could only define him as 'Son of God'.

When we come to Part IV and to St Paul's life and works we shall see how even he, the first great Christian theologian, had to struggle to answer the question of Jesus' divinity without making him into a 'second God'. He always called Jesus 'Lord' and not *Ho Theos* or 'The One God', but he also explains how he sees 'The Risen Christ' as fitting into the concept of the 'One God', just like the traditional Jewish concepts of the divine 'Word', 'Wisdom' and 'Spirit of God'. Yet Paul made it clear that Jesus was a distinct 'Person' within the one God and not annihilated within him. Although he did not define God as a 'Trinity of Persons, Father, Son and Holy Spirit', he implied that this was so.

Paul's case for this, the opening verses of St John's Gospel, and the many references that Jesus makes in his Gospel about his relationship with God the Father, convinced the very early Church that Jesus was the Second Person of a Holy Trinity. Thus by the end of the second century the Three Persons were described by the Roman lawyer and Christian writer Tertullian (c.155–c.220), as *'Consubstantialis'*, all of one substance.

Therefore from the very earliest days what developed later into the 'doctrine of the Holy Trinity' was implicit in the New Testament and had entered into the tradition of the Church. It was only later, in the fourth century, when the Eastern Church had to defend itself against the fierce rhetoric and criticism of many Greek clerics and monks, that a formal Trinitarian doctrine was defined at the Councils of Nicaea in 325 and of Constantinople in 381. This was a compromise answer to defend the tradition against a dangerous schism in the Church.

Some scholars today believe that it may be in the interests of the Church to define that doctrine again, so that it can be understood more clearly. One simple and helpful attempt at a new formula for this was made by the German theologian Hans Kung, the official theological adviser to Pope John XXIII at the Second Vatican Council, in his book *Christianity, The Religious Situation of Our Time* (1994). Unfortunately his teaching is now banned by the Roman Catholic Church as being too modern for the Curia to tolerate.

In his book *Crossing the Threshold of Hope* (1994), Pope John Paul II quotes the First Letter to Timothy: '*There is one God and one Mediator between God and men, the man Jesus Christ*' (2.5). When he was Archbishop of Canterbury Dr George Carey, now Lord Carey of Clifton, went further by describing Jesus as being '*translucent to God*'. Bishop Hugh Montefiore in his autobiography *Oh God, What Next?* called him '*transparent to God*'. This was also the description given by the Regius Professor of Divinity in Oxford, Keith Ward, in his book *A Vision to Pursue*. These all agree with the Gospels' picture that God is revealed to us through Jesus and therefore by knowing Jesus we can know the Father. These descriptions avoid the complicated Trinitarian

theology which few people can understand. So also does the definition of God by St Thomas Aquinas in the thirteenth century as '*complete in himself*'. This includes all Three Persons in God himself – Creator/Father, his Word (Jesus) and his Holy Spirit. This will be explained in the text on St Thomas at the end of the January Calendar.

The only reference to the Holy Spirit in Mark is when he gives John the Baptist's words about the one who is to come: '*I have baptised you with water; but he will baptise you with the Holy Spirit*' (Mark 1.8). One of the most important sayings in Mark's Gospel is in the first words that Mark records of Jesus. These are: '*The time is fulfilled, and the kingdom of God is at hand; repent and believe in the Gospel*' (Mark 1.15). What is easily missed, at least in the English translation, is what Jesus meant by '*repent*'. The English translation suggests a repentance like '*I am sorry, I won't do it again*', but the Greek word *Metanôeite*, that Mark used to convey Jesus' Aramaic word for 'repent', demands a much deeper form of repentance.

Had Jesus only meant a simple repentance, Mark would have used the milder Greek verb *Metamelia*. Instead, by using the strong form of the verb *Metanoia – Metanôeite*, which demands a more profound repentance, he showed that Jesus wanted a total moral revolution of heart and mind. His Gospel was a transforming Gospel, one that should change the world. That was far more demanding than the formal obedience to the old-style Jewish Law through which the Jews, especially the puritan sect of the Pharisees, felt that they would be 'right with God'. That is why Mark went on to show what Jesus meant by this deeper sense of holiness, which he illustrated in parables and through chance events as he spread his Gospel throughout Galilee.

This long-overlooked explanation was first exposed to the public in the 1920s by the French sage and theologian Père Guillaume Pouget (1847–1942). His life, *Portrait de Monsieur Pouget*, was written by the French Academician Jean Guitton and published by Gallimard in Paris in 1941 just before Pouget's death. Père Pouget was a Lazarist and professor, a famous savant of the Rue Du Bac in Paris in the 1920s. In spite of starting to go blind at the age of 57, he specialised in ancient languages, including Aramaic, the language spoken by Jesus. Many of his writings have been preserved and are quoted in Jean Guitton's book about him.

Père Guillaume Puget's explanation of Jesus' word for 'repent' or, in the French version *fâites penitence*, explains how revolutionary was Jesus' teaching and how mere obedience to the Jewish Law is not enough. This and Jesus' strong meaning for 'repent' makes nonsense of the claim by many modern critics that Christianity is no more moral than the traditional laws and ethics which had been developed in most societies. Mark therefore showed that Jesus' gospel was a transforming faith. Most of Mark's subsequent Gospel stories such as the forgiving of sins to the paralysed man and of the killing of the son of the owner of the vineyard, were there to show what Jesus meant by that transformation. Jesus' command to repent is therefore the key to the Good News that he preached.

A fourth important quotation, unique to Mark's Gospel, and one that must strike a chord in many a Christian heart, is the reply made to Jesus by the man who had asked Jesus to heal his epileptic son. Jesus had said almost mockingly: *'If I can! All things are possible to him who believes'*. Immediately the father replied *'I believe, help thou my*

'I believe; help my unbelief'. (Mark 9.24)

25

unbelief' (Mark 9.24). Thus Mark indicates the need to accept in faith the mystery of Jesus.

This saying *'help thou my unbelief'* was quoted in February 2000 by Cardinal Cormac Murphy O'Connor when he was made Roman Catholic Archbishop of Westminster. He then told some journalists that he often used the words of the father of the epileptic son as he himself prayed for better understanding in the face of difficult doctrinal problems.

A fifth important quotation from Mark comes immediately after the scene with the epileptic boy, when Jesus said: *'Anyone who welcomes me welcomes not me, but Him who sent me'* (9.37). This saying is also recorded in John's Gospel (12.49). This suggests that either John knew Mark's Gospel or else he had heard the saying himself. Jesus never claimed to be God. Once, when he was called *'Good'* (Mark 10.18) by a listener, Jesus replied: *'Why call me good? Only God is good'* (10.45).

Mark had a way of depicting the mystery of Jesus indirectly by occasionally lifting part of the curtain that conceals him, but without explaining it. He does this in a sixth set of verses quite early in his story of Jesus' ministry, when he tells us that Jesus' family thought his claims to forgive sins like God, meant that he was mad. He wrote that *'when his relations heard of this they sought to restrain him; they said "He is out of his mind."'* (Mark 3/12). These relations were named by Mark to include Jesus' mother Mary and his 'brothers and sisters', who were presumably children of a previous marriage of Joseph, or else cousins and members of his extended Jewish family. By including this incident in his Gospel, which none of the other Gospels mention, Mark invites us to ask ourselves whether Jesus really was mad, or whether he was a blasphemer as the Jews accused him of being. If he was neither mad nor a blasphemer, but a very devout Jew, as his teaching proved, then it follows that he must be exactly who he implied he was – one speaking with authority from on high.

The seventh of Mark's quotations is his version of Jesus' final words on the cross. Matthew also quotes them. They are sometimes claimed to be a cry of despair indicating Jesus' sense of failure: *'My God, my God, why have you forsaken me?'* (15.34). I cannot accept that these were words of despair. They come from Psalm 22 and if Jesus had not lacked the breath to finish the quotation, he would have been able to continue the psalm and give a message of hope and inspiration for the future by saying that: *'posterity shall serve him; men shall tell of the Lord to the coming generation, and proclaim his deliverance to a people yet unborn, that he has wrought it'* (Psalm 22.30–31).

It was after the crucifixion that Mark gave his own definition of Jesus in the words of the centurion who saw him die: 'Truly this man was the Son of God!' It is interesting that this quotation, common to all English translations from the sixteenth century onwards, differs from the French version, which says simply that *'cet homme était un dieu'* (note the small 'd' in 'dieu'). This French translation, perhaps more correctly, implies that a pagan Roman soldier in those days could not have thought in terms other than that of a pagan god, but a god nevertheless. This shows how easy it is for editors and translators to give different shades of meaning to the Gospel words.

Mark's record of Jesus' resurrection is the briefest of all the Gospel versions. When Mary Magdalene and Mary the mother of James and Salome had found the tomb of Jesus empty, Mark describes how *'a young man sitting on the right side, dressed in a white robe'* said: 'Do *not be amazed; you seek Jesus of Nazareth, who was crucified. He has risen, he is not here; see the place where they laid him. But go tell his disciples and Peter that he is going on before you to Galilee'* (Mark 16.1–17). Thus, typically, Mark leaves us with a mystery: *'Jesus is going on before you . . . '* We can never quite catch him up!

St Mark is believed to have left Rome after finishing his Gospel and to have travelled and preached in Palestine, ending up in Alexandria. It used to be claimed that he became the first bishop of that city, but the surviving records that we have of early bishops of Alexandria from 61 do not include his name. He is thought to have been murdered there by an anti-Christian mob late in the reign of Nerva in about 98 or early in that of Trajan.

In 829 what were alleged to be Mark's relics were bought by Venice. Mark replaced St Theodore as Venice's patron saint and Mark's lion symbol became Venice's emblem.

ST MATTHEW

The first Gospel in the New Testament and probably the second one to be written, has always been attributed to the disciple Matthew. This tradition is based on the fact that this Gospel gives the name Matthew to the tax-collector at Capernaum to whom Jesus said '"*Follow me*"' as Matthew '*sat at the tax office and he rose and followed him*' (Matthew 9.9). In Mark's and Luke's versions of the incident, he is called '*Levi the son of Alphaeus*' (Mark 2.14, Luke 5.27).

All three Gospels tell that Matthew was rich enough to give a great feast for Jesus and to which he invited many other tax collectors. In Matthew's list of 'The Twelve' disciples he is called '*Matthew the tax collector*' (Matthew 10.3) and he describes James as the son of Alphaeus, as also does Luke's Gospel (6.15) and Acts (1.13).

Whoever the author Matthew/Levi was, his Gospel shows that he was an educated man used to recording detail. This can be seen from his summary of Jesus' teaching in his Sermon on the Mount (Matthew 5–7). Perhaps Jesus chose him because he wanted someone experienced to note down his sayings and actions. Matthew the tax collector would certainly have been qualified to do this. I have already mentioned that Matthew, like Luke, included many quotations from the lost 'Q' document of Jesus' sayings as well as the results of his own researches.

As with the account of St Mark's Gospel, these notes are aimed only at showing how Matthew saw Jesus, what he taught and what followed at his passion and after his death. Matthew, like Luke, gives a traditional 'birth-story' to describe what the Early Church always regarded as a divine mystery. He shows how Joseph adopts Jesus after being told by the angel of the Lord that he should take Mary as his wife '*because she has conceived what is in her by the Holy Spirit. She will give birth to a son and you must call him Jesus ('He who saves') because he is the one who is to save his people*' (Matthew 1.20, 21). Matthew goes on to say that this fulfils the prophecy of Isaiah that '*a Virgin will give birth to a son and his name shall be "Immanuel", meaning "God-is-with-us"*' (Isaiah 7.14). An illustration for this is given below in Luke's version of this birth-story.

The early church community knew that Jesus was born of a woman as a normal human being. Also they knew from their reflections on his life, death and resurrection, that he came from God in a way no ordinary person had ever done. That is why they believed he had been '*born of the Holy Spirit and the Virgin Mary*', as the earliest creeds proclaimed. This clearly implies both Jesus' humanity and his divinity. Indeed there is scarcely a chapter in Matthew's Gospel that does not quote Jesus as saying that his words came from his Father. Matthew saw him as '*God with us*' – Emmanuel.

Today we have the problem of interpreting the tradition of the birth-stories of Jesus in the light of the discovery of DNA and knowing that a human male sperm is essential to the conception of any human. Whatever is the answer to the divine mystery over Jesus' birth, his total sinlessness suggests that his human nature was unlike the DNA chain of genes of any other human being.

Thus his genes, or at least one of them, differed from the normal. It does not ask too much of our faith or imagination to attribute this to the action of God's Holy Spirit. In other words the discovery of DNA can be seen to strengthen belief in God's historic intervention and initiative for us through Jesus. After recording Jesus' '*Good News*' that with him the Kingdom of heaven was at hand and a new era had begun,

Matthew gives a sweeping summary of Jesus' mission by saying: *'He went round the whole of Galilee proclaiming the good news of the kingdom and curing all kinds of diseases'* (Matthew 4.23).

The description of Jesus' actual teaching, for which Matthew is famed, is his account of Jesus giving his Sermon on the Mount to the disciples. This was aptly described by Sir Winston Churchill as *'the last word in Christian ethics'* (see Sir John Colville's diary for 18 May 1952 in *The Fringes of Power*, Vol.2). It is this sermon, or set of collected sayings, that brings out more clearly than Mark the revolution in he art and mind that Jesus demanded in his words *'repent and believe in the Gospel'*.

Jesus' preaching about a future life after death is illustrated in the opening words of the Sermon on the Mount, where Matthew quotes Jesus' *Beatitudes*. These tell that *'the poor in spirit'* shall inherit the kingdom of heaven (5.3), as will also *'those who are persecuted in the name of righteousness'* (5.10). The most revolutionary of his sayings in this sermon for his disciples was Jesus' command to *'love your enemies and pray for them that persecute you'* (5.44). Jesus also gave his interpretation of what Christian charity means – *'If anyone forces you to go one mile, go with him two miles'* (5.41).

After telling his disciples to pray *'Our Father . . . '* Jesus told them that *'If you forgive men their trespasses, your heavenly Father also will forgive you* (6.14). He also told them this: *'Do not lay up for yourselves treasures on earth, where moth and rust corrupt, but lay up for yourselves treasures in heaven'* (6.19, 20). He then gave them the 'golden rule': *'Whatever you wish that men would do to you, do so to them, for this is the law and the prophets'* (7.13). Another version of

this is in the apocryphal *Book of Tobit* (4.3).

As already described above at the beginning of the life of Peter, Matthew stressed Jesus' 'Sonship' in his description of the scene at Caesaraea Philippi as Peter exclaimed *'You are the Christ, the Son of the living God'* (Matthew 16.16). Matthew also implies in his Gospel that not only was Jesus someone even greater than the promised Christ, but also that in him the climax of the history of the Children of Israel was reached. He made it clear that the Jews would not recognise this and that 'others' would inherit the task of advancing the kingdom. He gave this message, taken from Mark, in the parable of the *'Wicked Tenants'* (21.33–45).

Jesus began this parable by saying that *'a householder who planted a vineyard, set a hedge around it, dug a wine press in it and built a tower and let it out to tenants. He then went away into another country. When the season of fruit drew near, he sent his servants to the tenants to get his fruit. The tenants took his servants and beat one and killed another and stoned another. Afterward he sent his son . . . but they said "This is the heir, let us kill him and have his inheritance". And they took him and killed him. When therefore the owner of the vineyard comes, what will he do to those tenants? They replied: "He will put those wretches to a miserable death and let the vineyard to other tenants who will give him the fruits in due season."'* Jesus then gave them the true meaning of his story – that the owner was their Lord and they the guilty ones. *'"Therefore the kingdom of God will be taken away from you and given to a nation producing the fruits of it"'* (21.33–45).

The Jews who heard him realised that Jesus was referring to them, because in their traditional code the Children of Israel were *'God's Vineyard'*. The parable was Jesus' way of telling them who he was, God's chosen coming to Zion as prophesied, and that they would deny him and kill him. Jesus told that parable after his entry into Jerusalem for the last time to show that with him the history of Israel was reaching its climax. This was blasphemy according to the chief priests who tried to arrest Jesus, but Matthew says *'they feared the multitudes, because they held him to be a prophet'*.

Matthew alone of the evangelists also tells how Jesus made it clear that he came from God. This was when Jesus, referring to himself, said that *'"When the Son of man [comes in glory to judge], he will say to the righteous: Come, O blessed of my Father, inherit the kingdom prepared for you since the foundation of the world; for I was hungry and you gave me food . . . thirsty and you gave me drink . . . a stranger and you welcomed me . . . naked and you clothed me . . . sick and you visited me . . . in prison and you came to me . . . As you did to one of the least of these my brethren, you did it to me . . . The righteous shall have eternal life"'* (Matthew 25.31–46).

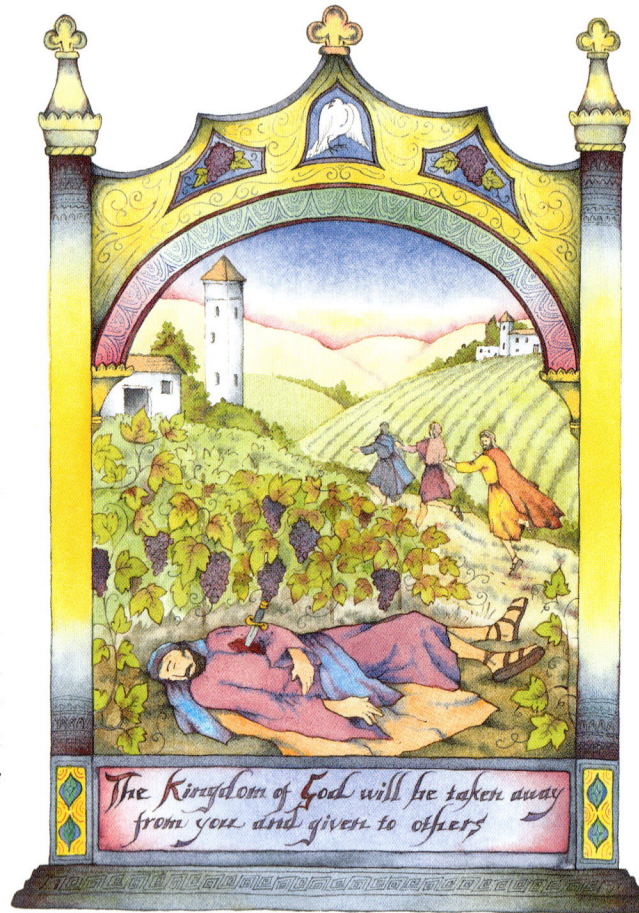

'The Kingdom of God will be taken away from you and given to others'.

According to Matthew, Jesus explained his purpose and that of his coming death at the Last Supper. After breaking the bread and offering his disciples the wine, Jesus says: *'"Drink of it, all of you; for this is my blood of the covenant which is poured out for many for the forgiveness of sins"'*(Matthew 26.27, 28).

Later, after Jesus had been betrayed and arrested, Matthew shows that Jesus did not deny to Caiaphas that he was *'The Christ, the Son of God'* (26.63). Like Mark, Matthew repeats the quotation from Psalm 22 as Jesus' last words.

Although Matthew also says little about Jesus' resurrection appearances, he does describe the visit by the two Marys to the tomb when they hear the news that *'he has risen, as he said . . . Tell his disciples . . . he is going before you into Galilee'* (28.17). Unlike Mark, Matthew describes the disciples meeting the resurrected Jesus on the mountain in Galilee and recounts how *'they worshipped him; but some doubted'* (28.17).

So, although Matthew leaves us with a mystery, his Gospel records at least a dozen different occasions when Jesus clearly indicated that he was acting for his heavenly Father.

ST LUKE AND HIS GOSPEL

Luke was a Greek and probably an early member of the Christian community at Antioch, where the disciples were first called 'Christians' (Acts 1.26). He is sometimes identified with the 'Lucius of Cyrene' (see Acts 13.1). He is described by St Paul at the end of his letter to the Colossians, written from Rome in about 62, as 'my dear friend Luke, the doctor'. In Paul's Second Letter to Timothy, probably written by a later disciple, Paul is described as saying from Rome that 'only Luke is with me' (II Timothy 4.14). According to Luke's Acts of the Apostles, we learn in the autobiographical 'we' passages from chapter 16 on, that Luke accompanied Paul on his third journey that ended in Paul's imprisonment in 58. Luke then went with Paul to Rome for Paul's trial before Caesar in 60. Luke was therefore in Rome with Paul, Peter and Mark at the time when Peter was dictating his gospel to Mark.

Luke's descriptions in Acts of key discussions earlier on between Paul and Peter suggest that he may have collected evidence from them both in Rome. In any case, the presence of St Peter, St Paul and the two evangelists in one place for more than a year makes it likely that they considered the need for a written Gospel in view of the risks they were running. Luke would have known that Mark was taking notes from Peter and may have been given a copy of his Gospel in 64. He then spent many years researching for his own much broader Gospel. This contains 19 of Jesus' parables. Most of them, like the parables of 'The Good Samaritan' and 'The Prodigal Son', are only found in his Gospel.

Luke also gives the birth-story of Jesus from Mary's point of view, while Matthew's seems to be from Joseph's. Luke wrote that 'Mary treasured all these things and pondered them in her heart' (Luke 2.19). The Holy Family in the stable are illustrated right.

'You will find the babe wrapped in swaddling clothes and lying in a manger'.
(Luke 2.12)

Luke's prologue to his Gospel says that *'many have undertaken to compile a narrative of the things which have been accomplished among us, just as they were delivered to us by those who from the beginning were eyewitnesses and ministers of the word. It seemed good to me also, having followed all these things closely for some time past, to write an orderly account'* (Luke 1.1–3).

Mary could possibly have been one of those witnesses known to Luke. If she had given birth to Jesus at the age of about 16, she would have been from 70 to 74 years old when Luke accompanied Paul and they stayed some time in Ephesus, where Mary is believed to have lived. Her alleged house can still be seen. Yet neither Luke nor Paul mentions meeting her, though she is thought to have lived there to a great age. Luke nowhere gives his sources. Whatever his source was for his account of Jesus' birth, he too emphasises both Jesus' humanity and his divinity.

Luke's Gospel is unique in giving Jesus' words in the synagogue at Nazareth about who he was and his purpose. After opening the book of Isaiah he read: *'"The Spirit of the Lord is upon me, because he has anointed me to preach good news to the poor. He has sent me to proclaim release to the captives, and recovering of sight to the blind, to set at liberty those who are oppressed, to proclaim the acceptable year of the Lord"'* (Luke 4.18, 19 quoting Isaiah 61.1, 2). These were the very attributes of the expected Messiah. After closing the book Jesus then confirmed his claim to the Messiahship by saying: *'"Today this scripture has been fulfilled in your hearing"'*. These words horrified his audience as blasphemous, so that he had to flee from them. It is therefore difficult not to believe, in spite of some critics' doubts, that Jesus saw his Messiahship as the role he had to play to fulfil his mission.

Soon after that episode Luke describes Jesus' 'Sermon on the Plain' (Luke 6.17–45) in a shortened version of Matthew's Sermon on the Mount. This contains many sayings which Luke and Matthew alone among the evangelists shared from what may have been the 'Q' source of Jesus' words. These included the command to *'"Love your enemies and do good to them that hate you"'* (Luke 6.27).

On the question of who Jesus was Luke records, like Matthew and Mark, that the imprisoned St John the Baptist asked him: *'"Are you he who is to come, or shall we look for another?"'* (Luke 7.19). Jesus, warned by experience, gives a cautious answer: *'"Go and tell John what you have seen and heard: the blind receive their sight, the lame walk, the lepers are cleansed and the deaf hear, the dead are raised up, the poor have the good news preached to them. And blessed is he who takes no offence at me"'*. Jesus then went on to explain who John was and, by implication, who he was himself. He did this by asking the people: *'"What did you go out into the wilderness to see? A reed shaken by the wind? A man clothed in soft clothing? . . . A prophet? Yes, I tell you – and more than a prophet. This is he of whom it is written: "Behold, I send my messenger before thy face, who shall prepare thy way before thee"'*. (Luke 7.25–28 quoting Malachi 3.1).

Luke alone explains the presence of Moses and Elijah with Jesus on the occasion of his Transfiguration which was witnessed by Peter, James and his brother John, the sons of Zebedee. Luke says the two prophets *'appeared in glory and spoke of his [Jesus'] departure, which he was to accomplish in Jerusalem'* (Luke 9.31). Thus, by recording the visible figures of the two dead prophets as actually talking, Luke perhaps shows that this dramatic event was anticipating how Jesus would also appear after his resurrection.

Luke, like Matthew, also describes the way Jesus taught his disciples the Lord's Prayer. He does this in chapter 11 and gives Jesus' own words of explanation: '"*Ask, and it will be given you*" (11.9). Then he adds significantly that "*if you then, who are evil, know how to give good gifts to your children, how much more will the heavenly Father give the Holy Spirit to those who ask him?"*'. This is the first time any of the evangelists actually mention the gift of the Holy Spirit.

Luke then gave Jesus' warning that following him would not be easy. He records Jesus' extraordinary words: '"*Do you think that I have come to bring peace on earth? No, I tell you, but rather divisions; for henceforth in one house there will be five divided, three against two and two against three*" (Luke 12.51, 52). In these words he warned that to follow the gospel would be a hard way of life. It would be too revolutionary for most people and would demand the sacrifice of many close relationships and traditions that they held dear. Jesus concluded by saying: '"*Whoever does not bear his cross and come after me, cannot be my disciple*" (Luke 14.27). Paul was one of the first to stress the importance of this.

Like the other synoptic gospels Luke tells how Jesus played the traditional role of the promised Messiah as he entered Jerusalem on an ass and the crowds shouted: '*Blessed is the King who comes in the name of the Lord! Peace in heaven and glory in the highest*' (Luke 19.38 quoting Psalm 118.26). Like Matthew, Luke emphasises Jesus' holy kingship, something even greater than the Jewish concept of Messiahship.

Luke's description of the Last Supper includes an important quotation by Jesus to his disciples concerning the life to come. In answer to their question he says: '"*You are those who have continued with me in my trials; and I assign to you, as my Father assigned to me, a kingdom that you may eat and drink at my table in my kingdom*"' (Luke 22.22, 29). Perhaps he was referring to his 'Second Coming' which he had described a few days before in the words of the prophet Daniel with: '*The Son of Man coming in a cloud with power and great glory*' (Luke 21.27 and Daniel 7.13, 14).

In Luke's Gospel little explanation is given by Jesus as to why he had to die, but at the Last Supper he said: '*This scripture must be fulfilled in me, "And he was reckoned among the transgressors", for what is written about me has its fulfilment*' (Luke 22.37 quoting Isaiah 53.12). This might also be taken as an allusion to the Book of Leviticus, chapter 16, when the Lord commanded Moses on the 'Day of Atonement' to sacrifice a goat, sending it out into the wilderness to die as a '*scapegoat*', bearing all the sins of the people of Israel on his back '*to a solitary land*' (Leviticus 16.22).

Luke does not mention this, but the concept of Jesus as a substitute sacrifice for others to obtain salvation for their sins became the accepted view. Therefore Christians have to look at this belief through first-century Jewish eyes in order to understand the 'Substitution' theory. It is not a concept that is in the least acceptable by modern notions of law. The first clear explanation of how Jesus saved us through the example of his unconditional love, was to be given in the twelfth century by the much-maligned Peter Abelard, famous for his love affair with Heloise. Abelard's solution will be mentioned in greater detail in the Calendar for August in the life of St Bernard of Clairvaux, whose hide-bound traditional arguments destroyed Abelard at his trial by French bishops for alleged heresy.

Luke gives Jesus' words at his trial before the Sanhedrin in answer to the question *'Are you the Christ?'* as *'"If I tell you, you will not believe; and if I ask you, you will not answer. But from now on the Son of man shall be seated at the right hand of the power of God"'*. When he was asked *'"Are you the Son of God?"'*, Jesus did not deny it, but simply said: *'"You say that I am"'* (Luke 2.67–70). Luke alone tells the story of the two thieves crucified with Jesus and how the 'good thief' (St Dismas) said: *'"Jesus, remember me, when thou comest into thy kingdom"'* (Luke 23.42). To which Jesus replied: *'"Truly, I say to you, today you will be with me in Paradise"'*.

Luke quotes Jesus' last words as *'"Father, into thy hands I commit my spirit!"'* (Luke 23.46). This is a quotation from Psalm 31.5. Jesus may have been mumbling several psalms and, as with the quotation given by Matthew and Mark, had Jesus had breath enough to finish that psalm he would have ended with this last message to encourage his disciples: *'Love the Lord, all you his saints! The Lord preserves the faithful, but he repays the arrogant with interest. Be brave, take heart, all of you who wait upon the Lord'*.

Luke records three reports of Jesus after his resurrection. The first is of how two men in white standing in the open tomb told Mary Magdalene and several other women that Jesus had risen. The disciples would not believe them. Later on two disciples met Jesus on the road to Emmaus, but they did not recognise him until after Jesus had broken bread with them and reminded them that it was *"necessary that Christ*

'Today thou shalt be with me in Paradise'.
(Luke 23.42)

should suffer these things and enter into his glory". The third sighting is when Jesus appeared through closed doors to the eleven apostles in Jerusalem and showed them his wounded hands and feet and then ate some fish. Jesus then told them: *'"Thus it is written, that the Christ should suffer and on the third day rise from the dead, and that repentance and forgiveness of sins should be preached in his name to all nations. And behold, I send the promise of my Father upon you; but stay in the city, until you are clothed with power from on high"'* (Luke 24.46–9 quoting Hosea 6.2).

Luke was not a witness to these post-Resurrection sightings, but he did not hesitate to provoke questions about their actual nature as they must have been described to him. He tells how Jesus vanished at Emmaus as soon as he was recognised and then that Jesus suddenly *'stood among them'* (Luke 24.36) in Jerusalem. His constant appearing and disappearing through walls and closed doors shows that Jesus' resurrected body did not conform to normal physical laws, although clearly something quite unique had happened; not a physical reconstruction, but something unexpected and mysterious.

These sightings all came unsought and convinced the apostles that by returning Jesus to them, God had vindicated his Son. They proved Jesus' victory over sin and death and demonstrated his unconditional love in his self-sacrifice for the sins of the world. Those who doubt their accounts should remember that the apostles could not go to their deaths while proclaiming the Resurrection, if they knew it to be a lie.

ST LUKE'S ACTS OF THE APOSTLES

The most dramatic event described by Luke in Acts is the sudden appearance of the Holy Spirit to the Apostles, Mary and other disciples at Pentecost, 50 days after the Resurrection. This inspired St Peter, according to Luke, to launch the Church with a brilliant sermon in which he gave the first 'oral Gospel' account of Jesus' life and mission. This caused 3,000 Jews to be baptised as believers in Jesus Christ the promised Messiah.

Luke could have heard the story of Pentecost from Peter in Rome. (The Pentecost scene is illustrated on the next page in an 'altar-piece'.) This suggests the thoughts that must have been uppermost in the minds of the Apostles as they awaited the coming of the Spirit. As they prayed and meditated, they may have pondered over the events of Jesus' life and what they had witnessed.

The events at Pentecost took place, according to Luke, about ten days after Jesus ascended into heaven. Pentecost was the Jewish Festival of Weeks. It took place 50 days after the Passover. Jews assembled for it in Jerusalem from many lands. Christians now celebrate this feast as 'Whitsunday', named from the old custom of baptising new converts dressed in white clothing on that day.

Mary and the Apostles were all gathered in an upper room in Jerusalem when 'suddenly a sound came from heaven like the rush of a mighty wind, and filled all the house where they were sitting. And there appeared to them tongues as of fire, resting on each of them. And they were filled with the Holy Spirit and began to speak in tongues, as the Spirit gave them utterance' (Acts 2.2–4). At the sound of this a crowd of Jews from every nation gathered round the house. They were amazed to hear the Apostles apparently speaking words in their different languages. They wondered how this came about and whether these people were drunk. St Peter was the first to realise what had happened. He stood up and addressed the crowd, explaining that they were not drunk 'since it is only the third hour of the day; but this is what was spoken by the prophet Joel: "In the last days it shall be, God declares, that I will pour out my Spirit upon all flesh, and your sons and daughters shall prophesy. And it shall be that whoever calls on the name of the Lord shall be saved."'

It was after this event that Peter, according to Luke, told the crowd that '"Jesus of Nazareth, a man attested to you by God with mighty works and wonders and signs which God did through him in your midst. This Jesus, delivered up according to the definite plan and foreknowledge of God, you crucified and killed. But God raised him up, having loosened the pangs of death, and of which we are all witnesses. Being therefore exalted at the right hand of God, and having received from the Father the promise of the Holy Spirit, he has poured out this which you now see and hear . . . Let all the house of Israel therefore know assuredly that God has made him both Lord and Christ – this Jesus whom you crucified."'

When the Jews in the crowd heard this they were cut to the heart. Peter then said to them '"Repent, and be baptised in the name of Jesus Christ for the remission of sins, and you shall receive the Holy Spirit"' (Acts 2.22–41).

Luke's account could be historical, since Acts records several other occasions when the Spirit descends upon new converts. It was not however the first time the Spirit had been given as St John records that Jesus came from his tomb and breathed the Spirit on the disciples alone.

The descent of the Holy Spirit at Pentecost

The experience of talking in tongues is far from unique then or nowadays among other faiths as well as Christians. It happens when a person or congregation has been so moved emotionally by prayers, exhortations and worship that they become filled with a sudden awareness of half-understood truths. Their mouths then gush out irrational words and phrases, as their minds attempt to express things that are still barely comprehensible to them. We shall see later what St Paul wrote about his experience of 'speaking in tongues'.

Before leaving the subject of Pentecost it may be helpful to quote some words of one of the greatest spiritual masters of the twentieth century, the Cistercian monk Thomas Merton (1915–68). In his diary for 25 April 1957 he wrote: '*Our life is a powerful Pentecost in which the Holy Spirit, ever active in us, seeks to reach through our imprisoned hands and tongues into the heart of the material world created to be spiritualised through the work of the Church, the Mystical Body of the Incarnate Word of God*'.

Pentecost changed the apostles from a group of saddened fishermen and peasants into the greatest band of religious teachers, whose followers were within a mere 280 years to convert the Roman Emperor, Constantine the Great.

ST JOHN THE EVANGELIST AND HIS GOSPEL

The Fourth Gospel, attributed in the second century to the disciple John the son of Zebedee and brother of James, pictures a far higher Christ than is given in the other Gospels. John's Jesus sometimes appears to be almost equal with God. Among John's 30 or so references to Jesus' relationship with the Father, Jesus says that '*"The Father is greater than I"*' (John 14.28). He says this even though he is also recorded as saying: '*"I and the Father are one"*' (John 10.30), '*"Before Abraham was, I Am"*' (John 8.58), and '*"I am in the Father and the Father is in me"*' (John 13.10). To the Pharisees these sayings were blasphemous claims to divinity, but they can also be seen as Jesus' way of proclaiming his Sonship by saying that he *'came from above'* (John 8.23) and that he had a special and almost parallel relationship with the Father.

John's Gospel therefore, written a generation after the others, shows how the evangelists' and the Church community's interpretation of the Gospel story had developed since the early days after Pentecost. This demonstrates how from the very earliest days the faith of the Church was a developing faith. This was so in the sense of the way its exponents' understanding of the gospel experience matured. There is for example some evidence in John's prologue for believing that he was influenced by the Greco-Jewish world-view of the Alexandrian Jewish theologian Philo and perhaps also by his contemporary St Paul in his Letter to the Philippians, written 30 years before John's Gospel. John's opening words are: '*In the beginning was the Word, and the Word was with God and the Word was God . . . and the Word was made flesh and dwelt among us*' (John 1.1–14). This prologue is John's symbolic equivalent of the birth stories of Jesus that had been written by

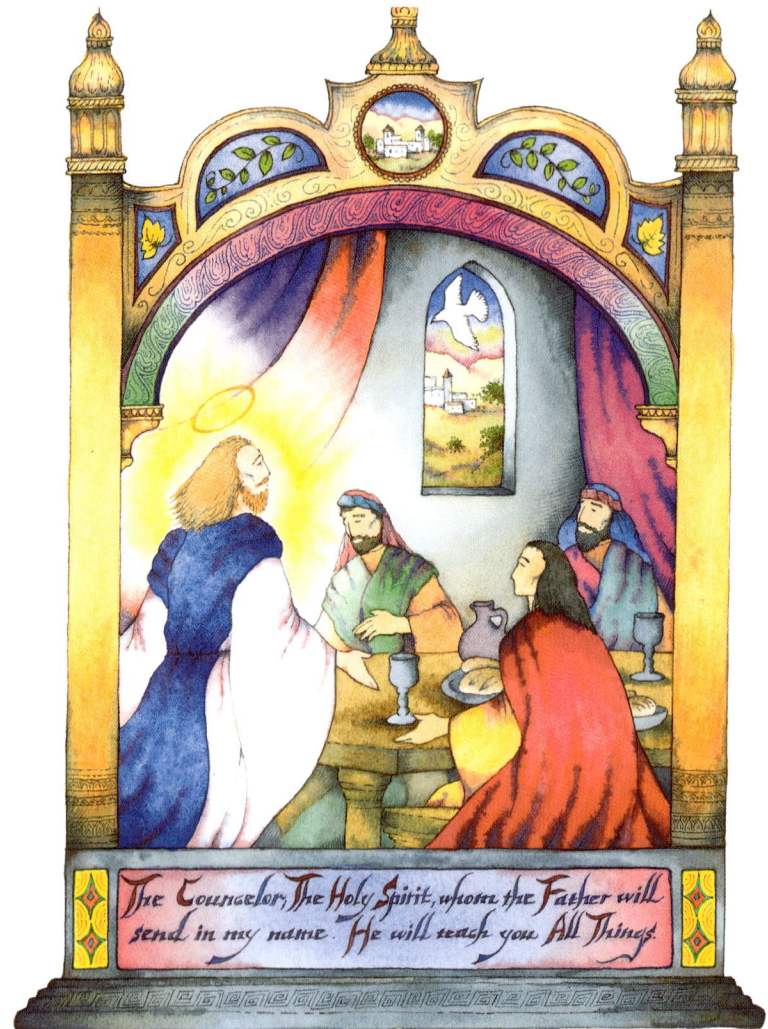

'The Counsellor, the Holy Spirit, whom the Father will send in my name, he will teach you all things'. (John 14.25)

38

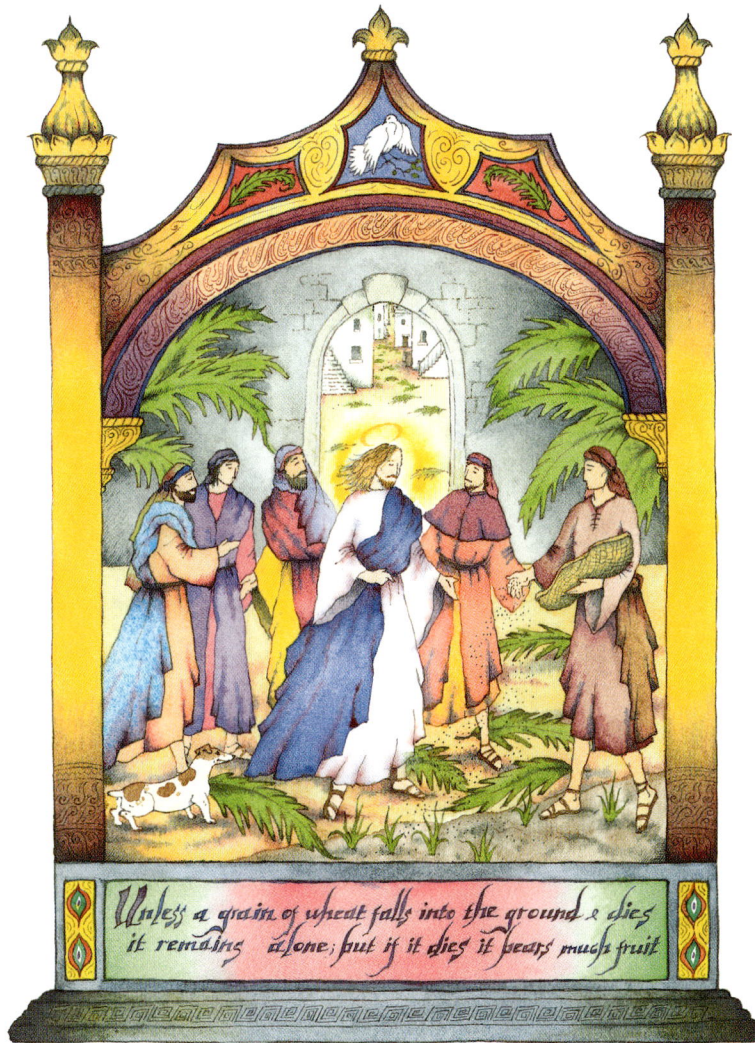

*'Unless a grain of wheat falls into the earth and dies,
it remains alone; but if it dies it bears much fruit'. (John 12.24)*

Matthew and Luke. It is designed to give his understanding of Jesus' nature and of God's purpose in revealing himself to the world through him. The words *'In the Beginning'*, as in Genesis, remind us that he is describing a new creation. By the 'Word' (or 'Logos') John implies Jesus' origin from above through the *Holy Spirit*. It was this *'Word made flesh'* who was Jesus of Nazareth, the man whom John described as *'the only begotten Son, who is in the bosom of the Father, he has made him known'* (John 1.18).

Thus John took the same revolutionary step as we shall see St Paul took, of reinterpreting the traditional Jewish concept of the One God. God was no longer to be talked of only in terms of his Spirit, or Breath, or as a Wind, Law, Wisdom and Will, but also as *'The Word of God'* revealed by Jesus. John's prologue also declares that Jesus not only revealed the Father, but that as *'The Word'* he had existed in God in a spiritual way since before creation. As for the Jesus known to the Church as the 'Risen Christ', he was now *'with God'*.

In view of the importance of John's Gospel, there are doubts as to whether it was written by John the disciple. It is clearly the work of someone who knew Jesus intimately. It was St Irenaeus of Lyons (c.130–200) who attributed both this Gospel and the Revelation of John to Jesus' disciple John the son of Zebedee and brother of James. These young men were called by Jesus the *'sons of thunder'*. When Jesus met them they were young, boisterous fishermen of perhaps 17 years of age, but they may also have been intelligent and favourites of his since he took only James and John with him and Peter to witness his transfiguration. There is no reason why John could not, as he matured, have been inspired by the Holy Spirit to become the learned evangelist by the age of 75 to 80. There is also one possibly autobiographical comment in John's Gospel, when he refers on three occasions to himself as *'the disciple whom Jesus loved'*. One of these times was once when he described the scene at the supper before Jesus was betrayed that *'there was leaning on Jesus' bosom one of his disciples whom Jesus loved'* (John 13.23).

St Irenaeus believed in St Polycarp's evidence, as was described in the text on the dating of the Gospels, that St John the disciple was the author of the fourth Gospel. As a young man he had heard from St Polycarp – Bishop of Ephesus, martyred in 156 at the age of 85 – that in his youth he had actually listened to St John preaching. This is quite possible since Polycarp was about 20 and John would only have been about 73 to 77 years old.

In this Gospel Jesus refers 17 times to our ultimate destiny as *'life everlasting'*, but unlike the other evangelists John only describes Jesus talking once about the 'Kingdom of God'. That is during his meeting with the secret Christian disciple Nicodemus, a member of the Sanhedrin. It was then that he told him *'"Except a man be born again, he cannot see the kingdom of God"'* (John 3.3). Jesus then explained that he meant being *'"born of water and of the Spirit"'*. He – or perhaps John – then explained that the Spirit was like the Wind: *'"The wind blows where it wills, and you hear the sound of it, but you do not know whence it comes or whither it goes; so it is with every one born of the Spirit"'* (John 3.8).

John's other unique contribution on the Spirit comes at the meal that Jesus held on the evening before the Last Supper at which he was betrayed and arrested. Although John describes Jesus at this meal as dipping bread into a cup (John 13.26), he makes no mention of any eucharistic ceremony. It was at supper that John describes Jesus promising his disciples *'"not to leave you comfortless: I will come to you. The Counsellor, the Holy Spirit, whom the Father will send in my name will teach you all things, and bring to your remembrance whatever I have said to you"'* (John 14.18).

Prior to this this Jesus had prepared the disciples for his forthcoming death by saying to them: *'"The hour has come for the Son of Man to be glorified. Truly, truly, I say to you, unless a grain of wheat falls into the earth and dies, it remains alone; but if it dies it bears much fruit"'* (John 12.23, 24).

With these words Jesus was implying the necessity for him to die so as to fulfil God's purpose and enable him to vindicate Jesus publicly by raising him again to send the Spirit back into the world. Jesus therefore added the explanation later that: *'"It is expedient that I go away, for if I do not go away, the Counsellor will not come to you; but if I depart, I will send him to you. And when he comes, he will convince the world concerning sin and righteousness and judgement"'* (John 16.7, 8).

In this way the Apostles were able in retrospect to understand that Jesus' death on the Cross was not a meaningless murder, but part of a single drama in God's plan, whose conclusion was the resurrection and ascension. Peter explained this at Pentecost. The other evidence for this is unique to John's Gospel, which records that Jesus said he was *'"sent into the world, not to condemn the world, but that the world might be saved through him"'* (3.17). He also said the famous words:

'"*Greater love has no man than this, that a man lay down his life for his friends*"' (John 15.13).

Jesus' words about himself, his Father and his mission are also illustrated by these quotations from John's Gospel: '"*As the Father has life in himself, so he has given to the Son to have life in himself*"' (5.26) and '"*The hour is coming when all that are in their graves shall hear a voice . . . and shall come forth*"' (5.28, 29), i.e. to judgement.

'"*I come in my Father's name*"' (5.47). '"*My doctrine is not mine, but his that sent me*"' (7.16). '"*I am from above: you are of this world*"' (8.23). '"*Before Abraham was, I am*"' (8.58), i.e. he pre-existed in the spirit before his incarnation. '"*My Father loves me because I lay down my life that I may take it up again. This command I received from my Father*"' (10.11–19). '"*Whoever loves me will be loved by my Father*"' (14.21). '"*The Father himself loves you, because you have loved me and believe that I come from God*"' (16.27).

The prelude to the second half of his Gospel starts with John's unique account of the raising of Lazarus in chapter 11. It was then that Jesus told Lazarus' sister Martha that '"*I am the resurrection and the life; he who believes in me, though he die, yet shall he live*"' (11.25). Unlike the other Gospels John does not record Jesus' transfiguration, perhaps preferring to use this story of Lazarus to prepare for Jesus' own resurrection.

John gives five pieces of evidence about Jesus' resurrection. The first is when Mary Magdalene, followed by Peter and '*the other disciple whom Jesus loves*' (i.e. John himself, John 20.2), discovered that Jesus' tomb was empty. The second is when Mary Magdelene met Jesus outside the tomb and thought he was the gardener, until he spoke and she recognised him, saying '"*Rabboni! Teacher!*"' (20.22). The third time is when Jesus met all the disciples except Thomas and breathed on them, saying '"*Receive the Spirit*"' (20.22). The fourth occasion is when all the disciples including 'doubting' Thomas were present. That was when Thomas, after seeing and touching Jesus' wounds, said to him '"*My Lord and My God!*"' (20.26). Modern Bible critics suggest that John's Gospel originally ended five verses after that. If they are right, then the fifth occasion, when John mentions Jesus after his resurrection, must have been added by editors later. This is John's chapter 21, when Jesus cooked breakfast for the disciples by Lake Galilee and told Peter '"*Tend my sheep*"' (21.16).

On the all-important question of 'Who was Jesus?' John quoted him as saying: '"*If you did know me you would know my Father also*"' (8.19). '"*I proceeded and came forth from God*"' (8.42). '"*I have not spoken to you of my own accord, but the Father who sent me commanded me what to say. And I know that his commandment is eternal life*"' (12.49, 50). These sayings are not claims to divinity, but clear explanations that Jesus was sent to reveal God in himself and to promise that our destiny was eternal life. It was in this sense that Jesus promised his disciples that "*You are my friends if you do what I command*" (15.14).

THE 'REVELATION' OF ST JOHN

It was St Irenaeus of Lyons in the second century who identified the author of 'Revelations' with St John the disciple and evangelist. John's name is mentioned three times in the book, including a reference to *'I John, your brother, who share with you in Jesus the tribulation and the kingdom and the patient endurance, was on the island of Patmos'* (Revelation 1.9), where he had been exiled for *'preaching Jesus'*.

The revelation that came to John was a vision brought by an angel. The whole book is a mixture of warnings of persecutions to come for the faithful, followed by the ultimate victory of *'The lamb'* – *'Christ'*. According to John, Jesus was the sacrificial lamb of the Passover, sacrificed for Israel's sins and the sins of the whole world. The language of the book is as beautiful as that of St John's prologue to his Gospel, but not all scholars are sure they were by the same author. The book has inspired the Church since the earliest days with an ideal picture of what life after the resurrection may mean. This vision is preceded by a description of the four creatures which became symbols of the evangelists. In the vision a voice then cried out to John: '*"Write what you see in a book"'* (Revelation 1.11).

'The Revelation of John' is filled with imagery linking the Old and New Testaments, leading up to a picture of the world to come: *'Then I saw a new heaven and a new earth; for the first heaven and the first earth had passed away, and the sea was no more. And I saw the holy city, Jerusalem, coming down out of heaven from God, prepared as a bride adorned for her husband; and I heard a loud voice from the throne saying "Behold, the dwelling of God is with men. He will dwell with them, and they shall be his people, and God himself will be with them; he will wipe away every tear from their eyes, and death shall be no more, neither shall there be mourning nor crying nor pain no more, for the former things are passed away." And he who sat upon the throne said, "Behold, I make all things new"'* (Revelation 21.1–5). That is to be an *Anastasis* on the grandest scale, with life being continued in a new form for all Creation.

'Receive the Spirit'.

PART FOUR

ST PAUL

'Take the whole armour of God'.

ST PAUL THE APOSTLE AND HIS LETTERS – INTRODUCTION

St Paul's Letters are the earliest Christian documents we possess. The two earliest letters, written in 48–49, are St Paul's Letters to The Galatians and his First Letter to the Thessalonians. St Paul is important because he was called by the risen Christ to be an apostle in about the years 35 to 37. He then became the first missionary to the Gentiles and the first great Christian theologian. In particular he explained the significance of Jesus' self-sacrifice on the cross, of his resurrection and of the work of the Holy Spirit. In St Peter's Second Letter it is said of St Paul's writings that 'some things in them [are] hard to understand' (II Peter 3.16). I will therefore quote again the words in the Preface of my learned friend the late Revd Basil Watson: 'If you can understand St Paul, you can understand Christianity'.

Paul's eight Letters only take a few hours to read, but they provide a life-time's food for thought. The Letters show that Paul often had to struggle in his attempts to define the relationship between Jesus and the Father and also to explain Redemption and Salvation. The Letters can often at first sight seem to be confusing. Because at times Paul takes different but complementary routes up the rugged mountain of faith, whose peak he admitted humbly to the Corinthians that he could not always see absolutely clearly: *'Our knowledge is imperfect and our prophecy* [Paul's word for 'interpretation'] *is imperfect; but when the perfect comes, the imperfect will pass away . . . For now we see in a mirror dimly, but then face to face. Now I know in part; then I shall understand fully. So Faith, Hope, Love abide, these three; but the greatest of these is love'* (I Corinthians 13.8–13).

Paul's Letters are particularly helpful to all who want to understand the working of the Holy Spirit. He writes of his own experience and understanding of the Spirit on about 60 occasions. That is four times as many references to the Spirit as there are in all four Gospels together. Paul told the Romans: *'the Spirit of God dwells in you'* and that when we pray and cry *'Abba! Father!' – 'it is the Spirit himself bearing witness with our spirit'* (Romans 8.9–17). We can find this to be true ourselves, if we really take time over our prayers and listen. It is then that we may get spiritual strength and understanding not only to achieve holiness of life, but to enjoy the fruits of the Spirit.

Paul explained to the Galatians that *'The fruit of the Spirit is love, joy, peace, patience, kindness, goodness, faithfulness, gentleness, self-control'*. He then said that *'those who belong to Christ Jesus have crucified their flesh with its passions and desires'* (Galatians 5.22–4). The importance of this need to crucify some of our natural and worldly passions was explained in a letter to me from Bishop Simon Barrington-Ward when he was Bishop of Coventry: *'Paul got it right by seeing the cross as the heart of the message, as did the writers of the Gospels which give a third to a half of their content to Jesus' passion and crucifixion. It is this that we need to seek to plant in the heart of the consciousness both of Christians and of people of all faiths, which is something different from seeking to make them what they are not'*.

Paul, who was not known by that name until after his dramatic vision of Christ before the gates of Damascus in about 34, was born as 'Saul', the son of a Jewish Pharisee and Roman citizen in the sea-port of Tarsus in Cilicia in about 10–15 BC. He was taught a trade, as were all Jewish boys. In his case it was that of a tent-maker. Paul practised that trade for two years to support himself and Luke in Ephesus in about 52AD. Prior to his conversion he had sat at the feet of the great Jewish theologian Gamaliel, seeking to learn the 'truth' about God and with the intention of becoming a Rabbi.

As the well-known stories about him in 'Acts' and his own letters record, while he was still called Saul he became a determined persecuter of the 'Jesus Sect' in the synagogues. He led the stoning to death of St Stephen, the first Christian martyr, outside the walls of Jerusalem in about 34AD (Acts 7). After that Saul's great moment came as he travelled to Damascus *'breathing out threatenings and slaughter against the disciples' (Acts 9.1) . . . 'As he journeyed, he came near Damascus. Suddenly there shone round him a light from heaven: and he fell to the earth, and heard a voice saying to him, "Saul, Saul, why do you persecute me?" And he said: "Who art thou Lord?" And the Lord said: "I am Jesus whom thou persecutes. Arise and go into the city, and you shall be told what you must do"'* (Acts 9.3–6).

Luke gives a fuller description of this in Acts (26. 13–23), when Paul tells the story of his conversion to King Agrippa, which suggests that the Risen Christ told Paul even more about himself and his mission.

Some scholars used to suggest that Saul's conscience had been suffering from doubts about what he was doing before he reached Damascus. His letters however show that his conversion after hearing Jesus' words was unpremeditated and instant.

Soon after his conversion and after learning more of the truth, Paul appeared in public, and *'preached Christ in the synagogues, that he was the Son of God'* (Acts 9.20). The Pharisees then forced him to flee from the city, whose walls he descended in a basket. His experiences after that are described in Paul's Letter to the Galatians, whom he told that he began by going far away into Arabia.

It was there that Paul seems almost certainly to have had further talks with the Risen Jesus, or else through the Spirit, because in his letter to the Galatians he wrote that: *'The gospel that was taught me is not man's Gospel, for I did not receive it from man, nor was I taught it, but it came by a revelation of Jesus Christ . . . I did not confer with flesh and blood, nor did I go up to Jerusalem to those who were apostles before me, but I went away into Arabia'* (Galatians 1.11–18).

'Saul, Saul! Why persecutest thou me?' (Acts 9.3–6)

ST PAUL IN THE FOURTEEN YEARS AFTER DAMASCUS

It was not until three years later in about 39 that Paul went to Jerusalem to meet Peter, James and John and discover if they approved of his teaching. After his favourable meeting with these apostles Paul returned to Syria and Cilicia to evangelise on his own. We learn from his Letters that he taught the gospel as far afield as Illyria or Dalmatia.

It was not until 14 years after his conversion that he again went to Jerusalem. Thus it was in 46–47 that Paul took Barnabas and his own Greek convert Titus with him to Jerusalem. There he met *'James and Cephas* [Peter] *and John, who were reputed to be pillars* [of the Church]' (Galatians 2.7). Paul describes that at his meeting with Peter and the others *'I laid before them the gospel I preach among the Gentiles, lest somehow I should be running in vain'* (Galatians 2.2). They approved and agreed that Paul *'had been entrusted with the gospel to the Gentiles just as Peter had been entrusted with the gospel to the circumcised'* (Galatians 2.7).

'The gospel I was taught came from a revelation of Jesus Christ'.
(Galatians 1.11–18)

ST PAUL'S LETTERS

At the beginning of his letter to the Romans Paul explains that he had been *'set apart for the gospel of God . . . the gospel concerning his Son, who was descended from David according to the flesh and designated Son of God in power according to the Spirit of holiness by his resurrection from the dead, Jesus Christ our Lord'* (Romans 1.1–4).

In this account Paul, the first Christian theologian, seems to imply a difference between Jesus the Son of man and Jesus the 'Risen Christ'. He also made Jesus' humanity clear when he told the Galatians: *'When the time had fully come, God sent forth his Son, born of woman . . . to redeem those who were under the Law, so that we might receive adoption as sons'* (Galatians 4.4, 5).

The key to Paul's theology stems from the *'Good News'* – *'The Gospel'* – that he received from the risen Jesus at Damascus. What he learned then and also during his meditations 'in Arabia', was that Jesus, while retaining his full identity as the Man of Nazareth, was now within the being of the One God of Jewish monotheism. He therefore, while retaining the belief in the One God, had to provide a new interpretation for the God of the Jews, *Yahweh ('YHWH')*, so that he could be understood as being eternally the source of the 'Word Incarnate'. Thus Paul's description agrees with that in John's prologue to his Gospel where he says that *'the Word became flesh and dwelt among us'* (John 1.14).

Like John therefore, Paul achieved this great advance in restating the nature of the One God of the Jews. He showed that God's Spirit revealed his 'Word and Wisdom' through Jesus of Nazareth. Thus he told the Corinthians: *'Yet for us there is one God, the Father, from whom are all things and for whom we exist, and the Lord, Jesus Christ, through whom are all things and through whom we exist'* (I Corinthians 8.6).

Paul explained this differently to the Colossians when he wrote of Jesus that *'He is the image of the invisible God, the first-born of all Creation . . . He is the beginning, the first-born from the dead . . . For in him the fullness of God was pleased to dwell, and through him to reconcile himself to all things, whether in earth or in heaven, making peace by the blood of his cross'* (Colossians 1.15–21). These words to the Colossians have been described as *'the most genuinely revolutionary bits of theology ever written'* by the Venerable NT Wright, now Bishop of Durham, in his book *What Saint Paul Really Said* (Lion Books, 1997). Thus Paul showed his belief that the one and only God was now known in terms at last of *'Father'* and *'Lord'*. However Paul never referred to Jesus as *Ho Theos* – 'God Himself', but always as 'Lord' *(Kyrios)* – *'God's mediator between God and men'* (I Timothy 2.5).

Paul defined Jesus in yet another way to the Philippians, emphasising his eternal pre-existence in the Father: *'Christ Jesus, who, though he was in the form of God, did not count equality with God as a thing to be grasped, but emptied himself, taking the form of a servant, being born in the likeness of men. And being found in human form, he humbled himself, taking and became obedient unto death, even death on the cross. Therefore God has highly exalted him and bestowed on him the name which is above everyone . . . and every tongue shall confess that Jesus Christ is Lord, to the glory of God the Father'* (Philippians 2.6–11).

For Paul, traditional Judaism was not enough. His meeting with Jesus at Damascus was an explosive discovery. He saw that with Jesus the new age, which he had previously believed *Yahweh* would institute at the end of time, had actually begun. That age had been launched on the Cross, as he told the Romans in the first six verses of his Letter to them. Paul then went on to tell the Romans that *'I am not ashamed of the gospel: it is the power of God for salvation to everyone who has faith'* (Romans 1.16).

Paul told the Corinthians: *'I delivered to you as of first importance what I also received, that Christ died for us in accordance with the scriptures, that he was buried, that he was raised on the third day in accordance with the scriptures, and that he appeared before Cephas and then to the twelve. Then he appeared to more than five hundred brethren at one time, most of whom are still alive . . . Then he appeared to James, then to all the apostles. Last of all, as to one untimely born, he appeared also to me'* (I Corinthians 15.3–8).

If we allow for duplications in the four Gospels, Paul therefore raises the list of sightings of the 'Risen Christ' to twelve occasions. Paul then says: *'Christ has been raised from the dead, the first fruits of those who have fallen asleep. For as by a man came death, by a man has come the resurrection of the dead. For as in Adam all die, so also in Christ shall all be made alive . . . The last enemy to be destroyed is death'* (I Corinthians 15.12–28).

Thus Paul recognised that Christ's death on the Cross and His subsequent Resurrection had a purpose and provided proof of what God has in store for us in heaven. The Resurrection is therefore of supreme importance. Indeed – as Paul realised and as the late Pope John Paul II wrote in his book, *Crossing the Threshold of Hope* (1994) – the Resurrection is the greatest single proof we have been given that God exists.

Having written of the future life, Paul then wrote *'How are the dead raised? What is sown does not come to life unless it dies. And what you sow is not the body which is to be, but a bare kernel – perhaps of wheat or of some other grain'* (I Corinthians 15.36–8).

John attributed the same argument of the seed of grain when telling of his need to die – as in the picture in Part III on John's life: *'What is sown is perishable, what is raised is imperishable . . . It is sown a physical body, it is raised a spiritual body . . . Thus it is written: "The first man Adam became a living being"; the last Adam became a life-giving spirit . . . Just as we have borne the image of the man of dust, we shall also bear the image of the man of heaven. So I tell you brethren: flesh and blood cannot inherit the kingdom of God, nor does the perishable inherit the imperishable. We shall not all sleep, but we shall all be changed. For this perishable nature must put on the imperishable, and the mortal nature put on immortality, then shall come to pass the saying that is written* [in Hosea 13.14]: *"Death is swallowed up in victory . . . O death where is thy sting?"'* (I Corinthians 15.35–55).

Paul told the Romans that *'now the righteousness of God has been manifested apart from the Law, although the Law and the Prophets bear witness to it, the righteousness of God through faith in Jesus Christ for all who believe. For there is no distinction; since all have sinned and fallen short of the glory of God, they are justified by his grace as a gift, through the redemption which is in Christ Jesus, whom God put forward as an expiation by his blood, to be received by faith . . . We hold that a man is justified by faith apart from works of the law'* (Romans 3.21–29).

Those words – *'He who through faith is just shall live'* (Romans 1.17 quoting Habakkuk 2.4) – released Martin Luther in 1511 from his fears that he would be damned; they showed him that *'the Just live by Faith'*. In order to stress this point in his German translation of the Bible, he made the words read: *'justified by Faith alone'*. In his commentary on Paul's Letter to the Romans he also said that though good works did not necessarily justify us, they should for true believers follow *'like cherries on a tree'*.

Paul went deeper than Luther was to do when writing about the way Jesus saved us. The Cross was the centre of his understanding of Jesus. Paul saw Jesus' voluntary sacrifice as turning shame into glory. This was proved by God's vindication of his action by raising him up at the Resurrection. Thus Paul told the Romans: *'While we were still weak, at the right time Christ died for the ungodly. Why? One would hardly die for a righteous man, though perhaps for a good man one will even dare to die. But God showed his love for us in that while we were yet sinners Christ died for us. Since we are therefore now justified by his blood, much more shall we be saved by him from the wrath of God. For if while we were still enemies we were reconciled with God by the death of his Son, much more now that we are reconciled shall we be saved by his life'* (Romans 5.6–11).

Paul explained this further: *'Do you not know that all of us who have been baptised into Christ Jesus were baptised into his death? We were buried therefore with him by baptism into death, so that as Christ was raised by the glory of the Father, we too might walk in newness of life. For if we have been united with him in a death like his, we shall certainly be united in a resurrection like his. We know that our old self*

was crucified with him so that the sinful body might be destroyed, and we might no longer be enslaved to sin. But if we have died with Christ, we believe that we shall also live with him. For we know that Christ, being raised from the dead, will never die'. It was perhaps these words that led St Irenaeus of Lyons and also St Gregory of Nazianzus in the second and fourth centuries to declare that with Jesus *'the Divine became human that we might become divine'*.

Paul exhorted the Romans *'to present your bodies as a living sacrifice, holy and acceptable to God, which is your spiritual worship'* (Romans 12.1). He had already, some three years before in 56, told the Corinthians the way to be saved – through Love. *'If I speak in the tongues of men and of angels, but have not love, then I am a noisy gong or a clanging cymbal. If I have prophetic powers and understand all mysteries and all knowledge, and if I have all faith, so as to move mountains, but have not love, I am nothing'* (I Corinthians 13.1, 2).In this Letter to the Corinthians Paul also wrote of a mystical experience that he had had after his stay in Arabia: *'I know a man in Christ who – fourteen years ago – was caught up in the third heaven – whether in the body or out of the body I do not know, God knows. And I know that this man was caught up in Paradise and heard things that cannot be told'* (I Corinthians 12.2–4).

Paul told the Philippians of the power of the Spirit to inspire and give us strength: *'I can do all things in Him who strengthens me* (Philippians 4.13). That is the strength of faith that we shall meet in the stories of the saints and other faithful. Faith can move mountains (I Corinthians 13.2). Paul also recognised that people can be so moved by the Spirit within them, that they cannot express themselves in ordinary speech, but may be so moved that they burst out in 'tongues' – as the apostles and others did at Pentecost. He discussed these 'tongues' in his letter to the Corinthians: '*Make love your aim and earnestly desire spiritual gifts, especially that you may prophesy. For one who speaks in tongues speaks not to men but to God, for no one understands him, but he utters mysteries in the Spirit. On the other hand, he who interprets speaks to men for their up-building and consolation, he edifies the Church. Now I want you to speak in tongues, but even more to interpret*' (I Corinthians 14.1–5).

'*He who speaks in tongues should pray for the power to interpret. For if I pray in a tongue, my spirit prays, but my tongue is unfruitful. What am I to do? I will pray with the spirit and I will pray with the mind also . . . I thank God that I speak in tongues more than you all; nevertheless in church I would rather speak five words with my mind, in order to instruct others, than ten thousand words in a tongue*' (I Corinthians 14.13–40). In spite of these qualifications Paul advised the Thessalonians: '*Do not quench the Spirit and do not despise prophesying, but test everything*' (I Thessalonians 5.19). That seems to mean we should test everything by the whole gospel. As Paul told the Corinthians: '*It is God who establishes us with you in Christ . . . he has put his seal upon us and given us his Spirit in our hearts as a guarantee*' (II Corinthians 1.21). '*Now the Lord is the Spirit, and where the Spirit of the Lord is, there is freedom. And we all, with unveiled face, beholding the glory of the Lord, are being changed into his likeness from one degree of glory to another; for this comes from the Lord who is the Spirit*' (II Corinthians 3.17, 18).

Having warned the Galatians against the evils of gratifying all desires of the flesh, for those who do so will not inherit the kingdom of God, Paul told them: '*Walk by the Spirit . . . The fruit of the Spirit is love, joy, peace, patience, kindliness, goodness, faithfulness, gentleness, self-control*' (Galatians 5.16–23). To these he added in his letter to the Colossians: '*Seek the things that are above, where Christ is seated. Put on then, as God's chosen ones, holy and beloved, compassion, kindness, lowliness, meekness and patience, forbearing one another and – if one has a complaint against another – forgiving each other; as the Lord has forgiven you, so must you forgive. And above all these put love, which binds everything together in perfect harmony. And let the peace of Christ rule in your hearts, to which indeed you were called in the one body*' (Colossians 3.1–16). These words are often read out to a newly married couple at their wedding ceremony.

Paul described his faith to the Corinthians in the context of the life to come: '*We know that if the earthly tent we live in is destroyed, we have a building from God, a house not made with hands, eternal in the heavens. Here indeed we may groan, and long to put on our heavenly dwelling, so that by putting it on we may not be found naked. For while we are still in this tent, we sigh with anxiety; not that we would be unclothed, but that we would be further clothed, so that what is mortal may be swallowed up by life. He who has prepared us for this very thing is God, who has given us the Spirit as a guarantee. So we are always of good courage; we know that while we are at home in the body we are away from the Lord, for we walk by faith – not by sight . . . So we make it our aim to please him. For we must all appear before the judgement of Christ, so that each may receive good or evil, according to what we have done in the body'* (II Corinthians 5.1–10).

To the Romans Paul wrote: *'The kingdom of heaven is not food and drink, but righteousness and peace and joy in the Holy Spirit'* (Romans 14.11). Paul always emphasised the happiness and joy that faith brings through the Spirit.

Paul also stressed the relationship between Father, Son and Spirit, as he did at the end of his letter to the Corinthians: *'The Grace of the Lord Jesus, and the Love of God and the Fellowship of the Holy Spirit be with you all'* (II Corinthians 13.14). That is a clear Trinitarian approach in its understanding of the relationship of the Three Persons united by love, as the 'Cappadocian Fathers' St Basil of Caearea, St Gregory of Nazianzen and St Gregory of Nyssa were to preach in the great debates that led to the Doctrine of the Trinity at the Council of Constantinople in 381.

In his First Letter to the Corinthians, written in about 58, Paul recorded the same words about the Bread and Wine that Jesus spoke at the Last Supper according to Matthew, Mark and Luke. He wrote that *'I received from the Lord what I delivered to you, that the Lord Jesus – on the night he was betrayed – took bread, and when he had given thanks, he broke it and said: "This is my body which is given for you. Do this in remembrance of me". In the same way also he took the cup – after supper – saying: "This cup is the new Covenant in my blood. Do this as often as you drink it in remembrance of me"'* (I Corinthians 11.23–26).

Paul also advised the Corinthians on the way the Holy Sprit guided different individuals: *'There are a variety of gifts, but the same Spirit; and there are varieties of service, but the same Lord; and there are varieties of working, but it is the same God who inspires them in everyone. To each is given a manifestation of the Spirit for the common good'* (I Corinthians 12.4–11).

Paul warned the Galatians against the evils of gratifying all desires of the flesh, since those who did so would not inherit the kingdom of God and told them to *'walk by the Spirit'*. He also told them that *'the whole law is fulfilled in one word, "You shall love your neighbour as yourself". But if you bite and devour one another take heed that you are not consumed by one another'* (Galatians 5.14).

Paul told the Ephesians how to approach their spiritual pilgrimage through life: *'Take on the whole armour of God, that you may be able to withstand in the evil day, and having done all to stand. Stand therefore, having girded you loins with truth, and having put on the breastplate of righteousness, and having shod your feet with the equipment of the gospel of peace; besides all these, taking the shield of faith with which to quench the fiery darts of the evil one. And take the helmet of salvation, and the sword of the Spirit, which is the word of God. Pray at all times in the Spirit, with all prayer and supplication'* (Ephesians 6.13–18).

PAUL'S POWERFUL ROMAN FRIENDS

Paul was skilled at cultivating powerful friends amongst governors, and guards officers. This enabled him to sow the seeds of Christianity at the heart of the empire, which would bear fruit over the two centuries following his death. In Cyprus in 47–48 the proconsul Sergius Paulus asked Paul to '*allow him to hear the word of God*'. As a result '*the proconsul believed . . . for he was astonished at the teaching of the Lord*' (Acts 13.7–12). In Corinth Paul was charged with blasphemy by the Jews and brought before the consul Gallio.

Gallio dismissed the case, saying: '*Since it is a matter of questions about words and names in your law, see to it yourselves*' (Acts 18.15). Gallio was obviously much taken with Paul, because he introduced him to his friend Burrus, commander of the Emperor Nero's Praetorian Guard. Thus when Paul arrived in Rome in 60 for his trial 'before Caesar', it was through Burrus that Paul gained access to the Imperial Palace. Paul confirmed this in his letter from Rome to the Philippians in 61–62, when he told them that the gospel '*became known throughout the Praetorian Guard*' (Philippians 1.13). In the same letter Paul also sent the Philippians greetings from '*all the saints . . . especially those in the imperial household*' (Philippians 4.22). Paul may also have been introduced into the palace household by Burrus' colleague Seneca, the senator and philosopher, who administered Rome with him in the early part of the youthful Nero's reign.

In spite of the many persecutions, there were always some Christians at court or acting as advisers to provincial governors like the Emperor Constantine's father Constantius in Britain at the end of the third Century. These converts included the highest officers of state and their wives, as well as knights and senators. Some of these were martyred, but the growing Christian influence among thoughtful Romans at Court encouraged the Emperor Philip the Arab (244–49) to be baptised. Philip and his empress even corresponded with the great Christian theologian Origen (185–256). He warned them to be careful, telling them that they were in danger – '*it is too good to last*'. It was shortly afterwards that Decius overthrew Philip and began the empire-wide persecutions of the Christians in 250, only exceeded by those of Diocletian at the end of the century after a 40-year gap.

Paul lived officially under house-arrest in Rome for two to three years, while his trial was being prepared for allegedly causing a riot by his speech to the Jews in Jerusalem. No record of him or his work exists after his last letters. He may possibly have gone on a mission to Spain, as he had told the Romans that he wanted to do '*after I have enjoyed your company for a while*' (Romans 15.24).

Paul certainly seems to have been absent from Rome during Nero's horrific massacring of the Christians, including St Peter, in 64. But Paul was a marked man by then, being one of the chief promoters of what to Nero's officers was a *superstitio illicita*. According to tradition Paul was seized and beheaded outside the Flaminian Gate of the city as he returned to Rome from a journey sometime in 65–67. He then may have been about 75 years old. He had kept the faith and '*run his race*'.

ST PAUL'S LETTERS TO ST TIMOTHY AND ST TITUS

Timothy and Titus were two favourite converts of Paul. The Letters to them may not be by Paul himself, but written later by one of his disciples in his style. They are called the 'Pastoral Letters'. Paul sent them on missions to several of his churches and made Timothy head of the Church in Ephesus and Titus the head of the Church in Crete. Timothy was martyred in Ephesus in about 97. According to tradition he was killed by a mob for protesting against a pagan festival. Titus died of old age as the first Bishop of Crete. These letters to Timothy and Titus are in the form of injunctions as to how to conduct themselves as church leaders. The first Letter to Timothy is filled with powerful words, which have inspired many Christians to be 'soldiers of Christ'. Some examples are given below.

'The aim of our charge is love that issues from the heart and a good conscience and a sincere faith' (I Timothy 1.5). *'This charge I commit to you, Timothy, my son . . . that you may wage the good warfare'* (I Timothy 1.18). By this Paul meant spiritual warfare for life is a spiritual battle between right and wrong and between love and hate.

'There is one God, and there is one mediator between God and men, the man Christ Jesus' (I Timothy 2.5). *'Fight the good fight of the faith, take hold of the eternal life to which you were called'* (I Timothy 6.12). *'Share in the suffering as a good soldier of Christ Jesus. No soldier in service gets entangled in civilian pursuits, since his aim is to satisfy the one who has enlisted him'* (II Timothy 2.3). *'Have nothing to do with stupid, senseless controversies; you know they breed quarrels* (II Timothy 2.23). *'All Scripture is inspired by God'* (II Timothy 3.16).

'The time of my departure has come. I have fought the good fight, I have finished the race, I have kept the faith' (II Timothy 4.6). *'The grace of God has appeared for the salvation of all men, training us to renounce irreligion and worldly possessions . . . to redeem us from all iniquity and to purify for himself a people of his own who are zealous for good deeds'* (Titus 2.11–14). *'He saved us, not because of deeds done by us in righteousness, but in virtue of his own mercy, by the washing of regeneration and renewal in the Holy Spirit, which he poured on us richly through Jesus Christ our saviour'* (Titus 3.5).

PART FIVE

FROM THE APOSTLES TO 451

The Scapegoat, bearing the sins of the world

INTRODUCTION TO PART FIVE

This brief survey aims to provide a historical background for the lives of the Saints and the work of the Spirit during a time of great change and great challenges in the first centuries after the death of the Apostles, whose fates are described in Table I (page 58).

The dates of the most important historical events in those centuries are first 313, when the Emperor Constantine I declared in Milan that there was to be freedom of religion throughout the Roman Empire; second, 325 and 381, when the Doctrine of the Trinity was declared at Nicea and finalised at Constantinople; thirdly 390, when Christianity was made the official religion of the empire by the Spanish Emperor Theodosius I; fourthly 451, when the Council of Chalcedon, on the advice of Pope St Leo I, defined the nature of Jesus Christ to be both wholly divine and wholly human.

THE RIVAL RELIGIONS FACED BY THE EARLY CHURCH

By the time of Constantine's decree in 313 it is estimated that between ten and 20 per cent of the population of the empire were Christian. The greatest number of these were in Greece, the near East and Egypt. The rival faiths, besides the worship of the traditional Roman deities, Judaism and the philosophies of the Greek Stoics and Epicureans, were the mystery religions of the Egyptian Isis and the Persian Mithras. Both the latter two faiths offered hope of a future life, which made them popular with the Roman soldiers.

There were also powerful groups of intellectuals who sought spiritual truths and were known as 'Gnostics'. This name comes from the Greek *Gnosis*, meaning 'knowledge', especially spiritual knowledge. The leader of these in Rome was a rich merchant called Marcion. He was attracted by St Paul's Letters because of the considerable attention that he paid to the Holy Spirit. Marcion was the first to publish a full set of St Paul's Letters and a truncated version of St Luke in 140.

In the second century the Gnostics published gospels of their own, attributing them to St Peter, St Thomas and others. In one of these they claimed that Jesus married St Mary Magdalene. Another, the *Gospel of Thomas*, denied that Jesus was crucified and said that *'only his image hung there'*. Four hundred years later the prophet Muhammad, founder of Islam, quoted those words in his Koran, which enabled him to reject the belief in the resurrection of Jesus.

The strongest new faith to rival Christianity was that of the Persian prophet Mani or Manaechius (c.215–274). Like Muhammad would do four centuries later, he claimed that he was the final *'seal of the prophets'*. He believed he had been called by God to found a religion that contained the best of all other religions. This led him to travel widely in the East and as far as China. He then chose the Persian deity Zoroaster, as well as Jesus and Buddha, as his top three religious teachers. He also, like the Gnostics, taught a dual version of the origin of the universe, according to which there were Good and Evil Principles. The good or Supreme God was aloof from the world and all material things, which were evil. The second and lesser God, Demiurge, was concerned with material things.

The Manichees were divided into the 'Perfects' and the lesser folk, or 'Hearers'. The souls of the Perfects were destined after death to abide with the Supreme God. The Hearers had to learn, through the Church's mystery rituals, how their souls could escape Demiurge to the abode of the Supreme God. St Augustine of Hippo joined the Manichaean Church when he was a student at Carthage, but left it after nine years.

TABLE I – THE FATE OF THE TWELVE APOSTLES

St Peter: He is believed traditionally to have been crucified upside down in Rome in 64, the treatment given to condemned slaves.

St Andrew: He was crucified in Greece on an X-shaped cross.

St James the Greater: Son of Zebedee and brother of St John. He was beheaded by Herod Agrippa I in 43 (see Acts 12.2). Claims that he evangelised at Santiago de Compostella date from the seventh century.

St John the Evangelist: Brother of James and son of Zebedee. Exiled to Patmos according to his book The Revelation of John, perhaps having looked after the Virgin Mary in Ephesus. Thought to have dictated the fourth Gospel in old age and to have died c.95–100.

St Philip: Recruited by Jesus at Bethsaida (John 1.43). At supper before the betrayal he asked Jesus to '*show us the Father*' (John 14.8). Believed to have been martyred at Heliopolis after evangelising in Phrygia.

St Bartholomew: May have been the 'Nathaniel' mentioned in John 1.45–51. Flayed alive in Armenia, whose Church he founded.

St Thomas: The 'doubting' Thomas of St John's account of the risen Jesus (John 20.24). Preached in South India and believed to have been martyred in Persia.

St Matthew: The tax collector called by Jesus in Capernaum (Matthew 9.9–13, Mark 3.18, Luke 6.15, Acts 5.27–32). May have written his Gospel in Antioch after reading St Mark's Gospel and sharing the 'Q' sayings of Jesus with St Luke. He is said then to have preached in Ethiopia and been martyred in Mesopotamia.

St James the Less: The son of Alpheus, but also referred to by Mark (6.3) as Jesus' brother and by St Paul in Galatians 1.9. He was head of the Church in Jerusalem and advised St Peter (Acts 15.13–21). He accepted Jesus as the promised Messiah but not as Son of God. He attended the synagogues and was close to the Chief Priest in Jerusalem.

James was martyred in 62 for refusing to deny Jesus as Christ. He was probably the author of the Letter of James. He was alleged by some gnostic gospels to have been kissed by Jesus as his successor. He may also have been connected with the Essene sect, whose non-Christian documents were found among the Dead Sea Scrolls in 1947. His followers fled from Jerusalem before it was besieged in 68.

A group of these followers, known as Jewish-Christians, were attacked as heretics in six sermons in about 395 by St John Chrysostom (347–407) who was Patriarch of Constantinople. In the 1930s the Nazi propagandists took these sermons to be evidence that the early Church was against all Jews, not just this small heretical sect.

St Jude or Thaddaeus: Mentioned in John 14.2. Possible author of the New Testament's Letter of Jude. Believed to have been martyred in Persia.

St Simon the Cananaean or the Zealous: Preached in Egypt and believed martyred with St Jude in Persia.

St Matthaias: Present in the upper room at Pentecost, before being chosen by lot to replace Judas Iscariot as an apostle (Acts 12.26). No more is known about him, but according to tradition he may have been martyred while preaching near the Caspian Sea.

THE PUBLICATION OF THE NEW TESTAMENT CANON OF SCRIPTURE

The publication of St Paul's Letters in 140 by Marcion made the leading thinkers of the Church realise that they had to publish an official set of Christian documents, which were considered to be genuinely of apostolic origin. This set of 27 documents formed the New Testament that we use today. Among those who decided on this selection were St Polycarp (c.69–c.155), the Bishop of Ephesus who said that as a youth he had heard St John preach, and Polycarp's friend St Irenaeus (130–c.200), Bishop of Lyons. St Irenaeus also wrote his book *Adversus Haereses* against the Gnostics, saying scornfully that they produced a new gospel almost weekly, claiming them to explain Christianity, but they were bad theology.

In 1947 a jar containing fifty Gnostic documents was found at Nag Hammadi in Egypt near the site of the monastery of St Pachomius (died 346). These manuscripts may have been hidden by monks from the monastery in 363 to save them from St Athanasius' religious police, who were sent out to destroy all heretical works. These documents included the so-called *Gospel of Thomas* and the *Acts of Peter*. The latter was the Christian novel which was referred to earlier in the life of St Peter in Part IV of this book.

The many early versions of the New Testament were thought by St Lucian (martyred 312) to be inaccurate. They were also written in such bad Latin that, as a student, the future St Augustine of Hippo could not take Christianity seriously. It was not until after Theodosius proclaimed Christianity as the religion of the State in 390 that Pope St Damasus I

(c.304–84) commissioned St Jerome (c.341–420) to produce an official translation of the Bible, using the oldest and most accurate scriptural sources in their original languages. Jerome established himself for this purpose in a nunnery at Bethlehem, where his researches were financed by St Paula and St Martina, two of the coterie of rich widows whom he had gathered around him in Rome.

Jerome was a difficult man who quarrelled with everybody. He was a ruthless critic, who rejected any document that he thought suspect and spent the rest of his life in producing the Latin Vulgate. At first he showered praise on the Greek translations and theological works of Origen (185–255), especially for his commentary on the gospel of St John and other writings (discussed in the January Calendar). Those writings had inspired the Cappadocian Fathers St Basil and St Gregory of Nazianzus during their campaign to agree the Doctrine of the Trinity.

However, in spite of his earlier praise for Origen, Jerome turned violently against him because he considered that some of his comments on the relationship between the Three Persons of the Trinity implied that they were three Gods. Jerome thus ignored the fact that Origen had already defined the Father, Son and Holy Spirit as *Homoôusion*, Greek for 'All of one substance', as was to be agreed at the Council of Constantinople in 381. In this way and although the doctrine of the Trinity was not defined until over 130 years after Origen's death, Jerome discredited a great religious explorer whose original works are now at last being praised by modern scholars.

THE ROMAN PERSECUTIONS OF THE CHRISTIANS

Unlike Judaism, which was licensed as a national faith, Christianity was regarded as an illegal superstition. Christians could therefore be condemned to death unless they rejected Jesus and cast incense before the altars of the imperial deities.

The first mass persecution of Christians was in Rome in 64, when the Emperor Nero killed them on a false charge of having set part of the city on fire. We also know from the Book of Revelation, that the early Church expected there to be an even greater assault on Christianity. This was probably the abortive one planned by the Emperor Domitian, who was killed in 96. After that the guide-lines for treating Christians were given by the Emperor Trajan (98–117) to Pliny the Younger, the governor of Bythinia. Pliny had asked for Trajan's advice in 109–111 because there were so many Christians in his province who were excellent citizens, that it would cause unrest if they were all tried and condemned. Trajan decreed that Christians were not to be hunted down and only tried if witnesses attended in person. Also they were only to be executed if they refused to worship at the imperial altars.

Other local governors often decided to seize and martyr Christians for reasons of their own. One example of this was when the governor of Lyons martyred its bishop and hundreds of Christians in the arena to provide entertainment for the citizens. The citizens of Lyons were not amused by the games and complained at the meanness of the governor. Another example was in 203, when St Perpetua and St Felicity were martyred in the arena at Carthage for refusing as to dress up in honour of a pagan festival. The story of their deaths by wild beasts, probably written by the Roman lawyer and Christian writer Tertullian (155–220), was publicised widely and impressed many who were not Christians.

The first empire-wide persecution was begun by the Emperor Decius in 250 and continued by his successors for several years. The victims included St Denis, patron saint of France, who was beheaded on the hill of Montmartre in Paris. The worst and longest persecution was begun by the Emperor Diocletian in 303, because his co-emperor Galerius claimed that Christianity weakened all the traditional Roman virtues. This persecution ended in 312 after Constantine's victory over his rival emperor Maximian at the Milvian Bridge outside Rome.

Before that battle Constantine is said to have had a vision. According to the story, which was illustrated in Arrezzo in a famous fresco by Piero della Francesca, Constantine had seen the sign of the cross in the sky and heard the words *'In hoc signo vinces'*. He took this to mean that he would conquer under the sign of the cross. He therefore had the Greek letters XP, signifying Christ, and a cross painted on the shields of his soldiers. After he had won his battle, Constantine decreed that, henceforth, all his legions should have this sign placed on a spear and carried before them on their marches. This did not mean that he was converted to Christianity, because he was not baptised until the eve of his death in 337.

Constantine had had a remarkable spiritual experience at that time and while he was searching earnestly for the God who would most favour Rome. He had thought that this God might be the Unconquered Sun, *'Solus Invictus'*, the source of his vision. After his victory he went a long way to accepting Christianity and showed his favour by paying for the ruined churches and Christian shrines in Rome to be restored. He followed this by his declaration in Milan in 313 that there was to be freedom of worship throughout the Empire.

ESTIMATING THE TOTAL NUMBER OF CHRISTIAN MARTYRS

It can be seen from the records of the saints in the Roman Calendar that 90 per cent of the saints of the first three centuries were martyrs. It is impossible to give an exact figure for the number of victims, as the names of many were known only to God. The example of the martyrs for the faith did, however, make a profound impression throughout the empire. Fidelity was the highest virtue in Roman society and the example of the martyrs made people examine the nature of the religion for which they had died. As a result Tertullian wrote that *the blood of the saints is the seed of the Church*.

Before the two great persecutions of Decius and Diocletian, the Christian theologian Origen (185–255) had written that the numbers of martyrs had been exaggerated and probably the total was not much more than 5,000. However Origen himself died in 255 from the effect of the tortures he had suffered during the persecution of Decius. Therefore

his figure for the number of martyrs did not include any of the victims from 250–313. Judging from the number of martyred saints listed in the Calendar for the periods covering those persecutions, the total number of Christian martyrs could have reached 20,000.

Diocletian's persecution was particularly severe in Rome, Asia Minor, Egypt and North Africa, but it was much milder in Spain, Gaul and Britain which were ruled by Constantius Chlorus, the father of the future emperor Constantine. He disregarded the edicts from Rome and continued to employ Christians in his administration. Even in Egypt the pagan population had tired of the constant attacks on the Christians. There is evidence supporting this in the autobiography of St Athanasius (166-167). He tells how his Christian parents were hidden from the Roman soldiers hunting for them by sympathetic pagan families, in their own homes.

THE SAINTS OF THE EARLY CHURCH

The early martyrs were the first Christians to be regarded as saints after the Apostles and Evangelists. These are sometimes known as the 'Red Martyrs'. Because they had shed their blood for the faith, they were deemed to have gone straight to heaven, having done all that they could humanly do. The practice of collecting the remains and ashes of the martyrs first began after St Polycarp was burned to death in 155. The relics of the saints were then placed under altars or in shrines to be venerated by the faithful in the belief that, being with

God, the saints could intercede for healings and other mercies. The later saints, who had not been martyred, are sometimes known as the 'White Martyrs', on the grounds that they had crucified themselves for the faith by giving up their ambitions and worldly desires. These saints were acclaimed by the local populations after getting the support of their bishops. The making of saints and their total numbers will be explained in the introduction to the 'Calendar of Saints' that follows this part of the book.

THE EMPERORS AND THE ARIAN HERESY 318-81

The last Christian to suffer martyrdom was St Lucian of Antioch in 312. He was a victim of Constantine's co-emperor Licinius, who was ultimately defeated by him. Lucian founded a theological school which examined the corrupt texts of Scripture then in circulation. He also promoted the literal meaning of the texts. This had led him into conflict at an academic level with the Church leaders, though he was reconciled with the Church before he died. However one of his most learned pupils, Arius, became a monk in Alexandria and promoted what became known as the 'Arian' heresy. This split the Church from about 318 for more than a century.

Arius claimed that although God is one, eternal and unbegotten, there was once a time when the Logos – Jesus, the Word and Son – 'was not', therefore Jesus was created and was only adopted as Son of God at his resurrection. This doctrine completely undermined the tradition of the Church that God was in three persons, Father, Son and Holy Spirit, or all of the same substance – *Consubstantialis*, as Tertullian had described, or *homoôusion* in Greek, as Origen had proclaimed.

Most of the bishops, many of whom were Constantine's courtiers, followed Arius. Therefore the schism in the Church so disrupted public affairs that the Emperor summoned a Church council at Nicea (on the opposite shore of the Bosphorus to his capital) in 325 to decide what orthodox doctrine should be. The Emperor presided. Largely due to the erudition of St Athanasius (296–373), who was then still only a deacon and secretary to the Bishop of Alexandria, the traditional doctrine of the Trinity was confirmed and Arius and the heretical bishops were exiled.

This was not the end of the matter. Constantine and his successors regarded the Church as a department of state. This caused them to interfere even over spiritual matters. The Arian controversy did not die down and therefore Constantine, in the interests of the State, ordered that Arian clergy should be allowed to celebrate the Eucharist in Orthodox churches. He also allowed Arius to return.

Athanasius, who had become Archbishop of Alexandria, stoutly refused to obey the Emperor and was exiled. This was the first of his five exiles during his more than 40-year reign over his diocese, as will be described in his life in the Calendar for August. This controversy was only settled at the Council of Constantinople in 381 through the efforts of the Cappadocian Fathers St Gregory of Nazianzus and St Basil of Caesarea. Their stories will be told at the end of the Calendar of saints for January.

HERESIES WHICH THE EARLY CHURCH HAD TO FACE

The distinguished theologian St Epiphanius, Bishop of Salamis in Cyprus, published a book in 370 in which he described no less than 70 rival Christian heresies, or major doctrinal differences, within the Church. He showed that the earliest of these began even amongst the Apostles and was caused by St James the Less, who was called Our Lord's brother. St James' unorthodox views on the nature of Jesus was outlined above in the table describing the fates of the different Apostles.

The worst of the heresies after that of Arius was the Monotheist controversy. This arose through the opposing views of the Schools of Antioch and Alexandria on the nature of Jesus. The Antiochans taught that he was both wholly divine and wholly human, while the Alexandrians, encouraged by St Cyril (376–444), taught that Jesus was wholly divine. This denied Jesus' humanity and therefore undermined the traditional doctrine that he gave his life for our salvation. The long-term ill-effects of this schism will be outlined below.

TEETHING TROUBLES OF THE CHURCH AND THE FOUNDING OF THE MONASTERIES

Having described how Christianity survived the persecutions and having outlined some of the problems it faced, it is time to show the state of the Church by 451, when the Council of Chalcedon was held (and which resulted in the Definition of Chalcedon), and to point out some of the problems that still remained. These will be covered in greater detail in the next part of the book, in the lives of the saints.

The victory of Christianity as a world faith was achieved in 390, when the Spanish-born Emperor Theodosius I (379–95) made Christianity the official religion of the Empire and ordered all pagan sacrifices to cease and all their temples to be closed. He also ended the long domination of the clique of Arian bishops at the imperial court.

By that time St Antony of Egypt (c.250–356) had, through his Desert Fathers, laid the foundations of the monastic movement. This was to be the great engine for spreading Christianity for over 1,000 years. Antony's life will be described in the Calendar for January, as also will be that of St Basil of Caesarea (c.330–79), who followed Antony's example by founding the first monasteries in the East.

By the middle of the fifth century the monastic system had been established in Gaul by St Hilary of Poitiers (c315–368) after he returned from exile in the East and had met St Basil. Hilary encouraged St Martin of Tours (316–397) to found monasteries at Ligugé and at Montpelier. These adopted the Rule of St Basil for organizing the lives of their monks. The other important monastic foundations in Gaul were the hermitages on the Isles de Lerins, about a mile from modern Cannes, that were founded by St Honoratus of Arles in 409 and the monastery of St Victor near Marseilles, founded in 414 by St John Cassian (c.360–433). During the next few centuries the followers of St Benedict of Nursia (c.480–c.550) founded many monasteries in Gaul, Germany, the Netherlands, Britain and Ireland. These were havens of Christianity in a sea of paganism.

Honoratus based his system at Lerins on a different set of rules, those of St Pachomius (died 346), a follower of St Antony in Egypt and his Desert Fathers. The importance of this is that the Egyptian and Greek monastic styles differed and they had a different system for deciding the date of Easter. This meant that when St Patrick (c.390–461), who had been trained at Lerins after escaping from slavery in 409, began his mission to Ireland in 432, he took with him the Egyptian system of dating Easter for his Celtic Church. This system and its humble approach to evangelising the poor, was therefore the one introduced by Irish monks to Northumbria two centuries later. It was because of this that the Anglo-Saxon Church suffered a major blow at the Council of Whitby in 664, when St Wilfrid (633–709), dazzled by his visits to Rome, forced it to agree to the Roman dating of Easter and the hierarchical structure of the Roman Church.

This was to be of far-reaching importance, since the Celtic Church style and way of evangelising was far less autocratic than that of the Roman Catholics. Many Anglo-Saxons were to regret this change, especially the learned Yorkshire monk Alcuin (732–804), who was the Emperor Charlemagne's chief adviser for educating his clergy. Alcuin criticised the grand style St Wilfrid had introduced into Britain by parading his retinue of priests in rich clothing. This was unlike the earlier Celtic missionaries in Britain like Bishop St Aidan of Lindisfarne (died 651). He always went on foot through his vast diocese of Northumbria, which stretched from the Humber to the Firth of Forth, and stayed in humble homes to preach so as to be close to the ordinary people.

Another perennial problem for the Church was, as has been shown above, the way the emperors interfered over spiritual matters. The saint who did most to oppose this was St Ambrose (339–397). He was elected Bishop of Milan in 374 and even made the Emperor Theodosius do penance for an act of great cruelty and injustice in slaughtering several thousand citizens of Thessalonica. He also told the Emperor Valentinian II that he was within the Church, but not above it. The Greek Orthodox Church would always remain a semi-department of state, but the Popes, the Bishops of Rome, gradually freed themselves from the Eastern emperors at Constantinople by the end of the seventh century. Nevertheless the relationship between the Papacy and the German Emperors would remain difficult even during the reign of Charlemagne, who Pope Leo III crowned King of the Romans on Christmas day 800.

The internal struggles in the Church over fundamental doctrine did not cease after the Council of Constantinople in 381. The Church school of Alexandria, supported by its Bishop, St Cyril of Alexandria (c.376–444), began to teach that Christ was wholly divine, thus ignoring his human nature and undermining the traditional doctrine of salvation. This was opposed strongly by the school of Antioch. This Monotheist doctrine spread rapidly and caused a fierce and at times murderous disagreement between its followers and the supporters of the Orthodox doctrine. Then in 451 the Council of Chalcedon accepted the ruling by Pope St Leo I the Great (died 461) that the nature of Jesus was both wholly human and wholly divine. Monotheism was therefore declared a heresy. This presented no problem in the West, but soon afterwards the Monotheists killed the Orthodox Archbishop who had been imposed on Egypt. From then on until the Muhammadan invasions of 638–648, the majority of Christians from Syria to Egypt were monotheists and opposed to Constantinople.

This was a tragedy for the Orthodox Church in the East. This great schism, and others that St Cyril and his uncle had caused by their political scheming, eventually had a fatal effect on the Church in the Middle East, causing it to lose the entire region and North Africa to Islam. This took place after 609, when Muhammad rejected Christianity, having found that there were at least six rival Christian sects teaching the gospel, while he had been searching for the one God for his Arab people. Although he accepted Jesus as a prophet, he could not accept Christianity because, as the Koran says, 'the sects cannot agree on the nature of the God they worship'.

This might not have happened if St Cyril of Alexandria, brilliant preacher though he was, had not attacked the Orthodox teaching of Antioch and the Patriarchs of Constantinople. He did this, like his uncle Theophilus, who was his immediate predecessor as Archbishop of Alexandria, because he was an ardent Egyptian nationalist and wanted to free Egypt from the control and taxation imposed by Constantinople.

The trouble with saints like St Cyril is that, great churchmen though they may be in some respects, they are like the champion tennis players, who sometimes serve as many double faults as they do aces. Even St Augustine of Hippo made great errors of judgement. For example he taught that the sexual act was evil. This was probably a hangover from his Manichaean days, but it has done much to inhibit and mislead social attitudes. Augustine was the greatest theologian in the West, as can be seen by his *Confessions* and his *City of God*, which outlined the ideal Christian society and guided the Church for 1,000 years.

However, Augustine pressed his doctrine of God's grace to such extremes, that he was forced to adopt a system of double predestination, that from birth we are all destined, no matter how hard we try, either to eternal life or to eternal damnation. Although the Church, encouraged by the monks of Lerins, condemned this as non-scriptural at the Council of Orange in 529, this belief had a discouraging effect on the faith. It was adopted by the Geneva reformer John Calvin in the sixteenth century and the Scottish theologian John Knox. As a result it is still held by most Presbyterian churches.

CHRISTIANITY AT THE START OF THE GREAT BARBARIAN INVASIONS IN THE FIFTH CENTURY

By the time the Visigoths from the Danube had sacked Rome in 410, the Vandals had crossed the Rhine into Gaul in 407 and destroyed everything on their path to Spain and North Africa. As St Augustine lay dying in 430, the Vandals were besieging his city of Hippo Regis. They then went on to take Carthage and Rome. Their leader Generic sacked the city and reduced the population from about half a million to less than 30,000. Other Germanic tribes followed the Vandals across the Rhine into Gaul including the Huns, the Burgundians and finally the Franks. The Saxons, meanwhile, had invaded and conquered most of Britain by 450. The Western Empire finally ended in 476, when the Gothic general Odovacar forced Romulus Augustulus to abdicate.

Yet the Church managed to survive and its missionaries converted the tribesmen to Christianity in the next two centuries, by which time the Irish missionaries had established over 100 monasteries from Gaul to the Alps and the Benedictine monks had spread their monasteries as far as Ireland, Britain and Eastern Germany. The Church was therefore able to resume its evangelising in spite of many set-backs, until by 1340 the Poles and Lithuanians were the last of the European peoples to become Christian.

The achievements and teething troubles for Christianity, that have been outlined above in earlier paragraphs, show how the Spirit gave strength to the faithful to face and overcome so many difficulties and set-backs. It therefore is appropriate to end this historical survey of those early centuries by quoting the words of six great Friends of God, whose words and wisdom are as relevant today as they were between the second and the fifth centuries.

Clement of Alexandria (c.150–220)

Clement of Alexandria wrote that '*The truth is to be found everywhere, because God implanted his image on all men at Creation. Following on the miracle of Christ's incarnation He, the Word, became the focus of the divine influence in the world. Thus Christ is God, the Ideal Man. That is true 'Gnosis' or Knowledge*'.

Origen (c.185–254/5)

Origen was Clement's pupil. Both were regarded as saints when they died. Their writings inspired the great Cappadocian Fathers St Basil and St Gregory of Nazianzus in the fourth century. However they were both deprived of their sainthood by the order of the Emperor Justinian I in the sixth century for political reasons. Their lives and teaching will be found in the January Calendar; meanwhile here is Origen's succinct definition of the purpose of the Church: '*The Church is the school of souls*'.

St Basil of Caesarea or 'The Great' (c.330–379)

St Basil made this wise and broadminded statement on the way God works through his Holy Spirit: '*Thou hast visited humanity in many ways. In the loving kindness of thy heart thou hast sent the prophets. Thou didst speak through thine own Son. There is no culture or religion that has not received and does not express a "visitation of the Word."*'

If only the Church had remembered these words, instead of damning every other faith as pagan, so much bitterness, hatred and warfare might have been avoided. All the world's faiths were inspired by the Spirit, as Pope John XXIII declared at the Second Vatican Council in 1962. This will be explained in greater detail towards the end of Part VII, 'The Unquenchable Spirit'.

Bishop Theodore of Mopsuestia (fifth century)

Bishop Theodore's see was the largest after Constantinople. '*Although there was only one person in Christ, there was a duality of natures, each nature, human and divine, was perfect as if joined in a moral union*'. This was the simple and wise answer to the almost 40-year quarrel between the orthodox views of the Antioch school and those of St Cyril of Alexandria over the nature of Christ.

St Isidore of Pelusium (365–449)

St Isidore was the abbot who trained St Cyril and who tried to control his excesses of zeal. These quotations are from his letters to Cyril: '*God values nothing more than love, for the sake of which he became man and obedient to death*'.

In the following words Isidore told Cyril of Alexandria to stop objecting to the sainthood with which the Church had honoured the victim of his brutal uncle Archbishop Theophilus, St John Chrysostom: '*Put a stop to these contentions; do not involve the living Church in a private vendetta prosecuted out of duty to the dead, nor entail her perpetual division under pretext of piety*'. In these words the exasperated Isidore criticizes Cyril for refusing to recognise St John Chrysostom as a saint because he was the victim of his uncle

Theophilus' outrageous scheming. If only Cyril had heeded Isidore!

In one of his many letters to his friends, Isidore tried to get his correspondent to leave off these pointless rhetorical and hair-splitting arguments and to concentrate on what really matters: '*If we are to overcome heretics, pagans and Jews by our doctrines, we are also to overcome them by our conduct, less when worsted on the former ground, and after rejecting our faith, they should show how unfavourably our lives compare with it*'. Mahatma Ghandi was to make exactly the same comment on Christianity in the 1930s.

In another letter Isidore once again argues against the futile debates about matters which in any case are divine mysteries: '*Always we need more people prepared to live in Christ than to talk about him. We are bound to know and believe that God is, not to busy ourselves as to what he is*'.

St Vincent of Lerins (died soon after 450)

St Vincent's well-known definition of the Catholic faith is often quoted: '*The Catholic faith is that which has been believed everywhere, always and by all*'. What however is never quoted by those in the Church's hierarchy who oppose changes, is this equally wise and profound saying with which Vincent continued: '*Is there then to be no progress of religion in the Church of Christ? Clearly there is to be progress, but it must resemble the growth of an infant to maturity, a growth which, through all the changes preserves its identity. The dogmas of the heavenly philosophy may by the operation of time be smoothed and polished. They may gain in the way of greater fullness of evidence, light and elucidation, but they must of necessity retain their integrity and essential features. Such has been the task of the Church in the decrees of the Councils, aimed at adding clarity, vigour and zeal to what was believed'.*

These quotations are all taken from the *Dictionary of Christian Biography* of the first eight centuries, published by John Murray in 1877–87. Unfortunately none of the present popular dictionaries of saints even mention St Isidore of Pelusium or St Vincent of Lerins, yet their words are as valid today as they were 16 centuries or so ago. The next part of the book, 'A Calendar of Saints', outlines the lives of 750 Christian heroes and heroines who have been made saints in the centuries leading up to our own. It is they, and other faithful witnesses who are not saints, who have preserved and developed the faith.

In recording the works of these Friends of God, special care will be taken to discuss the works of those who are particularly relevant to our world today.

PART SIX

A CALENDAR OF SAINTS

The Seven Heroic Saintly Virtues

INTRODUCTION: THE MAKING OF SAINTS

On hearing that I was writing about the saints, a lady asked me if they were made by God. I told her that apart from the Apostles, to whom Jesus said 'You did not choose me, but I chose you' (John 15.16), the saints are chosen by men, by the Church. Today the greater part of a pope's life is spent in the examination and selection of candidates for sainthood as examples of holiness.

Besides the proofs that are required of miracles that have been experienced by the faithful through venerating their names, the lifetime record of a candidate for sainthood has to show proof of heroic virtue in all of the seven saintly virtues. These are illustrated on page 69 as the four Classical virtues of Fortitude, Justice, Temperance and Prudence and the three Christian virtues of Faith, Hope and Charity or Love. In the illustration the figure for Prudence (bottom row, second from right) is not, as it may appear, looking at her face in a mirror but at what is going on behind and around her.

The Early Church recognised the Apostles and Evangelists as saints and then in the second century added to them those who had died for the faith as martyrs. In the next few centuries many other faithful witnesses were acclaimed as saints by local congregations for their heroic virtues and for spending their lives as 'white martyrs', living entirely for the faith and giving up worldly desires and ambitions. All these were venerated in the belief that they would be able to intercede with God for the petitioner to grant healing or other mercies.

Among the first saints to be recognised after the Apostles and martyrs were leading theologians and others who were renowned locally for their holy lives. These were chosen by public acclamation. Their sainthood then had to be confirmed by the local bishops. At the Second Council of Nicea in 787 it was decreed that every new altar should contain the relics of a saint. This led to an enormous demand for relics and this, in turn, caused a greatly increased number of local heroes and heroines to be recognised as saints.

The result was that by the tenth century there were, according to the massive *Bibliotheca Sanctorum*, at least 20,000 saints. These were in addition to those listed in the martyrologies drawn up in the fifth and sixth centuries by St Jerome, St Gregory of Tours and others.

In the tenth century the popes limited the numbers of new saints by insisting that only they had the authority to create them. The rules requiring proofs of miracles and heroic virtue described above were made at that time and they have been followed in principle ever since. The Papacy took some centuries to gain full control of saint-making, but the effect of the rules can be judged by the fact that only about 350 new saints were canonised between 1300 and 1950, when there were about 4,000 'universal' (as opposed to merely 'local') saints in the Roman Calendar.

Since 1950 the rules have been made less strict and the scope for sainthood has been broadened to take more account of holiness of life. The old custom of requiring that the petitioners answer the case of a 'Devil's Advocate' against their candidate has been dropped. As a result, in the past 40 years the popes have created over 1,000 new full saints and numerous *Beata* or 'Blesseds' (the first stage to becoming a saint). The main reason for this is the recognition of the need to provide examples of saintliness that are relevant to modern congregations.

'The Congregation for the Causes of Saints' in Rome is responsible for examining the evidence for making new saints, but the reigning pope makes the final decision. The Greek and Russian Churches have their own system for recognising new saints. Since the sixteenth century Reformation, the Protestant churches have not recognised any new saints. The reason for this is that they believe that veneration of such a great number of saints detracts from the worship of God. However, starting in the last quarter of the twentieth century, the Anglican Church has to include in the Church Calendars the names of some of their own heroes and heroines to be remembered as faithful witnesses and examples of holiness. In the monthly Calendars that follow this introduction their names and dates are inscribed in italics.

The choice of saints for inclusion in this Calendar has had to be limited for lack of space mainly to the great saints who changed things, and also to those who are interesting as examples of the great variety of ways in which saints have served God to advance his kingdom. The 800 saints that are included in this book represent about a fifth of those included in the official Roman Calendar and about four per cent of the much larger number in the *Bibliotheca Sanctorum*. This compares with the figure of just under two per cent that is covered by Gallup polls for testing demand for commercial products or for estimating support for political issues. Therefore it is suggested that this Calendar's selection is adequate for our main purpose in the book, which is to try and show how the Holy Spirit has been working through individuals in history.

Each of the monthly calendars that follow this introduction begins with an illustrated heading in the style used for medieval books of hours. These illustrate three or four saints whose feast-days are in the month. This is then followed by other illustrations with scenes from the lives of saints. These are designed in the form of tapestries or altar-pieces. The actual Calendars that follow give only the dates and briefest details of the saints. This is because the Calendars are meant to act not as detailed dictionaries but more like the war memorials one sees in churches and to show the remarkable variety of examples of holiness. In this way one can see how each monthly set of saints is a microcosm of the way the faith has been promoted and how Christian values have been demonstrated over 20 centuries.

The lists of feast-days in our Calendar are followed by more detailed texts on the important saints of the month whose lives and works provide special evidence of the way the Spirit has inspired them. In some cases additional illustrations have been included to help tell their stories. Attempts have also been made in most texts to emphasise what is relevant to our own times in the lives of various saints for the month. Their legacy of Christian values, built up in the layer upon layer of successive strata as in the formation of rocks, can be seen to produce the great range of Christian traditions on which our societies are based. These still persist today, sometimes more strongly than ever, in spite of the steady falling-off in church attendances which most denominations are experiencing.

JANUARY SAINTS

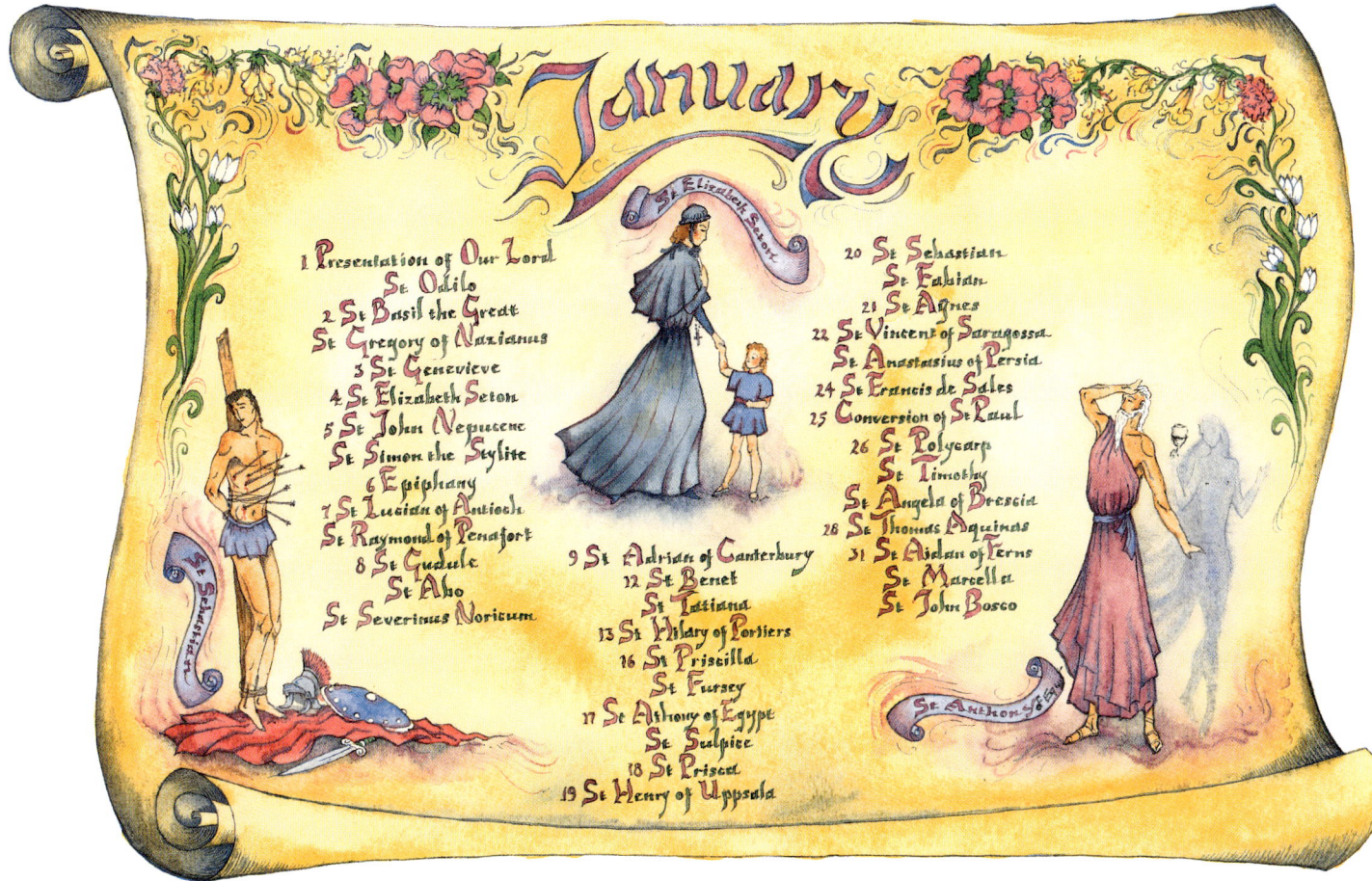

1 Presentation of Our Lord
  St Odilo
2 St Basil the Great
  St Gregory of Nazianus
3 St Genevieve
4 St Elizabeth Seton
5 St John Nepucene
  St Simon the Stylite
  6 Epiphany
7 St Lucian of Antioch
  St Raymond of Penafort
8 St Gudule
  St Aho
  St Severinus Noricum

9 St Adrian of Canterbury
12 St Benet
  St Tatiana
13 St Hilary of Poitiers
16 St Priscilla
  St Fursey
17 St Anthony of Egypt
  St Sulpice
18 St Prisca
19 St Henry of Uppsala

20 St Sebastian
  St Fabian
21 St Agnes
22 St Vincent of Sarragossa
  St Anastasius of Persia
24 St Francis de Sales
25 Conversion of St Paul
26 St Polycarp
  St Timothy
  St Angela of Brescia
28 St Thomas Aquinas
31 St Aidan of Ferns
  St Marcella
  St John Bosco

The three saints portrayed in this heading are **St Sebastian** (20 January), fourth-century Roman soldier-martyr; **St Antony of Egypt** (17 January), died 354, founder of the monastic ideal; and **St Elizabeth Seton** (4 January), canonised in 1975 as the first American-born saint. Their stories and those of the saints in the illustrations on pages 75 and 77 are told in the full Calendar that follows. In this illustration St Antony is being tempted with wine by a scantily clad lady. The picture of St Elizabeth depicts her in the habit that she chose for her nuns and which she described in a letter to her confessor. St Sebastian is shown pierced by arrows, the method by which he was martyred.

73

A DESIGN FOR A TAPESTRY FOR TWENTY-FIVE JANUARY SAINTS

The 25 saints from first eight centuries depicted opposite are in an imaginary scene of Paradise. The tent is meant to represent the early Christian concept of a veil between this world and the next.

The two saints shown at the sides are **Timothy and Titus** (both 26 January).

The saints shown in the top row, left to right are:

Simon the Stylite (5 January), Syria, fifth century; **Basil the Great** (2 January), fourth-century Greek bishop; **Gregory of Nazianzus** (2 January), bishop and friend of Basil; **Honoratus of Arles** (16 January), fifth-century bishop and founder of hermitages on the Isle of Lerins near Cannes in the south of France; **Pope Fabian I** (13 January), third-century martyr and missionary pope; **Hilary of Poitiers** (13 January), fourth-century bishop and theologian; **Felix of Nola** (14 January), fourth-century priest and hero; **Polyeuctus** (13 January), fourth-century soldier martyr; **Severinus of Noricum** (8 January) fifth-century missionary to the Danube region; **Adrian of Canterbury**, African abbot and teacher; **Fursey** (16 January), seventh-century Irish missionary to East Anglia and Gaul.

The saints shown in the lower and centre rows, left to right are:

Polycarp (26 January), second-century bishop martyr; **Vincent of Saragossa** (22 January), Spanish martyr, died 304; **Agnes** (21 January), child martyr, died 304; **Prisca or Prescilla** (12 January), third-century virgin martyr; **Lucian of Antioch** (7 January), theologian martyr, died 312; **Gildas** (29 January), sixth-century Welsh historian, missionary to Brittany; **Paula** (26 January) and **Marcella** (31 January) both helped finance St Jerome's translation of the Vulgate; **Genevieve** (29 January), fifth-century nun heroine of Paris; **Gudula** (8 January) noble lay Belgian martyr; **Abo** (8 January) eighth-century Muslim convert and martyr; **Anastasius the Persian** (22 January), seventh-century Zoroastrian convert and martyr.

Tapestry design for twenty five January saints of the first eight centuries

75

ALTAR-PIECE DESIGN FOR THIRTEEN JANUARY SAINTS

The saints shown at the sides are:

Raymund of Penafort (7 January), thirteenth-century Spanish Dominican canon law expert and friend of St Thomas Aquinas; **Angela Merici** (27 January) of Brescia, Franciscan tertiary who founded the Order of Ursulines.

The two saints at the top are:

Thomas Aquinas (28 January), thirteenth-century Dominican mystic and the most important Roman Catholic theologian, pupil of St Albert of the Rhine; **Francis de Sales** (24 January), Bishop of Geneva, mystic, missionary in the Alps, author of popular works on prayer.

In the central three rows are:

Pope Telesphorus (5 January), second-century martyr; **Ita** (15 January), Irish sixth-century abbess; **Sulpice** (17 January), seventh-century bishop of Bourges, who defended his flock against the Merovingian kings.

In the central row are:

John Bosco (31 January), nineteenth-century founder of the Salesians in Turin to train poor boys and girls in trades; **Philip of Moscow** (9 January), Patriarch strangled for criticising murderous tyrant Tsar Ivan the Terrible; **Benedict Biscop (or Benet)** (12 January), seventh-century British monk who founded two monasteries with important libraries.

In the bottom row are:

Seraph, of Sarov (2 January), nineteenth-century Russian mystic; **Odilo of Cluny** (1 January), eleventh-century abbot of Cluny who founded the 'Truce of God'; **Aidan of Ferns,** (31 January), seventh-century Irish bishop, pupil of St David of Wales.

Altar-piece design for thirteen January saints

77

JANUARY CALENDAR OF SAINTS' FEAST-DAYS

1st **ODILO** (963–1048): Abbot of Cluny. Promoter of the 'Truce of God', which was designed to end all military activities from November until April. He also founded All Souls Day to remember the souls of all the dead on 2 November. In these and other ways he spread the spirit of the gospel during a time of feudal violence.

2nd **BASIL the GREAT** (330–379): Greek bishop and theologian, trained in rhetoric in the School of Athens. Founded the monastic system in Cappadocia after visiting the Desert Fathers in Egypt. He resisted the attempts of the Eastern Emperors to impose the Arian heresy on the Church (i.e. denying the divinity of Jesus). Basil was a devoted follower of Origen's teaching and he supported St Athanasius' views in the fierce and hair-splitting debates over the definition of God as a Trinity. He was a social innovator who founded a Christian socialist community which he called 'Basiliad'. It had churches, workshops and also hospices for the poor and sick. (See also the text after this Calendar.)

GREGORY of NAZIANZEN (329–89): Colleague of St Basil and trained with him in Athens. Bishop and theologian of merit. His sermons on the Trinity and Salvation are quoted in this text after this calendar.

SERAPHIM of SAROV (1759–1833): Russian monk and influential mystic.

3rd **GENEVIEVE** (420–500): Nun and heroine, patron saint of Paris. Her prayers saved Paris from the Huns and she rescued it from being starved out by the Franks.

4th **ELIZABETH SETON** (1774–1821): Young New York widow and convert to the Catholic Church. She founded The American Sisters of Charity to start schools and was a pioneer of American primary education. Canonised 1975; the first American saint.

5th **SIMEON the STYLITE** (390–459): Popular Syrian hermit who lived on planks on top of a pillar to avoid the crowds. An oracle to visitors from East and West.

POPE TELESPHORUS: Martyred in 136.

6th **PETER of CANTERBURY**: Missionary with St Augustine of Canterbury; drowned in 607.

7th **LUCIAN of ANTIOCH**: Theologian and teacher martyred in 312. The heretic monk Arius of Alexandria was one of his pupils. This may account for Lucian being the favourite saint of the Empress St Helena, mother of Constantine I; both were proved to be weak on orthodoxy in spite of the decrees of the Council of Nicaea in 325.

RAYMUND of PENAFORT (1185–1275): Spanish Dominican whose list of conciliar and papal decrees was used for 700 years. A friend of Thomas Aquinas.

8th **SEVERINUS of NORICUM**: Fifth-century missionary to Austria.

GUDULA: Seventh-century devout and charitable lay woman martyr of Belgium.

ABO: Convert from Islam. Martyred in Iraq in 786.

9th **ADRIAN of CANTERBURY**: Died in 710. Black African Abbot of Monte Cassino. He twice, through humility, declined Pope St Vitalian's offer of the Archbishopric of Canterbury, but accompanied Archbishop St Theodore to Britain to help his work. He founded an important school for British clergy in Canterbury.

BISHOP JOHN NEPUCENE NEUMANN (1811–60): Emigrated to USA from his native Bohemia to work as priest to German emigrees. Bishop of Philadelphia. He founded the School Sisters of Notre Dame to teach and also care for orphans. The second American saint, canonised in 1977.

PHILIP of MOSCOW: Martyred in 1569 by Ivan the Terrible for criticising in public his murdering innocent people without trial. He told Ivan in a sermon in Moscow Cathedral that 'God rejects him who does not love his neighbour'.

10th **PAUL the HERMIT**: Died c.345 in Egypt. He inspired St Antony's desert life.

PETER ORSEOLO (927–87): Doge of Venice, retired to be a hermit.

WILLIAM LAUD (1573–1645): *Archbishop of Canterbury, opponent of puritanism, acknowledged the Catholic Church as a true Church, but denied papal infallibility. He tried to enforce a decent and uniform order in services so that 'the outward worship' was a witness to the true 'worship of the heart'. The foundation of his belief was the Bible and he believed that, when disputes on matters of faith arose, 'a lawful and free council, determining according to scripture, is the best judge on earth'. Executed by Parliamentary decree on 10 January in what was a politico-religious murder by the Puritans.*

12th **TATIANA**: Martyred c.303. Possibly identical with Sts Prisca and Martina.

BENEDICT BISCOP (or '**Benet**') (628–90): Monk and friend of St Wilfrid. He travelled to Rome five times to bring back manuscripts for his libraries in the monasteries he founded at

Wearmouth and Jarrow. The Venerable St Bede was one of his monks. He also imported sacred images, glass and pictures.

13th POLYEUCTUS: Roman centurion martyred for being a Christian convert, c.305. The main character in Corneille's drama of that name.

HILARY of POITIERS (315–367): Great Gallic theologian and bishop. Chief opponent of Arian heresy in the West. Friend of St Martin of Tours. See text after the Calendar.

GEORGE FOX (1624–91): *Founder of the Society of Friends or Quakers. See text on seventeenth-century Protestants in Part VII of this book, 'The Unquenchable Spirit'.*

14th MACRINA the ELDER Fourth century: Grandmother of St Basil. Basil's elder sister and helper; Macrina the Younger is also a saint of the Greek Church.

FELIX of NOLA: Died in c.260. A priest who rescued his bishop from prison during a persecution. Felix means 'happy'. There are over 20 saints with this name.

KENTIGERN (or 'Mungo'): Died in 612. Missionary to Scotland.

SAVA (1175–1235): Serbian archbishop and patron saint.

15th ITA (or 'Ide'): Died in 570. Abbess of Limerick, Ireland.

16th BERARD and COMPANIONS: Franciscans sent by St Francis to Morocco. They were martyred in 1220.

FURSEY: Died in 648. Irish missionary to Gaul, after evangelising in East Anglia.

HONORATUS of ARLES (350–429): Gallic monk who founded hermitage on the Isles de Lerins (1 km off Cannes) in c.409 after studying Egyptian and Cappadocian hermits. He probably taught St Patrick after his escape from slavery in Ireland. Lerins became a leading centre for theology, especially through St Vincent of Lerins (see April text).

17th ANTONY of EGYPT (c.250–356): Father of the monastic ideal through his founding of the Desert Fathers. See the story in the text after the Calendar.

SULPICIUS: Died in 647. Gallic bishop and hero.

18th MARGARET of HUNGARY (1242–70): Princess and Dominican abbess.

PRISCA: Martyred in 228. Possibly the same person as St Tatiana (see 12 January).

19th POPE FABIAN: Martyred in 250 in Rome in Decius' persecution, having sent a mission of seven bishops and several deacons to evangelise Gaul. These included St Denis.

HENRY of UPPSALA: English missionary bishop to Sweden. Martyred in 1260 in Finland.

WULFSTAN (1009–95): Saxon bishop of Worcester, supported King William the Conqueror after the invasion of 1066. Tried to outlaw the Bristol slave trade.

KING CANUTE IV of DENMARK: Died in 1086. He ravaged the coasts of Britain, but was devout. Murdered in church by rivals. Famous for many miracles alleged at his tomb.

20th SEBASTIAN: Legendary Roman centurion of Praetorian Guard, martyred in c.303 by being shot to death with arrows for refusing to deny Christ.

EUTHYMIUS the GREAT: Much-revered hermit who lived in the Jordan Valley in the fourth century.

21st AGNES: 12-year-old child martyred c.303 in Rome. Patron saint of children.

FRUCTUOSUS of TARRAGONA: Bishop martyred by Decius in Spain in 259.

22nd VINCENT of SARAGOSSA: Spanish deacon martyred in 303 after being tortured.

ANASTASIUS the PERSIAN: Zoroastrian convert to Christianity, strangled with his companions by order of Persian King Chosroes II in 628.

23rd JOHN the ALMSGIVER (560–619): Patriarch of Alexandria. Gave lavishly to hospitals and the poor in the city until the Persian conquest.

24th FRANCIS de SALES (1567–1622): Bishop of Geneva, evangelist, mystic, author of important and popular books on prayer of the heart. He filled the spiritual needs of a large and even international public. See also the text after this Calendar.

25th JUVENTUS and MAXIMUS: Officers martyred by Julian the Apostate in 363.

26th TIMOTHY and TITUS: St Paul's companions and bishops. See the text in Part II.

POLYCARP (68–156): Bishop of Ephesus. Had listened to St John preaching. Burnt alive for being a Christian and for refusing to deny Christ at his trial.

PAULA: Rich Roman matron devoted to St Jerome. She financed his researches while translating the Bible into Latin (the Vulgate) in Bethlehem. Died in 404.

27th **ANGELA MERICI of BRESCIA** (1475–1540): Children's teacher. Founded the teaching Order of Urselines at a time when education for girls was neglected.

28th **THOMAS AQUINAS** (1225–74): Greatest Roman Catholic theologian. See his story and works in the text after this Calendar.

29th **GILDAS the WISE** (c.500–570): Monk, historian of *The Ruin and Conquest of Britain*. Pupil of St Illtyd (6 November) in the Gower Peninsular of South Wales. He went as a missionary to Ireland and spent his later life in Brittany, founding a monastery there.

30th **BATHILD**: Died in 680. British slave who became Queen of the Frankish King Clovis II.

31st **MARCELLA**: One of St Jerome's rich Roman helpers, whose palace was on the Aventine Hill. She was killed during the sack of Rome in 410.

AIDAN of FERNS (or 'Maedoc'): Irish bishop who died in 626; a pupil of St David of Wales.

JOHN BOSCO (1815–88): Peasant who became a priest and modelled himself on St Francis de Sales. He Founded the Salesian Order in Turin to teach trades to unemployed boys. His schools and youth clubs also trained girls for jobs. The Order still operates world-wide. Also see his life in the text following the Calendar.

SUMMARY OF JANUARY SAINTS

The Calendar lists the feast-days of 59 saints of whom 20 were martyred and 11 were women. It also records two Protestant witnesses, Archbishop William Laud, beheaded by Parliament for supporting King Charles I, and George Fox, the founder of the Society of Friends, the Quakers.

The lives and works of two 'Friends of God' who are not included in the list of saints, **Clement of Alexandria** and **Origen**, are described in the following section. They taught in Alexandria at the end of the second and the beginning of the third centuries and had an important and lasting influence on the Greek Orthodox Church.

THE IMPORTANCE OF CLEMENT OF ALEXANDRIA AND ORIGEN

These two great theologians were so highly regarded by the Church in the East that, after their deaths in c.220 and 254, they were venerated as saints – but were later unfairly stripped of their sainthood for reasons of state. Their teaching was especially admired by the fourth-century Greek saints St Basil of Caesarea and St Gregory of Nazianzus whose lives, together with those of five other important saints featured in this Caldendar, are described immediately after this section.

Clement of Alexandria (c.150–220)

Clement was the teacher of Origen. He was, after St Paul, the first great theologian to influence the Greek Church. He based his thinking on the Platonic concept that the human souls returned after death to the Universal Soul, God. This enabled him to demonstrate the link between Christianity and the worlds of sense and intellect with which the Greek and Roman intelligentsia were familiar. The result was a fusing of Greek metaphysics and Christian gospel teaching, which gave the Eastern or Greek Church its Hellenistic style of thought.

One of Clement's innovations was to teach new believers that Christianity is a developing faith for each of us, as we progress on our particular spiritual journey. He showed that this progress was to advance up the ladder of faith towards understanding the relations between God and humanity.

This concept of the 'The Ladder of Ascent' would be developed further in the mystical teaching of the seventh-century St John Climacus (30 March) in his book of that name, written at St Catherine's Monastery beneath Mount Sinai.

Clement had to tread warily in his teaching in his divinity school at Alexandria, because he had to oppose the popular hotch-potch of gnostic ideas already mentioned in Part V of this book, and to show what true *gnosis* or 'wisdom' was. He taught that true Christian knowledge or 'illumination' came through the power of the Holy Spirit and that this, by the grace of God, was the way to perfection and holiness of life.

Clement, who had to flee from Egypt during a persecution in 200, wrote these words to warn his pupils about the false teaching of the Gnostics: *'The truth is to be found everywhere, because God implanted his image on all men in Creation. Following the miracle of Christ's incarnation He, the Word, became both the focus and climax of the divine influence in the world. Thus Christ is God, the Ideal of Man. That is the true* gnosis *or knowledge.'*

Origen (185–254)

At the age of 18 Origen was considered so brilliant a pupil of Clement, that the Bishop of Alexandria made him Clement's replacement as head of his divinity school. Origen's father Leonidas had been a victim of the persecution in 202. Origen taught in his school for 30 years, producing a massive output of books and translations of the Bible. He completed Clement's work and the Greek Fathers of the fourth century were to a great extent his disciples.

Origen's works explored boldly the important questions about the faith at a time when many matters of doctrine were still freely debated and would not be defined formally until the great councils a century later. This can be seen from his book *On First Principles*, in which he announced that what mattered most was for every Christian to be committed to the rules of faith laid down by the Apostles. These were as follows: faith that God is God both of the Old and the New Testaments; belief in the incarnation of the pre-existent Lord; in the Resurrection as proof of divinity and source of salvation in the Holy Spirit as one of the divine Triad; in the freedom of rational souls as discarnate sprits in the world to come; in the non-eternity of the world; and in a Judgement to come.

Origen was revolutionary in his teaching that outside these beliefs the educated believer is free to speculate and to interpret, and indeed has a duty to do so. This is a very modern approach to theology, the kind of imaginative exploration that has often offended the conservative authorities in the Church, who have always sought a fixed and unchallenged set of interpretations of what are still divine mysteries. Origen's pioneering approach was unique in its humility, for he regarded theology as a process of life-long research and not necessarily as producing definitive results. He saw himself as a theological explorer rather than a dictator of doctrine.

Origen wrote and taught a century before the great debate that established the official Doctrine of the Holy Trinity, but his writings, now mostly lost, were paraphrased by the Cappadocian Fathers St Basil and St Gregory of Nazianzus in their *Philocalia*. This synopsis shows that, like his contemporary the Roman lawyer and Christian apologist Tertullian (c.155–c.220), Origen taught the unity of all Three Persons of the Holy Trinity. In order to describe this Tertullian called their relationship *Constantiabilis* or 'All of one Substance', which Origen translated into Greek as *Homoousion*. The stern critic St Jerome,

writing almost a century after Origen's death, took his words to mean that the Father, Son and Holy Spirit are three independent divine beings and that Origen placed the three persons of the Trinity in a declining order. Origen could however hardly be blamed for this since Jesus himself had said, according to St John, that *'The Father is greater than I'*. Also, Jerome ignored the key point which Origen had made about the Incarnation. He described it as a fusion between the human Jesus and the divine Spirit as *'one of white hot metals and fire – all one'*.

The subject of the as-yet officially undefined Doctrine of the Trinity occupied only a fraction of Origen's output. His most original work was his study and interpretation of St John's Gospel. He showed that the Gospel should be read and understood at three different levels: the written meaning, the spiritual implications and the allegorical way the mysteries were expressed. This view matches the approach of modern theologians.

In spite of the critics in his own day, Origen was so influential that in 248 the Christian emperor Philip asked him to write an 'apology' proving the superiority of Christianity over paganism. Origen then produced his famous debate between a Christian and a pagan, *Contra Celsus*, in which he taught that the *'The Church is the School of Souls'*. That is still the church's purpose. In his writings he did not hesitate to shake traditional views that seemed to obfuscate the true purpose of particular books in the Bible. Origen was not afraid to make people think, which was probably all he was trying to do when talking about the relationship within the Trinity. In his *First Principles* Origen described what he believed to be the duty of the Church to teach: *'The Apostles left those who would deserve the higher gifts of the Spirit to examine the grounds of their statements. First there is the One God; second there is Jesus Christ himself, born of the Father before all creatures, there never was a time when the Son was not. Third there is the Holy Spirit, associated in dignity and honour with the Father and the Son; fourth the soul shall be rewarded according to his deserts; fifth the devil exists; sixth the world is not eternal; seventh the Scriptures are written by the inspiration of the Holy Spirit of God and they have not only one meaning, but also another meaning which escapes the notice of most people.'*

When Origen died in 255 of torture during Emperor Decius' persecution, he was acclaimed as a saint, as Clement of Alexandria had been before him. His remains were considered so holy that they were removed from his first burial place at Tyre and placed behind the altar in the Holy Sepulchre. No more sacred place was conceivable.

However, two centuries later, as the fierce debates rent the Greek Church over the Arian heresy and the nature of Christ, some of Origen's later disciples distorted his teaching. This led to violent disturbances. Criticism of Origen had already begun, with St Jerome unfairly saying that Origen was not sound on the Trinity. These disturbances eventually led the Emperor Justinian I to order in 543 that the Church should strip Origen and Clement of Alexandria of their sainthood.

The modern view of Origen's teaching is given in *The Oxford Companion to Christian Thought*. This says that *'Origen is always, in all his exegesis, a master of spirituality, according to his anthropology, human beings consist of spirit* (pneuma), *soul* (psyche), *and body* (soma). *The spirit which is in man is a participation in the Holy Spirit: it is the pedagogue of the soul, which becomes spiritual in proportion to its assimilation to the spirit.'* The *Companion* also says *'Finally, Origen is a great theologian, Augustine and Aquinas his only peers in Christian history'*.

His well-balanced approach to the divine mysteries cause modern theologians to study him more than any other Early Father. This is why it is appropriate to outline his thought at the beginning of this Calendar.

SEVEN IMPORTANT JANUARY SAINTS

St Antony of Egypt (c.251–356)

Antony founded the monastic way of life and teaching, which became the most powerful engine for spreading Christianity through Europe and the Greek world in the East. His call to serve God came when he was a newly orphaned youth aged 18. In church one evening in Alexandria he heard the story of Jesus and the rich young man who wanted to know how he could attain the kingdom of God and was told to sell all his goods, give to the poor and to follow Jesus. Antony went out and, after providing for the livelihood of his sister, he sold all his property, gave his money to the poor and left his home to live in an ancient ruined tomb in the desert. From there he began his mission. Antony is an outstanding example of how people are inspired to perform great works as the Holy Spirit literally speaks to them through the Scriptures.

St Antony lived for the next 20 years in the desert, meditating on the scriptures, growing his own food and resisting all the worldly temptations. These temptations afflicted him daily, according to his biographer St Athanasius. Antony also suffered from what became known as 'St Antony's Fire'. This was caused by the wild grains he used to make his bread. As a result of his wisdom and devout way of life Antony acquired fame as a religious counsellor. He attracted many pilgrims and several thousand disciples who came to join him and to live like him in the desert.

Antony impressed all his followers, known as the Desert Fathers, with the need to abandon worldly concerns if they wanted to understand the truth about the faith and a holy life. This did not mean that they had to live by begging, because Antony taught them to make ropes for ships out of the strong Nile papyrus plant and to make mats and baskets for sale in the towns, as well as growing their own food.

In his old age Antony established a monastery carved out of a rocky site near the Red Sea. There Antony started the regime which was later developed into the monastic way of life. This consisted of communal worship, work, study and prayer and was later made into 'Rules' by his follower St Pachomius (14 May), by St Basil and in the fifth century by St Benedict of Monte Cassino.

St Basil the Great (or of Caesarea) (330–379)

Before examining the lives and works of Origen's best-known fourth-century disciples, the Cappadocian Fathers St Basil the Great and Gregory of Nazianzen, it is necessary to summarise the situation that faced them and the Greek Church. In the 320's the Greek Church was split and the Western Church was threatened by the heresy publicised widely by the Alexandrian monk Arius – or Arianism. He denied the true godhead of Jesus Christ, claiming that the Son was created by the Father and therefore is not equal to the Father. In saying this he reversed Origen's claim about Jesus, made thrice in his writings, as St Athanasius was to point out, that *there never was a time when he was not*. In other words, Jesus existed within the nature of God before Creation.

The Council of Nicaea was summoned by the Emperor Constantine in 325 to decide between the Orthodox and Arian views. At the council most of the bishops were court place-seekers who had been appointed for political reasons after Constantine's declaration of freedom of worship throughout the Empire in 313. These nearly all supported Arius, but the ordinary clergy opposed his heresy. As was explained earlier in the historical summary in Part V, the Council of Nicea in 325 declared that all Three Persons of the Trinity were *'One God in Three Persons, all of the same substance'*. That is exactly what Origen had taught.

However, the problem did not disappear and its solution became the life tasks of St Basil, Bishop of Caesarea, his friend Bishop St Gregory of Nazianzus and Basil's brother Bishop St Gregory of Nyssa. Throughout their careers they bravely resisted the Arian heresy in defiance of the armed threats of various heretical emperors. Basil's scorn and determination once even shamed the heretic Emperor Constantius in his cathedral and drove out his soldiers. These three Cappadocian Fathers, so-named after their vast properties in what is now central Turkey, taught that the internal relationship of the Father, Son and Holy Spirit was one of mutual love.

Basil was trained in law and rhetoric at the School of Athens and came from a remarkable Christian family who owned large tracts of Cappadocia. Six others of the family were recognised as saints: his father Basil the Elder, his mother Emmelia, his grandmother Macrina the Elder, his elder sister Macrina the Younger, and his brothers Bishop Gregory of Nyssa and Bishop Peter of Sabate.

After leaving Athens to practice law in Antioch, Basil became dissatisfied with his profession and was introduced to the gospel by his sister Macrina the Younger. As he himself wrote later, within a year he was converted to Christianity and began his life's work. Of the spiritual experience that led to his conversion, Basil wrote: *'I awoke as out of a deep sleep to the marvellous light of the gospel truth, realising that I had wasted my life on superfluous studies'*. As a result he decided in 357 to study the ascetic life of the Desert Fathers in Egypt, the hermits who had followed St Antony. On his return to Cappadocia he and his friend Gregory of Nazianzus founded a number of small monasteries called 'Laura'. In later centuries these grew into substantial monasteries which eventually housed thousands of monks and became the chief means by which the faith was spread. They were also the centres for theological study and the source from which bishops were chosen.

The original Laura were built into the tufa rock in Cappadocia. As the numbers of monks increased, they carved deeply into the rock. Sketches of one of these rock-carved monasteries near modern Kaiseri (old Caesarea) and also of the wall-paintings in the chapel carved 360 feet below ground level, are shown on the next pages. In order to defend the monasteries from raiding barbarians from the Caucasus mountains and, after the seventh century, from the Muslim invaders, the entrances to the monasteries were concealed and could be closed by massive rolling blocks of stone. Huge galleries were also cut in the rock to store water and grain, to house the cattle and other animals and also to collect smoke from the fires to avoid giving their presence away.

The next two quotations are taken from Basil's book on the Trinity: *'When I speak of God it is of the Father, the Son and the Holy Spirit that I wish to speak, without diluting the Godhead beyond these limits, lest it introduce a whole tribe of divinities! The Father is the origin of all, the Son realises, the Spirit fulfils.*

Sketch of a rock monastery at Kaiseri (formerly Caesarea)

Everything exists by the will of the Father, comes into action by the Son and reaches perfection through the Spirit. The Spirit is in relation to the Father what the words are to the mind . . . In God the Father and in God the Only begotten Son we are contemplating only a single reality in the unchanging Godhead.'

'We declare we know God in his energies, but we hardly claim to approach him in his very essence. His essence remains inaccessible, whereas his energies reach down to us . . . The way to knowledge of God leads from the Spirit in unity to the Father. It also moves in the opposite direction; thus the fullness and holiness of the divine essence and its dignity come from the Father by means of the Son and the Holy Spirit.'

Finally, and far in advance of his times, Basil spoke these words in a sermon which gives a remarkably modern approach to the way God communicates with us: *'Thou hast visited humanity in many ways. In the loving kindness of thy heart thou hast sent the prophets. Thou didst speak through thine own Son. There is no culture or religion that has not received and does not express a visitation of the Word.'* Unfortunately this doctrine of the universal activity of the Spirit was never adopted by the Church. Nor was it taught for over 1,600 years until, in 1962 at the Second Vatican Council, Pope John XXIII declared that *'The seed of the Spirit can be seen in all the world's faiths today'*.

St Gregory of Nazianzus (329–389)

Gregory was St Basil's friend and had been a student with him in Athens studying rhetoric. He once said in a sermon about the Christian way of life in 361 that *'The true ideal is to be found in the lives of St Peter and St Paul'*. Gregory was reluctant to be made a bishop, always preferring a monastic life so that he could meditate. He worked closely with Basil on gathering the sources for their book *Philocalia*, on Origen's teaching. This had a profound effect on their contribution to the debates on the Doctrine of the Trinity which lasted from 325 to 381.

It was against Gregory's will that just before the Council of Constantinople in 381 he was persuaded by the Emperor Theodosius I to become Patriarch of the capital. Theodosius would accept no one else, so high was Gregory's reputation for orthodoxy and as a critic of Arianism. Gregory then wrote a poem to announce his purpose in becoming Patriarch in words that could almost be applied to our situation today: *'The New Rome* (Constantinople) *has passed through the death of infidelity* (i.e. Arianism). *I have come to defend the faith. What the people need now is solid teaching to deliver them from the spider's web of subtleties which have deceived them.'*

Gregory put this teaching into effect after the Council in five great sermons in 381, his 'Theological Orations': *'The Old Testament manifested the Father clearly, the Son only dimly. The New Testament reveals the Son and amplified the divinity of the Spirit. Today the Spirit lives among us and makes himself known clearly . . . The Son and the Spirit coexist with the Father, and without being separated in time, purpose or power all act together. What one does the others do also – but everything God does is done by the Spirit.'*

Gregory also spoke of human beings and souls, saying: *'The Father – as the Great Architect of the Universe – conceived and produced a being with two natures: visible and invisible. And so the invisible God created the human being, bringing forth the body from pre-existing matter which he animated with his own Spirit.'* Like Origen, Gregory understood that the human being is a temple of the spirit in which *'humanity is quickened by a flash from the Godhead'.*

Gregory followed Moses' account of the nature of God – *'I AM'* (Exodus 4.13), which he interpreted as *'I am existence itself'* or *'He Who Is'.* In one of his sermons in 381 he said: *'God is eternal existence. He actually contains himself. He enlightens our inner being – provided it has been purified – in proportion to our capacity to understand. He came down to earth out of compassion for humanity.'* Gregory's definition that God *'contains himself'* is another way of expressing the threefold doctrine of the Trinity. This definition can be compared below with St Thomas Aquinas' clear and simple definition of the Triad that forms the Trinitarian God: *'God is complete in Himself'.*

Gregory spoke these words on the naming of Jesus as 'Son of God': *'I believe that if he is given the name "Son", it is because he comes from the Father. He is called* Logos *because he is in relation to the Father and as the Son he makes known the nature of the Father. He is called the "Word" because he is everything. It is from him that we all receive the breath of life and the Holy Spirit'.*

Gregory gave the following moving explanation to suggest how Jesus' self-sacrifice on the cross and his resurrection had redeemed and brought salvation to all humankind: *'Christ's sacrifice is of praise, of sanctification, of restoration, by which he offered all of Creation to the Father so that he might bring it to life in the Holy Spirit. It is a Passion – the passing of Creation into the Kingdom of Life. But why was this blood shed for us? A Sacrifice? To whom was it offered? Why should the blood of his Son be pleasing to God – who would not accept Isaac's blood from Abraham? God accepts the sacrifice – not because he needs it but in order to carry out his human plan. We had to be brought back to Him by the humanity of his Son . . . Let us adore in silence. His sacrifice deifies the depths of human nature, of the Universe, of Being.'*

On the Eucharist, Gregory said: *'Jesus ate bread and so the bread was transformed into the body of the Word. Therefore the bread was transformed and that body was therefore raised to divine power. A similar change happens at the Eucharist, where the bread is hallowed by the word of God and prayer. It is formed at once into his body. So we say: "This is my Body".'* This is about the earliest theological account of what came to be called 'Transubstantiation' by the Roman Church from 1215.

Gregory's final sermon in 381 on the Incarnation, the Trinity and the Holy Spirit, is condensed into the following quotations: *'Jesus said, according to St John: "Though you do not believe me, believe my works, that you may know and understand that the Father is in me and I am in the Father"* (John 10.38). *The Son is thus equal to the Father and also what he was he remained at the incarnation; what he was not he assumed. God became man that we might become divine. The Holy Spirit is holiness. Had the Holy Spirit been absent from the Trinity, the Father and the Son would have been imperfect! The Spirit is of the same substance with the Father and the Son.'*

Gregory's definition of the Trinity and his statement that *'the Son is thus equal to the Father'* are, in spite of St Jerome's criticism, the same words that Origen had taught, whose works Gregory so admired. This and the fact that most of Origen's original manuscripts were lost,

Sketch of wall-paintings in monastery chapel at Kaiseri, 360 feet below ground

meant that St Jerome only had edited copies, which may not have been accurate.

Gregory resigned his office as Patriarch of Constantinople as soon as he could, having achieved his objective over the Doctrine of the Trinity at the Council of Constantinople in 381. He then retired to resume the monastic life that he had always wanted to practice.

St Hilary of Poitiers (c.315–68)

Hilary was born at Poitiers. He was self-taught as a Christian and theologian, as his words in his book *On the Trinity* reveal. He wrote it to attack the Arian heresy which had spread to the West. The book was written after he had been exiled by the Western Emperor for his support of orthodoxy. He was sent to the East and met St Basil in Cappadocia. He was then sent back to Gaul by the emperor for causing trouble preaching against the heresy!

Hilary's autobiography describes the thought process that led him to become a Christian. It is a spiritual journey that many modern believers will recognise as being similar to their own experiences. *'I began to search for the meaning of life. At first I was attracted by riches and leisure, but most people discover that human nature wants something better. I sought to know God better. Some claim there is no God at all and worship nature, which according to them came about by chance. Then I discovered the books written by Moses and the prophets, where God says: "Say to the people of Israel 'I AM' sent you!" (Exodus 3.14). I was filled with wonder at this perfect definition, which translates into intelligible words the incomprehensible knowledge of God – He who is!'*

'There is no place without God. From the greatness of the beauty of things comes a corresponding perception of the Creator of a Cosmos which means Adornment. Thus we can see God as Absolute Beauty.

I then learned that the 'Word of God', Jesus, was with him from the beginning. In him, without surrendering his divinity, God was made flesh. My soul joyfully received the revelations of this mystery. By means of my flesh, I was drawing near to God. By means of faith I was called to a higher birth from on high. I was thus assured I would not be reduced to a non-person.'

A 'Green Man' carved on St Afra's tomb, Poitiers, c.400

Hilary was elected Bishop of Poitiers. Through his gentleness and moderation he weaned most of Gaul from the Arian heresy. He was regarded as a saint in his lifetime. His tomb is in the cathedral at Poitiers which also contains that of his daughter St Afra (c.400) and has a carving on it of the 'Green Man':

Afra's tomb is interesting because of the apparently pagan design of the Green Man carved upon the side of the lid with vine leaves issuing out from his mouth. The explanation for this is that in Hilary's day the Green Man was the sacred symbol of the Celtic tree worshippers in the forests. The Green Man died in the Autumn and rose again in the Spring. The Christian interpretation of this to the pagans likened him to Jesus Christ, who also died and was resurrected. This tomb is the earliest representation of the many Green Men in Western churches, carved on pillars or in porches. They were put there to represent the Resurrection, to help the understanding of people in whom ancient myths still persisted and to remind them of their links with Nature and Creation.

The Life and Importance of St Thomas Aquinas (1225–1274)

The theologian and mystic Thomas Aquinas is shown praying in the top row of the third illustration of the January saints. The picture is meant to represent him having what he described as *a vision of heavenly truths which made everything I had written seem like so much straw'*. This happened near the end of his life and he never wrote again, which meant that he did not quite finish his greatest work, his *Summa Theologica*. Thomas also had many other spiritual and mystical experiences. These were unexpected and often happened at awkward moments, such as when he used to see the figure of Christ in the Host that he was handling at the Eucharist. Perhaps it was this that convinced him of the truth of the mystery of transubstantiation.

The lectures of Thomas Aquinas, the first true humanist, were popular with his Paris students and the Dominican Order to which he belonged, but they were not fully appreciated by the Church until many centuries after his death. Had his teaching on the nature of the human soul been accepted generally, it might have revolutionised the Church's teaching, influenced the future course of Western European history and enhanced ordinary people's understanding of the faith. However the hide-bound attitude of the traditionalists of feudal thirteenth-century society meant they were not prepared to accept all of his theology, nor the social implications of his analysis of the soul.

Thomas was nevertheless canonized for his lifetime's devotion to the faith by Pope John XXII in 1332. However, apart from their recognition by his own Dominican Order, Thomas' works did not become widely accepted until they were made compulsory reading for students in the seminaries in 1880 by Pope Leo XIII. Since World War II Thomas' writings have inspired Catholic 'Neo-Thomists' in ways that he would have thoroughly approved.

Thomas was born in 1225 into a noble family of Aquino, a town to the south of Rome. He was schooled in the Benedictine abbey of Monte Cassino and then sent to Naples University, which the Emperor Frederick II Hohenstauffen – known as *'Stupor Mundi'* – had founded a few years earlier. Thomas was a brilliant student and his family intended him to make a great name for himself in the service of the state, perhaps as a lawyer. They were furious therefore when Thomas felt called to serve God and joined the Dominican Order in 1243. The family seized and imprisoned him for a year. So highly did his Order regard Thomas' intellectual powers that they got the Pope to intervene and set him free. Thomas was then sent to Paris to study with the future St Albert the Great.

Albert was recognised as the most learned man in Europe, having studied all the sciences as well as theology and having produced original works on them all. In 1248 he and Thomas were sent to establish a Dominican teaching house in Cologne. They made a perfect partnership and helped each other to tackle the greatest spiritual problem that had faced the Church for centuries, the rediscovery of the lost works of Aristotle – his *On Nature, Metaphysics* and his books on moral and political philosophy. Until then Aristotle had only been known in the West for his Logic. His other works had been lost during the barbarian invasions from the fifth to the eighth centuries and had only been rediscovered by Arab Muslim philosophers in the eleventh and twelfth centuries. They had translated them into Arabic and provided commentaries on them in Cordoba, Arab capital of Spain, and the most cultured city in Europe.

By the thirteenth century the books had been translated into French. They immediately raised serious philosophical problems for traditional theologians. This was because Aristotle, the pupil of Plato, denied the creative part of God by saying that the universe was eternal. He also maintained that God was aloof from the world and indifferent to the fate of mankind. If accepted, this philosophy would undermine the whole basis of Christian belief and the doctrine of Salvation. At once arguments for and against multiplied, as the newly discovered works were debated by the faculty and students of the Sorbonne in Paris, where Thomas returned in 1252 to teach as one of the 14 Masters of the University. Thomas' lectures on Aristotle became so popular that they were held in the open air.

Thomas' conclusions from his studies of Aristotle's works rode serenely over the potential problems they raised for the Church. In his lectures he went to the very centre of what was at issue. He saw that the question about whether the Universe is everlasting was open to doubt. He then contradicted Aristotle's argument that there is only one active intelligence at work in the Universe, that of God. Against this Thomas taught that the active intelligence is not single but multiple. He then showed that the soul of man and his free will is his active intelligence and is entirely personal to himself. That is what makes man, man. Thus for Thomas each person is a world complete in themselves. Each one therefore has a right to develop towards perfection in their own way. This is God's gift of free will and so each person's soul or individual intelligence is the *Form*, in Plato's sense, of each human being and the source of their moral autonomy.

Thomas also taught that the soul, though embodied, is a spiritual body destined to return to God. In this way, Thomas adapted Aristotle's doctrines to Christianity. In particular Thomas challenged Augustine's (see August Calendar) depressing view of Predestination, that God willed from birth the fate of all either to eternal life or to eternal damnation. This made any claim that man has free will to do good or evil quite irrelevant as an incentive to live a holy life.

Thomas' next revolutionary teaching was his reinterpretation of the accepted definition of the Trinity which St Augustine had established in his fourth-century book *De Trinitate*. The Roman Church had adopted this as an article of faith. Augustine's explanation was a psychological one. He had argued that as God had made man *'in his own image'* (Romans 8.9), God was therefore immanent in all believers; Augustine had also taught that the nature of man was a Triad of *'Intelligence, Will and Wisdom'*, analogous to the *'The Father, Son and Holy Spirit'*. That definition was still being taught in Paris by Thomas' friend and rival, the Franciscan theologian St Bonaventure (see 15 July).

Thomas realized, after reading Aristotle's *Metaphysics* and *De Anima*, that St Augustine's explanation of the Trinity did not go deep enough, or explain the relationship between the Three Persons, which he, like St Basil and St Gregory of Nazianzus, believed was one of mutual love. He examined this by a totally original route, making it much easier for ordinary believers to understand the theology of how Jesus pre-existed within the Godhead before his incarnation.

Thomas' arguments and conclusions are only summarised here. First, Thomas' basic assumption on the nature of God as Trinity needs to be described. He gives this in his greatest work the *Summa Theologica*. He began by taking a route of his own. Starting with Aristotle's *Metaphysics*, Thomas came to the revolutionary view that the Divine Nature of God is complete in Himself (*'Ipsum esse per se subsistens'*). Thus his 'being' is identical with the substance and energy represented in its three modalities of Divine Person, Word and Spirit. That is a Trinity, three persons in one God.

It is easy to understand from this basic assumption that Thomas could go on to claim that God can, without dividing his divine unity, communicate his nature through his Word and Spirit and reveal himself to us through the human medium of Jesus Christ. Thus God was able to project his Word and Will in a way humans could understand. Thomas also wrote that the Word, Jesus, was not sent to us for his own sake, but that the Spirit might come to us also.

This is a simpler but more easily understandable concept than the compromise doctrine of the Trinity reached at Nicea in 325 and finalized at Constantinople in 381. It avoids the higher mathematical problem, outlined in the notes on St Basil above, which was designed to show that the crucified Jesus becomes part of the Godhead as the Second Person of the Trinity without his being made to appear as a second God. This is because Thomas' definition of the Divine Nature shows that He is here all the time, since God is complete in Himself in all his aspects, Father, Son and Holy Spirit.

The second most important of Thomas' inspirations concerned his view of man's free will and his soul, as described earlier. Thomas began to develop these first in his criticism of Peter Lombard's *Sentences*.

Since Bishop Peter Lombard (c.1100–60) wrote them the *Sentences* had become the theological text book for all clergy, especially in France. Its main contents were quotations from the writings of the Early Fathers. Most of these sayings were by St Augustine of Hippo. As we have seen, Thomas challenged Augustine with his own explanation of the Trinity. Then, with his own views on free will and the Soul, Thomas challenged the prevailing theology of man's soul and his relationship to God. In doing so he also challenged the basic feudal approach to human rights, which is why he was opposed by the hierarchy in the French Church.

Thomas started to do this in the first of his two greatest books – *Summa Contra Gentiles* in 1259. He wrote this book at the request of his friend in Rome St Raymond of Penafort, who wanted to use Thomas' teaching to help him evangelise Jews and Muslims in Spain. In the following years Thomas perfected his theme on the soul in his

Summa Theologica (1268–72), his greatest work. He wrote this in Rome after he had been appointed Master of the Sacred Palace in the Vatican. In this post Thomas was responsible for giving theological advice to the Roman Curia, which shows how highly he was regarded as a theologian by the forward-looking Papal Curia.

In his *Summa Theologica* Thomas posed and answered over 700 questions about the nature of God, the human soul, the problem of evil in the world and all aspects of the faith. Six centuries later his work was to become the authority on these subjects in the Roman Church. The subject is too great to be covered adequately here, which is why I have concentrated on Thomas' views about the Trinity, the soul and the creative spirit of every individual human being.

Thomas based his teaching on reason, and he supported it by faith. This can be seen in the example of his argument for the existence of God. He taught that our reason tells us that all creation must have a prime cause, as the first words of the Book of Genesis proclaim: '*In the beginning God created the heaven and the earth*'. Thomas saw proofs of God in design, through reason, experience and observation, just as some modern scientists have observed that the Universe and the Earth seem to have been designed especially to make life possible.

By his promoting of each person's God-given freedom to develop their capacities to the full, Thomas refuted the restrictive attitude of the medieval world. In this way Thomas became the first humanist, as the word is understood today. He thus did for theology what the eighteenth-century Frenchman Lavoisier did for chemistry – he broke the shackles of the past. Thomas taught a new way of looking at man.

In this he revived the teaching of the Early Fathers that the Spirit had been with us since the beginning. In doing so Thomas opened up the whole Pandora's box of the immense field of human rights, responsibilities and duties – fodder for philosophers and moralists to ponder over for centuries to come.

Thomas' theology of Salvation taught that Christ's death absolved all sins, because it was the death of God Incarnate and thus God's expression of his unconditional love for sinners. This definition was unacceptable to the old guard of the French Church. Thomas was therefore opposed in public debate in the Sorbonne by Bonaventure.

Bonaventure was also Thomas's friend, but unlike him he supported St Augustine's classical fusion of Christianity with Plato's metaphysics and ignored Aristotle and the problem raised by his works. King St Louis IX, who entertained them both in the Louvre, preferred St Bonaventure's approach, but nevertheless liked and admired Thomas. There is an account of a dinner given to Thomas and Bonaventure by the King during which Thomas, a courteous bear of a man whom everyone loved, suddenly relapsed into a brown study. The King immediately summoned a scribe to take down Thomas' words as soon as he ceased to meditate, lest some valuable thought was lost.

After Thomas' death in 1274 the resentful French bishops tried and condemned many parts of Thomas' works. They failed to gain the Pope's support, following the vigorous defence made by Thomas' old tutor and lifelong friend, St Albert. Even so, though he was canonised in 1323, Thomas' teaching was not as influential as it should have been until centuries later. The feudal world of the thirteenth and fourteenth centuries could not possibly understand the way Thomas saw each person's active intelligence or soul as the basis for God-given inalienable rights and responsibilities for all human beings. It preferred versions akin to St Augustine's. As for the 'rights of ordinary men', the peasants were not even regarded as human. Of all the great questions Thomas examined in his *Summa Theologica*, it is this subject which makes his theology so relevant to us today. This is why his book has been described by some modern scholars as the greatest theological work ever written.

Thomas' works were always taught by the Dominicans, though less forcefully from the fourteenth century onwards, as they were too heavily involved in administering the Inquisition. However in the sixteenth century St Ignatius of Loyala made his Jesuits study Thomas for their missionary work in Europe and overseas. Then again, in the turbulent seventeenth and eighteenth centuries, during the Enlightenment and the Age of Reason, Thomas was pushed into the background. It was not until the 1890s that the Roman Catholic Church, reeling from the effect of Charles Darwin's 1859 *The Origin of Species* and the subsequent development of evolutionary theories, realised that Thomas was a much-needed rescuer. He provided the lifeboat for the Church because he had argued that, as in Aristotle's studies of the inexplicable ways organs changed in different organisms, the act of creation was not complete in one action, but was continuous, as evolutionists believe. This belief could also be seen as underlying St Paul's picture to the Romans (chapter 8) of *'all creation groaning'* for the day when at last it will reach perfection.

The Life and Works of St Francis de Sales (1567–1625)

Francis de Sales was born to an aristocratic family in Savoy at the height of the Wars of Religion in neighbouring France. These wars had begun 40 years before, in spite of the fact that King Francis I had favoured some of the ideas of the Protestant reformers and encouraged the production of a French translation of the Bible. He had even made alliances with Protestant rulers against the Holy Roman Emperor Charles V. However Francis found that the Protestants were disturbing his kingdom by their over-enthusiasm and his throne was being threatened by the ruling house of Navarre, which was Protestant. The original mild and mainly intellectual reform in France against the influence of a degenerate papacy, with its intolerable taxation and insistence on choosing all new French bishops, turned from 1560 into a series of eight civil wars disguised as semi-religious conflicts.

The last phase of these wars began while Francis de Sales was still studying at the Jesuit college of Clermont in Paris between 1580 and 1588. Then in 1589 the Calvinist Henry Bourbon of Navarre became King Henry IV of France, but did not get control of Paris until 1593 after becoming a Roman Catholic. That was also the year in which Francis was consecrated as a priest after giving up his original plan to become a lawyer. A few years before that he had fallen into a deep depression concerning the fate of his soul. He asked himself much the same questions that had caused Martin Luther such agonies 80 years before and which were only relieved after he had read St Paul's words to the Romans: *'We hold that a man is justified by faith apart from works of the Law.'* (Romans 3.28).

Like Luther, Francis was deeply perplexed over the question of his own future salvation. This was because in his theological studies he had been driven to despair over the question of Predestination which the Calvinists had adopted from St Augustine of Hippo. Augustine had taught bluntly that from the beginning God had predestined some to eternal life and others to eternal damnation. Was there therefore no hope that an ordinary person like himself might be saved?

During his studies in Paris he had told his tutor that '*Only theology will teach me what God wants to reveal to me in my immortal soul*'. Francis then approached the problem of salvation more humbly and with greater love than the Calvinists. Far from seeing God like Calvin as a 'God of Wrath', he approached him as a 'God of Love'. In 1591 he went to the Paris church of St Etienne-des-Gres and prayed before a statue of the Virgin Mary:

'*Whatever happens, Lord, you hold everything in your hands, and all your ways are just and true. Though you have veiled my eyes before the eternal secret of predestination and reprobation, you, whose judgements are unsearchable, are a just judge and merciful father. I shall love you, Lord, at least in this life even if I am not allowed to love you in eternity. At least I shall love you here below and shall always hope in your mercy. Always I shall continue to praise you, whatever the angel of Satan may do to prevent me. Lord you shall always be my hope and salvation in the land of the living. If it is inevitable that I must be damned amongst the damned who will never see thy gentle face, let me at least be spared from the company of those who will curse your holy name.*'

As he finished his prayer Francis noticed a card on which was printed the words of St Bernard of Clairvaux's 'Memorare', which says '*Remember gracious Virgin Mary, that never was it known that anyone who fled to thy protection, implored thy help and sought thy intercession, was left unaided*'. Suddenly, as he recited these words, his whole being seemed to change. He felt as though a great sickness had been cured. A wonderful sense of spiritual and bodily peace came over him. He was a cured soul. He realised, as he himself recorded, that God had put him to the trial and had now taken that trial from him. He was literally 'born anew' in spirit.

Soon afterwards Francis decided to take Holy Orders and to devote his life to teaching the gospel as a priest in answer to what he believed to be his 'calling to serve God'. After his ordination in 1593 he received an offer through a cousin to be Provost of Annecy. The Pope consented and Francis accepted. The area above Annecy was the wild alpine region of Chablais. It was partly French and partly belonged to the Duke of Savoy. Its peasants had become converted to the Calvinism of Geneva, but the inhabitants were depressed by the lack of hope that it offered because of its doctrine of double-predestination.

For ten years Francis braved the wolves in the rough Alpine passes and threats of assassination and occasional physical attacks upon him. He preached his doctrine of the God of Love against that of the God of Wrath. He told the people that contrary to their belief '*Salvation is for all, but in a way and by means suited to the condition of human nature with its gift of free will*'. In other words God willed the salvation of all who believed, as had been revealed to him at St Etienne-des-Gres.

Thus Francis did not criticise their beliefs scornfully, as some others did, but took them a step further towards a more positive, better understanding in the light of his own spiritual trials and experience. In this way, preaching with love, he restored to those mountain people the hope that they had lost and brought the people of Chablais back to the Roman Catholic faith.

In the midst of this Francis had begun the first of his spiritual writings, his *Introduction to a Devout Life*, which was to be translated into many languages and give Francis a popular following in Paris and Rome. The book was sent as a present to King James I in England by the French Queen Marie de Medici. He received and read it with pleasure. Francis' literary success led him to be asked to travel to Rome where, after being examined on his theology by the learned Cardinal Bellarmine, he was made Bishop of Geneva by the Pope in 1603. On his way home to Annecy Francis' infectious Gallic sense of humour caused him to drive in his coach through the city of Geneva wearing his full episcopal robes, although this had been made officially out of bounds to him as a Roman Catholic by the Calvinist authorities of that republic. No one stopped him; nothing could!

Francis' book on the devout life and his later writings introduced a large audience to the benefits of what he called 'The Prayer of the Heart'. He showed them what true holiness of life meant and how it could be achieved

through actual contact with the Spirit through his way of mystical prayer. That is to say, by first driving out all worldly thoughts from one's mind. Like the early Greek mystics he taught the need for detachment from self-regard and total self abandonment to Christ. It was just what his wide public in France were yearning for as spiritual guidance. They were thirsty for it after so many years of war and religious controversy. They just wanted a clear and simple guide on the relation of the individual soul to God.

In his *Devout Life* and his *Treatise on the Love of God*, Francis showed that the advance towards perfection could be achieved by ordinary lay people, not only by priests. He said that it is wrong '*to exclude devoutness of life from among soldiers, from shops and offices, from royal courts and family homes*'. He then explained this by showing how '*Everything must be done through love, nothing by force. Obedience to God must be loved rather than disobedience feared – and he who preaches with love, preaches well*'. Francis did not want people to live too austere a life such as the Calvinists taught, but to dance and enjoy themselves. For this he received much criticism, but he persisted and spent many evenings by the lakeside at Annecy discussing and joking with the nuns of the Order of the Visitation which he had helped to found with his friend St Jeanne Francoise de Chantal (12 December).

In his lifetime Francis was regarded as a saint. When he died, a leading Calvinist of Geneva even said that '*If we honoured any man as a saint, I know of no one since the Apostles more worthy if it than this man*'. Another great admirer of Francis was his younger contemporary and friend the future St Vincent de Paul (27 September). In his evidence to those examining Francis' candidature for sainthood in 1665, Vincent wrote how Francis '*ardently wished to imitate the Son of God. So clearly did he model himself on Our Lord, as I have myself seen, that many a time I asked myself with astonishment how a mere creature could reach so high a degree of perfection, given human frailty.*'

Francis was one of the few in the Church who were not afraid of the impact on the faith of new scientific discoveries. Foremost among these were those of Galileo that the earth and planets orbited the sun and not the other way round as the Alexandrian mathematician Ptolemy had taught 1,500 years before. Galileo's book containing his discovery had been declared heretical by the Church because it no longer placed man at the centre of God's creation. Galileo was forced to retract his statements and was put under house arrest and threatened with execution. Towards the end of his life Francis paid a visit to Galileo to show him his support for his works. He was introduced by Cardinal Bellarmine, who had begged Galileo to avoid offending the Roman Curia by toning down some of the theological implications of his discoveries. Francis was canonised in 1665, made a Doctor of the Church in 1877 and patron saint of journalists and writers in 1923.

St John Bosco (1815–88) – A modern style of saint

John Bosco was brought up in a peasant family by his widowed mother in Piedmont and became a priest in 1841. He discovered the need in his parish in the suburbs of Turin to teach a trade to the crowds of uneducated and unchurched youths. Hundreds of them were attracted to the evening work-classes that he arranged in his chapel. He also took into his home apprentices to be taught a trade and to be looked after by his mother.

John Bosco's success with this mission won considerable financial support for his work and brought in many voluntary helpers from Turin. Inspired by the spirit of St Francis de Sales, who had advocated the application of prayer to every walk of life, John Bosco called these helpers 'Salesians'. Today the Salesian Order, which he founded, has

spread through Italy and abroad, founding Christian centres to teach many trades. They do this by providing religious guidance in both life and work. Many charities were founded with similar objectives with these aims in Britain and elsewhere by the end of the nineteenth century and have since developed many forms of youth clubs. John Bosco was canonised in 1934 – a saint for the modern world.

Conclusions on the importance of these nine Friends of God

The saints and faithful witnesses discussed above, provide a good cross-section of what it means to live a holy life and to have been inspired by the Spirit. It is therefore a stupid error for Protestant churches to ignore the example of the saints. Even Martin Luther recommended studying the lives of the saints if they were well written, and which were not just hagiography.

John Henry Newman said in one of the last sermons in St Mary's Church in Oxford before he was received into the Roman Catholic Church in 1845: *'The New Testament authors only take us so far, leaving us with the duty to interpret'*. We can follow this process in action through the lives of the saints as they brought about changes in thought and practice. Not least among these was Origen's message about prayer that *'he prays unceasingly who combines prayer with the necessary duties of life'*.

St Basil taught that God is indefinable and that while we cannot approach him in his essence we can at least *'know God through his energies'* – that is through his works, his creation. Indeed as the late Bishop of Lynn, Bill Llewellyn, noted in the margin of one of his books *'to try to define God or even to think about Him, is only to diminish Him'*. In any case such definitions only raise more unanswerable questions. The strongest rational argument for God as the ultimate creative reality is in existence itself since absolute nothingness is inconceivable.

From Basil we also learned that, contrary to the Church's teaching in succeeding centuries, *'there is no culture or religion that has not received and does not express a visitation of the Word'*. He also pointed out that man is *'both microcosm and microtheos'* – a spark of the divine is within us; man is greater than just man. On this same subject Gregory of Nazianzus wrote: *'humanity is quickened from the Godhead'* and that *'God is eternal existence . . . He became man that we might become divine'*.

Thomas Aquinas showed us that there is not just one single active intelligence in the world, but that it is multiple, since through God's grace we have freedom of will. This is our personality or 'Form' which is what makes each person an individual as it is our God-given right to strive for perfection according to our innate abilities. That is a thoroughly modern idea.

Between them these nine holy people, including Clement of Alexandria and Origen, have left us a legacy of Christian thought that is as relevant to our time as it was to theirs. As we look to the future and the need to work for a better world, it is therefore comforting to record, as I do in Part VII of this book, the way that clergy of different denominations have been inspired to do great work by the Spirit. As an example of how that actually happens today, I will now describe how a modern clergyman in the City of London fulfils in his pastoral work the ideal that Origen described 1800 years ago in his book *First Principles*. My friend, Prebendary David Burgess MA, a Chaplain to the Queen, Vicar of the Guildhall Church of St Lawrence Jewry in the City of London and Chaplain of the Girdlers' Company, has given me permission to tell the following account of an important aspect of his work in the City.

In answer to a question that I had put to him, David told me that he had often noticed how leading City bankers and others came to his church for a short lunch-time service or an organ recital and then remained in their pew to meditate. After they had been sitting there alone for a while, he would ask them whether he could help them in any way. He then often found that they were seriously stressed and would take him into their confidence as they explained their problems.

These often came about through stress caused by the intensity of their work. Some of them were deeply involved in making decisions at very high levels that would affect the lives of thousands of people. After sharing their thoughts with him, and then listening to David's quiet approach, based on the way Christ might have answered their problem, they would thank him and leave the church seemingly more at ease and strengthened spiritually.

What delighted me about David's story was that such a thing could happen amidst all the financial bustle of the City of London. What also excited me was that David was following an ancient pastoral practice of the Church that has always existed quietly behind the scenes because, as Origen wrote: *'the Church is the school of souls'*.

FEBRUARY SAINTS

February

1 St Brigid or St Bride
2 St Joan of Lestonnac
3 St Anska St Blaise
  St Laurence of Canterbury
  St Andrea Corsini
4 St Gilbert of
  Sempringham
  St Joan of Valois
5 St Agatha
6 St Dorothy
  St Paul Miki
  St Theodore
  the General

St Dorothy   *St Joan of Valois*

Apollinaria
10 St Scholastica
11 St Benedicta of Ariane
12 St Julian the Ferryman
13 St Polyeuctus
14 St Valentine
15 St Sigfried of Sweden
16 St Elias
17 St Finan. The
  Seven Founders
18 St Colman
19 St Mesrop
21 St Peter Damian

22 St Margaret of Cortona
24 St Montanus & St Lucias
25 St Ethelbert of Kent
26 St Porphyry of Gaza
27 St Leander
28 St Oswald of Worcester

St Cuthman   *St Valentine*

The four saints portrayed in this heading are remembered for widely different reasons. They are **Dorothea** (6 February), a virgin martyr who died in 303; **Princess Joan of France** (4 February), foundress of an order to promote peace between rival dynastic factions in fifteenth-century France; **Cuthman** (8 February), an Anglo-Saxon missionary of the eighth century; **Valentine** (14 February), Roman bishop-martyr of the third century. Of these four saints, Joan of France was not canonised until 1950.

ALTAR-PIECE DESIGN FOR EIGHTEEN FEBRUARY SAINTS

Shown in the central scene are:

The martyrdom of **Paul Miki and the Japanese Christians** (6 February), who were crucified in Nagasaki in 1597.

In the top row left-hand group are:

Agatha (5 February), third-century Sicilian virgin martyr; **Montanus and Lucius** (24 February), martyred in 259 in Carthage; **Theodore the General** (7 February), Greek soldier martyr of the early fourth century.

Shown at top centre is:

Brigid (1 February), Irish abbess of the fifth century.

Shown in the top right group are:

Scholastica (10 February), fifth-century abbess; **Ethelbert, King of East Anglia** (20 February) martyred in 794; **Gilbert of Sempringham** (4 February), eleventh-century monastic founder; **Joan of Lestonnac** (2 February), abbess in Bordeaux, seventeenth century.

Shown centre right to bottom and left side are:

Blaise (7 February), Armenian vet and healer, fifth century; **Cyril and Methodius** (14 February), brothers, ninth century, invented cyrillic alphabet for the Slavs; **Leander** (27 February), seventh-century Spanish bishop baptising the king of the Visigoths; **Peter Damian** (21 February), monk and Church reformer, Italy, eleventh century; **Benedict of Aniane** (11 February), being told by Charlemagne to organise the monasteries in his empire; **John de Britto** (4 February), seventeenth-century Jesuit missionary and martyr in India; **Catherine dei Ricci** (13 February), sixteenth-century Florentine nun and visionary.

Altar-piece design for eighteen February saints

FEBRUARY CALENDAR OF SAINTS' FEAST-DAYS

1st **BRIGID or 'Bride'** (c.450–523): Revered in Ireland as 'The Mary of the Gaels'; made abbess in Kildare by St Patrick and niece of St Macartan (24 March).

2nd **JEANNE de LESTONAC** (1556–1640): Niece of the essayist Michel de Montaigne. She founded the teaching sisters of Notre Dame de Bordeaux.

THEOPHINE VENARD (1829–91): French missionary martyred in Viet Nam.

3rd **BLAISE**: Fourth-century Armenian bishop. Legendary healer of animals.

LAURENCE of CANTERBURY: Died in 617. Successor to St Augustine of Canterbury. He failed to win over existing Celtic bishops to Roman practice.

ANSKAR (801–65): Monk of Corbie in Picardy. Sent on mission to Danes and Swedes, but this failed to convert them. He then became a successful bishop in Hamburg.

4th **PHILEAS**: Egyptian bishop martyred in 306.

ALDATE: Bishop martyred in 577 by Saxons at Deorham.

GILBERT of SEMPRINGHAM (1085–1189): A Lincolnshire vicar who founded the Gilbertine Order. This community of monks and nuns began in his village and formed an order which spread rapidly, having men and women's houses side by side – in the ancient Celtic and early British style. They provided orphanages and leper hospitals. He was arrested by Henry II for sending support to the exiled Archbishop St Thomas à Becket.

JOAN of FRANCE (1464–1505): Hunchback daughter of Louis XI. Her marriage to Duke of Orleans who became King Louis XII was not consummated as he found her too ugly and divorced her. She retired to Bourges to do good works and founded the Nuns of the Annunciation to work for peace in France and concord between enemies.

JOHN de BRITTO (1647–93): Portuguese Jesuit beheaded for criticising a Rajah's polygamist practices. He fell foul of court politics.

5th **AGATHA**: Third-century martyr in Catania, Sicily.

6th **DOROTHEA**: Third-century martyr of Caesarea in Cappadocia. Legend that a bystander mocked her on her way to execution and asked her to send him flowers and fruit when she went to her heavenly garden. After her execution the fruit and flowers came to him from heaven. He immediately declared himself a Christian and was promptly executed as well.

ISIDORE of PELUSIUM (365–449): Eminent ascetic abbot and guide of souls. His 2,000 letters were preserved and published in 1638. They give a fascinating picture of him and the troubled times in which he lived. See fuller story at the end of this chapter.

AMAND of MAASTRICHT (584–679): Missionary bishop who reproved King Dagobert I for having forcibly baptised pagans.

MEL: Fifth-century monk made a bishop by St Patrick.

VEDAST: Died in 539. Bishop of Arras. Prepared Frankish King Clovis for his baptism. Has church dedicated to him in London because of Arras cloth trade.

PAUL MIKI and 25 JAPANESE MARTYRS: Crucified together by Shogun of Nagasaki in 1587, because he feared that the large Christian community founded 50 years before by St Francis Xavier would destroy the Shinto religion. Today there is a strong Christian community in Japan led by a Japanese cardinal.

7th **THEODORE the GENERAL**: Early fourth-century martyr. First patron of Venice.

RICHARD: Died in 720 in Lucca. Devout father of Anglo-Saxon missionaries Willibald and Winebald (7 July and 18 December). Believed in Lucca to be 'King Richard'.

RONAN: (1) A sixth-century Cornish monk who went to Brittany and became a bishop. (2) A seventh-century Scottish hermit and curer of souls.

8th **KEW**: Fifth-century Cornish virgin dedicated to Christ.

CUTHMAN: Late eighth- or early ninth-century missionary whose legend is that he came over the Downs to the village of Steyning in Sussex, wheeling his old mother in a cart and then built a church there to convert pagan inhabitants. His church was rebuilt by King William I as St Andrews after he had killed King Harold at Hastings in 1066. Harold had seized back the priory and church of Steyning after his predecessor Edward the Confessor had given it to Normandy. William made this his excuse for waging a Holy War. The Church has a very fine Norman nave, the gift of the victorious King William I.

JOHN of MATTHA: Died in 1213. Founded Trinitarian Friars to ransom prisoners taken by the Saracens.

9th **APOLLONIA:** Christian virgin burnt alive by Alexandrian mob in 249.

TEILO: Sixth-century Welsh bishop who accompanied Cornish bishop Sampson to Doi in Brittany from Cornwall.

10th **SCHOLASTICA** (480–543): Abbess twin sister of St Benedict of Nursia who founded the Abbey of Monte Cassino (11 July).

CONGAR: Sixth-century Breton saint with Cornish links.

CAEDMON: Died in 680. Shepherd poet who became monk of Whitby in Yorkshire.

POPE GREGORY II: Died in 731. Opposed Eastern emperor's edicts against icons. Sent St Boniface of Crediton (5 June) to evangelise Germany from Mainz.

BENEDICT of ANIANE (780–821): Organised abbeys in Charlemagne's empire under strict Benedictine rule to preside over and control local government.

12th **JULIAN the FERRYMAN:** Legendary. Probably based on St Christopher (25 July). His name was used widely as patron of hospitals founded in middle ages.

MARINA: No known date. Said to have lived as a monk in a male habit.

13th **CATHERINE dei RICCI** (1532–90): Florentine nun and visionary. Tried to have Savonarola canonised as martyr. Her case for him was encouraged (2002) by Pope John-Paul II. Much of a pope's time is spent in examining the causes of potential saints.

14th **VALENTINE:** Second-century bishop or priest believed martyred on Flaminian Way outside Rome. Ancient tradition made him patron saint of lovers because birds were believed to pair off and mate on this day.

CYRIL and METHODIUS (827–69 and 815–85): Greek apostles to the Slavs. Driven out by Frankish missionaries for political reasons despite the pope's backing.

15th **SIGFRID:** Died in 1045. English apostle to Sweden who baptised St Olaf (29 July).

16th **ELIAS and COMPANIONS:** Martyred in Caesaraea in 303.

JULIANA: Virgin martyred near Naples in 304.

17th **FINAN:** Died in 661. Celtic monk of Iona who succeeded St Aidan (31 August) as Bishop of Lindisfarne in Northumbria. Baptised Penda, Saxon king of East Anglia.

SEVEN FOUNDERS: Seven leading thirteenth-century Florentine laymen opposed to the Cathar heresy and the loosened morals of their region's community and who founded the Servite Order in 1259 dedicated to serve the Virgin Mary which has since spread into many parts of the world.

*On 17 February 1974 the Anglican Archbishop of Uganda, **Janani Luwum** was murdered by the usurper President Amin for criticising his unjust killings. A martyr for justice.*

18th **COLMAN of LINDISFARNE:** Celtic bishop, died 676. Would not accept Roman usages instead of Celtic practices after St Wilfrid's (12 October) victory for the former at Council of Whitby in 663. He retired to the isle of Inishboffin off the Galway coast of Ireland and founded an abbey there and in Mayo.

'FRA ANGELICO' (1387–1455): Dominican monk and leading Florentine painter. He prayed as he painted the gospel mysteries. Canonised in 1984.

19th **MESROP** (345–439): Founded Armenian Church with St Isaac the Great (9 September). He created the Armenian alphabet for his gospel translations.

20th **ULFRIC:** Died in 1154. The Wiltshire 'hunting parson' who retired to be a hermit.

SIMEON SHARDROST: Persian bishop martyred by Zoroastrians in 342.

21st **PETER DAMIAN** (1007–72): Forceful monk of St Romuald's order (7 February). Active in stirring up what he saw as a lazy church that needed renewal. Pope Gregory wanted the discipline of the Church improved after two centuries of anarchy in Rome during which seven popes were murdered. He made Damian Cardinal of Ostia. In the picture he is reproving an idle bishop for playing chess.

22nd **MARGARET of CORTONA** (1247–97): Mistress of a Tuscan noble, who devoted herself to charity after his death. In spite of gossip she made many converts.

23rd **POLYCARP:** See story under his old feast-day (26 January).

MILBURGA: Died c.700. Welsh princess who founded Wenlock Abbey.

WILLIGIS: Died in 1101. Peasant who became chancellor of Emperor Otto II and Archbishop of Augsburg. He also preached the gospel in Denmark and Sweden.

24th MONTANUS and LUCIUS: Martyred with others at Carthage in 259.

25th KING ETHELBERT of KENT (560–616): Welcomed St Augustine to Kent in 597 and was converted by him. Built first St Paul's cathedral in London; converted King of East Saxons.

WALBURGA: Died in 779. Sister of Saints Willibald and Winebald (7 July and 18 December), Anglo-Saxon missionaries to Germany. Made Abbess of Hildeheim. Her powers over sorcery are still celebrated annually as Walpurgisnacht.

26th PORPHYRY of GAZA (352–420): Hermit of the Egyptian desert who gave his Jerusalem property to charity. Made bishop of pagan Gaza, but had to use troops to control angry mobs. His patient teaching succeeded in winning them over to Christianity.

27th LEANDER: Died in 600. Bishop of Seville. Converted king of the Visigoths.

28th OSWALD of WORCESTER (925-992): Danish, trained at Fleury in France. Bishop of Worcester and then Archbishop of York. Helped Archbishop of Canterbury St Dunstan (19 May) restore monasteries ruined during the Danish invasions.

29th JOHN CASSIAN (360–435): Greek monk and scholar. His Roman feast-day is 23 July. He defended St John Chrysostom (13 September) against fraudulent accusations of Empress Eudoxia and Archbishop Theophilus of Alexandria (St Cyril's uncle). Pope Leo I used Cassian to examine the charges of heresy raised against Patriarch Nestorius by Cyril of Alexandria.

Cassian agreed with Cyril but neither he nor Pope Leo wanted him to hound Nestorius out of the church as Cyril succeeded in doing (see the story in St Isidore's life after the Calendar). Casssian retired to Marseilles where he founded a monastery. There he wrote his famous *Institutes* on the right ordering of monastic life, which influenced the monastic system for centuries. He wanted his monks to strive to achieve the purity of heart by which men can see God.

SUMMARY OF FEBRUARY SAINTS

Twelve of the 56 saints with feast-days in February are martyrs and 13 are women. The most interesting of these saints is **St Isidore of Pelusium** (6 February). He was the most learned, outspoken and spiritual critic of the uncharitable fifth-century Greek clergy whose arguments led to a major schism in the Eastern Church.

It was due to this that Muhammad wrote in the Koran that the *'Christian sects cannot agree over the nature of the God they worship'* and preferred his own spiritual insights for the ideal God for his Arab people. Had Isidore been listened to, Arabia and the whole of the Middle East might have become Christian. His story therefore is of such importance that it is given at length below.

ISIDORE OF PELUSIUM

Isidore of Pelusium was born in Alexandria into a family of high rank. He is one of the most neglected saints of his time and his name is even omitted from the two most popular English dictionaries of saints. Pelusium was an important port on the Eastern mouth of the Nile delta.

After being educated in Athens to the highest Greek literary and religious standards Isidore became a hermit among the 5,000 inmates of the monastic cells on Mount Nitria in the Egyptian desert. It was during his early days there in 392 that the Emperor Theodosius I declared Christianity to be the official religion of the Empire. Through his learning and wisdom Isidore was chosen to be abbot and was then given the task by Archbishop Theophilus of Alexandria to educate his gifted nephew Cyril. Cyril is today venerated as one of the most learned of the Greek saints in spite of the many controversial and uncharitable acts during his career.

After teaching Cyril for five years, Isidore sent him back in 403 to his uncle, saying that he took too worldly an approach to his faith for him to become a monk. Not long afterwards Isidore, who was highly critical of the worldly, nationalistic and flamboyant influence of Archbishop Theophilus, left his monastery and retired to the important port of Pelusium. He was however so highly respected that he was able to turn himself into an oracle whose advice on spiritual matters was sought by many leading people of his day – emperors, abbots, bishops, monks of the rival schools of Antioch and Alexandria, and influential courtiers of the Eastern Roman Empire. He also attracted to Pelusium many followers who, like him, were disgusted at the bitter quarrels and misguided religious policies of those days. He carried on an immense correspondence at the highest levels, trying to correct these trends and especially to guide Cyril, who had become Archbishop of Alexandria in succession to his uncle in 412. By then Cyril had helped his uncle's schemes to support the tyrannical Empress Eudoxia's plot to have St John Chrysostom (13 September), reforming Patriarch of Constantinople, judged unjustly as a heretic, exiled and driven to his death in 407.

Isidore's correspondence over the period from his retirement until his death in 449, five years after that of Cyril, reads like a series of first-class 'leaders' such as might be published by newspapers today. Just over 2,000 of these letters were preserved by his followers the 'Sleepless Monks' in Athens after his death. These were translated into Latin and published in five volumes in 1638. It is from this source that we can follow the course of the misguided and shameful story of what has been described, rather too kindly, as 'the teething troubles' of the early Greek Church in those years. It is also a story that some modern biography will hopefully one day tell in full, since it would bring out clearly how misguided the Church had been and how much more respect there might be for it had the doctrines advocated by Isidore been accepted.

He devoted his life to the service of truth in the Orthodox faith and his life-story helps to illuminate the disputes which split the Eastern Church during the years leading up to the Council of Chalcedon in 451. It was those disputes, especially the rejection by the Egyptian Church and the late Cyril's followers that led to the disastrous and murderous schism in the Greek Church between the Orthodox believers and the 'Monotheists'. That split was between those who held that Christ had two natures, one human and the other divine, and those who supported

Cyril's original view that Christ had only one divine nature.

The seriousness of this almost academic dispute about what is really a divine mystery, can be judged by the fact that it eventually led to there being two separate Christian Churches in the East, one that included Egypt, Mesopotamia and Syria and the other based on Constantinople. This led to the loss to Christianity of the whole of the Middle East and North Africa after the rise of Muhammad at the beginning of the seventh century, as will be explained below

The quotations and accounts from Isidore's letters that are given below are taken from their English translations in the *Dictionary of Christian Biography*. The letters show that Isidore acted as a restraining influence on the brilliant though aggressive theologian Archbishop Cyril of Alexandria, whose excessive zeal and worldly ambitions as an Egyptian nationalist split the Greek Orthodox Church. In spite of Isidore's criticisms, Cyril always revered him, even when his former tutor reminded him how *'very few bishops take the trouble to live up to the standard of the Apostles'.*

Isidore's letters cover many subjects, ranging from criticism of the gluttony of the monks and their neglect of manual labour, to remonstrating at an Emperor's attempt to take away the privilege of sanctuary. He also wrote to the Empress Pulcheria, the wife of Theodosius II and future saint, complaining of the conduct of some of her imperial envoys who had compromised their Christianity in the negotiation of a treaty. He told her husband on his accession to the throne that he should *'combine mildness with authority and that he who is invested with rule ought himself to be to ruled by the laws'*. He also accused a palace chamberlain of inconsistency by *'being glib with scripture and mad after other peoples' property'.*

His comments provide a fascinating picture of the ruling society of those days, but his important contributions to the theological debates of the time were strictly orthodox. His main concern with these was to see that justice prevailed in the disputes and trials which divided the Church. Above all, he emphasised the need for Charity and Love. To one bishop, a great friend, he commented that *'God values nothing more than love, for the sake of which he became man and obedient unto death'.*

Two great church questions brought Isidore into collision with Cyril after he had become his superior and patriarch of Alexandria. The first was related to St Chrysostom's memory as being worthy of veneration by all faithful Christians. Although Cyril's uncle Theophilus, aided by Cyril himself had secured Chrysostom's deposition and fatal exile, the future saint Pope Leo I the Great (10 November) on the advice of St John Cassian (29 February), had found him guiltless of the crimes of which he was falsely accused. Chrysostom had died in exile in the Caucasus before he heard this news. After hearing Rome's verdict, Theodosius II and Pulcheria prayed publicly for forgiveness and all Greek churches were instructed to add Chrysostom's name to their list of martyrs. The order also excommunicated all churches who failed to do so, but the arrogant Cyril in Egypt refused to obey the order. Isidore therefore rebuked him in a letter.

In this letter, Isidore called Chrysostom *'Holy John'*. Isidore was always correct in the way he addressed his superiors in the Church. He therefore began the letter by saying: '*I am your son, since you represent the great St Mark*' (traditionally the first Bishop of Alexandria), but after that he did not mince his words: '*Put a stop to these contentions: do not involve the living Church in a private vendetta prosecuted out of duty to the dead, nor entail her in perpetual division under pretence of piety*'. Cyril gave way and the threat of his own and of Egypt's excommunication was removed.

The other great matter over which Isidore had to restrain Cyril was during the series of trials that led to the deposition for heresy of the Patriarch Nestorius. They also resulted in fierce struggles between the rival schools of theology in Antioch and Alexandria over the definition of the natures of Christ. This is where Isidore's letters shed valuable light on the Eastern Church's troubles in the first half of the fifth century. These troubles were inherited from the earnest questioning by some Greek bishops, monks and theologians in the fourth century, which had been condemned as heretical. Some idea of the problem can be seen from the estimate of Bishop St Epiphanius of Salamis (7 June) in his book in 370, that there were still over 70 Christian heresies. What was at issue was an attempt to produce a watertight definition of Christ's human and divine nature so that it protected the unity of Christ's authority on earth for our salvation. This involved the further issue that, unless that authority could be seen as both human and divine, the gospels became simply a masterpiece of idealism and moral teaching.

The schism between Cyril's supporters of a single nature, the divine, for Christ, which became known as 'Monotheism' and the Antiochan and orthodox tradition of the two natures in Christ endangered the unity of the Empire. This caused the Emperor Theophilus II in 427, a time when he was threatened by the Goths in the north and by Persians in the East, to seek a Patriarch for Constantinople who would bring order to the Church and rid the city of heretics. He chose a monk of the School of Antioch, Nestorius, who had gained a reputation as a sound and popular orthodox preacher. He began his first sermon before the Emperor by saying: '*My Prince, give me the Earth purged of heretics and I will give you Heaven in recompense! Assist me in destroying the heretics and I will assist you in destroying the Persians!*'

Nestorius began by driving out heretical monks and abbots without mercy and so made many enemies. Then the inevitable happened, as it always did in the argumentative atmosphere of Greek theologians. Nestorius' favourite deacon preached on the subject of Jesus' nature and declared that it was unsafe to call his mother Mary by her traditional title of 'Mother of God' – *Theotokos*. She was really the 'Mother of Jesus' – *Kristokos*. This was only meant to support the belief in the human nature within Jesus of Nazareth. Nevertheless Nestorius' enemies at once cried out that Jesus' divinity was being denied and called upon him to revoke this heresy. Nestorius, who was a great preacher but a rather broad-brush theologian, tried to calm the storm by preaching three sermons to explain what was meant by his deacon. In these sermons he attempted inadequately to explain his Antiochan School's definition of Jesus' nature. This only made matters worse, since the hair-splitting ability of Greek rhetoricians to destroy any argument was taken up by Cyril of Alexandria, who was only too keen to attack both Antioch and the pre-eminence of the See of Constantinople.

What should have been a quiet academic debate flared up into a theological and national crisis, a fire whose flames were stoked by the combustible natures of the Greeks and Egyptians and the total lack of charity of the Egyptian nationalist Archbishop Cyril. The Antiochan school, taught through Theodore Bishop of Mopsuestia, the largest Greek see, that *'Although there was only one person in Christ, there was a duality of natures. Each nature, human and divine, was perfect and joined as if in a moral union'*. This was supported by his pupil Bishop John of Antioch. John wrote that *'The way the union of Our Lord's nature was achieved is a mystery. But it must be in such a way that the fullness and freedom of his humanity was preserved. Otherwise he could not be free to decide through his own free will to sacrifice himself on the Cross for our Salvation. That is why the Father vindicated him by raising him to life.'*

Isidore wrote to one of Nestorius' detractors saying that in his view the right way to describe Jesus of Nazareth was *'God Incarnate'*. That would differentiate his person quite clearly from that of God the Father. It was, after all, not God who died on the cross, but the man Jesus, who gave back his Spirit to God. However Cyril and the other opponents of Nestorius were in no mood to listen to such common sense.

Cyril and the Alexandrian School taught that after the incarnation in Mary's womb, Christ had only one nature and that Nestorius' and Antioch's definition of a moral union of natures meant that Jesus was two persons, not one! To Cyril this difference in words was fundamental. He leapt into the fray, obtained copies of Nesotorius' sermons and declared his own opposed views. He said that *'I preach the singleness of Christ's nature. Having said that I need to explain what is meant by the title "Theotokos" of his mother Mary. I affirm that it does not mean "Mother of the Godhead!" She was mother in regard of his manhood of he who, being in the form of God, had assumed the form of a servant and, being the Lord of Glory, condescended to die on the Cross. Now, if it be true, as we believe, that Christ was God, it is by consequence no less true that Mary was "Theotokos". If she was not rightly so-called, her Son was but a human individual, external to the divine nature and not in a true sense the Emmanuel foretold by Isaiah.'*

It can be seen from this how Cyril concealed his political aim under a glib theological cloak to discredit Constantinople. Isidore's simple solution for Mary's title was to call her *'Mother of God Incarnate'*. This was more helpful in that it made Jesus' nature clear, as the human through whom God had chosen to reveal himself. That was all that Nestorius had wanted to explain. The ferocity of Cyril's prosecution against Nestorius was, as Isidore's letters pointed out, partisan and unchristian. Cyril sent copies of Nestorius' sermons to Pope Celestine and asked him to demand that Nestorius repudiate his words or else be deposed. The Pope did not know Greek and it took two years before a papal answer was given. With the aid of his theological advisor St John Cassian, the Pope agreed with Cyril and told him to go ahead and demand a statement from Nestorius withdrawing his words on the Virgin Mary and, failing that, to have him tried and deposed. Cyril, however, went much further than the Pope had intended and made a list of demands which no churchman of the Antioch School, or indeed any orthodox cleric, could possibly accept. A major row ensued and the Emperor was forced to arrange for the matter to be tried at Ephesus in 431. It was an unseemly affair. Cyril went ahead with the trial before Nestorius' chief witnesses and supporters could arrive from Antioch.

Shocked by reports of Cyril's behaviour, Isidore remonstrated with him:

'Prejudice does not see clearly; antipathy does not see at all. If you wish to be clear of both these affections of the eyes, do not pass violent sentence, but commit causes to just judgements. For many at Ephesus accuse you of pursuing a personal feud instead of seeking the things of Jesus Christ in an orthodox way.'

Isidore also wrote to the Emperor Theodosius II, whose ministers were always interfering in Church affairs. He urged him to restrain his ministers from dogmatising on religious matters upon which they were not equipped to judge. He also urged Cyril to cease to stress the *'singleness of Christ's nature'*. He told him that *'To assert only one nature in Christ after Incarnation is to take away both – either by a change of the divine or an abatement of the human'*. He begged him to accept the authority of St Athanasius for the phrase *'from Christ's two natures'*, the divine and the human.

Cyril ignored Isidore's advice and his ruthless attack succeeded in having Nestorius deposed and exiled after the exasperated man had exclaimed that he could *'never accept a baby of two or three months as God!'* If only he had accepted Isidore's definition of *'God Incarnate'* he might have saved himself and avoided a lasting and harmful split in the Church. Instead Nestorius was deposed and exiled. He took his supporters with him and established his own Church in Syria, from where it had such a remarkable success that it spread as far as Mongolia and comprised over 250 bishoprics.

This dispute over the title of Mary also had one interesting consequence a century later. Jesus' mother was described as *Kristokos* by Nestorius' Church, this later agreed with the Koran's version of Mary as the mother of Jesus. This therefore enabled the Muslim Caliphs in Baghdad from the seventh century onwards to support the Nestorian Church whose missionaries could act as a barrier to their enemies the Zorastrians in Persia. It was only with the Mongolian invasions in the thirteenth century that the Nestorian Church was forced to retreat. It now only exists as the small Syrian Church today.

Cyril's success over Nestorius' trials at Ephesus did not end the matter. The bickering between the two schools continued until the Emperor Theodosius ordered a compromise to be agreed between Antioch and Alexandria in the interests of securing internal unity in the realm. Cyril finally agreed with John of Antioch to drop his view of the *'singleness of Christ's nature'* and signed a compromise agreement that Jesus *'In the last days was for us and our salvation born of the virgin Mary according to Manhood. For this there took place a union of two natures. This union was without confusion and we confirm the Virgin Mary to be* Theotokos, *because God the Word was incarnate and made man AND from his very conception united himself to the temple (i.e. the body) assumed from her.'*

This compromise agreement shows how Cyril never sincerely revoked his former position. Nor was Isidore convinced of the genuineness of his acceptance of this formula and told Cyril that he must write to his bishops and explain why his agreement with John was consistent with what he himself had taught previously. He said that if he did not do so, his bishops *'would accuse him of being swayed by vainglory over agreement instead of imitating the great athletes of faith'*. Cyril was such an athlete, and he wriggled out of his difficulty by appearing to accept both definitions! In writing to allay his bishops' scandalised feelings he said: '*I can still maintain that our traditional orthodox faith in this city holds good – namely that after the union the two natures became one – the Incarnate Nature*'.

This cover enabled the Egyptian Church to cling on to their 'one-nature' monotheism and they never truly accepted the compromise. Twelve years later in 451 at the Council of Chalecdon, after both Cyril and Isidore were dead, an even worse split occurred under Cyril's successor Archbishop Dioscoros. As will be explained in the text on Cyril's life in the June Calendar, the Egyptian bishops rejected the 'two-nature' decisions at Chalecdon, murdered their Orthodox archbishop, and converted all Egypt, Palestine, Syria and Mespotamia to the Monophysite heresy. Thus by the beginning of the seventh century, when Muhammad was preaching his Islamic faith, there were in and around Arabia many different Christian churches, all of whom, as Muhammad pointed out in his Koran, disagreed on the nature of the God they worshipped.

Isidore did not live to see the disasters that followed for the Orthodox Church and the Empire, but in one of his last letters he summed up what the Greeks needed to do: '*If we are to overcome heretics, pagans and Jews by our doctrines, we are bound also to overcome them by our deeds, lest, when worsted on the former ground, and after rejecting our faith, they should show how unfavorably our lives compare with it*'.

The tragedy of St Isidore, as Bishop Simon Barrington-Ward has told me in a letter, is that '*some theologians seem always to have preferred arguing about the mystery of Christ's nature as a fusion of the divine and human, rather than demonstrating that fusion in their own being. Always we need more people prepared to "live in Christ" than to talk about him incessantly, let alone argue about him*'. In despair, Isidore wrote: '*We are bound to know and believe that God is – and not to busy ourselves as to what he is!*'

Many of the bitter and sometimes murderous disputes that have disturbed and split the Churches in the past 1,600 years might have been avoided if only there had been more saints as wise and as gifted with common sense on spiritual matters as St Isidore.

As already mentioned, much of the argument about these points of faith and the confusion which so disturbed the Church was caused by the different meanings that the Antiochans and Alexandrians gave to the Greek word for 'nature', as Philip Hughes pointed out in his brilliant *History of the Church* (see Vol. I, pages 237 and 248). The Antiochans used the word *physis* for 'nature', whereas the Alexandrians (and the Monophysites) used it to mean 'person'. They were therefore, unknown to each other, arguing from different standpoints. Also Cyril did not make very clear the distinction he drew between 'nature' (*physis*) and 'substance' (*hypostasis*). This exposes the utter pointlessness of such arguments and the danger of taking up positions over the meaning of words, something which was too often to split the Church over other definitions in later centuries to the despair and confusion of the faithful.

By treating the life of this neglected saint St Isidore at length, I have shown the damage caused by St Cyril, who is nevertheless venerated greatly by the Orthodox Church. When we come to looking in the June Calendar at Cyril's life and character, he will be seen as the most double-faced Janus-like character. However in making such judgements on Cyril or any saint, one needs to remember that they lived in difficult and dangerous times.

MARCH SAINTS

This heading for March portrays three saints who are remembered especially in England, Wales and Ireland: **Pope Gregory I 'The Great'** (12 March), who sent St Augustine of Canterbury on the first Roman Catholic mission to Britain in 597; **Patrick** (16 March), who founded the Irish Celtic Church; **David** or **Dewi** (1 March), sixth-century bishop and Patron Saint of Wales; Saint Gregory is included in the March Calendar because his feast is celebrated by Anglican Churches on 12 March and this date is in the Anglican *Book of Common Prayer*. However the Roman Calendar changes of 1969 altered his day to 3 September. In any event, it is appropriate to place him early in the Calendar, given his important role in the formative years of the Catholic Church.

ALTAR-PIECE DESIGN FOR THIRTEEN MARCH SAINTS

Shown in the central scene is:

John Climacus (30 March), seventh-century Abbot of St Catherine's monastery in Sinai, and author of the mystical book *The Ladder of Ascent*.

Shown in the scenes from top left and round to the right are:

Perpetua and **Felicity** (7 March), being martyred in the arena at Carthage in 203. **Gregory of Nyssa** (9 March), fourth-century Greek bishop and theologian, brother of St Basil. **Sophronius** (11 March), theologian and Bishop of Jerusalem surrendering the city to the Caliph Omar in 638; **Euphrasia** (13 March), who gave her property to the poor and gave up the world to became a nun, doing the meanest tasks; **Cuthbert** (20 March), Anglo-Saxon Bishop of Hexham, who became a solitary on the Isle of Farne, famed as a worker of miracles and for his holiness; **Queens Matilda** and **Cunegond** (3 March): Matilda was Empress of Henry I ('The Fowler') in the tenth century; Cunegond was Empress of Henry II of Bavaria in the eleventh century. Both were zealous supporters of the Bendictines. **Catherine of Bologna** (9 March), fifteenth-century abbess and visionary; **John of God** (8 March), sixteenth-century Portuguese soldier convert who devoted his life to the care of the sick, supporting himself as a wood-merchant; **Louise de Marillac** (15 March) seventeenth-century foundress in France; **John Ogilvie** (10 March), Jesuit martyred in Edinburgh in 1615.

St Perpetua & St Felicity

St Gregory of Nyssa

St Sophronius

St John Ogilvie

The Ladder of Divine Ascent

St John Climacus

St Euphrasia

St Louise de Marillas

St Cuthbert

St John of God

St Catherine of Bologna

St Matilda & St Cunegonde

Altar-piece design for thirteen March saints

MARCH CALENDAR OF SAINTS' FEAST-DAYS

1st **DAVID (or 'DEWI'):** Sixth-century Welsh Bishop and patron saint. One of St Illtyd's (6 November) pupils on the Gower peninsular of S.Wales. His mother was St Nun (3 March). His daffodyl emblem was worn as a distinguishing mark in battle by Welsh soldiers.

2nd **CHAD:** Died in 672. Anglo-Saxon bishop famous for the humility with which he accepted his demotion from Archbishop of York in place of St Wilfred, to being Bishop of Lichfield on account of the Celtic instead of Roman style of his consecration.

3rd **MARINUS:** Soldier martyred in c.260 under Diocletian.

NON or NONNA: St David's unmarried mother, a victim of rape by a Welsh chief. She became a nun in Cornwall and retired to Dirinon in Brittany where she is buried.

WINWALOE or GUENELOE: Sixth-century missionary with St Budoc (8 December) from Cornwall to Brittany, where he built a monastery at Landevennec. Famous for his typically Celtic self-mortifications.

CUNEGOND (978–1033): Empress of Holy Roman Emperor Henry II. Founded a nunnery at Cassel. Very stern abbess. Voltaire named the princess in *Candide* after her.

AILRED of RIEVAULX (1100–67): Cistercian abbot, famed for his spirituality and convincing sermons. In his early career he was a priest at King St David of Scotland's court. In spite of delicate health he was made second abbot of St Bernard of Clairvaux' monastery at Rievaulx. The monastery grew to 150 monks and 500 lay brothers under his rule and made five other foundations in Scotland and England. He became important nationally and was chosen to preach at Westminster Abbey for the Translation of St Edward the Confessor. He wrote a treatise on friendship, *Speculum Caritatis*, and also the life of St Ninian and the northern saints.

THE BLESSED MOTHER KATHERINE DREXEL (1858–1955): Rich American foundress of The Sisters of the Blessed Sacrament especially for Indian and black people who were neglected by the Church due to segregation laws. Forerunner of Martin L. King. Beatified 1989 (see Kenneth L Woodward's *The Making of Saints* (Chatto and Windus, 1990) for an interesting study of the process of her Cause).

4th **ADRIAN of MAY:** Irish bishop burned by Danes on Scottish Isle of May in 875, which became a famous place of pilgrimage. King St David of Scotland (24 May) built a monastery for Benedictines there in his memory in the eleventh century.

PRINCE CASIMIR (1458–84): Prince of Poland banished by his father King Casimir IV for refusing to take up arms against any Christian lands while Christians were in danger from the Turks. Died at Vilna. Canonised by Leo X in 1521. Patron Saint of Poland and of Lithuania.

5th **CIARAN of SAIGHIR:** Late fifth-century Irish bishop, who may have been consecrated by St Patrick. Legends abound about his working with wild animals, badgers and foxes. This was typical of the Celtic saints. Founded monastery at Ossory, where many Irish kings are buried. Fine ruins remain.

PIRAN: Died in 480. Irish or Welsh monk who settled in Cornwall. Patron of tin-miners. His cult was popular both in Cornwall and Brittany.

6th **FRIDOLIN:** Sixth-century Irish missionary to Poitiers. He also evangelised in the Rhineland, Switzerland and Austria. His relics at Sackingen attracted many pilgrims.

7th **CHRODEGANG of METZ:** Died in 766. Bishop of Metz and minister of Charles Martel. Persuaded Pepin the Short to drive the Arian heretic Lombards from Italy, thus creating the Papal State under Pope Stephen III. Charlemagne adopted his rules for his monasteries and bishoprics.

BALDRED: Eighth-century Northumbrian hermit. Lived on the Bass Rock off the coast. His prayer for the removal of a dangerous reef was granted. It is still marked on Admiralty charts as 'Baldred's Rock'. His faith had literally 'moved a mountain'!

BILFRITH: Eighth-century hermit and goldsmith, famous for his gold and silver binding of the Lindisfarne Gospels containing intricate and lovely Celtic illuminations.

COLETTE or NICOLETTE (1381–1447): Daughter of a poor carpenter of the Abbey of Corbie in Picardy. She became a Franciscan tertiary after having visions to go and reform the Order of Poor Clares founded by St Clare of Assisi (11 August).

PERPETUA and FELICITY: Died in 203. Young mother and her servant killed by wild beasts in the arena at Carthage, as Tertullian described – see the text following the Calendar.

8th **JOHN of GOD (1495–1550):** Portuguese atheist soldier who was called to serve God at the age of 40 to work for the poor and sick. He began by peddling sacred books and pictures to earn funds. Then, after a breakdown in 1539, he established a hospital in Grenada and worked selflessly for the physical and spiritual welfare of his patients. See illustration. He is a patron saint of hospitals and the sick.

9th GREGORY of NYSSA (335–95): Bishop and younger brother of St Basil (3 January). See illustration and, after the Calendar, the story of his life in Cappadocia, Turkey.

CATHERINE of BOLOGNA: (1413–63): Court lady of the Duke of Ferrara. She became a nun and had many spiritual visions. See illustration above.

FRANCES of ROME: (1384–1440): Lay woman married with children. Her many mystical experiences had a profound religious influence on Roman society. She founded the Order of Oblates in 1436 with her friends to look after the poor and suffering.

10th FORTY MARTYRS of SEBASTEA: Soldiers of the XIIth Legion who refused to obey Licentius' order in 320 to renounce Christianity. Constantine executed Licentius.

JOHN OGILVIE (1574–1615): Scottish Jesuit convert and priest, betrayed and hung at Edinburgh Castle as a traitor even though he was always loyal to King James.

11th SOPHRONIUS (555–638): Orthodox theologian and abbot, born in Carthage. He taught as an Orthodox theologian in Carthage, Rome and Alexandria. At the age of 80 he opposed the Monothelite heresy (single will for Christ) which the Emperor Heraclius had adopted to try and unite the opposing Orthodox and Metaphysites (only a single nature for Christ, divine rather than human). He was made Patriarch by the people of Jerusalem, but was forced to yield the city to the Muslims in 638. See the illustration above.

EULOGIUS of CORDOBA: Priest martyred by Muslims for trying to save a Muslim girl convert to Christianity from being executed.

12th POPE GREGORY I ('The Great') (540–604): This is his old feast-day, changed in 1969 to 3 September. His picture in the heading shows him with the Anglo-Saxon slaves who inspired him to send St Augustine of Canterbury's mission to Britain to establish the Catholic Church. See his life story in the text after the Calendar.

MAXIMIILIAN: Soldier martyred in 295 in Algiers.

SIMEON the new theologian (949–1022): Monk of Constantinople who took Byzantine mystical theology to its peak. He followed the mystical tradition of St John Climacus (30 March) and St Maximus the Confessor (13 August). His title of The New Theologian denotes the Eastern Church's opinion of him as second only to St John the Evangelist and to St Gregory of Nazianzus (3 January).

13th EUPHRASIA (382–412): Egyptian orphan who abandoned her engagement to be married, gave her property to the poor and became a nun. She took on all the menial tasks to punish herself for her desire to return to the world. Jealous nuns accused her of being conceited and hypocritical, but she won them over with her gentle patience.

14th MATILDA or MECHTILDE (895–968): Empress of Henry I ('The Fowler'). Popular for her love and charity for her people, but she was treated cruelly by her princely sons.

15th LONGINUS: According to tradition, the centurion who speared Christ's side on the Cross. Longinus' alleged lance was 'discovered' by the bogus Peter the Hermit at the siege of Antioch during the first Crusade (1097). This deceit had a dramatic effect in raising the crusaders' morale.

LOUISE de MARILLAC (1591–1660): Born in the Auvergne. Widow of courtier of Louis XIV. Helped St Vincent de Paul (27 September) found The Daughters of Charity.

HOFBAUER (Clement-Marie) (1751–1820): Viennese priest driven out by anti-Catholic Joseph II. Converted Protestants and Jews in Poland. Returned to teach the poor.

16th MARTYRS of NORTH AFRICA: The many third-century martyrs.

17th JOSEPH of ARIMATHEA: Organised Jesus' burial.

PATRICK (385–461): Roman-Briton who founded the Irish Celtic Church. See illustrated story below after this Calendar.

WITHBURGA: Died in 743. Daughter of King Anna of East Anglia. Solitary hermit nun at Holkham, Norfolk, before founding nunnery. Her symbol in art is a tame doe. The park at Holkham today is famous for its deer. It belongs to the Earl of Leicester.

GERTRUDE of NIVELLES (620–59): Abbess of monastery for monks and nuns founded by her mother on advice of St Amand (6 February). Her sister St Begga (17 December) helped the Irish St Fursey (16 January) and his brother in their work in Gaul.

18th CYRIL of JERUSALEM (315–86): Bishop thrice exiled for his orthodoxy against Arian heresy. Mistrusted the hair-splitting differences over the relations of the Three Persons of the Trinity, but agreed with St Athanasius (2 May) on the definition of *Homoousion* – 'of the same substance'. He commented on opponents: 'They mean what we mean but differ over words!', thus pointing out the typical fault of the fierce theologians of those days.

FINAN of ABERDEEN: Sixth-century disciple of Kentigern (14 January).

KING EDWARD THE MARTYR: Died in 978. Son of King Edgar, murdered at Corfe Castle by his half-brother's retainers with the connivance of his mother and her party who opposed the influence of the monasteries.

19th JOSEPH: Husband of the Virgin Mary.

20th CUTHBERT (634–87): Anglo-Saxon monk of Lindisfarne and bishop. Adored by his priests for his holiness. He preferred a hermit's life to that of being a bishop. They took his incorrupt body with them to the site of Durham Cathedral just before Lindisfarne was destroyed by Danes in 793. The Lindisfarne Gospels are associated with him. He became the most popular saint in northern Britain. His tomb is in Durham Cathedral.

21st ENDA: Born in Meath, Ireland. Died in 530. After being a soldier he was trained as a monk in Ninian's (26 August) monastery in Galloway before returning to Ireland and founding monasteries in the Boyne valley. His Irish monasticism had immense influence in Wales.

NICHOLAS von FLU (1417–87): Swiss patriot of Lucerne. Became a hermit with his wife's approval. People flocked to him for temporal and spiritual advice. His advice to Lucerne's rulers prevented a war.

On this day in 1554 Archbishop of Canterbury **Thomas Cranmer** *was burned alive in Oxford by Queen Mary I, the fanatical Roman Catholic daughter of Henry VIII and his divorced wife, Queen Catherine of Aragon.*

22nd POPE ZACHARIAS: Died in 752. Got the Frankish Pepin the Short to attack the Lombard invaders of Italy. Supported St Boniface of Crediton (5 June) in Germany.

23rd TORIBIO of LIMA (1538–1606): Law professor at Salamanca, made president of Inquisition by King Philip II and later Archbishop of Lima in Peru. Revitalised the neglected education of the Indian population. His example spread all over South America.

24th CATHERINE VADSTENA (1331–81): Daughter of the mystic St Bridget of Sweden (23 July). Helped her found the Bridgetine Order.

MACARTEN: Fifth-century Irish bishop, the first made by St Patrick. He is said to have been the uncle of St Brigid. The evidence for that is the history written two centuries later by the monk Muirchu, who may have been currying favour with the O'Neills.

25th FEAST of the ANNUNCIATION of the VIRGIN MARY

DISMAS: The name of the 'Good Thief' crucified with Jesus according to St Luke.

ALWOLD: Died in 1058. As Bishop of Winchester he devoted cults to St Cuthbert (20 February) and to St Swithun (2 July). Renowned for being unusually abstemious for a Saxon.

26th BRAULIO (590–651): Bishop of Saragossa. After St Isidore of Seville (4 April) he was the most respected churchman in Spain before the Muslim conquest.

LUDGER: Died in 869. Frisian missionary trained by St Boniface's followers. Made Bishop of Munster. Evangelised Westphalia better than Charlemagne's forced baptisms.

WILLIAM of NORWICH: Probably fictitious. A body found in 1144 was alleged to have been that of a boy killed at a Jewish ritual. The story of this rumoured martyrdom was spread to help raise funds for Norwich Cathedral. The appeal failed because pilgrims preferred to visit the Wishing Well of Our Lady of Walsingham 25 miles away.

27th JOHN the EGYPTIAN: (305–94). A carpenter of Assyut in Egypt who became a hermit only a little less famous in his own day than St Antony of Egypt.

RUPERT of SALZBURG: Died in 710. Bishop of Worms and Salzburg. Evangelised Bavaria and developed its saltmines.

28th ALKELDA of MIDDLEHAM: Saxon princess strangled by Danes in 800.

29th JONAH and BERIKJESU: Converts martyred horribly in Persia in 327.

MARK of ARETHUSA: Fourth-century teacher alleged to have been stabbed to death by the pens of his pupils. See also St Cassian of Imola (13 August) for similar story.

GLADWYS and GWYNLLOW: Eccentric sixth-century Welsh couple who ran naked on the beach in all weathers as a penance. They were stopped from doing this after many years by their son St Cadoc (25 September), who did not consider this practice holy.

BERTHOLD and BROCARD: Frankish hermits who founded the Carmelite Friars on Mount Carmel. They died in 1198 and 1231 respectively.

30th JOHN CLIMACUS: Died in 649. Abbot of St Catherine's monastery at the foot of Mount Sinai. He was an important theologian on the art of mystical prayer, the technicques for which are described in his *The Ladder of Ascent*. His full life-story is given below.

31st ACACIUS: Bishop of Antioch during the Emperor Decius' persecution. Arrested in 251, he swore he was loyal to Rome. At his trial the Roman governor enjoyed debating the nature of God with him so much that he released him.

SUMMARY OF MARCH SAINTS

The 68 saints in this Calendar include 16 martyrs and 17 women, three of whom were visionaries. The rest of this chapter will concentrate on seven of the March Saints about whom we know most: **St Perpetua** and **St Felicity, St Gregory of Nyssa, St John Climacus, St Patrick, Pope St Gregory I 'The Great'** and on one Faithful Witness not mentioned in the Calendar, **St Isaac of Nineveh** who is important for his spiritual writings. He is not recognised as a saint by the Orthodox or Roman Churches since he belonged to the Nestorian Church (see details for this Church under the text on St Isidore of Pelusium at the end of the February Calendar).

IMPORTANT MARCH SAINTS

St Perpetua and St Felicity

These two, a young wife and mother and her servant Felicity, were condemned to be killed in the arena at Carthage for refusing as Christians to put on special fancy dress and to take part in a pagan festival at Carthage in 203.

The story of their martyrdom in the arena was widely publicised in the Church and probably was written by the Roman lawyer and publicist Tertullian. He became a Christian in 193 and wrote a famous defence or 'Apologia' for the faith and several criticisms of heretical doctrines. He is famed for his comment that *'The seed of the Church is the blood of the martyrs'* – *Semen est sanguis Christianorum*. He himself was not recognised as a saint because he became a member of the Montanist sect in 207. This North African sect was an early example of a breakaway Christian community. They were followers of Montanus, who sought inspiration directly from the Holy Spirit. They trusted in what was revealed by members speaking in 'tongues' in the belief that the existing Church was not spiritual enough. In every other respect Tertullian was orthodox. This community survived until the time of St Augustine of Hippo.

The reason for including this story here is that Tertullian's description of the martyrdom gives a vivid account of the ceremonies that took place in the Roman arenas when Christians were sent to be mauled and killed by wild beasts. It also demonstrates the amazing bravery of the martyrs. The two girls were imprisoned. Perpetua had some remarkable visions and was able to hand over her own child to a Christian foster-parent as well as the infant born in prison to her pregnant maid Felicity. The show in the arena began with a parade of the wild beasts led by the

Venator. Then the girls entered the arena from the dungeons beneath the seats. The two girls were bare-breasted. The crowd were horrified and insisted that the ceremony could not start until their breasts were covered. The two victims sang hymns as they walked in, convinced that they were about to go to heaven. The game-wardens drove in two wild cattle, which charged Perpetua and knocked her over with their long horns. She was in a state of ecstasy, seemingly oblivious of her painful wounds, but Felicity helped her to stand. The two were then taken out of the arena to the dungeons, while the second 'act' was prepared.

The girls were then led into the arena together with a young male Christian, who was attacked by a leopard. He was killed. His body was removed and the girls were again sent into the dungeon beneath the tiers of the onlookers' seats. The third 'act' soon began. This was a parade of trainee gladiators with swords and full armour. The girls were then sent into the arena alone, so that the gladiators could practice their trade by learning how to kill them. Perpetua's executioner was so incompetent that she had to guide his sword to her throat. Once the act had fnally been completed, the girls' bodies were dragged out of the arena by the heels, just as is done today with the corpses of bulls following a Spanish bull-fight, whose ceremonies seem to copy those of the gladiatorial arenas.

St Gregory of Nyssa (335–95)

Greek bishop and brother of St Basil the Great (1 January). Like his brother and their friend St Gregory of Nazianzus, he was a theologian and doughty opponent of the Arian heresy which denied the doctrine of the Trinity that the Risen Christ was equal with God. In the picture in the altar-piece illustrated at the start of this Calendar, St Gregory is shown writing his book after being imprisoned by the Arian heretic Emperor Valens.

Gregory's belief in the human soul being implanted with the seed of the Holy Spirit is described in his book *On Virginity*: '*What came about in bodily form in Mary, the fullness of God shining through Jesus Christ, takes place in a similar way in every soul that has been made pure. The Lord does not come to us in bodily form, but dwells in us spiritually and the Father takes his abode with him.*'

Like St Bernard of Clairvaux (20 August) Gregory was fascinated by the poetry of King Solomon's *Song of Songs* and its message about love. In a sermon on the song Gregory likened true love to the '*yearning of the soul for God*'. He called the soul 'she': '*She is no longer satisfied with the cup of wisdom. She wants to see the whole process to the place where the mystery of wine is performed. Once she has entered there she aspires still more highly. She seeks to be put under the banner of Love – for St John says "God is Love".*' So the soul ever aspires to attain higher things.

Gregory, like the other two Cappadocian Fathers, Basil and Gregory of Nazianzus, describes his own experience of prayer. In writing his *Life of Moses* Gregory explained how the soul needs to rest in its contemplation and to forget worldly concerns and illustrated this by his own mystical experiences in prayer, which involved him in a journey from light to darkness. He describes Moses' ascent of Mount Sinai as an example of the way the mystery of God may appear to the seeker: '*At first the revelation of God is made to Moses in light. Then God speaks to him in a cloud. Finally Moses climbs higher and he contemplates God in darkness.*' This story of Moses inspired many poets and writers. Among them was the unknown sixth-century author who is called Denis the Areopagite. He shows how through the '*unknowing darkness*' a person's intellect may be transcended to unite himself with the living God.

One unknown fourteenth-century English poet and mystic also wrote on this theme in his *Cloud of Unknowing*, which he ended with these cautionary words: '*With Love you shall find Him, but with thinking, never*'. The Irish theologian John Scotus Erigena (810–77) also used this theme to remind us that belief must come before reason.

Gregory of Nyssa also tells us that once we believe and then seek, the more aware we become of hidden objects. It is a process of private exploration, carried out in all humility. This '*leads us to what is hidden*' and although much may be revealed by the reason, the key to true understanding, the only way to advance to knowledge of God, is through '*Love*'.

In one of his last sermons Gregory gave this message: '*You have the ability within you to see God because "The Kingdom of God is within you" (Luke 17.21). He who has formed you, also put into your being immense power. He encloses you in the image of his own perfection, just as the mark of a seal is impressed in wax. Your inner staring at first obscured God's image, but if you rediscover the beauty of the image that was put in you at the beginning, you will obtain within yourself the goal you desire. No one has ever seen God. In fact that part of his nature that is invisible becomes visible through his "energies" that are revealed in his nature.*'

St John Climacus (died 649)

Just over two centuries after Gregory of Nyssa, John Climacus, a widower from Egypt, became a hermit at the monastery of St Catherine at the foot of Mount Sinai, which had been built partly for defensive reasons by the Emperor Justinian in the sixth century. The sketch below shows St Catherine's as it is today. It contains a fine collection of Byzantine eleventh- to twelfth-century icons.

St Catherine's monastery today at the foot of Mt. Sinai

John Climacus wrote his book *The Ladder of Ascent* after years of meditation. He was elected abbot of St Catherine's and was given the name 'Climacus' in honour of his book. The book, which he describes as a training manual for beginners, describes the way to achieve perfection as far as it is possible in this world through 30 stages of contemplation and prayer.

John Climacus says that the most fruitful prayer begins with the need to break off thought from the world. He then advises us how to do this: '*Let your calling to mind of Jesus be continuously combined with your breathing and you will then know the meaning of silence. The remembrance of Christ's suffering cures the soul of rancour, so confused is it by Christ's love. Love is greater than prayer. Prayer is one virtue amongst others, whereas love contains them all.*' The prayer he and later followers recommend is adapted from St Luke (18.13): '*God, be merciful to me a sinner*'.

The form of the 'Jesus Prayer' is: '*O Lord Jesus Christ, Son of God, be merciful to me a sinner*'. If said slowly and in time with one's slow breathing and then repeated 50 times or more, this prayer does bring one peace and brings one a little closer to God. One can then listen, meditate, pray in silence and progress to understanding. The Greek mystics believed that it would help even beginners, as Climacus says, to climb the various stages through '*Purification*' and '*Illumination*' to a momentary '*Union*' with God's presence in the uncreated light that existed before Creation and at Christ's Transfiguration.

This is a well-known process of prayer, in each stage of which the mind's attitude changes and it is practised by mystics of all the world's great faiths. It gives a sense of obedience, of repentance and of a revolution in heart and mind. It helps by fighting against passions such as vainglory, sloth and pride to attain the corresponding virtues of gentleness, silence, vigilance and detachment from possessions. This discipline, in its Christian version, culminates in bringing the mind close to God through a sense of simplicity, and humility to the goal of faith, love, charity and hope.

The prayer should be said in one's heart in silence; as Climacus says: *'the friend of silence comes close to God. In secret he converses with him and receives light.'* He therefore shows that prayer is a conversation with God, as St Bernard of Clairvaux will be seen to explain in the August Calendar. This sense of speaking with God in private was also experienced by St Teresa of Avila (15 October) and described in her autobiography as *'Prayer for me is like a conversation with Him Who loves us'.*

The Ladder of Ascent was the precursor of many versions of spiritual progress through prayer. Two Greek saints who developed this mystical theology further were the thirteenth-century monks St Gregory of Sinai (27 November) and St Gregory Palamas (14 November). Two books on mystical prayer by the sixteenth-century St Teresa of Avila are still widely read today – *The Way of Perfection* (1566) and *The Interior Castle* (1577). A symbolic and narrative approach to the ideal of spiritual progress towards Christ is *Pilgrim's Progress*, written in prison by the Puritan John Bunyan in 1678. Another record of spiritual progress was made by The Blessed Cardinal John Henry Newman in his *Grammar of Assent* (1870). Both of these are described in Part VII.

Isaac of Nineveh (c.630–c.700)

Isaac was a Syrian anchorite and monk who was made bishop of the Nestorian Church in Nineveh. He then retired to a hermit's life in Iraq to record his most famous work, his *Ascetic Treatises*. These writings were collected for the book by his faithful disciples after Isaac had gone blind. They have been increasingly studied by modern scholars both in the East and the West. Like John Climacus, he taught that perfection,

that is to say *'becoming close to Christ'*, cannot be attained without some break with the world.

Yet in saying this Isaac realised how difficult and impractical this ideal must be for busy pastoral priests and for lay people busy with their lives. He advised nevertheless that progress can be made through prayer, just as we have seen in the case of St Francis de Sales in the text at the end of the January Calendar. Isaac suggested the following prayer for those who found his plan difficult: *'Lord Jesus our God who wept for Lazarus and shed tears of grief and compassion, accept my tears of bitterness . . . By thy suffering assuage my suffering. May thy soul, which thou didst give back on the Cross to thy Father, lead me by grace to thee. I have wandered far from thee. Do thou set out in quest for me. Lead me back to thy pastures and to the sheep of thy flock.'*

Isaac wrote that we must be humble: *'Humility is the ornament of the Godhead. The "Word" clothed himself in it when he became man. Therefore anyone who wraps themselves in it truly makes themselves like Him. So therefore, when you come before God's presence in prayer, be in your thought like a tiny creature or a lisping child. And in his presence make no pretence of knowledge. Approach God rather with the heart of a child. Go into his presence to receive the loving care with which fathers look after their children, and you will feel in your senses the power of Him who is with you.'*

Isaac understood the anger and passions that sometimes possess us and the inner turmoils which can oppress us: *'It is by fighting against passions that one prevents them entering the heart. That is achieved by gratification of conscience, by the knowledge with which the soul is filled and by the memory of one's own acts of contemplation.'*

He also wrote on the depression and despair that can affect us all at times: *'Sometimes our soul is engulfed in waves and drowned. Then whatever we give ourselves to, whether to reading or scripture or prayer, whatever we do we are increasingly imprisoned in darkness. It is an hour filled with despair and fear. The soul is utterly deprived of hope in God and the consolation of faith. It is entirely filled with anguish. But those who have been tested by the distress of such an hour know that in the end it is followed by a change. God never leaves the soul for a whole day in such distress, for then hope would be destroyed. Rather he allows it to emerge soon from darkness.'*

Blessed are those who endure such temptations. For great will be the stability and strength to which they will come after that. However it is not just in one hour or at a stroke that such a combat is concluded. Gradually grace comes to take up its dwelling completely in the soul. There is a time for trial and a time for consolation.'

Isaac showed how we can experience God through contemplative prayer: *'It is at the moment when we are praying and pleading with God, talking to him and striving to gather our thoughts from many directions, that we are open to God alone. Filled with God we may begin to comprehend the incomprehensible. For the Holy Spirit breathes on us until in the height of concentration the very motion of prayer stops. Our spirit, in wonderment, is struck with amazement. It then forgets its own desires and petitions. It is no longer of this world. It no longer distinguishes between body and soul and the things of memory. As the godly St Gregory of Nyssa said: "Prayer is the purity of the spirit. It stops of its own accord when the light of the Holy Spirit overwhelms it in wonder".'*

The highest attainment of prayer, when it becomes spontaneous and continuous, as with St Francis of Assisi (4 October), is also described by Isaac: *'When the Spirit dwells in a person, from that moment when a person becomes full of prayer, he never leaves him. For the Spirit never ceases to pray in him. Thus the prayer of silence is pure, since the thoughts are divine motions and the workings of the heart and intellect have been purified.'*

Isaac shows that the goal of prayer is Love: *'Love comes from meeting Him. Knowledge united with God fulfils every desire . . . One who has found love feeds on Christ every day. At every hour that person becomes immortal thereby. Jesus said: "Whoever eats this bread that I shall give him shall never see death." (John 6.52). "God is Love" (1st Letter of John 4.8). Therefore those who live on love receive from God the fruit of life. They breathe, even in this world, the air of resuscitation, because Love is the Kingdom.'*

St Patrick (c.385–c.461): The Legend and the Saint

The Roman Catholic Bishop of Downpatrick in Northern Ireland told me that *'all we know for certain about Patrick is written in his* Confessio *and in one letter to a British chief who had killed some of his monks and converts. Copies of these two documents, together with two biographies written two centuries after his death by the seventh-century monks Murchiu and Tirechan are in the ninth-century* Book of Armagh *in the library of Trinity College in Dublin.'* The Bishop has decorated his cathedral with fine mosaics of Patrick's legends. When asked how true they were he said in 1996 that: *'You have to have a great imagination to believe that – but they are all about driving out paganism'*.

Patrick's *Confessio* and the two biographies show that he dedicated his life to taking the gospel to Ireland. Yet he has often been a cause of controversy due to the legends that were woven around him. These and the criticisms of some early twentieth-century historians have tended to obscure his true greatness and achievement. We need to examine these before we can see the true St Patrick. In doing so we must remember the purpose and humility of Patrick's *Confessio*, written in his old age.

Patrick begins his *Confessio* with these words: *'This is my confession before I die. I must not hide the gift of God.'* He then combines praise and thanksgiving and gives an account of the gospel he took to Ireland, together with occasional details of his life. Judging from the number of years he gives in it for various periods in his early life, Patrick was probably born in 385–90.

Before examining the *Confessio* we need to consider the claims by some critics that there was not one Patrick, but two, three or even seven of them! Yet no critic has yet been able to provide any convincing evidence for this. Nor can they get away from the fact that only the one true Patrick could possibly have written the *Confessio*. We can therefore feel safe in rejecting these criticisms.

Patrick tells us that he was born in Bannaven Taburniae and that his father was a Decurion or local Roman-British civil servant and also a Christian deacon. No one has been able to ascertain the position of Bannaven. It has been suggested that it might be almost anywhere from the Scottish borders to the Lancashire coast or by the Severn estuary. Muirchu says it was near the Western Sea. If it was near the mouth of the River Severn, that could account for the British legend that Patrick visited Glastonbury, famous in the Arthurian stories.

Patrick starts the actual story of his life by saying: *'I was about sixteen years old and did not know the true God. I was taken into captivity in Ireland with thousands of people . . . I deserved this fate because I had turned away from God; we neither kept his commandments nor obeyed our pastors, who used to warn us about our salvation. The Lord there made me aware of my unbelief that I might turn away from my sins and turn wholeheartedly to the Lord my God. He watched over me before I got to know him and before I was able to distinguish good from evil.'*

Patrick says that after his capture he was sold to a farmer in the west of Ireland and made to look after his sheep in the hill pastures. He interrupts his story to outline his own profession of faith in God.

This shows he was well trained and versed in the doctrines of the Holy Trinity and of God's Grace. It is his frequent references to Grace which indicate clearly that he was not taught or made a priest in Britain. This is because by that time the British Church had adopted the heresy of the monk Pelagius. This denied that God's free-gift of grace was required before anyone could come to a true belief and so be saved. According to Pelagius, people could merit salvation by personal endeavour, pulling themselves up by their own boot-strings. This denied the sovereignty of God, which Patrick knew to be paramount, as his *Confessio* indicates.

The story will be told below of Patrick's escape from slavery and also the case for believing that he spent 20 years studying to be a priest in

St Patrick kidnapped by Irish pirates

Gaul. Before describing that we need to deal with the criticism that the quality of Patrick's Latin prose in his *Confessio* is so crude that he could not possibly have spent so many years in Gallic monasteries. On this question there are three things to be said in his defence. First, he admits frankly that *'anyone can see from my style of writing how little training in words I got'*. Secondly Patrick's quotations from the Bible in his description of the gospel he taught are verbatim from the pre-St Jerome version of the Vulgate, whose Latin style, as St Augustine of Hippo complained, was particularly crude. Thirdly, the critics are mostly scholars from Oxford, masters of Ciceronian prose, a style far superior to anything that Patrick could have learned from the provincial Latin 'patois' of the Gallic monks.

Patrick's story begins: *'When I came to Ireland I tended herds every day and I used to pray up to one hundred times a day and at night, even in times of snow, frost and rain. In my sleep one night I heard a voice saying to me: "It is well that you fast. Soon you will go to your own country . . . ". Again, I heard a voice saying: "Your ship is ready".'* Patrick then describes how after six years as a slave he escaped and made his way some 200 miles from Mayo to a port, which may have been Cork. He persuaded some sailors to take him on board their trading ship before they sailed from Ireland. If the date of his birth is accepted as having been between 385 and 390, then he would have left Ireland in about 408.

His journey was difficult: *'After three days at sea we came to land and for 28 days we made our way through deserted country. Our supplies ran out.'* However after some time marching through the land they found a herd of swine, as Patrick had prophesied to the sailors, and so were saved from starving. Some critics maintain that their landfall must have been in Britain. The suggestion by one critic that the travellers wandered in a circle in a fog in the west of Britain for 28 days can be rejected as absurd. They could not have marched for that time in Roman Britain without finding a human habitation! Nor would sailors used to navigation have been so stupid as to have marched in circles as has been suggested. It seems more likely that they landed either in Brittany or in Normandy, or further south near La Rochelle. At that time the northern route across Gaul from the Rhine to the Pyrenees had been devastated by the successive hordes of invading Vandals from across the Rhine in 407–9. Not a soul or a beast was left alive in any village from Laon westwards.

It is at this point in the Dublin copy of the *Confessio* in the *Book of Armagh* there is a complete break in the story. This shows that Patrick's account suddenly goes off at a tangent. He writes that: *'Again a few years later I was in Britain with my kinsfolk, who welcomed me'*. His account thus leaves a gap of about 18–20 years. Without mentioning those years, the copy of the *Confessio* goes on to describe a dream in which Patrick heard the *'Voice of the Irish'* calling him *'to come back and walk among us'*. A little later on the copy shows Patrick saying: *'I would dearly love to go also to Gaul in order to visit the brethren'*. He would not have said this unless he had spent some time in Gallic monasteries, as the biography by the monk Muirchu claims, but which the copy in Dublin omits, probably because that section of the confession was missing.

Because of this we must fill the gap in Patrick's life in Gaul by relying on the traditional accounts compiled by the two monks. Muirchu says

St Patrick's escape to Gaul and the Isle of Lerins

that on his arrival in Gaul, Patrick travelled to Rome before settling for some years in the hermitages founded in about 409 by St Honoratus on the Isle of Lerins, one mile out at sea from Cannes. He was then taken by St Gregory of Auxerre to his church just south of Paris, where he was ordained as a priest in about 418. From there, after serving ten years with St Gregory, Patrick returned to Britain. We do not know the date of this, but it may have been in the company of St Gregory who was sent to Britain by Pope Celestine I in 428 to convert the British clergy from their Pelagian heresy.

This would have only been the start of Patrick's campaign to take a mission to Ireland, which he succeeded in doing in 432. His request to do this as a bishop was turned down by the British clergy. Instead, a mission was sent to Ireland under St Palladius by Pope Celestine I in 431 on the advice of the historian Bishop St Prosper of Aquitaine. This failed within a year, leaving the field open to Patrick, who seems to have sailed to Ireland a year later on his own authority.

Patrick's estimated routes to and from Gaul are shown in the sketch maps opposite and on the following page. The first map shows Patrick's route in red and that of the Vandals in purple. The second map shows Patrick's estimated return route from Lerins via Auxerre to Britain and eventually to Ireland between 428 and 432.

There is one other interesting and possibly conclusive piece of evidence to support the case for Patrick having been taught at Lerins. As *The Times Atlas of History* shows, Lerins is the only monastic site in Europe to have been founded direct from the Desert Fathers in Egypt. This means that the Gallic saint Honoratus may have studied the monastic system there as well as in Cappadocia before settling at Lerins. This would account for the way Patrick's Irish Church and later Irish monasteries, unlike the Roman or Gallic ones, practised the severe asceticism of the Desert Fathers. This Egyptian influence may also explain why Patrick's Church used a different way of dating Easter to that of Rome until the eighth century.

Muirchu's account of Patrick's travels says that he was consecrated in 432 at Auxerre as missionary bishop for Ireland by St Gregory. But there is no evidence for this even in St Prosper of Aquitaine's record of this period. If Patrick had been made a bishop officially, he would have said so in his *Confessio*, but the only mention he makes of his being a bishop is in the letter to the British chief Coroticus. In this he says: '*I declare myself to be a bishop. I believe most firmly that what I am I received from God.*' This suggests that Patrick did leave Britain on his own authority, believing he had been called to go to Ireland by God as a missionary bishop and went there in spite of his rejection by the British Church.

In his *Confessio* Patrick says that he '*was not in Britain at the debate*' which the British Church held about request for his mission as a bishop to Ireland. He was on a visit to Gaul. He then explains that although God '*chose me to be his helper, I was slow to accept the promptings of the Spirit. The Lord showed kindness to me a million times because he saw that I was ready, even if I did not know what to do about my position because of the number of people who were blocking my mission. They used to discuss me amongst themselves behind my back: "Why does this fellow throw himself into danger among enemies who have no knowledge of God?"*'

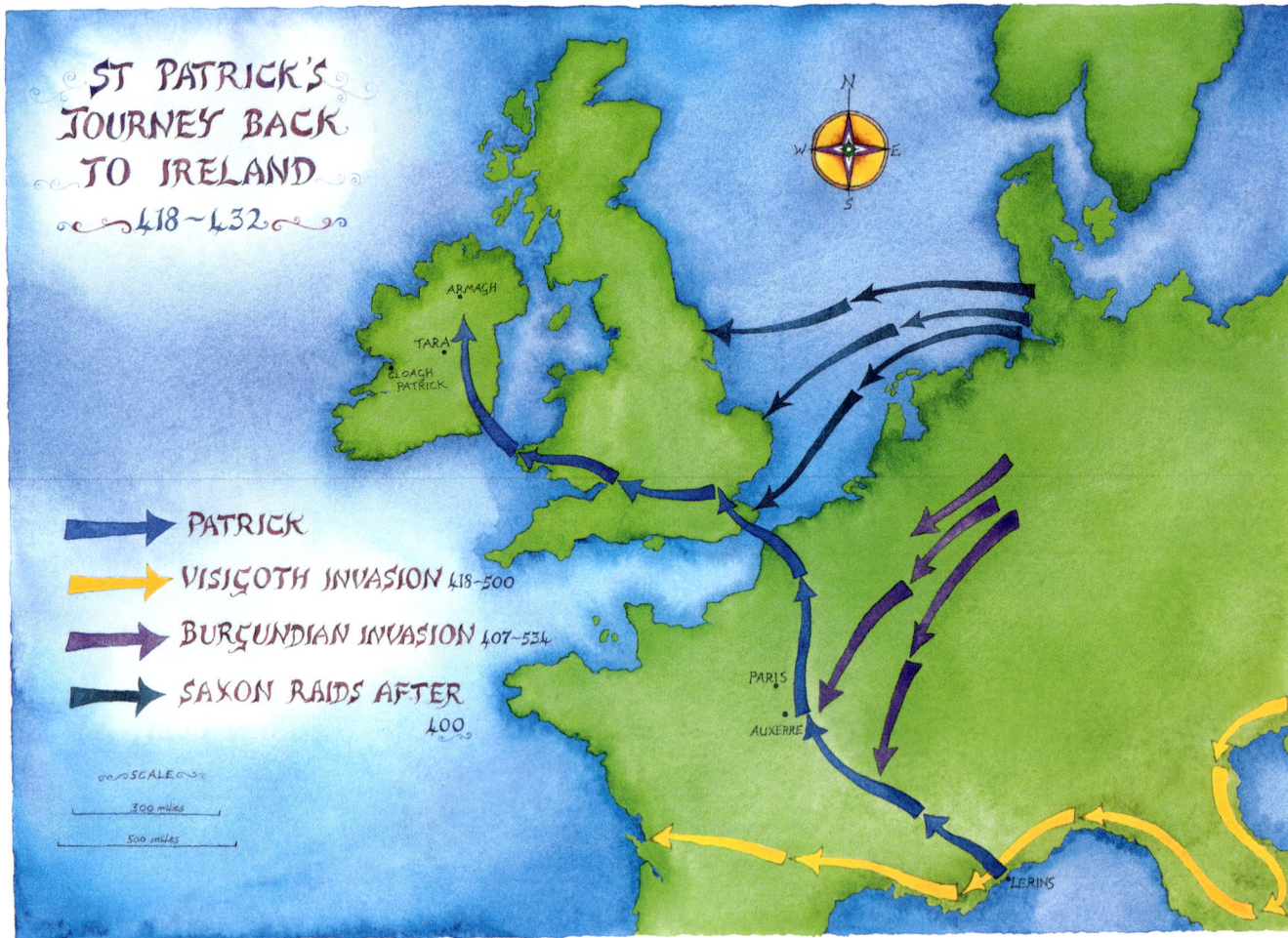

St Patrick's return journey to Ireland

Patrick considered that the British clergy's refusal to make him a bishop for Ireland was because he lacked education and also because of a youthful sin that he had confessed to a friend. He then expressed his regret for not having made his decision to go to Ireland earlier, confessing that *'I failed myself to realise in good time the grace that was in me. It is obvious to me now what I should have done earlier.'*

According to the traditional story Patrick first landed in Ireland in Wicklow at the mouth of the Liffey, but received a poor reception. He then sailed north and landed at Saul in Armagh. This was in the kingdom of a descendant of Neil of the Nine Towers in whose reign Patrick had originally been made a slave. Patrick told him about his plan to take the gospel to the Irish Christians he had known as a lad. They were probably, like him, captured slaves or descendants of captives, the ones he had heard calling for him in his dreams.

The king granted him land for his first church at Saul. From Saul Patrick is said by Muirchu to have gone to Connaught, where he had been a slave. Then in 433, as Easter approached, he went to the Druid circle of upright standing stones on the Hill of Tara, north of the river Boyne, to confront Loeghaire the High King of Ireland. The legend is then told of how the King and his druids were waiting in the stone circle for the sacred moment as the sun rose on the dawn of the Spring Equinox. The King had ordered that no lights were to be shown or fires lit. Patrick and his companions climbed the Hill of Slane within sight of Tara and lit a huge fire, perhaps by burning a hayrick. The King sent soldiers to extinguish the fire. They arrested Patrick and took him before the King, who demanded to know why he had broken the law. According to Muirchu's account the magical tests on Patrick by the Druids failed, and

so the High King gave him permission to preach his gospel in the Kingdom of Loehgaire. This story may be partly a myth devised to explain the extraordinary success of Patrick's mission and the speed with which he gained the King's permission to preach his gospel. However it does fit in with what little we know of the state of Ireland and the Druids at that time when the Druids were losing power, as the Irish no longer believed in their magic. Some such confrontation must have taken place between Patrick and Loeghaire and also many times elsewhere with other clan kings and princes. Otherwise Patrick's mission would have been stillborn as he could not have got the message accepted that he was preaching about an even truer light than the one for which the King and the Druids were waiting at dawn on the Spring equinox.

Patrick made Armagh his headquarters and delegated bishops to administer the churches. His first bishops were St Macarten of Armagh (6 March) and Mel of Clogher (6 February). The remarkable result of his mission was that within less than 30 years and despite assaults, beatings, robberies and being chained and imprisoned, he laid the firm foundations for his Celtic Church in the middle of Ireland, in the west in Mayo and in the north in Armagh.

We do not know for certain whether he chose the most famous Irish nun and foundress, St Brigid, whom Muirchu claims was St Macarten's niece, but Patrick's Church was very much a family affair. This gave it its strength, as he used his knowledge of the Irish tribal customs to select leaders for his schools for the men and women from the princely families and heads of the clans. The Irish population then has been estimated at 250,000, divided into a 100 clans, each with its king. Within less than 50 years of Patrick's death many monasteries were founded. They

St Patrick wins the support of the High King in Ireland

became famous for their scholarship, as the beautiful Celtic illuminations of the gospels in the *Book of Kells* in Dublin reveal. Patrick says that this success only came through God's grace: '*I thank God for enabling me to bring so many thousands to Him*'. He achieved this through the charismatic power of his own faith, which appealed to the spiritually hungry Irish. He also admitted humbly how at times it was only God's great love for him that had carried him through many difficulties. In acknowledging this he wrote in his *Confessio* that '*I was like a stone lying in deep mud and He that is mighty lifted me up*'. He also confessed to God his own original lack of attention to religion, saying '*it was the Lord who opened the senses of my unbelief*'.

Patrick had no help from outside in founding his Church. Ireland was cut off from Rome by the barbarian invasions, though by the end of his mission, or shortly afterwards, the Irish monks exchanged fruitful visits with the Welsh. Patrick tells us in his *Confessio* how the British clergy despised him. He really did found his Church alone.

Despite this, apart from the lives written by the two seventh-century Irish monks, Patrick is scarcely mentioned by historians until the Normans were encouraged to bring peace to Ireland in the twelfth century by the English Pope Adrian IV. The Venerable St Bede does not mention his name in his seventh-century *History of the English Church and People* because, as a supporter of the Council of Whitby's decision to replace the Celtic with the Roman Catholic rites, he ignored the Irish. Bede was only concerned with Britain, though he praised highly the Irish St Aidan of Lindisfarne, who came in 635 from St Columba's monastery on Iona to restore Christianity in Northumberland after the Saxon invasions had destroyed it. The only early mention of Patrick by

name is in a note in a record by St Adamnan (died 628, see 23 September). Adamnan was descended from St Columba's grandfather and he refers to '*Patricus nostra pater*'.

Patrick's legacy can be seen in the fruit that his work bore in the three centuries after his death. One only has to compare the religious vacuum that existed before he came to Ireland with the missionary zeal of the monks such as St Ciaran (9 September), whose foundations grew up from Patrick's tribal churches and later Celtic monasteries. Their missionary zeal in the sixth to eighth centuries took them to Brittany, Normandy, Burgundy, the Rhine, Switzerland and North Italy and even to Fulda in Bohemia, founding more than 100 monasteries, as the map on page 134 shows. They achieved this without once drawing a sword or making forcible baptisms, as the emperor Charlemagne was to do in Saxony. In his old age Patrick fasted for 40 days on the mountain that has been named after him – Croagh Patrick – which rises half a mile above the coast of Mayo and where he is said to have had many visions. This scene is illustrated below.

After his fasting Patrick returned to Saul, where he had first landed in 432. He died there on 17 March in 461 and it became his feast-day when at last in the seventeenth century this Celtic saint was included in the Roman Calendar of Saints. He is depicted here as a great missionary saint who drove out the reptiles, symbolic of paganism, from Ireland and as he holds the trefoil leaves of shamrock in his hands to indicate the Trinity. This myth, the story of the shamrock and the hymn 'St Patrick's Breastplate' date from two centuries after his death. Yet they demonstrate the simple style of Patrick's teaching in a land where sorcery and demons continued to be part of the popular culture for

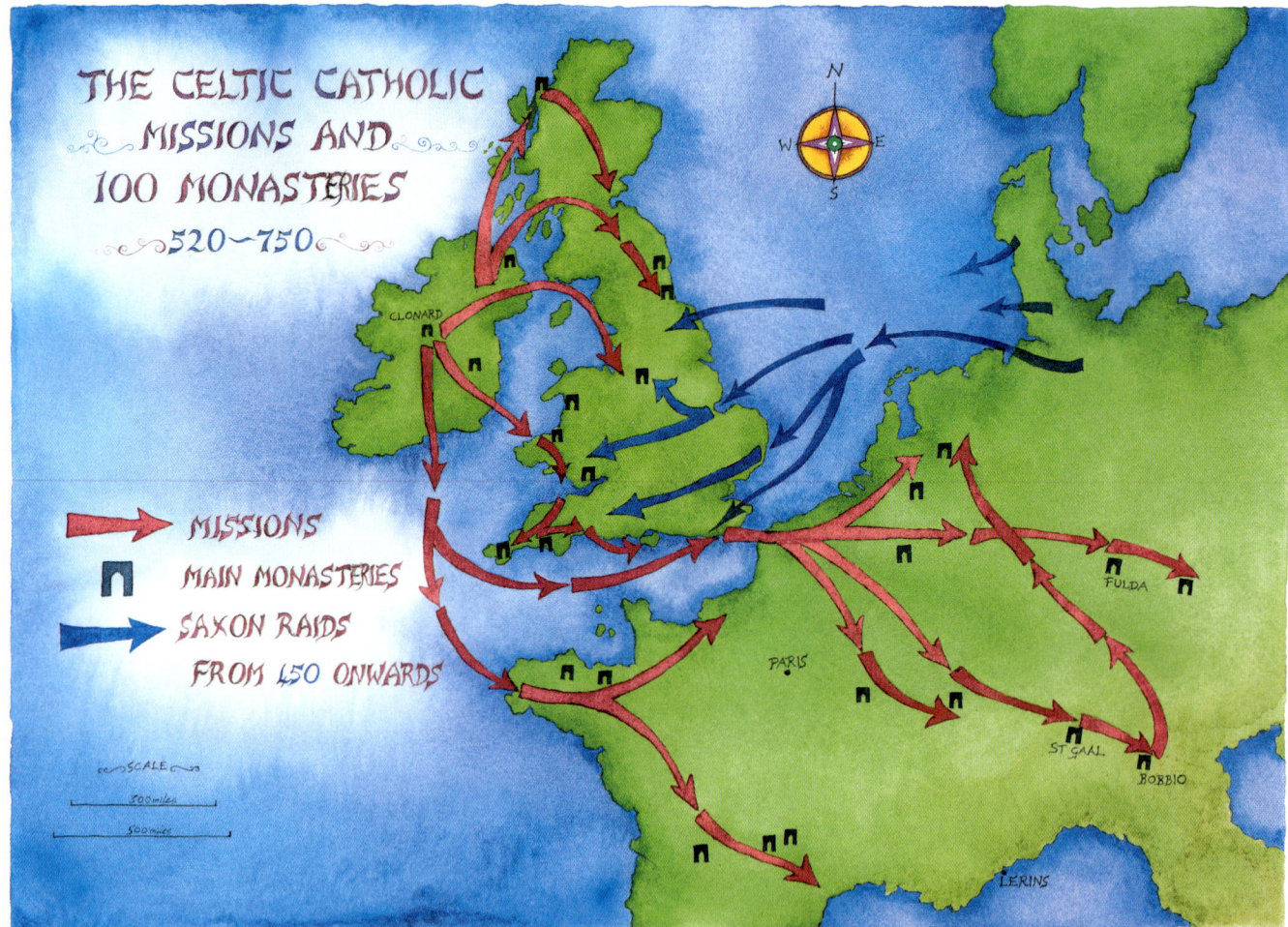

THE CELTIC CATHOLIC
MISSIONS AND
100 MONASTERIES
520~750

CLONARD

MISSIONS
MAIN MONASTERIES
SAXON RAIDS
FROM 450 ONWARDS

SCALE
300 miles
500 miles

PARIS

FULDA

ST GAAL
BOBBIO

LERINS

Irish and British mission routes and monasteries in Europe many centuries after him. Patrick's Church was absorbed into the Roman Catholic Church by the end of the eighth century. Its monasteries were almost obliterated by the Viking invasions of the ninth century, but his spirit lived on as firm as ever and they were rebuilt, only to be ruined again by Henry VIII, leaving beautiful ruins in the Shannon valley.

One can experience the atmosphere of the old Celtic Church by climbing Croagh Patrick and standing where Patrick stood over 1500 years ago. One can feel the wind in one's face and look out, as he must have done, over the many islands of Clew Bay where the sea duck nest and the skeins of wild geese swing out across the ocean according to the season on their annual migrations. Before the climb one can also pick fresh oysters, plump and sea-sweet from the rock pools along the shore beneath the hill at low tide, as Patrick may have done.

Almost certainly, if you go there, you will also hear groups of school-children being led by their nuns and chanting Patrick's hymn: '*I bind unto myself this day the strong name of the Trinity*'. You may also be fortunate enough to hear a priest repeating Patrick's prayer: '*May the strength of God guide me this day; and may his power preserve me. May the wisdom of God instruct me; the ear of God hear me; the word of God give sweetness to my speech; the hand of God defend me; and may I follow the way of God.*'

Pope St Gregory I (540–604)

In his picture in the decorative heading at the beginning of this chapter Gregory is shown with flaxen-haired Anglo-Saxon children. This recalls the words attributed to him when he saw them in the slave market in Rome and enquired where they came from. He was told they were Angles from Britain. '*Non Angliae sed Angelae!*' he said, meaning they looked like angels. It is believed that this is what made him decide to send a mission to Briton to convert the people to the Roman Church. In 596, seven years after the start of his papacy, he sent a party of monks to travel to Britain under the Benedictine monk and future Saint, Augustine of Canterbury. On the way Augustine asked permission to delay his journey because of the disturbed state of Gaul. Gregory ordered him to continue and he reached Kent in 597.

St Patrick driving out the reptiles and holding out the shamrock, symbolic of the Trinity, on Croagh Patrick

Gregory thus played an important part in the development of the Church in Britain, which had suffered greatly from the Saxon invasions after the Roman army had left in 410. Gregory's main importance however lay elsewhere. He revitalised the Church after the inroads of the Barbarian tribes in the fifth and sixth centuries. He also made the Church and Rome independent of the imperial court at Constantinople, even though this did not go unchallenged until the kidnapping and martyrdom of Pope St Martin I in 655 by a revengeful and heretical emperor (see the April Calendar).

Gregory's early career was in the law and he became the chief civilian magistrate in Rome before joining the Benedictine order at the age of 35 in 575. Four years later he was sent as papal agent to Constantinople. He spent six years there before returning to his monastery in Rome and where he became Chief Papal Secretary. In 590 he became the first monk to be elected pope, but was reluctant to fill the post as he preferred his monastic life.

In 592 the Lombards crossed the Alps into Italy and reached the gates of Rome. The Byzantine Emperor's legate fled and this left Gregory to face the enemy alone. He persuaded them to retire to the North by agreeing to pay them an annual tribute in gold. This marked the beginning of the end of Constantinople's rule over Rome. Gregory then secured the future and finances of the Church by his administrative reforms of the Church's lands around Rome.

Gregory's diplomatic experience helped him to improve relations with the Visigoth invaders and rulers of Spain through his friend Bishop St Leander (27 February). He also reproached the Merovingian rulers in Gaul, where the Church and its congregations were being oppressed. He implored Queen Brunehild to correct the vices of her court clergy. He then continued his policy of establishing Rome as the head of the Western Church by laying down rules in three councils of bishops that he summoned in the ten years to 601 to ensure Rome's control over the election and direction of the pastoral care of all bishops. He also circulated to them his homilies on the gospels and insisted on reforms in the monasteries whose discipline had become lax. There was no aspect of the Church's affairs which he left unattended.

As Gregory was so involved in administration, it is difficult to imagine how he was able to provide the much-needed spiritual guidance in those troubled times. However he did so, even in Ireland, which had been virtually cut off from contact with Rome since St Patrick's day by the barbarian inroads from across the Rhine. He wrote to the Irish bishops to warn them against the interference of the warring tribal kings, but he was also tolerant of the differences between the Celtic Church and Rome in many aspects of conduct and liturgy.

Among these differences was the Irish way of celebrating Easter on a different day from Rome, which they had inherited from St Patrick's day and the Egyptian Church's practice which he imported from his training in the Isle de Lerins. This was to be the subject of a friendly dispute between Gregory's successor and the Irish missionary abbot St Columbanus (21 November) in his monastery at Bobbio which he had founded in Northern Italy.

Gregory carried out an extensive correspondence with St Augustine in Britain. He instructed him not to destroy the pagan Saxon temples, but to turn them into churches. He also told him to organise the British Church into two archbishoprics, Canterbury and York, each with twelve suffragen bishops.

It was through his influence in Constantinople that his successor Pope Boniface III succeeded in persuading the Emperor Phocas to declare that *'The Apostolic see of St Peter, that is the Roman Church, is the head of all Churches'*. For all these reasons, Gregory's 14-year pontificate is regarded as second to none in the influence of Western Christianity. He is also famous for the changes he introduced in the music of the Church. He founded a school of singing in Rome and endowed it with farms. This school invented the 'Gregorian Chants', a development from the four scales introduced over 200 years before by St Ambrose (7 December).

Gregory wrote an exposition in Greek of the Book of Job in which he expounded its historic, allegoric and moral meaning. He also published 40 of his sermons including the famous one delivered during the plague in Rome in 690, when he was still reluctant to accept the papal throne. It was his vision of an angel standing on top of Hadrian's tomb by the Tiber, that he took as a sign that the great plague, which had attacked the population of Rome, was ended.

The final tribute to Gregory as a great pope is the way he regarded his own mission as Bishop of Rome and said *'I am the servant of the servants of God'* *(Servientor Servientium)*. This is still the title and motto given to every new pope. Gregory is counted as one of the Four Fathers of the Western Church, the other three being St Ambrose, St Augustine of Hippo and St Jerome.

APRIL SAINTS

April

1 St Hugh of Grenoble
2 St Mary the Egyptian
  St Francis of Paola
3 St Richard of Chichester
4 St Isadore of Seville
5 St Vincent Ferrer
7 St John Baptiste Dela
   Salle

11 St Gemma Galgani
12 St Zeno of Verona
13 St Martin I
16 St Bernadette of Lourdes
17 St Robert of Chaise Dieux
19 St Alphage
   St Leo IX
21 St Anselm

St Bernadette of Lourdes 1858

23 St George
24 St Euphrasia Pelletier
25 St Mark the Evangelist
27 St Zita
28 St Peter Chanel
29 St Catherine of Siena
30 St Erconwald (13th May) St Pius V

Soldier Martyr   St George

St Mark

The decorative heading for the April Calendar illustrates three saints who between them span nearly 20 centuries: **St Mark the Evangelist**, **St George** the fourth-century soldier martyr, and **St Bernadette of Lourdes**, the mid-nineteenth-century visionary who was canonised in 1933.

ALTAR-PIECE DESIGN FOR TEN APRIL SAINTS

Shown in the central scene is:

St Anselm (21 April), eleventh-century Italian abbot of Bec in Normandy, and Archbishop of Canterbury and theologian.

In the nine scenes from top left and round to the right are:

Zeno of Verona (12 April), fourth-century bishop standing before the magnificent tenth-century bronze doors of his abbey. Pope Martin I (13 April), maintaining the Catholic faith against the heretic Byzantine emperor's decree insisting on the Monothelite heresy (one will, the divine, for Christ). Martin was kidnapped, imprisoned and martyred for his opposition; Archbishop Alphege of Canterbury (19 April) being martyred by the Danes in 1012; Robert of La Chaise-Dieu (17 April), having a vision of the future abbey that would be raised over his hermitage in the Auvergne, the founder of a famous order to help pilgrims going to the shrine of St James at Compostella.

Bishop Hugh of Grenoble (1 April), riding towards one of the bridges he built to improve communications in his diocese; St Vincent Ferrer (5 April), helping to end the papal schism at Avignon; Catherine of Siena (29 April), telling Pope Gregory XI to leave Avignon and return to Rome in 1377.

Pope Pius V (30 April) sending letters to excommunicate Queen Elizabeth I of England; Gemma Galgani (11 April) nineteenth-century Italian domestic servant having one of her many visions. Canonised 1940.

Design for an altar-piece for ten April saints

APRIL CALENDAR OF SAINTS' FEAST-DAYS

1st HUGH of GRENOBLE (1053–1132): A pupil of St Bruno (6 October) He became Bishop of Grenoble, reformed a run-down diocese and built roads and bridges.

GILBERT of CAITHNESS: Died in 1245. Archdeacon of lawless Moray region of Scotland. Mastered rebel earls, built hospitals and a cathedral. Many pilgrims to his relics.

2nd FRANCIS of PAOLA (1416–1507): Founded Franciscan Minim Friars. Famed for miracles, he served Louis XI and Charles VII of France and negotiated peace with Spain.

3rd AGAPE, IRENE and CHIONIA: Martyrs burnt alive in Macedonia in 304.

RICHARD of CHICHESTER (1197–1253): He was Chancellor of Oxford University and then elected Bishop of Chichester. As an advocate of the Church's independence from the Crown, King Henry III refused to accept his election and seized the Cathedral's lands. Richard fled to France, but was later allowed to return. He was strict with clergy and attacked corruption, but was generous to the poor. Legend tells of the miracle of his accident with the communion chalice which fell but spilled no wine. Richard supported the cause of the Fifth Crusade. He is famed today for his prayer which includes the words: *'Lord may I daily love Thee more dearly and may I daily draw nearer to Thee'*.

4th ISIDORE of SEVILLE (560–636): Succeeded his brother Leander (27 February) as bishop. He continued his brother's conversion of Visigoths from Arianism. He was also a prolific writer on religious, historical and scientific subjects and famous for his *Encyclopaedic Etymologies*.

BENEDICT the BLACK (1526–89): Son of Nubian slaves in Sicily. Became a Franciscan and superior of the lay brethren. Patient and dignified in the face of public insults about his colour. Popular religious counsellor though illiterate. Canonised in 1807.

5th VINCENT FERRER (1345–1419): Born in Spain of an English father. Became a Dominican aged 17. A powerful itinerant preacher. Helped end Avignon papal schism.

6th WILLIAM of AEBELHOLT (1127–1203): Parisian canon who became Abbot of Aebelholt in Denmark, which he reformed. Had great religious influence on the Danes.

7th JEAN-BAPTISTE de la SALLE (1651–1719): Became a priest in 1678. Dedicated his ife to teaching poor children. Founded Brothers of Christian Schools at Rheims and for teachers in Paris. These De La Salle Brothers are now widespread in France and overseas.

9th MARY the EGYPTIAN: Fifth-century penitent prostitute, who became a hermit in the Palestine desert after seeing a vision in Jerusalem. Her gospel came by divine inspiration.

WAUDRU: Died in 688. Lay woman of Mons in Belgium who devoted her life to the care of the poor and sick. Her parents, husband and four children were all made local saints.

10th HEDDA of PETERBOROUGH: Died in 870. Abbot martyred with all his monks by the Danes of the 'Great Army' which had killed King St Edmund Martyr.

11th GUTHLAC (673–714): East Anglian hermit in the fenlands round Crowland, who lived like the Desert Fathers and had constant spiritual temptations. He cared for wild animals and birds, saying: *'Men should set an example of patience even to wild animals'*.

STANISLAUS of CRACOW (1030–79): A martyr revered in Poland after rebuking King Boleslav II for his disorderly private life and being murdered at the king's command.

GEMMA GALGANI (1878–1903): Laywoman who believed her spinal TB was cured after her prayers to St Gabriel Possenti (27 February). She had many remarkable spiritual experiences and also received well-attested marks of the stigmata. She was canonised in 1940 solely for her holiness of life.

12th SABAS the GOTH: Church leader in Rumania. Tied to a stake and drowned by pagan Gothic ruler in 372. Buried at Caesaraea as a martyr by St Basil (2 January).

ZENO: Died in 372. Great preaching bishop of Verona. His church there is well worth visiting to see its magnificent bronze doors and the paintings inside.

13th CARPUS, PAPYLUS and AGATHONICE: Martyred by being burnt alive under Marcus Aurelius. Carpus was Bishop of Pergamon. The others were his brother and sister.

POPE MARTIN I: Starved to death in Crimea by Emperor Constans II in 655, after being kidnapped from Rome for refusing the order to support the Monothelite heresy. He was supported by St Maximus the Confessor (13 August) in his defence of orthodoxy. The Church in Rome ignored the exiled and starving Martin and his urgent pleas for food, electing another pope in his place. He died a martyr to the true Catholic faith.

14th BENEZET of AVIGNON (c.1163–84): Shepherd-boy who had a vision in 1178 to build a bridge over the Rhone at Avignon. He got lay help for this project but died before the work was finished. He was buried in a chapel on the bridge. The chapel and half the bridge were swept away by floods in 1669. Benzet's body was recovered and found to be incorrupt. He was made a saint and patron of Avignon. The bridge is now being restored.

15th PATERNUS: Fifth-century bishop near Cardigan in Wales.

16th MAGNUS (1075–1116): Earl of Orkney. Captured by Norwegian invaders. He escaped and was treacherously murdered by his cousin Haakon. Venerated as a martyr and for his piety. Norwegian sagas about him depict Magnus as a hero against violent pagans.

BERNADETTE of LOURDES (1844–79): Famous for her visions of the Virgin Mary and the healings at Lourdes which attract millions of pilgrims yearly. See her story in the text after the Calendar.

17th DONAN and COMPANIONS: Donan was one of St Columba's (9 June) companions on Iona. He and his monks founded a monastery on the Hebridean Isle of Eigg. They were burnt to death in their church by pirates on Easter eve, 618.

ROBERT of LA CHAISE-DIEU (1001–67): A canon of St Julian's (28 August) church in Brioude in Auvergne, France. He founded a hermitage in the hills above the town and called it Casa Dei (now La Chaise-Dieu). See his story in the text after the Calendar.

STEPHEN HARDING: Died in 1134. Englishman schooled at Sherborne Abbey in Dorset. Helped St Robert of Molesme (29 April) found the important Abbey of Citeaux in Burgundy in 1098. He became the third Abbot of Citeaux and served there for 25 years dealing with the great problems of construction on swampy ground. He wrote two documents – *Exordium Cisterciencis* and *Carta Caritatis* ('The Map of Charity'). These became the models for the constitutions and spiritual purpose of all subsequent Cistercian houses. He founded 12 of these houses, but the greatest number – over 1,000 Cistercian houses – was the work of St Bernard (20 August) who, as a young man, Stephen appointed Abbot of Clairvaux. St Bernard succeeded Stephen as head of the Order.

18th APOLLONIUS: Died in 183. Roman senator tried by the Senate after being betrayed as a Christian by his slave. At his trial he advised the senators to reject man-made idols which had neither life, reason nor virtue. In comparison he showed how Jesus had revealed the word of God and taught a transforming morality and faith. Apollonius said *'The true life is the life of the soul'.* He also explained that because Jesus had redeemed the world from sin, there was no need to fear death. He thus gave the same message as had been given 18 years before by St Justin Martyr (1 June) at his trial before a governor. Apollonius was condemned to death.

19th CAEDWALLA: Died in 689. Saxon King of Wessex by conquest. Gave St Wilfrid (12 October) land on the Isle of Wight to found a church after he had been deposed as Archbishop of York by St Theodore, Archbishop of Canterbury. The king abdicated to go to Rome to be baptised by Pope Sergius. He died there still wearing his baptismal clothes.

ALPHEGE (953–1012): Archbishop of Canterbury when the Danes seized the city and took him prisoner. They demanded an enormous ransom for him and other important prisoners. He refused to pay for his own release, but had the ransom paid to release the others. The Danes were furious and pelted him to death with ox bones.

POPE LEO IX (1002–54): As a deacon he commanded the troops given by his bishop to put down rebellious Lombards. In 1048 Emperor Henry III chose him as pope. He travelled through Italy and France holding synods to reform abuses in the Church. In this he was a forerunner of the reforms under St Gregory VII (25 May), which were to free the papacy after 200 years from the control of the murderous Roman aristocracy. He worked closely with national kings and the emperors. This did not always work, as Pope St Gregory VII (25 May) was to find out after him. Pope Leo had to lead a papal army against Norman invaders. For this St Peter Damian (21 February) criticised him to his face, saying: *'Emperors but not popes should go to war, even for the Church!'*

20th AGNES of MONTEPULCIANO (1268–1317): As a nun and young abbess in Tuscany she had so many visions of Christ and Mary that the citizens of Montepulciano asked her to found a nunnery in their city. She agreed and chose the Dominican Order. The convent prospered under her mystical faith and ardour. St Catherine of Siena (29 April), herself a mystic who lived a generation later, admired her greatly.

21st ANSELM (1033–1109): Italian monk and theologian who became Abbot of Bec in Normandy. He spent the happiest and most fulfilling 34 years of his life there writing his three guides to the faith for his monks. He was then made Archbishop of Canterbury by the Norman King William II of England. See his story in the text after the Calendar.

22nd CONRAD of PARZHAM: Bavarian Capuchin and Franciscan lay-bother who died in 1894, canonised in 1934.

23rd GEORGE: Believed to be a soldier-martyr in Diocletian's persecution. The most popular Greek soldier, hero and saint. Only legends are known about him. St Jerome included him in his fourth-century martyrology. He was discovered for the West during the crusades and in the fourteenth century was made patron-saint of England and the Order of the Garter. See his story in the text after the Calendar.

ADALBERT of PRAGUE (956–97): Bishop opposed by a powerful nobility. He was encouraged by the Emperor Otto III to envangelise the Magyars whose invasions had devastated Central Europe. He had some success and inspired St Boniface of Querfort (19 June) to continue his work and so go to his martyrdom. Adalbert met his own martyrdom at the hands of the Prussians while preaching at Königsberg.

24th IVO (or YVES): Early sixth century, but no date. Believed to have been a bishop of St Ives in Cornwall, but he may never have existed.

MELITUS: Died in 624. One of St Augustine's missionaries to England. He was made Bishop of London and then (the third) Archbishop of Canterbury. Brought the message to Augustine from Pope Gregory I that he should destroy the Saxon idols but turn their temples into churches.

EUPHRASIA PELLETIER (1798–1886): Born in the Vendée in France. She became a nun at Tours and founded at Angers The Institute of the Good Shepherd to do rescue work for women in moral danger. She overcame much criticism patiently and with determination. Her Order now has over 100 convents in four continents. Canonised 1940.

25th MARK the EVANGELIST: First century. St Peter's secretary in Rome and author of the first gospel to be written, probably in about 63–64. See his life in Part II of this book.

26th ANACLETUS (or CLETUS): Third Bishop of Rome, martyred in the first century.

RIQUIER: Died in 645. Converted by Irish missionaries he saved from an Amiens mob. Became a priest in England and then founded an Abbey at Celles in Flanders. He was famous as a forthright preacher who reproved King Dagobert I for immorality.

STEPHEN of PERM (1346–96): Founded a monastery at Rostov. Missionary bishop who invented alphabet to proclaim the gospel in the Urals.

27th PASCHASIUS RADBERTUS: Died in 865. Abbot of Corbie in Picardy. In his work *The Lord's Blood* (831), he gave a theoretical explanation of why the bread and wine at the Eucharist appeared unchanged after becoming Christ's Body and Blood at the consecration. He called them *'visible accidents'*. In about 860, a monk of his monastery called Ratrumnus wrote in answer that the bread and wine are mystical symbols within which a power is seen only by faith. These two books started a debate which eventually led to the Roman Catholic Church confirming Paschasius' views and incorporated them in the Doctrine of Transubstantiation at the fourth Lateran Council in 1215. Protestant Reformers in the sixteenth century mostly followed the opinion of Radbertus.

ZITA (1118–78): Servant at Lucca, who took food for the poor in spite of her employer's objections. She had many supernatural experiences. Patron saint of servants.

28th VITALIS: Third-century martyr from Bologna. Famous basilica dedicated to him at Ravenna.

PETER CHANEL (1803–41): Marist missionary martyred by cannibals in Fiji.

29th HUGH of CLUNY (1024–1109): He became Abbot at 25 and made Cluny the most powerful force in the Church for reform for over a century. He advised six popes and gave counsel to St Anselm during his exile from England.

ROBERT of MOLESME (1027–1110): Cistercian abbot who founded Citeaux.

PETER the MARTYR (1205–52): Dominican friar killed while preaching against the Cathars.

CATHERINE of SIENA (1347–80): A mystic who dedicated her life to being a holy virgin from childhood. She was the last of her mother's 25 children. She became a Dominican tertiary and a powerful influence and guide to souls in Siena. She had visions which led her to go to Avignon to persuade Pope Gregory XI to take his papacy back to Rome. She is now joint patron saint of Italy together with St Francis of Assisi. Her house in Siena has been preserved and is illustrated after the Calendar in the text of her life.

30th MARIAN and JAMES: Martyred in Numidia in 259.

POPE PIUS V (1504–72): He is the archetypal Counter-Reformation hero to Roman Catholics. He was the severest Grand Inquisitor before becoming pope in 1566. His election was mainly due to the advice of St Charles Borromeo (4 November) that he would make the strong and determined pope needed to put the decisions of the Council of Trent on Church reforms into effect. He faced a situation in which 40 per cent of Europe had deserted Rome and Catholicism was in retreat. He therefore had little time for spiritual guidance and based his policy on enforcing obedience.

Pius oversaw the introduction of the Council of Trent's Catholic Missal and Breviary to replace the multitude of daily services for many saints. He swept Italy clean of all reformist cliques, rewarding the Medici Duke with the title of Grand Duke of Florence for betraying a number of leading intellectuals who were attracted by the ideas of the Reformers. His support of Mary Queen of Scots and her plot to kill Queen Elizabeth I of England led to a persecution of Catholics and their agents as traitors. Pius excommunicated Elizabeth in 1570. He is said by some Catholic writers to have followed a lenient policy towards Protestants. However the truth is, as his correspondence reveals, that he ordered Spain and the Emperor to *'kill more heretics'*. The Spanish governor of the Netherlands, the Duke of Alba, began a reign of terror against the Dutch Protestants. According to the Dutch historian Grotius over 100,000 civilians – women and children as well as men – were slaughtered in the Netherlands. The St Bartholemew's Day massacre of over 5,000 protestants in Paris and other French towns occurred three years after Pius' death, but it illustrates the ruthless attitude among Romans Catholics that Pius' Counter-Reformation caused.

Pius was a warrior-pope in spite of his personally austere life. He master-minded the raising of a great fleet under Don John of Austria which destroyed the Turkish invasion fleet in the Adriatic at Lepanto in 1571. His reign was edified by the saintly St Philip Neri (26 May), who gave help to poor uneducated men in Rome, to the sick and to pilgrims. Pius did what he felt he had to do against the reformers and to rally his Church, just as Sir Winston Churchill had to do against an implacable enemy in 1940–45. His portrait by Velasquez in the Palazzo Doria in Rome depicts his ascetic, cunning and ruthless face. To modern non-catholics he represents the spirit that led to the killings and religious warfare of the late sixteenth and the early half of the 17th centuries. Pius was not canonised until 1742, 140 years after his death.

SUMMARY OF APRIL SAINTS

The April Calendar lists the feast days of 53 saints, of whom 24 were martyrs and 11 were women.

The most important April Saint is St Mark. His life has already been described in Part III, 'The Apostles and Evangelists'. The lives of five other saints for this month who are also important are described in the following notes. They are **St George, St Anselm, St Robert of La Chaise-Dieu, St Catherine of Siena** and **St Bernadette of Lourdes.**

St George (died c.303)

There are no written records about St George, who may have been either a soldier-martyr, as the Greek tradition maintains, or else a most devout layman who died for the faith in about 303 during Diocletian's persecution. His name was unknown in the West until the accounts of the main legends about him were brought back by the returning crusaders after finding that more churches were dedicated to him in the East than to any other saint.

The earliest of these churches was dedicated to him in his alleged birth-place Lydda in Palestine as early as 50 years after his death. The earliest written record that we have of George was made by the scholarly St Jerome in his early fifth-century martyrology. He described him as *'a true soldier of Christ'*. The returning crusaders reported the many remarkable legends that were attached to his name. The best-known one is that he had saved a Christian princess in Syria from being sacrificed to a dragon. After he had killed the dragon, perhaps a symbol of evil, he refused the offer of a great reward and is said to have asked that the money should be given to the poor. Other tales were also told of him, some of which were painted in frescoes on church walls, especially in Sussex, in the twelfth century. Two of these near Pulborough and just north of Brighton depict him being crushed to death on a wheel. Another famous one is a Russian icon of him showing him being stood in a frozen pool and then tied to a red-hot brazen bull before being beheaded.

In the fourteenth century he was depicted with the emblem of a red cross on a white background. He was then adopted as the Patron Saint of England and also of the German state of Hesse. In 1348 the English King Edward III (1327–77) made him the patron of his Order of the Garter, restricted to the monarch and 25 Knight Companions. The motto of the Order is *Hon y soit qui mal y pense* ('shame on him who thinks ill of this'). King Edward dedicated to him the beautiful new chapel that he built at Windsor Castle.

Because of the lack of contemporary evidence about him the Roman Catholic Church removed St George from its list of Universal Saints in its 1969 calendar reforms. George was then demoted with 13 other saints including St Catherine of Alexandria and St Blaise as only 'auxiliary saints'. However St George is too precious a symbol of Christian charity and virtue to be demoted. He was therefore restored once more as a Universal Saint in 1999.

St Robert of La Chaise-Dieu (1001–67)

The story of Robert of La Chaise-Dieu takes us right into the heart of the Auvergne, where a very individual style of religious fervour developed from the tenth century onwards. This was linked to and developed with the massive pilgrim movement that arose in those days.

The abbey and town of La Chaise-Dieu, which St Robert founded, is in the high hills about 100 kilometres south-east of Clermont-Ferrand. The abbey is the most important foundation in the beautiful and rugged province of the Auvergne, whose forested volcanic hills and sheltered valleys were the traditional strongholds of the ancient Gauls in times of danger. Through the life of St Robert and the earlier saints of the Auvergne we can trace a continuous thread of the progress of

Christianity in France from its first beginnings in 250 and right up to the present day.

St Robert was born in the Chateau de Turlande to the south of St Flour in the Auvergne. He became a canon of the church of the third-century martyr St Julian in Brioude, in the plain below the 3,000-foot high plateau, where La Chaise-Dieu now stands. Julian was one of the converts of the Roman deacons St Nectaire and St Baudime who accompanied the seven missionary bishops, including St Denis, sent to evangelise Gaul in 250 by Pope St Fabian (20 January). The year 250 saw the start of the Empire–wide persecution of Christians. These two saints survived when their bishop was martyred by the Romans at Clermont and made their way to the ancient volcanic highlands of the Auvergne, where they evangelised the whole region.

In 1043 Robert left Brioude to become a hermit in the hills above the town. This *Casa Dei*, as he called it, soon attracted many other hermits. The hermitage was sited on the direct route over the mountains from the Rhone Valley on the pilgrim way to the shrine of St James of Compostella in Spain. It also led to the shrines of St Nectaire and St Beaudime. It was to save the shrine at Compostella from being overrun by the Muslims that the Emperor Charlemagne had sent three expeditions two centuries earlier. In the last of these there took place the famous rearguard action at Roncevaux where Roland and his force fought and died to a man to save the rest of the army.

The pilgrims needed to be housed and fed as they crossed the mountains on their way to the shrines. Therefore St Robert established lodgings and a hospital for them. Robert came from a family who were related to St Gerald of Aurillac (13 October), who had built an abbey at Aurillac in the southern Auvergne at the end of the ninth century and which was taken over by the Benedictine monks of Cluny. These Cluniacs were the chief promoters of the pilgrim ideal to help the faithful repent of their sins and to meditate, discuss and seek salvation. Cluny became a powerful supporter of Casa Dei. St Robert extended his work to provide shelter for the pilgrims on their way to the Pyrenees. His work impressed Pope Alexander III, the predecessor of Pope St Gregory VII (25 May), and he richly endowed Casa Dei. More gifts and more endowments after Robert's death enabled his Order, known like the people of the modern town as *Cassadiens*, to build ten more monasteries and to establish 395 small priories to lodge the pilgrims along their route as far as Burgos in Spain. Pilgrims following the route today can still stay in some of these places. St Robert was canonised in 1070, 26 years before the first Crusade was summoned.

The construction of the magnificent Abbey at La Chaise-Dieu was completed in the fourteenth century. Like most of the churches in the Auvergne along the pilgrim route it had a specially broad gallery to house the pilgrims above the nave. The Abbey's greatest treasure is the set of fifteenth-century Flemish tapestries depicting the entire *Bible des Pauvres*. This is divided into panels and covers 200 feet of the walls of the nave above the choir-stalls. The tapestries tell the story of how everything that happened in the New Testament was foretold in the Old Testament. The tapestries were designed to tell the bible-story to those who could not read. They were hidden during the Franco-German war of 1870 and again in 1940. They have since been beautifully restored.

Sketches of images of three Vierges en Majesté
in Auvergne

The abbey is now served by the modern Order of St Jean, but the care of the buildings, as for all French cathedrals and churches since the French state appropriated all Church property at the start of the twentieth century, is the responsibility of the State.

There are many fine churches in the region around Clermont-Ferrand and to the south. These nearly all have pilgrim galleries and columns with fine carvings of the stories of the saints to whom they are dedicated – St Nectaire and St Beaudime for example, whose shrines have long been the objects of pilgrimages. One other feature, unique to these Auvergne churches, is the collection of carved and painted wooden statues of the Virgin and child.

The wooden statues date from the tenth century and each one used to contain a jewel and a saint's relic. Their main feature is that the Virgin is seated on her throne as the 'Queen of Heaven', holding a very grown-up looking child Jesus with a book of the gospel in his hands. These statues are known as *Les Vierges en Majesté*. Sketches of three of the statues from the Auvergnat churches of Orcival, Vauclair and Massiac are shown above.

St Anselm (1033–1109)

Anselm was born to a noble Lombard family in Aosta and entered the Benedictine monastery of Bec in Normandy at the age of 30. His Prior there was Lanfranc, who preceded him after the Norman conquest of England as Archbishop of Canterbury. For the next 30 years Anselm lived the happiest years of his life. It was there that he wrote the theological and philosophical works that, characterised as they were by his use of rational argument, earned him the title of 'the father of Scholasticism'. This approach to theology influenced the Church until the time of St Thomas Aquinas in the thirteenth century.

Anselm followed the example of the Irish theologian John Scotus Erigena (810–77), who taught that belief has to come before reason. Anselm believed, however, that the power of human reason was so great that it could investigate even the divine mysteries. He was the greatest theologian after the fourth-century St Augustine of Hippo. Anselm spent most of his life contemplating the truths of the faith which gave him so much spiritual, moral and aesthetic pleasure.

His three greatest books, written for his monks, are the *Monlogion* (or *Meditation*), the *Proslogian* and *Cur Homo Deus?* ('*Why the Man-God?*'). His approach to theology is explained in his prayer '*I long to understand something of thy truth, which my heart believes and loves. I do not seek to understand so that I may believe, but I believe in order to understand.*' Another important example of Anselm's advice is that '*A person's spiritual journey lasts the whole way through life*'.

In the *Proslogion* Anselm outlined one of his other important contributions to theology – his proof for the existence of God: '*Even a fool has an idea of a Being greater than which no other can be conceived; therefore such a Being must really exist, for the very idea of such a Being implies its existence*'. This argument, known as the Ontological Proof, was later seen by Thomas Aquinas to be at fault because it was tautological and Thomas preferred to rely on his famous five proofs that were all based more or less on experience of God. However Anselm had already replied to this line of criticism by saying that '*If God only existed in the mind, it would be possible to think of something greater than he*'.

Anselm was compelled by King William II of England to leave Bec and become Archbishop of Canterbury in 1093. However almost immediately the relations between him and the king broke down over the archbishop's insistence that the monarch '*should honour the Church as the Bride of Christ*'. He wrote this in a letter to William's Queen Matilda as William demanded total submission of the Church to him, as all the Norman kings were to do after him. Serious disagreements between them over Church rights and lands followed. After two years of disputes with the king the other bishops deserted Anselm and he was forced to flee the country and seek support from Pope Urban II in Rome, whose election William had refused to accept, supporting the rival anti-pope, Clement III, instead.

Pope Urban had launched the First Crusade in 1096, in which England took no part. He took the opportunity of Anselm's exile in Rome to ask him in 1098 to attend the Council of Bari and to try and resolve the differences between the Roman Catholic and Greek Churches over the procession of the Holy Spirit – the *Filioque Clause*. This clause, added to the Creed in the ninth century in the West, said that the '*Holy Spirit proceeded FROM the Father AND the Son'.* The Greeks refused to adopt this *'and the Son'* and the disagreement over this had caused the two Churches to cease to be in communion with each other in 1054. This clause still divides the two Churches.

Anselm began his argument to defend the clause by starting from the common doctrine of the two Churches that the Three Persons of the Trinity were distinct from the one Godhead. However he failed to persuade the Greeks to accept the teaching that the Cappadocian Fathers had supported (see the January Calendar), namely that the Holy Spirit did indeed proceed from both the Father and the Son.

On the perennial problem of the existence of evil in a world created by a good God, Anselm followed St Augustine of Hippo's definition that *'evil is nothing but absence of Good, or Good wilfully and wrongly directed'.* He did not go quite as far as Augustine in saying that God allowed evil to exist in creation so that over time good might come out of it. Anselm applied this to the way that sinfulness and imperfections in the human mind led eventually to better understanding and moral progress. It was through this line of argument that Anselm also said that in human beings Original Sin is not in the seed, but is inevitable when the foetus reaches a point where the infant has a rational soul, since through God-given free will it can then choose between right and wrong.

In his book *Cur Homo Deus*, written in exile in Rome, Anselm was the first theologian to attempt to show how the reality of God's existence is bound up with the very nature of human understanding. He said that faith is nothing, unless it is made active by love. His main argument in the book concerned the necessity for a Being who was both God and man to make the full satisfaction on the cross for the sins of the world, which had offended God's honour. A simple pardon by God for all our sins was not possible. Anyway, how would it be proclaimed and accepted by the world?

Anselm's case for the way by which humankind was redeemed from sin and achieved salvation through Jesus on the cross, was that this required an unprecedented act of sacrifice. But a sacrifice to whom? Anselm believed in Satan or Satanic influences, but he said that Satan had no rights over mankind in this matter as others had claimed. Therefore the sacrifice was not made to Satan. Instead Anselm took a contemporary feudal approach, saying that the reason for the sacrifice was to restore God's honour, which had been lost by Adam's disobedience.

Anselm based this concept on the feudal justice system which decreed that a payment had to be made if a dishonour was to be redeemed. In this case the sin was so great that the only possible payment was one in which Jesus' human life was sacrificed for the sins of humanity. God could then demonstrate his love for humanity by raising Jesus to life again and thus vindicating him and his conquest over death on behalf of us all. In this way, according to Anselm, God's honour was restored. This is the least convincing of Anselm's ideas, but it was well suited to the popular understanding in his day, even though it did make Jesus a substitute victim for others. His argument does not compare with the case made for Jesus' sacrifice by St Gregory of Nazianzus in the fourth century, which was described in his sermon quoted earlier at the end of the January Calendar.

The substitution theory is not an argument that is acceptable to modern concepts of justice. Nor did it satisfy Peter Abelard (1079–1142), Anselm's younger contemporary. Abelard, who was later condemned by St Bernard of Clairvaux for his views, maintained with his followers that Jesus' prime purpose was to set an example of the way human life should be lived. Abelard taught that it was for Jesus' example of indescribable and unconditional love in dying voluntarily for our sins, that he was vindicated by God at the Resurrection, a much simpler point of view than either St Anselm's or St Bernard's. It is one that makes most sense to many today.

Anselm remained in Italy until King William 'Rufus' was killed while out hunting in 1100. William's son Henry I summoned Anselm back. The king resumed the same disagreements over Church properties and rights and the authority of the Crown. Anselm was again forced to flee for his life and stayed abroad from 1103–6. He then spent three final peaceful years in Canterbury, but failed to fulfil his plan to complete a book on the soul.

Anselm's greatest achievement was to set the whole Church thinking anew and to try and answer some of the mysteries of faith by a rational approach – his 'scholasticism'. His work and popularity were assisted by his sincerity and originality and his social ability to tell a good story. The novelty of his thought can be seen in this prayer, written nine centuries before any ideas about having women as priests:

'Jesus, as a mother you gather your people to you, you are gentle with us as a mother with her children. Often you weep over our sins and our pride. Tenderly you draw us from hatred and judgement. You comfort us in sorrow and bind up our wounds. In sickness you nurse us and with pure milk you feed us. Jesus, by your dying we are born to new life. By your anguish and labour we come forth in joy. Despair turns to hope through your sweet goodness. Through your gentleness we find comfort in fear. Your warmth gives life to the dead. Your touch makes sinners righteous. Lord Jesus in your mercy heal us. In your love and tenderness remake us. In your compassion bring peace and forgiveness. May your love prepare us for the beauty of heaven.'

St Catherine of Siena (1347–80)

Catherine was a spiritual phenomenon who lived in the most warlike and troubled times in Italy when the papacy had removed itself to Avignon in France. She was the youngest of the 23 children of her father, a rich dyer of Siena. She was beautiful and vivacious, but refused to contemplate marriage and lived her whole life in the fine family house next door to a Dominican church. From childhood she spent many hours each day in prayer and many spiritual experiences are recorded of her.

These included the description in her *Dialogo* or autobiography of her mystical marriage to Christ and of the pain of the stigmata which she received, though without visible lesions.

She became a Dominican 'Tertiary' and all her life she was guided by Dominican confessors. She had boundless energy and the conviction that God meant her to help reform and restore the Church and to inspire the absentee Pope Gregory XI in Avignon to return to Rome and end the civil wars that were ruining Italy. To this end she believed she was guided by the Virgin Mary, to whom she talked in several visions. The historian Philip Hughes described her as follows in the third volume of his *History of the Church* (1955): '*Catherine was a power. The radiance of her unearthly personality gathered an extraordinarily broad collection of followers, men and women, friars, tertiaries, poets, artists, nobles and plebeians, married and single, most of whom she had converted, all of whom she instructed, and all of whom were the one great means of the apostolate that was her life*'.

Catherine conducted an extensive correspondence with popes, kings, emperors and bishops. Her fine family house still stands in Siena as the sketch here shows; it contains an imaginary scene of the vivacious young Catherine receiving a group of her many visitors.

During Catherine's short life there was continual warfare between the Italian city-states and the papacy. The Visconti family in the North and Florence were the Pope's chief enemies. Catherine was horrified at the death and destruction and wrote in 1372 to her friend the papal legate in Bologna: '*Make Charity the foundation of all your acts . . . Peace! Peace! Peace! Dearest Father make the Holy Father consider the loss of souls more than cities; for God demands souls more than cities.*'

Catherine sent the Pope stern criticisms of the loose living, nepotism

Sketch of St Catherine's house in Siena, with an imaginary scene of her receiving young people seeking her advice

and simony at Avignon. She called the cardinals and bishops there '*wolves and sellers of divine race*'. She thus re-enacted St Brigid of Sweden's (23 July) challenge to the Pope a few years before: 'Be a man!' and she anticipated the words of the reformer Martin Luther 150 years later. She also wrote to the Pope: '*Alas that which Christ won upon the hard wood of the Cross is spent on harlots*'. When the war became worse in 1376 eighty more Italian cities including Florence deserted to the Visconti. Catherine travelled to Avignon and in an interview with the Pope she told him her knowledge of a secret that only he knew, but which God had revealed to her. She told him that in a prayer in 1370 he had promised to return to Rome if elected pope. Gregory was astounded at this, because he had told no one of his dream. Although he pointed out to Catherine the difficulties that he faced, especially with Florence, he did make plans to return to Rome. He landed there in 1377 and died within a year, having made no progress towards a peace.

On Gregory's death the Roman mob rose up and attacked the Cardinals gathered in the Vatican to elect a new pope. They demanded with threats of death that only an Italian pope was acceptable to them. It was the old story all over again, repeating what had driven the popes to take refuge in Avignon 70 years before. The Cardinals hastily elected the Italian Archbishop of Bari, who was not even a Cardinal. He chose the name of Urban VI and at once, from having been for 20 years a loyal supporter of the papal court at Avignon, underwent a complete personality change. He cursed and threatened all who came near him, swearing that he now had power to depose kings and emperors. The Cardinals realised their error. They declared the election had been made under threat and was invalid. In place of Urban they elected a Frenchman who took the title of Clement VII and established himself at Avignon. Urban condemned him as a heretic. Thus started over 40 years of schism with two Popes, one reigning in Avignon and the other in Rome.

Catherine believed her holy duty was to support Urban as God's elect. Just as the martyr St Thomas More was to do 150 years later, she refused to regard the personality and behaviour of the pope as a reason to withhold her loyalty, which was owed to the occupant of the seat of St Peter in Rome as Christ's Vicar. She wrote to Urban from Florence, where she had been sent as ambassador to pursue peace by Gregory XI: '*You have the greatest need of being founded in perfect Charity, with the peace of justice . . . letting the pearl of justice glow forth from you united with mercy*'.

She then wrote to all the cardinals who had elected Clement VII, saying: '*Even if he were so cruel a father as to hurt us with reproaches and with every torment from one end of the world to another, we are still bound not to forget nor persecute the truth*'. To the leader of the cardinals she wrote: '*Now they have contaminated the faith and denied the truth; they have raised a schism in the Holy Church that they are worthy of a thousand deaths*'.

Catherine's mission to Florence failed and so did her attempt to reunite the Church. She died of a stroke on 29 April 1380. That day was to become her feast-day after her canonisation in 1461, forty three years after the papacy had been united in Rome in the person of Martin V. By then the diplomatic power of the papacy had been almost fatally weakened. The popes did not begin to recover their full power and respect as world spiritual leaders until after the unification of Italy in 1870, and even then not fully until after World War II, when Rome was made safe under the Republic of Italy and the United Nations. Then a new and a more hopeful age may have begun for the Church of Rome and for all the other Churches. Catherine was named a Doctor of the Church in 1970 and is joint patron saint of Italy.

St Bernadette of Lourdes (1844–79)

By the end of 2000, sixty-eight physical cures had been proved and accepted by the strict and extensive tests of official French Government officials at the site at Lourdes, where the peasant girl Bernadette Soubirous had had a series of 18 visions of the Virgin Mary in 1858.

To these miracles must be added the countless spiritual healings at Lourdes, one example of which is described below. It may be suggested that from the point of view of faith and life eternal these spiritual healings are even more important than the physical cures. In the last analysis, all those who are cured physically have eventually to die, but the records at Lourdes do not give any account of their deaths.

Bernadette was the daughter of an unemployed miller. She was small, backward and slow to learn anything at school. Her teachers said that in her religious classes she had never learned about the doctrine of the

Immaculate Conception which had only recently been decreed by Pope Pius IX. One day at the age of 14 she was sent with her younger sisters to collect driftwood along the river Gave at Lourdes. In a cave by the river she had the first of her visions of the Virgin, who introduced herself to her, rather strangely, by her Catholic title, saying: *'I am the Immaculate Conception'*. Bernadette reported her experience and the words that she alone had heard, but she was disbelieved. She visited the cave 17 more times. She was sometimes accompanied by others who saw nothing except Bernadette talking.

Bernadette reported several conversations; in one of these the Virgin told her that a great basilica would be raised at Lourdes. On one occasion 'her Lady' gave Bernadette a rose and on a another she told her that if she scrabbled with her hands in the floor of the cave, she would find a spring of water. Bernadette did so. This previously unknown spring appeared and has flowed amply ever since to provide cups of its water to the queues of pilgrims.

Friends of Bernadette's family visited the site and were convinced that Bernadette had taken part in a miracle. In spite of long and agonising questioning by her school teacher and the clergy, Bernadette held to her story of the events she had witnessed and answered that she had never before heard of the Immaculate Conception. The people of Lourdes were convinced of the miracle and flocked to the Gave to taste the water in the hope of being cured of various ailments. One woman claimed that she had been cured of a painful limp and soon even the pharmacy in Lourdes was selling bottles of the water from this 'holy' stream.

The Church authorities objected. The cave was closed with wooden boards and guards were placed to keep the crowds away. The water from the stream was tested by experts. They found it contained no special minerals. Was the whole thing invented by the strange imagination of this backward child? There had been several other such visionary claims in her area, but Bernadette still kept to her story, claiming no special virtue except that 'her Lady' had spoken to her.

Then the Empress Eugènie sent from Paris for a bottle of the well water to give her son, the Prince Imperial, who was suffering from a fever. The boy was cured and immediately the crowds broke into the cave once more. In 1858 the story of the healings and the mass pilgrimages to Lourdes began.

In 1866 the Church authorities decided to send the devout Bernadette to be admitted as a nun to the convent of the Sisters of Charity at Nevers. The Convent superiors were unconvinced about her visions, but she submitted to their strict regime. Then, always in weak health, she became increasingly a victim of asthma. She never claimed any special virtue for her visions, but never wavered from her conviction of their reality, accepting her increasing infirmity as her lot. The Basilica which the Virgin had foretold was built at Lourdes, but Bernadette did not attend the ceremony of its dedication. She died of her illness in 1879.

Millions of pilgrims journeyed each year to Lourdes and in 1934 I saw hundreds of crutches and plaster casts of hearts nailed above the cave by the faithful, grateful for the healings they believed they had received from drinking cups of water from the well that Bernadette had discovered. Broad asphalt paths were laid to the cave along the Gave riverside and a huge trade had begun in images and other mementoes in stalls along its sides. The crutches and other thank-offerings have now been cleared away, but the trade in postcards and plastic and plaster objects continues and over three million pilgrims go to Lourdes each year.

The story of a recent (1993) spiritual healing after a pilgrimage to Lourdes was told me by my friend Mrs Molly Millard-Barnes, an intrepid ocean-racing yachtswoman, who is also a part-time Franciscan Tertiary. In this capacity she volunteers to escort sick people to Lourdes. On one occasion she accompanied a very difficult, ungracious and ungrateful patient, who was always complaining. He was suffering from a fatal muscular disease. She managed to get him safely by train to Lourdes and got him the requisite blessing and glass of holy water at St Bernadette's spring. On the journey home the train was halted in a siding for many hours, due to some trouble further up the line.

There was no restaurant car and the patients all became very thirsty. The condition of the sick man in my friend's charge became serious. So she went along the line to the engine and managed to find water to make him some tea. By the time she got back to her patient, the tea was only tepid. She began to apologise to him, expecting the usual acid comment and complaint. Instead he beamed at her and said: *'I just don't know how to thank you and all the others who help us. You are quite wonderful'.* On hearing this and seeing him smile for the first time during the whole trip, she almost dropped the tea.

The man appeared to have undergone a complete change of character. A year later Mrs Millard-Barnes visited her patient in hospital and was told by the staff that he had become the most perfect patient – happy, considerate and patient. He had been cured spiritually. The devil inside him had indeed been banished.

Bernadette was not canonised in 1933 for the miracle of her visions or for the cures attributed to the spring that she discovered, but for the way she responded to her experiences, for her humble simplicity and her trusting faith.

MAY SAINTS

May

1. St Philip, St James
   St Peregrinus Laziosi
2. St Athanasius
3. The Invention of the Cross
   Our Lady of Luzon
4. St Gothard, St Florian
5. St Hilary of Arles
8. St Peter of Tarantaise, St Acacius
   10. St Isidore

11. St Asaph
    St Pancras
14. St Matthias
16. St John Nepomonk
19. St Dunstan, St Celestine IV
20. St Bernadine of Sienna
23. St Ivo of Chartres
    St William
    of Rochester

St Joan of Arc at Orleans 1429

24. St David of Scotland
25. St Gregory VII, The Three Marys
26. St Augustine of Canterbury
27. The Venerable Bede
28. St Germanus of Paris
    St Bernard of Montjeux
29. St Bona of Pisa
30. St Ferdinand III, St Joan of Arc

Driven from Rome by Emperor Henry IV & the Normans

St Gregory VII

St Dunstan crowns King Edgar at Bath 976

St Dunstan (19 May), tenth-century Saxon Archbishop of Canterbury is shown (right) crowning King Edmund I with the traditional square Saxon crown; Pope St Gregory VII (25 May), eleventh-century heroic pope, is being driven from Rome after calling in the Normans under Guiscard to help him in his struggle against the German Emperor, Henry IV. In the centre is St Joan of Arc (30 May), a visionary who led the French to victory against the English; she was martyred in 1431. St Joan is co-patron saint of France with St Denis.

ALTAR-PIECE DESIGN FOR TWELVE MAY SAINTS

Shown in the central scene is:

St Athanasius (2 May), the fourth-century theologian and Archbishop of Alexandria. He is holding the creed that was attributed to him.

In the scenes from top left and round to the right are:

St Germanus of Paris (28 May), protecting his flock against the attack of his Frankish king; St Pancras (12 May), martyred in 304 during Diocletian's persecution, his tomb is by the Via Aurelia north-east of Rome. King Ferdinand III of Spain (30 May) about to attack a Moorish city in southern Spain c.1240; King Eric of Sweden and King David of Scotland (18 and 24 May), who lived in the eleventh and twelfth centuries. Isidore the Farm-servant (10 May), eleventh-century devout farm-worker and patron-saint of Madrid; St Gothard (4 May), tenth-century abbot and bishop who founded the travellers' hospice on the St Gothard Pass in Switzerland; St Bona of Pisa (29 May), twelfth-century pilgrim captured by Saracens, ransomed and became the first guide for pilgrims on the route to the shrine of St James of Compostella; Bernard of Montjeux (28 May) searching for travellers lost in the snow; The Venerable Bede (25 May), eighth-century monk of Northumbria writing his *History of the English Church and People*; St Augustine of Canterbury (27 May), who was sent by Pope Gregory the Great to Britain to establish the Roman Catholic Church in 597.

Design for an altar-piece for twelve May saints

159

MAY CALENDAR OF SAINTS' FEAST-DAYS

1st **BRIEUC**: Sixth-century Welsh missionary to Brittany, who founded a monastery near Treguier. He was one of scores of Welsh, Cornish and Irish missionaries to Gaul. The Breton port of St Brieuc is named after him.

ASAPH: Early seventh-century bishop of North Wales.

ULTAN: Brother of the mid-seventh-century Irish missionaries to Gaul St Fursey (16 January) and St Foilan (31 October). He became abbot of Les Fosses.

2nd **ATHANASIUS** (296–373): As a young deacon he was the chief orthodox theologian at the Council of Nicea in 325, when the Arian heretics who denied the divinity of Christ were defeated and the doctrine of the Holy Trinity was formalised. He became Archbishop of Alexandria in 328. He spent a lifetime defending the orthodox faith against Arianism and was five times exiled by heretic emperors. His life is described after this Calendar.

3rd **PHILIP** and **JAMES THE LESS**: Apostles, whose lives are described in Part III of this book. Philip is believed to have preached and been martyred in Phrygia. James the Less was a 'brother' or a member of Jesus' extended family who led the Church of Jerusalem. He was thrown from the temple roof and killed by the Sanhedrin in 62.

THEODOSIUS of KIEV (1002–74): Much revered 'staretz' or Russian spiritual father, who was an abbot who founded a band of monks in a cave to which pilgrims still go.

4th **GOTHARD** (960–1038): Abbot in Bavaria who was made Bishop of Hildesheim in 1022. His foundations included hospices for the poor at St Moritz. The alpine pass of St Gothard is named after him.

5th **HILARY of ARLES** (400–449): Monk of the Isle of Lerins who was made Bishop of Arles in succession to his cousin St Honorius (16 January). Arles was an important centre for the Church in Roman Gaul. Hilary held the Gallic Church together during the barbarian invasions, but his zeal and independence offended Pope Gregory the Great.

6th **MARIAN** and **JAMES**: Martyred in Constantine (Numidia) in 259.

EDBERT: Bishop of Lindisfarne in Northumbria from 688 to 698. Very learned and charitable according to the historian the Venerable St Bede (25 May). Buried in St Cuthbert's tomb.

7th **JOHN of BEVERLEY**: Died in 721. Bishop of York. Took special care of the poor and handicapped according to Bede and Alcuin, the Yorkshire scholar at Charlemagne's court.

8th **PETER of TARANTAISE** (1102–74): Cistercian abbot who was made bishop of the Alpine see of Tarantaise by Count Amadeus I of Savoy. He built a hostelry for travellers at the St Bernard pass – see St Bernard of Montjoux (25 May) – which gave them free soup and bread. Sent by Emperor Alexander III to make peace between the English King Henry II and Louis VII of France. Much admired for his sanctity.

On this day the Anglican Church remembers **Dame Julian of Norwich** *(1342–1416). She has attracted a popular cult as a mystic and visionary; admirers include both Roman Catholics and Protestants. See the text after the Calendar for information about her life and works and for a summary both of her famous book* Revelations of Divine Love *and of the writings of other fourteenth-century English mystics.*

9th **ANTONINO PIEROZZO** (1390–1459): A Dominican who was made Prior of St Marco in his home town of Florence in 1420. In 1446 he became Archbishop of Florence, having at first refused through humility to receive such a high office. He removed most of the court and servants of his magnificent palace and fed the poor copiously from his kitchens. He remained in Florence during the plague of 1448–9 after the leading citizens had fled. He roamed the streets on a donkey laden with food and the Host for the sick.

10th **ISIDORE the FARM-SERVANT** (1070–1130): Devout farm-worker near Madrid, famed for his holiness and miracles of healing. Patron saint of Madrid. His feast is celebrated in the USA on 25 October.

ANTONINO of FLORENCE (1389–1459): Vicar-general of the Dominicans. Founded the famous convent of San Marco in Florence, decorated by St Fra Angelico's masterly frescoes. He was the first to teach that money in commerce or industry was capital and not usury. This helped the rising Medici. He was generous and lived simply.

11th **COMGALL** (517–603): Irish soldier who became Abbot of Bangor. He accompanied St Columba (or 'Comcille'; 18 February) of Iona to evangelise the Picts of Scotland.

ASAPH: Sixth-century bishop and founder of the Welsh Church in Flintshire.

MAIEUL (906–94): Abbot of Cluny in Burgundy in 965. Made his monastery a powerful influence in the Church at a time when Rome was in anarchy.

FRANCIS di GIROLAMO (1642–1716): Jesuit priest in Naples. He worked for the poor, galley-slaves, sinners and children in danger. Many alleged miracles.

12th PANCRAS of ROME: Martyred c.304 and buried beside the Via Aurelia. Nothing is known of him, but oaths taken at his tomb were believed to have special sacredness.

NEREUS and ACHILLES: Soldiers who refused to fight after their conversion. Martyred. No known date. They were said to have been attendants on Flavia Domitilla, cousin of the Emperor Domitian, whom he exiled and then had burnt as a Christian.

EPIPHANIUS of SALAMIS (c.315–403): Learned monk elected Bishop of Salamis in Cyprus. A strong defender of orthodoxy in the Arian squabbles of the Greek Church. His book *The Medicine Box* describes over 70 Christian heresies that existed before and during his lifetime. He died in his ship on the way back to Cyprus from Constantinople after discovering that the Empress Eudoxia and Archbishop Theophilus of Alexandria (St Cyril's uncle) had rigged the trial of St John Chrysostom, whom he found innocent.

GERMANUS of CONSTANTINOPLE (634–733): Patriarch who refused to obey the Emperor Leo III's edicts against images and icons. He said that *'Whenever we reverence images and paintings of Jesus, we worship not painted wood, but the invisible God'.*

13th ERCONWALD: Died in 693. Bishop of the East Saxons who reconciled St Wilfrid (12 October) with the Archbishop of Canterbury, St Theodore (19 September).

ANDREW FOURNET (1752–1834): A priest who refused to take the oath of the civil constitution during the French Revolution. He was arrested for continuing his ministry, but escaped by hiding in a coffin. With St Elizabeth Bichier des Anges (28 August) he founded The Daughters of the Cross. This grew to 60 teaching convents in the post-revolutionary revival of the Church in France.

14th MATTHIAS: The Apostle elected at Pentecost in place of Judas Iscariat (Acts 1.26). Nothing else is known of him for certain, but tradition names him as a martyr.

PACHOMIUS (c.290–346): An ex-soldier who joined St Antony's (17 January) Desert Fathers. He was the first to organise these hermits in monasteries under strict rules of common life and worship. He founded 11 monasteries and two nunneries in Egypt. It was at Nag Hammadi near the monastery of St Pachomius that in 1947 a collection of 50

heretical and gnostic gospels was discovered in a buried earthenware jar. They are believed to be part of a library hidden by the monks from St Athanasius' police, whom he sent out in 367 to destroy heretical documents. They included the gnostic *Gospel of St Thomas*. This declares that Jesus did not die on the Cross, which only had his image. This is the claim that Muhammad quotes in the Koran, where he also denies Jesus' Resurrection.

CARTHAGE: Died in 637. Irish abbot of Lismore, who founded a monastic school.

MARY MAZARELLO: Died in 1881, canonised in 1951. She was helped by St John Bosco (31 January) to found The Daughters of Mary to help Christians fulfil social and spiritual needs such as the training of girls for suitable trades.

15th DYMPNA: Legendary Irish woman killed by her father at Gheel near Antwerp for being converted to Christianity. Her cult, founded in the thirteenth century, many centuries after her alleged death, is still celebrated at Gheel where she is patroness of the insane.

16th HALVARD: Killed in 1043 in Norway while trying to rescue a girl accused falsely of theft. He is patron saint of Oslo – a martyr who died in defence of innocence.

BRENDAN the VOYAGER (c.486–578): Brought up as a monk by St Ita (15 January) in Kerry, Ireland. Founded the monastery of Clonfert in Galway. A tenth-century legend of Brendan's Voyage tells how he sailed with his monks to 'The Land of Promise' in the Atlantic, which was probably the Canary Islands. He is said also to have evangelised in West Britain and Brittany like so many other Irish, Welsh and Cornish monks at that time.

HONORIUS of AMIENS: Sixth-century bishop after whom the Rue St Honore in Paris and also in Versailles are named.

SIMON STOCK: Died in 1265. English prior of the Carmelite Order, which had been founded on Mt Carmel in the twelfth century by St Berthold (29 March) and St Brocard (2 September). Stock consolidated the Order's teaching position in the universities of Paris, Bologna, Oxford and Cambridge. His vision of the Virgin Mary led to the *Scapular Devotion*, popular amongst Roman Catholics.

JOHN of NEPOMUNK (1345–93): Vicar-General of Prague murdered by Wenceslas IV of Bohemia for frustrating his plans to interfere with Church appointments. Wenceslas had him half burned and then chained in a sack and thrown into the river. The legend that he was executed for refusing to reveal a confession of Wenceslas' queen is false. See the July Calendar for an illustration of his martyrdom.

17th PASCHAL BAYLON: Died in 1592: A lay Franciscan brother of exceptional holiness.

18th POPE JOHN I (c.446–526): In the last year of his life, aged 80, he was compelled by Theodoric the Ostrogoth, the barbarian and Arian heretic King of Italy, to go to Constantinople and persuade the Emperor Justin to cease persecuting the Arians and to return their churches. John only succeeded in ending the persecution. On his return to Ravenna, Theodoric fell into a great rage with him for not recovering the Arian churches and accused him of treason. Pope John was so shocked that he died shortly afterwards. The faithful treated him as a martyr. Many miracles were alleged at his tomb.

ERIC of SWEDEN: Died in 1160. King of Sweden who was killed in battle at Upsala by a Danish prince leading rebel troops. He was venerated as a martyr in the Nordic tradition that those who die in battle go to Valhalla.

19th DUNSTAN (909–88): The greatest Saxon Archbishop of Canterbury. He was a relation of King Alfred the Great who captured London from the Danes in 903. Jealous factions and intrigues drove him from the royal court in 933 and he decided after a severe illness to become a monk. In 943 the new King Edmund I made him Abbot of Glastonbury and commissioned him to restore the monasteries and churches which had been ruined by the Danes.

Helped by two of his friends, St Ethelwold of Winchester (1 August) and St Oswald of Worcester (28 February), Dunstan restored the monasteries as the backbone of the national Church. King Edmund was succeeded in 946 by King Edred and Dunstan became his Chancellor. He improved the country's civil administration radically until he was forced into exile at Ghent in Flanders during the brief reign of King Edwy (955–7),where he studied the Benedictine system that he was later to adopt in England. A revolt replaced Edwy by King Edgar in 957 and in 960 he made Dunstan Archbishop of Canterbury and handed over to him the whole administration of the kingdom.

The illustration in the heading for the month shows Dunstan crowning King Edgar. Part of the ceremony that he devised is still used for British Kings and Queens. Dunstan's policy was to establish the royal authority, uproot heathenism, reform the clergy and educate the laity.

Dunstan's lasting achievement was to bind all these elements together through his creation of a national code of conduct in the Benedictine style for all monasteries and nunneries which then, through their farms and workshops and schools, became integrated with the local life of the people. This system flourished until it began to decline in the fifteenth century and was finally destroyed by King Henry VIII from 1534 to 1538, when he appropriated the lands of all monasteries.

The great tragedy of Dunstan's life was the murder of King Edgar's son, St Edmund Martyr (18 March) by his half-brother Ethelred and his step-mother, the leaders at court of the anti-monastic party. Ethelred became king and forced Dunstan out of the royal court and into retirement at Canterbury. There he impressed everyone by his devoutness and the way, when at prayer, he *'seemed to be talking to the Lord face to face'* like Moses in the *'tent of meeting'* (Exodus 33.11). It was said of his 42 years as Archbishop of Canterbury that they were the golden age of the British Church.

CELESTINE V (1214–96): An 80-year-old hermit elected as a stop-gap pope in 1294, after the cardinals had failed to agree for two years on a successor to Nicholas IV. He was too simple to cope with the complexities of politics in Rome. He also encouraged the followers of the late Abbot Joachim da Fiore and his prophesies that the world was approaching a new age, the 'Age of the Spirit', following the 'Ages of God the Father and that of the Son'. He was compelled to resign his office by the cardinals, who elected the imperious Boniface VIII in his place. Dante placed Boniface among the worst sinners in his Hades in his *Divine Comedy*. Boniface imprisoned Celestine, who died five months later. He was made a saint in 1980 by the late Pope John-Paul II.

20th BERNADINO of SIENA (1380–1444): A Franciscan friar and brilliant popular preacher who roamed Italy wearing the badge *IHS* to denote his devotion to Jesus. He moved the crowds both to tears and to laughter by his sermons in which he denounced the party strife that was the great evil of the day in Italy. His preaching was said to have produced one of those periods when the rule of Jesus made visible progress in society.

21st GODRIC the HERMIT (1069–1170): An English trader and ship's captain before becoming a hermit after pilgrimages to Rome, Jerusalem and Santiago de Compostella. He walked barefoot across Europe to Palestine and helped rescue King Baldwin I of Jerusalem after a battle. For a while he lived with hermits in the desert beyond Jordan and then returned to

Durham to live in a hut in the forest and grow his own food, as his hero St Cuthbert had done. He gained a reputation for holiness, clairvoyance and prophesy, which attracted many distinguished visitors including St Ailred of Riveaux (12 January). He took rabbits, field mice and even a stag into his hut in freezing weather and wrote lyrical poetry. He also inflicted severe penances on himself to repent for what he considered to have been a disorderly early life.

RITA of CASCIA (1381–87): She was the widow of a cruel husband whom she had suffered patiently. She retired to became a nun at Cascia in Umbria. So many supernatural events occurred to her that a popular cult arose. She was canonised in 1900.

ANDREW BOBOLA: A Polish Jesuit priest who was martyred barbarously in 1657 near Pinsk by Cossacks for encouraging the union of the Orthodox and Roman Catholic Churches. Bishop St Josaphat of Polotsk (12 November) suffered martyrdom for the same reason.

23rd DESIDERIUS: Died in 607. Bishop of Vienne in France who was murdered after rebuking King Thierry II of Burgundy for his dissolute life. He is venerated as a martyr.

IVO of CHARTRES (1014–1116): A Benedictine monk of Bec in Normandy who became Bishop of Chartres in 1090. He was imprisoned by King Phillip I for refusing to recognise his bigamous wife, whom Phillip had seized from her husband. Pope Urban II secured his release. He denounced the financial exactions on France by the Roman Curia, but was a moderating influence in the disputes with Rome about investing laymen as bishops.

EUPHROSYNE of POLOTSK: Died in 1173 in Jerusalem as a recluse. She was a Duke's daughter from Byelorussia, who copied sacred books to sell for charity.

24th VINCENT of LERINS: A learned monk of the Isle of Lerins who died c.450. In his book *Comminitorium* he denounced St Augustine of Hippo's (28 August) definition of Predestination as meaning that God destines some people from the beginning to eternal life and others to eternal damnation. Vincent said this was unscriptural. In this book he analysed the entire Catholic faith. His most important words on the faith and on its development are given in the text following this Calendar.

KING DAVID of SCOTLAND (1085–1153): The son of Queen St Margaret of Scotland. He is regarded as a hero in Scotland for his barbaric raids on the North of England in 1335–38 and as a saint for his founding many bishoprics, monasteries and churches in Scotland. Like most royal saints he was not convincingly holy.

25th ZENOBIUS of FLORENCE: Died in c.350. Learned Bishop of Florence.

THE VENERABLE BEDE (673–735): Monk of the Northumberland monasteries of Wearmouth and Jarrow, which were founded by St Benedict Biscop (12 January). He was Benedict's most distinguished pupil and used the libraries he had built up to help him compile his famous *History of the English Church and People*. St Boniface of Crediton and of Mainz (5 June) wrote after Bede's death that *'a light of the Church, lit by the Holy Spirit, has gone out'*. In 1899 Pope Leo XIII made him a Doctor of the Church.

POPE GREGORY VII ('The Great') (1021–85): Before becoming pope, Gregory was known as Cardinal Hildebrand. He carried out the much-needed reforms begun by his predecessor – the Church had become lax in every way after two centuries in which popes were made and unmade by the emperors or installed and sometimes murdered by the Roman nobility. Gregory built up an efficient Curia in Rome to centralise the Church's administration, providing a system that survived even the century-long 'Babylonian Exile' of the papacy in Avignon after 1305. It was through the officials of the Curia and Gregory's papal legates in every European capital that the policies and spiritual aims of the popes were directed.

The greatest problem with which Gregory had to deal was the refusal of the German Emperor Henry IV to obey his commands to leave the final choice of German bishops to him. Gregory insisted on this to ensure the spiritual well-being of the universal Church and to end the custom whereby rulers chose their own favourites as bishops and abbots even though they were only laymen. Henry's refusal to give in to the Pope's demands caused Gregory to excommunicate him and compel him to come and do penance in the snow before the Castle of Canossa. Henry's submission was only to give him time to deal with a rival in Germany, after which in 1081 he besieged Rome. Gregory held out for four years in the Castle of St Angelo for four years until William Guiscard and his Norman and Saracen troops drove off the Germans and sacked the city. He then fled in despair to Sorrento, where he died in 1085 believing, quite wrongly, that he had failed in his life's mission.

MADELEINE SOPHIE BARAT (1779–1865): Barat was educated by her brother Louis, who was a priest. In 1801 she was sent to teach in the first house at Amiens of The Society of the Sacred Heart. She was made prioress and ruled the community for 63 years. She was modest, attractive and inspired by a strong religious spirit. She established girls' schools for the Sacred Heart Society in the USA, England and ten European countries. She was canonised in 1925.

26th PHILIP NERI (1515–95): As an ordinary layman he devoted himself from 1538 to the religious education of the crowds of young men in Rome whose moral welfare was being totally neglected. He spent much time in prayer and in 1544 he had an intense spiritual experience of what he described as Divine Love. In 1548 he founded a lay brotherhood called The Confraternity of the Holy Spirit to help his work and to assist pilgrims and the sick in Rome. In 1551 he became a priest and was renowned as a confessor and for reading hearts. In 1575 he founded The Congregation of the Oratory, named after the oratory he had built over his church of St Giralomo. It was in this church that the first 'Oratorios' – musical compositions for solo voices and choruses – were sung. His unconventional preaching often attracted criticism. Unlike the ex-Grand Inquisitor Pope St Pius V (30 April), who ruled the city at that time, Philip played down the idea of an austere life. Instead he promoted a life of joy and the love of God and man. He died 13 years after Pius, having done more for the religious life of Rome than anyone that century.

27th AUGUSTINE of CANTERBURY: Died in 605. Missionary bishop sent with 40 monks in 597 by Pope Gregory the Great to spread the Catholic faith in Saxon England. His mission was welcomed in Kent by King Ethelbert (25 February), whose wife was a Burgundian Christian, though he was a pagan. Ethelbert was Augustine's first important convert. By that time the early British Christian Church had been almost wiped out by the Saxons, except in Cornwall, South Wales and Northumbria, where the old Celtic Church was restoring the faith. The Roman style of worship was not welcomed by the few remaining British bishops, who considered Augustine to be too superior towards them, not unlike their previous Roman conquerors. However with the aid of King Ethelbert a cathedral of St Paul was founded in London and through Ethelbert's influence the Saxon King of Essex became a Christian. Guided by Pope Gregory Augustine planned two Archbishoprics at Canterbury and York and twelve lesser sees. At Gregory's suggestion Augustine did not destroy the Saxon temples, but broke up their idols and turned the buildings into Churches. By the time he died, the Roman Church was on a sound footing in England.

28th JULIUS of DUROSTORIUM: A Roman soldier martyred in Bulgaria in 302.

GERMANUS of PARIS (496–576): Abbot of St Symphorian at Autun who became Bishop of Paris in 556. He tried fearlessly to end the civil strife in the city and also to curb the vicious Frankish kings.

BERNARD of MONTJEUX (996–1081): As Canon of the cathedral of Aosta he was responsible for the Alpine passes. He spent 40 years looking after them and the people of the valleys. He also built hospices for travellers at the summit of the passes. These became known as the *Petit St Bernard* and the *Grand St Bernard*. He endowed these hospices and his 'St Bernard' dogs aided travellers lost in the snow.

29th ALDATE: Died in 577. Early British bishop killed by the Saxons at Dereham.

BONA of PISA (1156–1207): After experiencing visions of St James the Greater of Santiago de Compostella (25 July) she spent her life on pilgrimages. She went first to Jerusalem in 1170, where her father was on a crusade. She was shipwrecked and captured by Muslims on the way back, but was ransomed. She then became an official guide on the pilgrim route to Compostella in Spain. She went on foot across France 12 times by the routes on each side of the Massif Centrale to the Pyrenees. As we have seen in the story of St Robert of La Chaise-Dieu (17 April), the churches had provided hostelries for the crowds of pilgrims all along the route. She died of exhaustion in Pisa and has now become the patroness of air hostesses.

30th KING FERDINAND III (1199–1252): King of Leon and Castile who regained Andalusia from the Moors. He began his campaign filled with the intolerant outlook that had been instilled in Spain by the Cluniac and Cistercian Orders. After his victory he got rid of most of the prosperous Moorish population and so ruined the economy. This forced him to be more tolerant. He left Grenada as the last Moorish kingdom in Spain. This was finally conquered in 1492, 140 years after his death. He was popularly regarded as a saint but was not canonised until 1671 – the only Crusader to be thus honoured other than King St Louis IX of France (25 August).

St JOAN of ARC (1412–31): Visionary saviour of France in the Hundred Years' War against England. Second patron saint of France after her canonisation in 1920. She was a pious daughter of a substantial farmer at Domremy in Champagne. At the age of 14 she heard the 'voices' that were to guide her life. She attributed them to St Catherine of Alexandria and St Margaret (or 'Marina') of Antioch – the legendary favourite of the first crusaders. They told her to 'save France', which was then engaged in the Hundred Years' War against England. She sought out the Dauphin of France (the future King Charles VII) at his castle of Chinon and in a remarkable interview she convinced him and his bishops and commanders that she was a true visionary inspired and sent to them by God.

They dressed her in armour and made her leader of the French army which then, under her command, relieved the siege of Orleans. Joan was wounded, but continued to inspire the French troops and after a further victory she led the Dauphin to be crowned King at Rheims.

Joan's faith never wavered though her voices told her that she did not have long to live. She was captured by the Burgundians as she attempted to save her army's rearguard in a battle. The French king, now Charles VII, failed to rescue her and the Burgundians handed her over to the English in Rouen to be tried by the Church as a heretic for claiming divine guidance. She was found guilty and burned to death. Although Joan was regarded as a saint in France, she was not canonised until 1920. She is now joint patron saint of France with St Denis (9 October).

31st PETRONILLA: An early Roman martyr, a member of the family of Domiltilla.

SUMMARY OF MAY SAINTS

This Calendar for May gives the feast days of 67 saints of whom 18 were martyrs and 9 were women. The text that follows reviews the lives of **St Athanasius** and **St Vincent of Lerins,** as well as discussing the English mystic, **Dame Julian of Norwich.**

THE SPIRITUAL IMPORTANCE OF TWO MAY SAINTS AND ONE ENGLISH MYSTIC

St Athanasius (c.295–373)

St Athanasius was the son of Christian parents who were hidden by pagans in Alexandria to save them from Diocletian's persecution. As a brilliant student of theology he was chosen to be the secretary and adviser to his bishop and exerted a strong influence at the Council of Nicea in 325. This council, presided over by Constantine the Great, rejected the claim of the monk Arius and many bishops who denied the eternity of the world and the *'uncreatedness of the Son'*. By then Athanasius had already published his first book. In this he was the first to examine scientifically the chief circumstances of the life of Christ. This was the foundation of his life-long struggle to defend the orthodox faith and tradition.

St Gregory of Nazianzen, who survived him to lead the Council of Constantinople in 381 and to confirm the decisions of Nicea, said in his obituary of Athanasius that at Nicea he was *'Foremost among those who were in attendance and did his utmost to stem the plague of Arianism'*. Gregory said that *'the face of this diminutive man was that of an angel. His readiness as a disputant and his richness as an interpreter of the Holy Scriptures made him already a great power at a great crisis.'*

Athanasius was elected Bishop of Alexandria in 328 at the age of 33. He was exiled five times by heretical emperors, but each time he returned. His first exile to Treves on the borders of Germany was ordered by Constantine the Great for his refusal to give Holy Communion to Arian Christians. He wrote to the emperor that *'It cannot be right to admit persons to communion who invented a heresy contrary to the truth and who were anathametised at Nicea'*. It was at Treves, when Arianism was again rife and supported by the emperors, that he exclaimed that he was *'Solus in Mundum'* in his standing up for the true faith.

Athanasius' books on the faith and against heresy asserted that the divinity of the Saviour had been foretold in many places in Scripture. He confirmed the nature of Jesus' unique Sonship, which was required by the Doctrine of Redemption or Salvation. This was attested by the consciousness of the Church although, as he informs us, he was far from imagining that any form of human thought could adequately represent a Divine Majesty. He was convinced that the formula *Homoousion* or *Consubstantial* – 'All three of the same substance' – explained correctly the sense that Jesus was truly the Son of God and was a test of adherence to the Scriptural Christology. It is from these words that the Creed attributed to him is derived and which he is shown proclaiming in the altar-piece design above: *'The Godhead of the Father, of the Son, of the Holy Spirit, is all one. The glory is equal, the Majesty eternal.'* He never wavered from his belief that *'nothing is more certain than that Jesus was in the full force of the words "God Incarnate", perfect God and perfect man, the very God in the flesh and the very flesh in the Word.'*

Athanasius met the aged St Antony of Egypt when the old man struggled across the desert to Alexandria and outfaced the imperial governor to defend the faith against Arianism. After Antony died he wrote his biography, which was to have such a profound effect on St Augustine of Hippo that he changed his loose way of life and converted to Christianity (see the Calendar for August Saints).

During the first of his five exiles Athanasius appealed to Pope Julius in

Rome for support, which was given unequivocally. At times his life was in danger and the Emperor Constans ordered that he should be beheaded. Fortunately Constans was killed by a rebel general and the sentence lapsed. Athanasius continued his work, writing to his friend Serapion, Bishop of the Upper Nile, that contrary to the opinion of many in the Church the Holy Spirit was rightly included as a divine person in the Trinity.

It was also in this letter (written in a cave where he was in hiding with the Desert Fathers), that he described the Trinity vividly: *'The Trinity is like a fall of water. The Father is the source, the Son is the pool into which it flows and the Spirit is the river that takes it out into the world. All three are the same substance.'*

The Holy Trinity likened to a fall of water – all the same substance

Athanasius twice nearly lost his battle. The first time was when Pope Liberius gave way to the imperial threats at the Council of Rimini in 359 and proclaimed a doctrine in support of Arianism. Liberius was forced to retract later by the bishops, who were led in the West by St Hilary of Poitiers.

The second time that Athanasius was almost overwhelmed was during the reign of Julian the Apostate, when the Arian Archbishop George was imposed on Alexandria. The people of Alexandria rose up and killed George. The Emperor Julian, who despised Christianity, merely rebuked the citizens, saying that *'this was just a Galilean dispute'*. However he allowed Athanasius to return, though not to resume his office as Archbishop. Even during his exile at that time Athanasius had sent word to his flock to encourage them, saying that *'This cloud will soon pass'*. He was proved right when Julian was killed in Persia in 363. Julian's last words according to Bishop Theodoret of Cyrrhus were: *'Thou hast conquered, Oh pale Galilean!'*

The last few years of Athanasius' life were spent peacefully in Alexandria, where he died on 2 May 373. In spite of the importance of his struggle and the bitter disputes in which he became embroiled, Athanasius had a reputation for great affection and tenderness and he always acted where possible as a peacemaker. Even when he had to use sharp words, he was always charitable. The early seventeenth-century Anglican theologian Dr Hooker described the *'deep religiousness which illuminated all his studies and controversies by a sense of his relations as a Christian to his Redeemer'*. Cardinal John Henry Newman included among Athanasius' gifts *'his firmness with discretion and discrimination'*.

St Vincent of Lerins (died c.450)

St Vincent (24 May), who died shortly after 450, was a hermit on the Isle of Lerins which produced many early bishops for Gaul. He may have known St Patrick (17 March) who spent over 15 years at Lerins and who almost certainly studied for the priesthood there.

St Vincent's book *Comminitorum* shows how his community at Lerins was concerned with theological studies on a broader front than those that occupied the Greek theologians of his time. While accepting and analysing the traditional faith, he looked much further ahead than the Greeks and was the first to proclaim that Christianity was a developing faith. His conclusions on this are important.

Vincent gave the classic definition of the faith, which has been quoted by theologians ever since: *'The Catholic Faith is that which has been believed everywhere, always and by all'*. Thus he combined scripture and the tradition that interpreted it. But Vincent then went further and gave this original explanation, asking the question: *'Is there then to be no progress of religion in the Church of Christ?'* His answer, which is rarely given by conservative theologians even today in their criticisms of new interpretations of the scriptures, is truly illuminating: *'Clearly there is to be progress, but it must resemble the growth of an infant to maturity, a growth which, through all the changes preserves its identity. The dogmas of the heavenly philosophy may by the operation of time be smoothed and polished. They may gain in the way of greater fullness of evidence, light and elucidation, but they must of necessity retain their integrity and essential features. Such has been the task of the Church in the decrees of Councils, aimed at adding clearness, vigour and zeal to what was believed.'*

These words ought to have been accepted as the Magna Carta for all who interpret the gospels on behalf of each new generation of Christians. However the Roman Church has always been reluctant to follow Vincent's advice on new ideas and concepts, even if they were supported by scientific evidence. The trial and condemnation of Galileo in the seventeenth century is an example of this hidebound attitude. Galileo's works were still on the Index of forbidden books at the beginning of the nineteenth century.

However by the mid-twentieth century the Church was no longer at war with science. In 1958 Pope Pius XII acknowledged that *'the Big Bang theory of the creation of the Universe is in accordance with the description in Genesis'*. This more modern attitude was confirmed by the 'Bringing-up-to-date' policy of Pope John XXIII at the Second Vatican Council in 1963. This trend was taken a step further by the late Pope John-Paul II in 1998, 140 years after the publication of Charles Darwin's *The Origin of Species*, when he admitted that the discoveries of science did suggest that the human race may have originated from earlier forms of life.

It can therefore be seen that Cardinal Newman's historical analysis showing that Christianity is a 'developing Faith', as St Vincent had taught over 1,400 years before, had been ignored by the Roman Catholic Church. In view of this it is remarkable that neither of the two most popular English dictionaries of saints mention St Vincent of Lerins.

Dame Julian of Norwich (1342–1416) and the English mystics

Dame Julian and the other fourteenth-century mystics mentioned below are important because they and their popularity illustrate how deep was the faith of the ordinary people once Europe had at last become fully Christian. This was achieved when Lithuania became officially Christian after its union with Poland in the fourteenth century.

Before describing Dame Julian's life and her spiritual experiences as told in her book *Revelations of Divine Love*, it may be helpful to say a little about mysticism in all religions. All mystics believe they encounter a reality in the depths of self during their spiritual experiences. They feel that they meet 'something other' that is transcendent and apart from themselves. They also know that this cannot be explained rationally, though at least it tells us about the human mind and its relation with that ultimate reality known as God. Some of the mystics, as we have seen with the Greeks such as St John Climacus (30 March), developed special techniques of prayer to help them encounter a presence which transfigured their heart. This happened after they had gone through a process of purification and illumination which led them to a momentary union with God. This spiritual experience gave them ineffable satisfaction and confidence in faith.

Mysticism, like art, is an imaginative and creative attempt to find a meaning and value to human life. Followers of the world's main faiths, Christians, Jews, Muslims, Hindus and to some extent Buddhists have these mystical experiences. Roman Catholics believe that these graces come to only a limited number of special souls. Even then they need guidance to help them to avoid the dangers to the mind that are encountered on the way. Until the middle of the twentieth century, Protestants disregarded the claims of the mystics, but the writings of Dean Inge of St Paul's Cathedral (1860–1954) and the spiritual experiences of the modern mystic Dorothy Kerin (1889–1963), the foundress of the Anglican healing centre at Groombridge in Sussex, have attracted a considerable following and interest. The life and work of Dorothy Kerin is described near the end of Part VII of this book – 'The Unquenchable Spirit'.

Dame Julian of Norwich's mysticism was unique in its form and spiritual experience. She was probably a nun or else had been taught by nuns before her faith caused her to immure herself for the rest of her life as an Anchoress inside the church of St Julian in Norwich. It is however not clear from her writings whether she had her first revelations before or after she arrived at St Julian's, having dedicated herself to the Church and begun to give spiritual advice to her many visitors and to the pilgrims who came to see her.

Dame Julian wrote her first account of her experiences, *A Shewing of God's Love*, shortly after they had occurred in 1373 when she fell apparently fatally ill at the age of 31. She had been ill for several days, steadily weakening and everyone could see that she was dying. A priest gave her the Last Rites. He also held before her eyes a crucifix. She gazed upon this and suddenly felt her illness leaving her body. She fell into a deep trance and for about five hours received 15 consecutive visions of Christ, with blood streaming from his head as he hung on the cross, of the Virgin Mary and of the Trinity. She listened to Jesus explaining to her the meaning of these 'shewings'

When she awoke from her trance, she felt her sickness return. She then had a sixteenth 'shewing' or vision of Christ, during which she spoke to Jesus. This time the illness did not return. Mother Julian then lived for another 40 years, spending 20 of those years meditating on her remarkable experiences. She recorded her memories, thoughts and her conclusions in her book *The Revelations of Divine Love*.

The following precis and quotations tell her story: *'These revelations were shown to a simple uneducated creature on 13th May 1373'*. She tells how before this she had prayed for three gifts – to have an understanding of Christ's Passion, to suffer a physical illness at the age of 30 and to receive three wounds from God.

These were the wounds of true contrition, of genuine compassion and of a serious longing for God. She had also felt before her illness that her life had been paltry and short and she had prayed: *'Good Lord, let the end of my life be to your glory'*. She then surrendered herself wholly to God's will. Her desire for a serious illness had already been granted, so after seeing the priests' crucifix and the feeling that a cure was taking place in her body, she said that *'It occurred to me that I should ask for the second gracious gift – that my body might experience and understand Jesus' blessed Passion'*.

During the first revelation Julian saw blood trickling down from Jesus' crown of thorns. She blessed God for showing her this and also for showing her *'our blessed Lady in a spiritual manner and as a simple humble young girl'*. Jesus then showed her something which no person is likely to have thought of by themselves. This was a tiny hazel-nut in the palm of her hand and about which he said: *'This is all that is made. It lives on and will live on for ever because God loves it'*. Julian realised from this that it had three essential properties – *'that God made it, that God loves it and that God preserves it. So every single thing owes its existence to the love of God'*.

Julian then records a typical mystic's thought and says *'Yet I cannot say what this Creator, Preserver, Lover is, until I am united with him in my essential being'*. After a few more revelations Julian said of herself: *'I am not a good person because I have had this revelation, but only if I love God more perfectly'*. She also described how these visions came to her in three ways, *'with the eyes of my body, by a word that was imaginatively conceived in my mind and by spiritual visions . . . I saw in my mind God concentrated on a point. By this vision I understood that he is in all things . . . and my heart became filled with fear as I thought "What is sin?"'*

Obviously Mother Julian had been well taught by some Catholic person steeped in the Church's understanding of those days, because she went on to reflect that: *'nothing happens by chance or luck but everything is caused by the providence and wisdom of God'*. According to her reflections 20 years after the event, perhaps under the influence of St Augustine of Hippo's fourth-century teaching, she wrote that *'God foresees everything, so that what is an accident or luck to us, is quite different for Him'*.

In her talks with Christ she heard him comfort her with the words *'All will be well!'* Towards the end of her record of her 16 visions Mother Julian writes more and more like a theologian, commenting on problems such as the existence of evil and of how prayer unites the soul. She again seems to have been influenced indirectly by Augustine's teaching as she writes on the Trinity: *'God is eternal Truth, sovereign Wisdom, eternal Love and he is uncreated. Man's soul has been created by God and has the same qualities, only they are created' . . . 'Our soul is created to be God's dwelling and the dwelling of the soul is God' . . . 'Yet until our soul has attained its full potential, we cannot be entirely holy.'*

Much of Mother Julian's record of her visions and meditations reads as though she was passing on standard answers to the kind of questions that theologians were asking or teaching in her day. Even so, we can see from this how greatly her visions inspired her subsequent thinking and understanding. That, after all, is what they were about. As anyone who has had even the least spiritual experience knows, it may take years before its significance becomes clear. Perhaps the most modern thinking in Mother Julian's record is the way she sees the Trinity as Motherhood. She wrote that: *'God, who is All-Wisdom, is the Mother of our nature together with the Love and Goodness of the Holy Ghost. This is all One God . . . I saw the activity of the whole blessed Trinity and in my vision I understood these three attributes – Fatherhood, Motherhood and Lordship . . . In our Father Almighty we are sustained, made joyful and redeemed. The Second Person sustains, restores us human beings, for he is our Mother, Brother and Saviour. Also, in our Lord the Holy Spirit we have our reward. Thus our life is threefold – we have a Being, we have our Development and third we have our fulfilment. The first is Nature, the second Mercy, the third is Grace.'*

It is doubtful if there were ever many copies of the English book of this Norfolk recluse. Most may have been destroyed after the dissolution of the monasteries in 1534–37. It was not until 1877 that a copy was made from an MSS of her book in the Bibliothèque Nationale in Paris. Since then her church of St Julian, destroyed by bombing in the war, has been restored and has become the centre of an active promotion of Mother Julian as a remarkable visionary, perhaps one to be recognised as a saint. Certainly the twentieth-century Cistercian monk and spiritual writer Thomas Merton said that he preferred her writings to those of St John of the Cross. There is no record of any other visionary or miraculous healing of a woman in English history since Mother Julian's day until that of Dorothy Kerin at the beginning of the twentieth century. Her story will be told in Part VII of this book.

The other important fourteenth-century mystics are St Bridget of Sweden (23 July); the Fleming John Rysbroeck (1293–1381), founder of the Order of the Brotherhood of the Common Man, of which the writer Thomas à Kempis was a member (see Part VII of this book); the German Abbess St Gertrude the Great (1256–1302), (16 November); the Germans Martin Eckhart (who died in 1327), John Towler (who died in 1361) and the Blessed Henry Suso (born in 1295).

Then there are three famous English mystics – Richard Rollo of Hampole (1290–1340), Walter Hilton (who was the author of *The Ladder of Perfection and* who died in 1326*) and, lastly, the unknown author of *The Cloud of Unknowing*. The latter describes the hidden God of whom even Moses only saw his back in the cloud on Mount Sinai. The poem ends with the advice on the way to find this God: *'With love you will find him, but by thinking, never'*.

JUNE SAINTS

June

1. St Justin
2. St Blandina St Elmo
   St Erasmus
3. Martyrs of Uganda
5. St Boniface of Crediton
6. St Jarlath of Tuam St Norbert
7. St Meriadoc
   St Robert of Newminster

9. St Columba
   St Pelagia of Antioch
11. St Barnabas
12. St Eskil, St Leo III
13. St Anthony of Padua
14. St Methodius of Constantinople
15. St Vitus
17. St Alban St Botolph
    St Harvey

19. St Boniface (Bruno) of Quefort
    St Juliana of Falconieri
22. St Thomas More, St John Fisher
23. St Etheldreda (Audrey)
24. Birth of St John Baptist
26. St John & St Paul of Rome
27. St Cyril of Alexandria
28. St Irenaeus of Lyons
29. St Peter & St Paul

St Peter & St Paul 62-64 AD.

1885 Martyrs of Uganda

St Alban (c.209)

The picture heading illustrates the Apostles **St Peter** and **St Paul** (29 June) who were martyred under Nero in Rome in 64 and c.67; **St Alban** (22 June), the first British martyr (c.209); **St Charles Lwanga** (3 June) and the Catholic martyrs of Uganda, who were burnt alive in 1885–87.

ALTAR-PIECE DESIGN FOR FOURTEEN JUNE SAINTS

Shown in the central scene is:

Justin Martyr (1 June), being tried by a Roman Governor and refusing to deny Christ.

In the nine scenes from top left and round to the right are:

Barnabas (11 June), martyr and cousin of St Mark, stoned to death at Salamis in Cyprus while preaching the gospel; **Irenaeus of Lyons** (28 June), returning to Lyons as the new Bishop after the massacre in the arena of all the Christians in 177; **John** and **Paul of Rome** (26 June), a sketch of the fresco in their villa beneath the Church of Giovanni Paulo in Rome. They had been beheaded as Christians by Justin the Apostate and are shown entering Paradise through the walls of the imaginary tent that divides this world from the next; **Cyril of Alexandria** (27 June), at the Council of Ephesus in 431 which he forced to condemn and banish the Patriarch Nestorius; **Columba** (9 June), Irish missionary arriving at the Isle of Iona to preach to the Picts in 561; **Nicetas** (22 June), Greek missionary teaching the Goths along the Danube, c.410.

The next panel (bottom left) shows four sixth-century Celtic saints:

Jarlath (6 June), founder of the Irish bishopric of Tuam in Galway c.550; **Harvey or Hervé** (17 June). Born blind in Brittany in the sixth century. Abbot of Plouvien at Lanhourneau; **Kevin** (3 June), died 600, founded abbey of Glendalough, Wicklow, Ireland. **Petroc** (4 June), important sixth-century missionary from Wales to Cornwall, many churches dedicated there to him. **Queen Clotilda** (3 June), wife of the Frankish King Clovis whom she persuaded to be baptised by St Remi at Rheims in 596. She is shown with her son the future St Cloud; **Botolph** (17 June), popular seventh-century Anglo-Saxon bishop. Many churches were dedicated to him in the Middle Ages.

Altar-piece design for fourteen June saints

ALTAR-PIECE DESIGN FOR NINE JUNE SAINTS

Shown in the central scene is:

Boniface of Crediton (5 June), shown planting a pine, the first 'Christmas Tree', to represent the symbolic evergreen for the eternal Christ after he had cut down the sacred oak at Geismar which the tree-worshippers venerated as the 'Green Man'.

The scenes from top left and round to the right show:

Martial of Limoges (30 June), made a bishop in Gaul by Pope Fabian in 250. He preached for 40 years, escaping capture by the Romans; **Erasmus** or 'Elmo' (2 June), martyred c.303 at Formiae near Rome as his entrails were wound onto a windlass; **Columba** (9 June), this is a repeat scene to emphasise his importance and those of his successors as abbot in taking the gospel and Celtic Church to Scotland and Northern Britain after 561; **Methodius of Constantinople** (14 June) Bishop Patriarch being flogged by order of Michael II for refusing to ban icons of Christ and saints in the ninth century; **Pope Leo III** (12 June) crowning the Emperor Charlemagne King of the Romans on Christmas Day, 800; **Boniface of Querfort** (19 June) missionary bishop martyred near the Russian border in 1009; **Adalbert of Magdeburg** (20 June) blessing Princess Olga of Kiev on his first abortive mission to Russia in 961; **Antony of Padua** (13 June) preaching in c.1225 when his finest psalter was stolen and which he prophesied rightly would be returned.

Altar-piece design for nine June saints

JUNE CALENDAR OF SAINTS' FEAST-DAYS

1st **JUSTIN MARTYR**: Greek philosopher and Christian preacher in Rome tried by the Governor in 165 for refusing to deny Christ. His great contribution to teaching Christian thought was to demonstrate its reasonableness as the perfect philosophy. He also showed how the Greek philosophers, because of their understanding of God, were in effect *'Christians before Christ'*.

2nd **BLANDINA**: A Christian slave-girl martyred with 160 companions by wild beasts in 177 in the arena at Lyons. This martyrdom was part of a purge of Christians made by the Emperor Marcus Aurelius who had believed wrongly that Christians in the army were refusing to bear arms. The governor of Lyons had chosen wild beasts to kill the Christians in order to save the cost of hiring gladiators. The audience thought the sport poor and demanded professional combats in future.

ERASMUS (or 'ELMO'): Legendary martyr in Syria c.303 whose entrails were wound out of his body onto a windlass – hence his becoming patron saint of sailors. The electrical discharges seen on ships' mastheads in storms are called 'St Elmo's Fire'.

3rd **KEVIN**: Died c.612. Founded Abbey of Glendalough in Wicklow (Ireland). Disciples flocked to his school there. Famed, like many Irish saints, for his love of nature.

CLOTILDA: Died 545. Widow of Frankish King Clovis. Saved the lives of two of her grandchildren after their uncle King Childebert murdered their elder brothers. Under her influence her young grandson St Cloud (7 September) gave up his claim to the Frankish throne and became a priest. Both are revered as saints in France.

UGANDA MARTYRS, CHARLES LWANGA and others: Burnt alive by King Mwanga of Buganda between 1885–87. Lwanga had protested at the king's pederasty. The victims were his Christian pages. The Catholic missionaries, the White Brothers, said they went to their deaths singing hymns like the early Christian martyrs. Also martyred at that time was Bishop James Hannington, Anglican Bishop of Equatorial Guinea.

4th **PETROC**: Sixth-century itinerant preacher who founded an abbey in Cornwall after travelling there from Wales. Many Cornish and Devon churches are named after him.

FRANCIS CARACCIOLO: Died 1608. Founded the Lesser Clerks Regular in Italy as part of a movement started by St Cajetan (8 August) to reform the teaching of clergy after the Council of Trent.

5th **BONIFACE (or 'WINFRITH') of Crediton and of Mainz** (675–754): Born in Devon, he became an indefatigable missionary to the Low Countries, the Franks and Germany. He was called 'Boniface' by Pope Gregory II on account of his cheerful face. Gregory thought so highly of his missionary and his administrative abilities that he made him Archbishop of Mainz. He was martyred by robbers in Frisia while conducting a confirmation service. He became patron saint of Germany. His history is told in the text after the Calendar.

6th **JARLATH**: Fifth-century Irish bishop, the third to be appointed by St Patrick.

NORBERT (1080–1134): This courtier to a Rhineland prince was 'born-anew' and converted after a narrow escape from death. He was ordained as a priest and was afflicted with the reforming zeal that takes over many late converts. Pope Gelasius II helped him found the reforming order of The Premonstratensian Canons named after the valley of Premontré in Flanders. The canons were itinerant preachers. He was made Archbishop of Magdeburg in 1126 and brought much-needed reforms to his see.

7th **MERIADOC**: Sixth-century Welsh missionary to Cornwall, who then went to the Vendée in France, where he is still venerated.

COLMAN of DROMORE: Late sixth-century Irish bishop. Old Irish lists include 230 saints named 'Colman'.

ROBERT of NEWMINSTER (1110–59): Yorkshire monk who studied in Paris. He became a Cistercian and was one of the founders of Fountains Abbey in Yorkshire, one of the most beautiful of all English monastic sites. St Bernard of Clairvaux cleared him of a false charge of over-familiarity with a girl.

8th **MEDARD** (c.470–560): Bishop of Tours famed for his knowledge of the weather and agriculture. He ruled in Normandy. On his feast-day the most exemplary girl in the parish is crowned with roses and given a purse of money. This ceremony is still celebrated in the Norman village of St Mar d'Egrenne near Domfront.

WILLIAM of YORK: Archbishop who died in 1154. A member of the noble Fitzherbert family. He was chaplain to King Stephen. He was accused of simony and unchastity by a minority in his diocese in 1140 at the time of his election as archbishop. Both sides appealed to the pope. He was supported by St Bernard and the Yorkshire Cistercians and was cleared of the charges on oath. The next pope, Eugenius III, deposed him and he retired to be a monk in Winchester, but was restored to York in 1154. He died that year, perhaps of poison. Miracles were claimed at his tomb, as recorded in the 'William Window' in York cathedral. He was canonised in 1227.

9th COLUMBA or COMCILLE (521–97): A member of the royal O'Neill clan in Ireland. Trained as a monk by St Finnian of Clonard (12 December). He founded monasteries at Derry and Kells. He left Ireland after a dispute with another monastery over an alleged stolen psalter in 565. He took 12 monks with him to symbolise Jesus and his disciples to evangelise the Hebrides. He based himself on the Island of Iona off Mull and converted many Picts. He corresponded in verse with the Druid bards of Ireland. His life was written by his successor as Abbot of Iona – St Adomnan (23 September).

PELAGIA of ANTIOCH: Virgin martyr, died in 304. According to St John Chrysostom (13 September) she was only 15 when she threw herself off a roof to avoid being raped by soldiers.

10th ITHAMAR: The first Anglo-Saxon Archbishop of Canterbury. Died in 660.

11th BARNABAS: A Jewish Cypriot recorded in Acts 11.24 as *'a good man, full of the Holy Spirit and of faith'*. He looked for Paul at Tarsus and brought him to Antioch to be with the Christians there. That was also the first time the disciples were called Christians (Acts 11.26). Barnabas accompanied Paul on his first missionary journey to Cyprus. He brought with him his young cousin John Mark (25 April), the future evangelist. He is believed according to tradition to have been martyred in Salamis, Cyprus, in 61.

12th POPE LEO III: Died in 816. He crowned Charlemagne Roman Emperor on Christmas Day 800. This action may have been planned earlier at Charlemagne's headquarters at Paddeborn in discussions which included the emperor's Anglo-Saxon adviser Alcuin. Leo meant this first coronation to ensure that the emperor became the secular sword and protector of the Church. It never worked out like that. Charlemagne himself and the later emperors, who became elected as 'Holy Roman Emperors' by seven German Electoral Princes, nearly all tried to control the Church for centuries to come. Leo was not canonised until 1773. Alcuin, who founded the entire education system for clergy in Charlemagne's empire and retired as the learned Bishop of Tours, has not yet been made a saint in spite of his great virtues and wise guidance of the Gallic Church.

ESKIL: English bishop and martyr in Sweden, 1080. He had accompanied St Sigfrid's

(12 February) mission and was stoned to death for stopping a pagan festival.

13th ANTONY of PADUA (1193–1231): Portuguese theologian who became a Franciscan. Francis of Assisi sent him to teach friars in Bologna and Padua. He also preached in France and Rome, where his preaching was hailed as opening 'the jewel case of the Bible'.

Like all popular saints he attracted many legends. He is also famous for the occasion when a valuable psalter was stolen. Antony prophesied that it would be returned. This happened and Antony is now invoked as a finder of lost possessions.

14th METHODIUS of CONSTANTINOPLE: Died in 847. Bishop venerated for his support of sacred images and icons during the second iconoclastic persecution which Emperor Michael II had instigated. Michael had him flogged and imprisoned for seven years. The Empress Theodora became regent in 842, freed Methodius and made him Patriarch of Constantinople. He called a council which restored veneration of icons.

15th VITUS: Martyred in South Italy in c.303. Patron of sufferers from epilepsy and nervous diseases – hence St Vitus' dance.

16th CYR (or Cyriacus) and JULITTA: Their legend tells that Cyr was a three-year-old-boy who was taken by his widowed mother Julitta from Iconium to Tarsus in c.304 to escape the persecution. They were caught and Julitta was tortured. Cyr then attacked her persecutors and was executed with her. St Cyr was the name given to Madame de Maintenon's school for young ladies near Versailles in the reign of Louis XIV. That also became the name of the famous French military academy.

TIKHON of ZADONSK (1724–83): Made Bishop of Voronezh, but retired to a monastery through ill-health in 1767. He gave spiritual guidance to many and money to the needy. He said that *'to live in Christ is to walk in love'*. His letters show how he sought inspiration not only from the Early Fathers but also from Lutheran and Anglican authors. He was made a Russian saint in 1860.

17th HARVEY (or Hervé): Popular saint in Brittany. Sixth-century legend says he was born blind, the son of a British bard. He became Abbot of Plouvien.

BOTOLPH: Died c.680. Popular and learned saint in medieval England where many churches were dedicated to him. He founded a monastery at Boston in Lincolnshire.

18th MARK and MARCELLIAN: Martyred in Rome, c.290. Their tomb is in the decorated catacomb of St Balbina on the Appian Way.

ELIZABETH of SCHOENAU: Died in 1164. Nun and visionary. Inspired the legend of St Ursula (21 October). Friend of the mystic St Hildegard of the Rhine (19 September).

19th GERVASE and PROTASE: Names given to relics of unrecorded martyrs found by St Ambrose (7 December) near Milan after having a vision.

ROMUALD (950–1027): Florentine Cluniac monk who taught the virtues of giving up the world and leading a life in solitude in the style of the Desert Fathers as a way to attain salvation. In doing this he aimed to reform and restore monastic life, which had become lax in Italy. He founded a monastery at Fonte Avellana in Tuscany, where Saint Peter Damian (21 February) was a disciple and extended his ascetic ideal throughout Italy.

BONIFACE of QUERFORT (974–1009): One of St Romuald's (see 19 June) monks near Ravenna, where he heard a call to take up the missionary work among the Prussians after the martydom of St Adelberg of Prague (23 April). He was consecrated bishop for this purpose by Pope Sylvester II, but political difficulties caused him to be sent to evangelise the Magyars and Pechenegs of South Russia instead. He there again met fierce opposition and was martyred.

JULIANA FALCONERI (1270–1341): A tertiary member of the Servite Order founded by her uncle St Alexis (see the 'Seven Founders', 17 February). She founded the Servite Order of Nuns to do good works.

20th ADELBERT of MAGDEBURG: Died in 981. In 961 at the request of Queen St Olga of Kiev (11 July) he led a mission to Russia. Olga's son killed several of his missionaries and drove Adelbert back to Mainz, where he was made Archbishop in 968 to evangelise the Slavs and Wends.

21st MEWAN (or Meen): Sixth-century disciple of the British missionary St Samson (28 July). He followed him and St Austell (28 June) via Cornwall to Brittany. He founded a monastery at St Meen which became a popular medieval centre for pilgrims. Patron of St Mewan in Cornwall.

ALOYSIUS GONZAGA (1568–91): Son of an Italian marquis. He was disgusted in his youth by the violence and licentiousness of the nobility and became a Jesuit novice in 1585. He died of a fever caught while working in a hospital in Rome. St Robert Belarmine (17 September) praised his extreme holiness. Canonised in 1726.

22nd ACACIUS: Alleged martyr with 10,000 Armenians at an unknown early date. Their story resembles that of the Theban Legions (22 September), and was popular in Germany and with the crusaders.

ALBAN: First British martyr c.204–9. An unbaptised Romano-British soldier of Verulanium (St Albans) during the persecution in 209. He helped a Christian priest by exchanging his clothes with him. Alban was arrested and put to death. Before his martyrdom Alban had been preparing for baptism.

NICETAS: Died in 414. Missionary bishop to Goths and Dacians along the Danube. He expounded the Apostle's creed to them and encouraged them to sing psalms. According to modern scholars he may have written the 'Te Deum'.

PAULINUS of NOLA (353–431): Born in Bordeaux and married to a Spanish wife. Inspired by the ideals of the gospel they sold their property in 390 and gave the money to the poor. Paulinus became a priest . In 395, having given up marital relations, they took up a monastic form of life at Nola in Italy, where Paulinus dedicated a church to St Felix of Nola (14 January). He also provided accommodation in the church for the crowds of pilgrims. He corresponded with St Ambrose (7 December), St Augustine of Hippo (28 August), St Victricius (7 August) and St Martin of Tours (11 November). He was elected Bishop of Nola in 409.

BISHOP JOHN FISHER and **SIR THOMAS MORE** (1469–1535 and 1478–1535): Both were beheaded for alleged treason to King Henry VIII.

Fisher was Bishop of Rochester and an enthusiast for papal reform. At a commission for Church reform in Rome he said *'If the Pope (Leo X) does not mend his ways, God will soon do it for him'*. He opposed vernacular translations of the Bible on the grounds that giving an English Bible to the common people was like giving an open knife to a baby. A friend of More, he, like many others in his day, was torn between his traditional religious beliefs and dislike of the way they were being practised by Rome. He defended Queen Catherine of Aragon against the king's plea to divorce her. Henry VIII was enraged at this by the way his bishops openly preferred to obey Rome rather than their king. For him this was nothing less than high treason.

More suffered in the same way. A distinguished lawyer, Speaker of the House of Commons and briefly Chancellor for Henry, he was also a humanist and friend of Erasmus, who dedicated to him his critical attack on the decadent papacy and monasteries in his book *In Praise of Folly*. More was a dedicated traditionalist who believed that the popes should still be honoured as Christ's Vicars on Earth regardless of the way they behaved. This brought him into conflict with the King when Henry split with Rome over his divorce, married Anne Boleyn and declared himself Supreme Governor of the Church in England. More, who had written half a million intemperate and narrow-minded words attacking William Tyndale's English translation of the Bible, refused to recognise the King as head of the Church. He could easily have paid lip-service to this, but bravely faced death on the scaffold instead. Further details are given in the text below the Calendar.

23rd **ETHELREDA (or Audrey)** (630–79): Daughter of King Anna of the East Angles in Britain. St Wilfrid (12 October) secured her release from an unconsummated marriage to a king's son. She then founded a double monastery for men and women at Ely in 672 on the site of the present cathedral. She was the most revered of female Saxon saints.

24th **MAXIMUS of TURIN** (c.350–c.415): He became Turin's first bishop in 397 and held a council of Gallic bishops in 398. One hundred of his surviving sermons show him to have come into conflict in the Piedmont with rural paganism.

25th **FEBRONIA**: Virgin martyr who died in c.304. She chose death rather than marriage to the son of the Prefect of Mesopotamia.

26th **JOHN and PAUL of ROME**: Believed to have been courtiers put to death for their faith in Rome by the Emperor Julian the Apostate, c.363. The evidence for this is in the remains of their villa, which was also a church, beneath the beautiful Church of St Giovanni e Paulo dedicated to them on the slopes of the Celian Hill. The walls of their villa are painted with Christian signs including the fish and an early fresco of their execution, which is also sketched in the illustration in the heading to this month's Calendar.

27th **CYRIL of ALEXANDRIA** (380–444): A controversial character who followed his unpleasant and arrogant Uncle Theophilus, destroyer of St John Chrysostom, as Archbishop of Alexandria. Much has already been said about Cyril in the April Calendar in the text of his tutor St Isodore of Pelusium (6 February), who tried to temper his excesses during his intrigues against Nestorius and the Antiochan monks. It is obvious from these accounts that although Cyril may be considered by the Greek Church as a theologian of importance and as a successful and popular preacher in Egypt, he lacked charity. Through this he and his disciples and successors caused the fatal schisms in the Greek Church which laid open the way for Muhammad to refuse to accept Jesus as son of God. He gave his reason for this in his Koran, saying that the Christian sects could not agree on the nature of the God they worshipped. Further comment on Cyril is given in the text below this Calendar.

28th **IRENAEUS of LYONS** (c.130–202): A theologian born in Ephesus. He followed the teaching of St Polycarp (26 January) and said that as a young man he had listened to him and known that Polycarp, when he too was a young man, had heard St John the Evangelist preach as an old man. In his book *Against Heresies* Irenaeus refuted the claims of the Gnostics, saying contemptuously that '*New versions of their so-called gospels are produced almost daily*'. He was referring to such works as *The Gospel of Thomas*, *The Gospel of Peter*, *The Acts of Peter*, *The Apocalypse of Peter* and many others. Some of these were really religious novels designed to act as theological studies, but were nevertheless, in Iranaeus' view, only '*bad theology*'. Irenaeus was absent from Lyons on a mission to Rome when the great massacre of Christians and their bishop Pothinus took place in 177. He was made Bishop of Lyons immediately afterwards and continued his writing on theology. He was the first to write that '*perhaps the bread and wine do indeed become the body and blood of Our Lord after their consecration. This is because of their remarkable efficacy and effect on all who partake of the sacraments.*'

Irenaeus played an important part in selecting the final canon of books for the New Testament, insisting – following St Polycarp's teaching – on the inclusion of the Gospel of St John and St Paul's Letters. He may have died as a martyr in the persecution of 202.

AUSTELL: Cornish sixth-century disciple of St Samson (28 July) and missionary companion with him and St Mewan (Meen) (21 June) to Brittany, where he died after founding a church at St Austell in Cornwall.

29th **PETER and PAUL**: Martyred in Rome in 64 and 67. Their stories and writings have already been described in Parts III and IV of this book. St Peter was believed by Bishop Papias in about 135 to have dictated much of St Mark's Gospel to him, when he acted as his secretary in Rome in c.62–64. St Paul (see Part IV) was the first great Christian theologian, as his Letters show. In these he tells and explains far more about the Holy Spirit than all four evangelists together.

30th **THE MARTYRS of ROME:** A feast-day to remember the 1,000 or more martyrs killed by order of Emperor Nero, who accused the Christians falsely of setting fire to Rome in 64.

MARTIAL of LIMOGES: One of the six bishops sent by Pope St Fabian (20 January) to evangelise Gaul in 250, just before the Emperor Decius began a severe persecution of the Christians throughout the empire.

Martial became Bishop of Limoges, where he reigned for nearly 40 years, the only one of the six bishops not to be martyred. He had many narrow escapes. There are many remarkable legends about the numerous marvels he achieved.

SUMMARY OF JUNE SAINTS

There are 53 saints in this Calendar, 24 were martyrs and 11 were women. The text that follows looks at the lives of **Cyril of Alexandria** and **St Thomas More**.

A CRITICAL VIEW OF ST CYRIL OF ALEXANDRIA AND ST THOMAS MORE

Cyril of Alexandria (380–440)

Cyril is highly regarded as a saint in the Greek Orthodox Church and was even made a Doctor of the Church by Pope Leo XIII in 1881, possibly in an attempt to please the estranged Orthodox community. There was another and far from saintly side to him which these Churches ignore. Like his uncle Theophilus, whom he succeeded as Archbishop of Alexandria, he was a fanatical Egyptian Nationalist and determined to challenge the power of the Byzantine influence of Constantinople and the theology of the Greek theologians of the learned school of Antioch. His deceitful scheming and discreditable actions in these matters have already been described in the letters of St Isidore of Pelusium in the February Calendar, who told Cyril that he was too worldly to be a monk and sent him back to his uncle the archbishop in Alexandria.

In addition to these faults and in spite of his popular sermons in his See of Alexandria, he roused the rabble of that city to such an extent that they committed the most atrocious crimes. These included the murder of the gracious female Neo-Platonist philosopher Hypatia, whom the mob sliced to death with sharpened shells. They also burned down Jewish synagogues together with their congregations. His uncharitable attack on Patriarch Nestorius of Constantinople caused a major split in the Church, which lost it the chance to evangelise from Mesopotamia to Mongolia – as Nestorius' followers succeeded in doing. Most damaging of all to the unity of the Greek Church was Cyril's suspect theology on the nature of Christ. He declared that Christ had only one nature, the divine, thus ignoring his humanity. Cyril eventually agreed to the two natures of Christ, after St Isidore of Pelusium had

admonished him (as we saw in the February Calendar). However Cyril wrote an equivocal letter on the subject to his bishops with the result that they refused to accept the orthodox two-nature view of Pope Leo I and the Council of Chalcedon in 451 and murdered the orthodox Archbishop of Alexandria. They then founded a monophysite church which spread through Palestine and much of Asia Minor.

The schism between the Orthodox Church and the Monophysites split the Byzantine Empire and was, together with the exiled Patriarch's Nestorian Church and the Jacobite Church that broke from it, the real legacy of St Cyril to the Greek Church. The Church eventually split into six rival Christian sects. It was therefore not surprising that Muhammad rejected Christianity and Jesus as Son of God in his search for the One God for his Arab people, even though he described the Virgin Mary reverently in his Koran as the Maid Mary to whose womb God had sent his Spirit. Thus, through the initial splits caused by Cyril, Islam became, as St John of Damascus was to describe it in the seventh century, an extreme form of Christian heresy.

Because of Cyril's record it is not easy to agree with Cardinal John Henry Newman's defence of Cyril, which dismissed his errors and deeds and maintained that *'we may hold Cyril a great servant of God, without considering ourselves obliged to defend certain passages of his ecclesiastical career'*. That seems too bland, because, as Cyril's record shows, those *'certain faults'* were grave and showed that Cyril had had none of the six heroic virtues later declared by the tenth-century popes to be essential for sainthood. Cyril's aims were probably as much political as doctrinal, as he wanted to free Egypt from the imperial control and taxes.

St Thomas More (1478–1535)

Thomas was without doubt a learned, able, devout and brave man, but he also, in his hide-bound and uncritical approach to every aspect of tradition, represented the one aspect in the religious debate of his time that made him blind to all the needs for reform, including the translation of the Bible into the vernacular.

This may seem unkind towards a truly great man, but greatness is not necessarily a saintly quality. He was a distinguished lawyer and judge, Speaker of the House of Commons, briefly Chancellor and friend of King Henry VIII and the famous author of *Utopia*, his ideal of a Christian state. He is also credited with being a Renaissance Man and the humanist friend of Erasmus of Rotterdam, who dedicated to him his own best-selling book *In Praise of Folly*, which mocked and criticised the monasteries and monks as being greedy, out of date and failing in their duties.

In spite of this literary association, More's humanism was only skin deep. His *Utopia* for instance, which is almost unreadable today, describes an extreme sacerdotal totalitarian state, such as we would abhor today and which exists in Iran. He could not accept any new ideas and was so infuriated by William Tyndale's English translation of the Bible that he published a tirade against it that was filled with half a million words of angry and petty objections to some of Tyndale's now most treasured words. As Chancellor he saw nothing wrong in having accused heretics brought for questioning to the cellars in his house in Chelsea which were equipped with instruments of torture.

His hidebound approach to tradition and his belief that the Church could not err, made it impossible for him to consider the case for any reforms in the Church. He believed that the Pope must be honoured as Christ's Vicar on earth, regardless of the way he behaved. So Thomas found himself defending a morally unchristian and fraudulent pope as the case for the King's divorce was debated. When the exasperated King finally threw off allegiance to the papacy and made himself supreme governor of the English Church, which was still to be Catholic, Thomas could not recognise the King as head of the Church. This was treason in the eyes of King Henry and so he suffered the supreme penalty on the scaffold.

He was given every chance to pay lip-service to Henry's claim to be Supreme Governor of the Church, as his wife and many others tried to persuade him to do. His refusal to do so, or to perjure himself, is greatly to his credit. He was one who never changed his mind on what he regarded as fundamental. This made his theology fall far short of the ideals expressed by St Victor of Lerins 1,000 years before, who, as we saw at the end of the February Calendar, had refused to accept that there could be no progress in religion.

Although we may criticise him for this attitude, we must admit that right to the end Thomas kept to his highest ideals and was true to himself, a *'man for all seasons'*. He deserves therefore our unqualified respect as a man who died for his faith as he saw it. The way the final decision came for Thomas was described in a short biography by his son-in-law William Roper, *The Mirror of Vertue in Worldly Greatness, or the Life of Sir Thomas More*. A copy of this belongs to my sister-in-law Charmian (née Roper), a direct descendant of William, who had married Thomas' daughter Margaret. The small book records William's conversation with Thomas after his examination by his judges at Lambeth, following Thomas' inclusion in the Parliamentary Bill of Attainder for Treason. William and Thomas were being rowed back to the family manor on the river bank in Chelsea (in what is now 'Roper's Gardens').

William's account begins with Thomas' final words to his judges, when he replied to their threats by saying: '"*My Lords, these terrors be arguments for children and not for me*". *Then took Sir Thomas More his boat toward his house at Chelsea, wherein by the way he was very merry, and for that I was nothing sorry, hoping he had gotten himself discharged from the Parliament bill. When he landed and come home, then walked we alone in his garden together, where I, desiring to know how he had sped, said: "I trust, Sir, that all is well because you are so merry". "It is so indeed, son Roper" quoth he. "I never remembered it!" – "Never remembered it!" said I; "A case that toucheth you so near, and us all for your sake! I am sorry to hear it, for I verily trusted, when I saw you so merry, that all had been well". Then said he "Wilt thou know, son Roper, why I am so merry?" "That would I gladly Sir", quoth I. "In good faith I rejoiced, son" said he, "that I had given the devil a foul fall, and that with those lords I had gone so far as without great shame I could never go back".'*

Even then there was a chance that he might not be beheaded for treason, because the King and the judges were debating whether to let Thomas off the death penalty on the grounds that he was, otherwise than over the oath, the most loyal of the King's servants. However '*at these words Queen Ann, by her importunate clamour, so sore exasperated the King, that, contrary to his former resolution, he caused the oath to be administered to Sir Thomas*', which he was bound to refuse to take, thus condemning himself to death. He simply said to William: '*Son Roper, I thank our Lord, the field is won*'. He had chosen death for his faith as he understood it. That decision reveals him as a saint and martyr of truly heroic virtue.

JULY SAINTS

1 St Oliver Plunkett
2 Visitation of The Blessed Virgin Mary
3 St Thomas the Apostle
11 St Benedict of Narsia
12 St Veronica
15 St Bonaventure
   St Swithun

16 St Helier
17 The Scillitan Martyrs
20 St Margaret
22 St Mary Magdalene
23 St Bridget of Sweden
   St Apollinaris of Ravenna
24 St Christine

St Christopher

25 St James (of Compostella)
   St Christopher
26 St Anne
27 St Celestine I
   St Pantaleon
29 St Olaf
31 St Neot
   St Ignatius of Loyola

St Bridget of Sweden

St Olaf King of Norway 1016

The three saints depicted in the heading for July are **St Christopher** (25 July), third-century martyr, popular as patron saint of travellers, but legendary; **King St Olaf of Norway** (29 July), Viking mercenary and eleventh-century martyr, buried at Trondheim Cathedral; **St Bridget (or 'Birgitta') of Sweden** (23 July), fourteenth-century visionary and monastic foundress who is shown demanding that Pope Clement VII return to Rome from Avignon and make peace between France and England.

ALTAR-PIECE DESIGN FOR TWENTY THREE JULY SAINTS

Shown in the central scene are:

Bonaventure (15 July), Franciscan theologian in Paris c.1255 preaching to St Louis XI and St Thomas Aquinas.

Shown from top left and round to the right are:

Silas or **Silvanus** (13 July), scribe for St Peter and St Paul; **Aaron** and **Julius** (1 July), and **Margaret** and **Christine** (20 and 24 July); **Prosper of Aquitaine** (7 July), fifth-century historian. **John Cassian** (23 July and also 29 February), fifth-century theologian and abbot; **Helier** (16 July), the martyr of Jersey in the Channel Islands; **Andrew of Crete** (4 July), eighth-century archbishop; **Edith of Tamworth** (15 July), **Modwenna** (6 July), tenth-century saint of Burton-on-Trent; **Rhiddian** (8 July), sixth-century priest on Gower Peninsular of Wales; the scene shows Druid standing stones around today's church. **Neot** (31 July) tending King Alfred who had been defeated by the Danes and burned the cakes! **Swithun** (15 July), ninth-century Bishop of Winchester, being buried. **Mildred** (13 July), seventh-century princess of Mercia and abbess; **Audrey** or **Ethelreda** (23 July), seventh-century Northumbrian royal widow, made Abbess of Ely by St Wifrid; **Emperor Henry II** (13 July) and **Ulric** or **Wulfric** (4 July), Bishop of Augsburg for 50 years, died in 973. First saint to be canonised under new papal criteria for the seven heroic saintly virtues.

Four tenth-century Russian Saints: **Princess Olga of Kiev** (11 July), her grandson **Prince Vladimir** (15 July) and his martyred sons **Boris** and **Gleb** (both 24 July).

Altar-piece design for twenty three July saints

189

ALTAR-PIECE DESIGN FOR TEN JULY SAINTS

Shown in the central scene are:

Benedict of Norcia (11 July), handing his rules for the conduct of his monks to his prior outside his abbey of Monte Cassino c.525.

In the scenes from top left to right are:

St **Thomas the Apostle** (3 July) seeing Jesus' wounds and also **St Thomas** taking the gospel to South India; **St James the Greater** (25 July) asleep with St Peter and his brother John, while Jesus experiences his Transfiguration. Also, the Cathedral of St James of Compostella. **St Veronica** (12 July), wiping Jesus' face on his way to be crucified; **St Mary Magdalen** (12 July), recognising the newly risen Christ; **St Martha** (29 July), serving Jesus and two apostles at Bethany; **St Victor** (21 July), died c.290, scene of his tomb near Marseilles; **Pope St Celestine I** (27 July), commissioning St Palladius in 431 to go on his abortive mission to evangelise Ireland; **St Germanus of Auxerre** (31 July), fifth century, consecrating St Patrick as a priest.

Altar-piece design for ten July saints

ILLUSTRATIONS OF FIVE MORE JULY SAINTS

In the top row are:

Elizabeth (Isabel) of Portugal (8 July) making peace between Portugal and Spain in 1336; **John of Nepomunk** (16 May), being thrown into the river in 1393 at Prague, chained in a sack, for allegedly refusing to report his Queen's confession to King Wenceslas IV.

In the middle row are:

Ignatius of Loyola (31 July) having a vision of the Trinity as a perfect three-note chord of music; Ignatius of Loyola writing his famous Spiritual Exercises.

In the bottom row are:

Oliver Plunkett (1 July), Catholic Archbishop of Dublin being condemned to death in 1681 for treason on the false evidence of Titus Oates; **Laurence of Brindisi** (21 July) leading the Emperor's troops against the Turks in Hungary in 1601.

Altar-piece design for five July saints

JULY CALENDAR OF SAINTS' FEAST-DAYS

1st **AARON and JULIUS**: British martyrs at Caerleon in Monmouthshire, mid-third-century.

JUNIPERO SERRA (1713–84): Spanish Franciscan missionary to Mexico and California. Beatified by Pope John-Paul II as the third American saint.

OLIVER PLUNKETT (1625–81): Archbishop of Armagh (Ireland), friend of Charles II's Queen Catherine of Braganza. Falsely charged with treason by Titus Oates, and hanged – a political murder.

2nd **BLESSED VIRGIN MARY**: Feast of the Visitation.

3rd **THOMAS the APOSTLE**: See the details of his life in Part III – 'The Apostles and Evangelists'. He is believed to have evangelised as far as South India.

4th **ULRIC of AUGSBURG** (890–973): Bishop for 50 years. First saint to be canonised under the papal rules for the need to have been heroic in all seven Saintly Virtues.

ELIZABETH (or Isabel) of PORTUGAL (1271–1336): Daughter of the King of Aragon, named after her distant relative St Elizabeth of Hungary (19 November).

She wed King Denis of Portugal at the age of 12. Very pious, she founded schools, hospitals and homes for fallen women. Personally intervened and prevented war between Portugal and Spain. Became a Franciscan Tertiary after her husband's death. Canonised in 1626.

ST. ATHANASIUS the ATHONITE (920–1003): Hermit of Trebizond who became first abbot of monks who had settled on Mount Athos in Greece.

MODWENNA: Seventh-century virgin hermit of Burton-on-Trent. May be identical to Irish St Monenna, who settled as a hermit in Scotland.

ANTONY ZACCARIA: Died in 1539, canonised 1897. Physician who became a priest to heal spiritually as well as physically. Founded the Barnabites in Milan.

6th **MARIE GORETTI** (1890–1912): Devout peasant girl of Ancona who was stabbed to death fiercely resisting a rapist. Made a saint in 1950 as a martyr for Charity. Her murderer became a monk after 27 years in jail and watched her canonisation.

7th **PROSPER of AQUITAINE** (390–445): Theologian and recorder of contemporary events in Gaul. Advised Pope Celestine I to send St Palladius (9 July) on his abortive mission to Ireland. Upheld St Augustine (28 August) on Grace and against Pelagianism.

8th **RHIDDIAN**: Welsh priest of the Gower peninsular in the sixth century. Established his church in a Druid circle of upstanding stones. The stones are still visible; they are shown in the illustration above.

9th **PALLADIUS**: Died in 432 after Pope Celstine I (27 July) sent him as first bishop to Ireland in that year. He failed to impress the southern Irish and may have died in Scotland.

10th **ALEXANDER**: Second century. One of seven martyred sons of St Felicity (23 November). She and her sons had refused to cast incense to the Roman gods.

ANTONY of the CAVES (983–1073): After living as a hermit in the Balkans and Athos he settled in a cave near Kiev. He attracted others, thus founding the first Russian monastery.

11th **BENEDICT of NORCIA** (480–547): Regarded as father of Eastern Monasticism at Monte Cassino after leaving Rome in disgust at its licentiousness. His *Rules for Conduct* of monastic life were based on those of St Pachomius (15 May) and the Desert Fathers; they later became the model for Western monasteries. The Benedictine Order and its related monastic orders became the engine for spreading Christianity.

OLGA (879–969): Princess of Kiev in Russia and wife of Prince Igor. After his murder in 957 she became a Christian and through Emperor Otto I she invited St Adalbert (20 June) to preach the gospel in Kiev. In spite of pagan opposition the Kievan Church was established on a sound basis by her grandson Prince Vladimir (15 July). Her great-grandsons Boris and Gleb (24 July) were murdered.

12th **VERONICA**: Legendary follower of Christ who is said to have wiped his face with a fine cloth as he carried his cross. Her name means 'True Image'. An ancient veil in Turin Cathedral has the image of a face – maybe that of Jesus. Veronica's action is depicted in all series of the 'Stations of the Cross' in Catholic churches.

JOHN the IBERIAN Died in 1002: A Georgian who founded the monastery on Mount Athos.

13th **SILAS (or Silvanus)**: With St Paul on his second missionary journey (Acts 16). He probably acted as his secretary, just as he also did for St Peter in Rome (Peter's 1st Letter).

MILDRED: Died c.700, the daughter of a Welsh prince and a Kentish princess. Educated in a French nunnery and became abbess of nunnery in Thanet, Kent.

HENRY II (973–1024): Taught by St Odilo of Cluny. Elected Holy Roman Emperor in 1014.

He made the German monarchy secure. On Odilo's advice he helped reform the Church. He and his Empress St Cunegond (3 March) encouraged the Benedictine style of monasteries.

FRANCIS SOLANO (1544–1610): Franciscan friar sent to evangelise Peru. He saved many slaves from drowning when his ship foundered. He had great success with Indians and Negroes.

14th CAMILLUS (1550–1615): Italian soldier and gambler who was converted by a sermon in 1575. Shocked at the state of hospitals in Rome, he founded the lay Servants of the Sick. He was helped by St Philip Neri (26 May).

NICODEMUS of the HOLY MOUNTAIN (1748–1810): Greek scholar and monk of Athos. Produced the *Philokalia* in 1792 to record the spiritual writings of the Early Fathers. Canonised in 1955 by the Greek Orthodox Church.

15th SWITHUN: Died in 862. Bishop of Winchester and adviser to Saxon kings. Out of humility he insisted on being buried half inside and half outside the cathedral porch. A violent thunder storm broke out as he was buried. This led to the well-known belief that if it rains on this day it will rain for 40 days!

EDITH of TAMWORTH: Tenth-century English nun, probably a royal princess.

VLADIMIR (955–1015): Prince of Kiev and grandson of St Olga (11 July). Was baptised in 989 in order to wed a Byzantine princess. He then gave up his dissolute life to impose Christianity on Kiev. He was generous to the poor, mild to criminals. He is regarded with St Olga as one of the founders of the Russian Orthodox Church.

BONAVENTURE (1221–74): Italian Franciscan contemporary at Paris University of the Dominicans St Albert (15 November) and St Thomas Aquinas (28 January) during the reign of King St Louis IX (14 August).

Followed traditional church approach of St Augustine (28 August) to Plato's philosophy in contrast to Albert and Thomas' teaching of the soul developed from Plato's pupil Aristotle. They were all friends of St Louis. Bonaventure became Master General of the Franciscans and reorganised the order so that it could own property.

16th HELIER: Sixth century. Born in Belgium. Became hermit on Isle of Jersey, where he was murdered by pirates. The island's capital is named after him.

BLESSED KATHERINE TEKAKWITHA (1656–80): Made local saint in USA by John-Paul II, the first North American Indian saint. Her Algonquin mother had been baptised at Three Rivers, Quebec, but was taken by raiding Iroquois to New York and espoused to a Mohawk chief. She produced a daughter, Katherine, whom she brought up as a Christian. Jesuit priests helped Katherine to escape to Montreal after suffering from smallpox, so that she could safely practice her Christian faith. She dedicated herself as a virgin to Christ and lived a life of austerity and charity, dying bravely of a chest disease. Her example led to a strong revival of religious fervour among Christian Indians.

RAINELD: Sister of St Gudula (8 June). Martyred in pirate raid on Saintes in 680.

17th THE SCILLIUM MARTYRS: c.180. Seven men and five women carrying satchels containing St Paul's letters were arrested at Scillium in North Africa. They refused to deny Christ and were beheaded immediately. Theirs is the earliest such record or 'Acta'.

NARSES the FIRST (326–74): Bishop of Armenia and father of St Isaac the Great (9 September). Trained at Caesarea, St Basil's see. May have died of poison after rebuking local Armenian king.

ALEXIS: Holy beggar who died in Eddessa (Syria) in c.430. It was then found that he was the son of a Roman patrician who had left his rich wife on their wedding day after an unwanted marriage. He went to live in Syria to share his alms with the poor. A popular legend in the middle ages.

KENELM: Died in 811. Heir to Saxon king of Mercia, but murdered by his sister at the age of seven after his father's death. Regarded as a martyr in the middle ages.

18th ARNULF of METZ (582–641): Although a layman and courtier he was made Bishop of Metz. Became tutor to Frankish King Dagobert. Arnulf's son wed St Begga (17 December), daughter of Pepin of Landen. Through her he was therefore an ancestor of the Carolingian dynasty. He retired to a monastery in the Vosges.

19th MACRINA the YOUNGER (327–79): Elder sister of St Basil (1 January) and St Gregory of Nyssa (9 March), whom she influenced strongly to become Christian after their schooling in Athens. She led a religious community in Pontus (Turkey). Her grandmother St Macrina the Elder and her mother St Emmelia are both regarded as Greek saints.

20th MARGARET of ANTIOCH: No date. Legendary virgin martyred for refusing to wed a pagan governor. A popular cult developed around her in the middle ages.

WILGEFORTIS (or 'Uncumber'): No date. Legendary patroness of unhappy wives. Sworn to virginity she is said to have grown a beard to avoid a forced marriage. Her angry father crucified her. Her name 'Uncumber' means to get rid of, and it was given to her as she was venerated by wives wishing to get rid of cruel or tiresome husbands. The best-known statue of her was put up by King Henry VIII in the chapel he built his father Henry VII in Westminster Abbey. She is portrayed complete with beard.

21st VICTOR: A soldier martyred c.290 near Marseilles. His tomb became a popular place of pilgrimage in Gaul.

LAURENCE of BRINDISI (1559–1610): Capuchin monk born in Brindisi, Italy. An expert linguist, he carried out many semi-diplomatic and preaching tasks for the Vatican and his order. Pope Clement VIII sent him to convert Jews in Italy. He then established the Capuchin reform in Germany, Prague and Vienna. The Emperor Rudolf II commissioned him to unite the German princes against the Turks and as the army chaplain-general he led the troops into battle in 1601 armed only with a cross. He was made papal legate to Spain and founded the Capuchins in Madrid. He died in Lisbon on a mission to have the Spanish viceroy in Naples replaced and for help to be sent to the oppressed poor Neapolitans. Canonised in 1881, he was made an Apostolic Doctor by Pope John-Paul II in 1959. His shrine at Brindisi attracts many pilgrims.

22nd MARY MAGDALENE: Christ's follower who anointed his feet before the Last Supper and met the Risen Christ in the garden outside the Tomb.

23rd JOHN CASSIAN: His Western Feast-day, see story under Greek day, 29 February.

APOLLINARIS of RAVENNA: Early bishop and martyr stoned to death by a mob. Famous sixth-century churches in Ravenna were dedicated to him and have beautiful mosaics on the walls.

BRIDGET of SWEDEN (1303–73): See story above (under chapter heading).

24th CHRISTINA: Early fourth-century virgin martyr at Bolsena, Tuscany, Italy. Also a Greek: St Christina of Tyre. The first may be legendary. The legends of both say she died after torture.

BORIS and GLEB: Younger sons of Prince St Vladimir of Kiev. Devout Christians murdered in 1015 by their elder half-brother to secure his succession to Vladimir.

25th JAMES the GREATER: Apostle and brother of St John, these 'sons of Zebedee' were nicknamed 'sons of thunder' by Jesus for their youthful boisterousness. The brothers were taken by Jesus to witness his Transfiguration. James was beheaded by Herod Agripa II in 44, the first apostle to die for the faith (see Acts 12.2). In the eighth century his relics were claimed to have been translated miraculously to Compostella in Spain, which as Santiago de Compostella became a famous place for great pilgrimages in the middle ages from all over Europe, and still is. Charlemagne campaigned three times in Spain to save the shrine from the Saracens.

CHRISTOPHER: Martyr of unknown date. His legend tells how he carried a child across a ford, but found it became so heavy that he could hardly move. The child then said to him: *'You have been carrying the whole world, because I am Jesus Christ, the king you seek'.*

26th JOACHIM and ANNA: Believed to have been the parents of the Virgin Mary.

BARTHOLOMEA CAPITANO and VINCENTIA GEROSA (1807–33 and 1774–1847): Founded together the Sisters of Charity of Lovere, their home in Lombardy, to teach young girls to be nurses along the principles of St Vincent de Paul (27 September). Canonised 1950 after their foundation had spread widely.

27th PANTALEON: Died in 304 in Bythinia. A phial of his blood is at Ravello, south of Naples. It liquifies like that of St Januarius (29 September).

POPE CELESTINE I: Elected Pope in 422, died in 432. Joined St Augustine of Hippo in condemning the British monk Pelagius' heresy that we can achieve salvation by good works because God's grace is innate within us. He also agreed with St Cyril of Alexandria that Patriarch Nestorius was wrong to refer to the Virgin Mary as 'Mother of Christ' instead of 'Mother of God'. He did not support Cyril's extremist measures against Nestorius. He sent St Palladius (7 July) to Ireland in 431, where he failed to win converts.

AURELIUS and NATALIA: Martyred in 852 in Cordoba, Spain, for being converted from Islam.

28th SAMSON (480–565): Educated and ordained by St Illtyd (6 November) in the Gower

Peninsular of Wales. Abbot of Caldey Island, then evangelised in Cornwall. A vision caused him and St Kew (8 February) and St Asustell (28 June) to sail to Brittany, where Samson built a monastery at Dol. He became a bishop and signed himself 'Samson, sinner and bishop' on a document at the Council of Paris in 557.

29th MARTHA: Sister of Lazarus and Mary, Jesus' friends at Bethany. See John 11 and l2 and Luke 10. Patron of housekeepers and lay sisters. It was to her that Jesus said '*I am the resurrection and the life*', after she had confessed to him '*I believe that thou art the Christ, the Son of God*'.

SIMPLICIUS, FAUSTINA and BEATRICE: Martyred in Rome in c.304.

LUPUS of TROYES (383–479): Married the sister of St Hilary of Poitiers (13 January) and became a monk in St Honorius' community on the Isle of Lerins, off Cannes. He may have met St Patrick (17 March) there, or possibly with St Germanus of Auxerre (31 July), whom he accompanied to Britain in 428 to deal with the Pelagian heresy. He became Bishop of Troyes and was an important influence in Gaul during the Barbarian invasions in the fifth century.

KING OLAF of NORWAY (995–1030): Viking mercenary who made himself king of Norway, but was defeated by the Anglo-Danish King Cnut. He was killed trying to regain his throne and was buried as a martyr in Trondheim Cathedral.

30th PETER CHRYSTOLOGOS: c.400. Bishop of Ravenna, who tried to make the controversial Abbot Eutyches of Constantinople see sense before the Council of Chalecedon in 451 and accept the classic orthodox definition of the nature of Christ promulgated by Pope St Leo – that He had two natures in harmony, Divine and Human. Eutyches' single-nature heresy was condemned at the Council. Peter influenced the Empress Galla Placida who built the lovely church of St John at Ravenna. He was made a Doctor of the Church in 1727.

31st NEOT: Ninth-century hermit in Cornwall, associated with King Alfred's burned cakes.

GERMANUS of AUXERRE (373–448): A married Gallo-Roman lawyer, who was made Bishop of Auxerre against his will in 418. May have taken St Patrick (17 March) with him as a protector on his journey from Lerins through the lines of the invading Visigoths and Burgundians to Auxerre in c.420.

Germanus twice visited Britain – in 428 and 434 – to quell the Pelagian heresy. According to St Bede (25 May), he led the British forces in 434 and set up the ambush where they defeated a Pictish and Saxon raid.

IGNATIUS of LOYOLA (1491–1556): The founder of the Society of Jesus – 'The Jesuits'. His mystical experiences, his struggle to educate himself and achieve papal recognition for his Society eventually had an immense impact on the Roman Church and the world.

Ignatius gained widespread and powerful support for his missionaries and educators both in Europe and overseas. When he died a magnificent baroque church, 'The Jesu', was built by his Order in Rome, complete with a glorious painting of his apotheosis in the dome. He is so important that a longer text on his life is given below, after this Calendar.

SUMMARY OF JULY SAINTS

This Calendar gives the feast-days of 67 saints, of whom 20 were martyrs and 21 were women. In the text that follows I look at the life and work of **St Ignatius of Loyola.**

ST IGNATIUS OF LOYOLA (1491–1556)

Ignatius was a Basque nobleman, born at his family home of Loyola in Spain. As a young man he became a soldier and sought glory in battle. He was so badly wounded in his leg while defending Pamplona in 1519, that he was forced to retire home and stay there many months during which he made a very slow recovery, but was lamed for life. During this time, as he records in his autobiography, he sought consolation by reading the only two books in his family's castle of Loyola. One of these was a life of Jesus and the other was on the lives of the martyrs.

As Ignatius meditated on these he gradually underwent a complete personality change and became a born-again Christian. Hitherto he had been inspired by a romantic ideal to emulate only military heroes, but now, although only 28 years old and too disabled to fight as a soldier, he began to experience a long period of darkness of the soul. At first he felt he was incomplete and imperfect, both physically and morally. Then after meditating for several months, he realized that his way forward was to seek glory in a different way, by dedicating his life to the service of Christ.

He had no clear idea as to how he would do this, except that he must begin by giving up everything connected with his previous life-style. Ignatius therefore abandoned his fine clothing, adopted a pilgrim garb and made his way to Montserrat on the borders of Catalonia. There he established himself as a hermit in a cave by a river. For a year he starved himself rigorously, though he was sometimes given food and shelter by some kind ladies who lived in a town nearby.

Perhaps as a result of his starving himself he began to have terrible dreams and also many visions. All the time he thought about the life and Passion suffered by Jesus and experienced several remarkable visions of the Trinity. In one of these he saw the Trinity explained to him as three harmonious notes of a chord of music. He had many mystical visions later in life, including one on his way to see Pope Pius III in Rome in 1537 in which he saw Christ and the Eternal Father and heard the Father say to the Son: '*I wish you to take this man for your servant*'.

Before this Ignatius had, in his spiritual experiences in his cave, gone through the threefold process common to mystics of all faiths during their periods of prayer. These are self-purification, illumination and realisation or moment of union with the ultimate reality, God.

With his faith strengthened and enlightened in this way, Ignatius took the most original and important practical steps that would lead him to his future way of life. He achieved this after long and deep thought in which he concentrated his mind on Christ's Passion. He then analysed the images that came to him again and again during these meditations, which he treated as a method of training himself and he wrote the first draft of what later became his *Spiritual Exercises*. These helped him to strengthen his faith and to broaden his understanding of what the gospel meant as a way of life.

The *Spiritual Exercises* became the cornerstone for his whole approach and that of his future followers in their service of Christ. The exercises are designed for three weeks' study and contemplation. They are still followed today not only by Roman Catholics, but also by adherents of other Churches. They lay down a discipline which has to be followed privately for several weeks at a time. Their aim is to teach the meaning of Salvation by experiencing in meditation every detail of Christ's Passion, so as to compass the whole meaning of his suffering and resurrection. This requires serious effort by the individual who is undertaking these exercises, but it helps to concentrate the mind and enable the individual to broaden his or her understanding and greatly to strengthen faith.

This kind of exercise and meditation can and should be applied by anyone, not necessarily Roman Catholic, who sincerely wishes to examine their faith. The fact to remember is that faith does not often come without working at it. It is perhaps therefore not out of place to point out here that this is as true of one's relationship with God as it is true for relationships between husband and wife. Marriages are only truly happy and successful if one works at them. Thus all happily married couples know that if one party makes a serious effort, then love will ensure that the other partner will respond and they will become closer than ever before.

So also in spiritual relations, if one takes a step forward, then God, through his love for us, will respond by also taking a step to meet one and one finds that one's faith and understanding make a leap forward.

Ignatius left Spain to make a pilgrimage to Jerusalem, but found that his calling was not to the Holy Land. He returned to Spain, studied in Barcelona and there he practiced his urge to evangelise. This drew the attention of the Inquisition and he was arrested and questioned. The Dominican Inquisitors found nothing diabolical in his experiences, but they advised him to study more academically in a university. He therefore made his way slowly to Paris to study for a Master's degree.

In Paris he met four other mature students who were approaching their studies like him as mystics. One of these students was the future St Francis Xavier (see 3 December). Having found that they were all of a like mind, Ignatius and these four men then bound themselves to a private order, dedicating themselves to Poverty, Charity and Obedience and called themselves 'The Company of Jesus'. With Ignatius as leader and having added three more to their numbers, they adopted a military style and a spiritual aim – to serve Christ.

After further pilgrimages, during which Ignatius gathered more companions, the little party of seven men went to Rome to dedicate their Society of Jesus to serve Pope Pius III and all future popes in their struggle for the Catholic faith and against the Reformers and Protestants. Pope Pius realised, after questioning Ignatius, that his 'Company' was just the kind of organisation that he wanted to help him embark on what was to become the Roman Catholic Church's counter-reformation. In 1540 therefore Pope Pius III gave Ignatius his permission to found the Society of Jesus, whose members were soon to be known to the world as 'Jesuits'.

Ignatius established the Society's headquarters in Rome and was allowed by the Pope to draw up its constitution. Ignatius soon found men of all classes to join him and they raised the substantial sums of money that would be needed to prepare his missionary activities throughout Europe and to the furthest corners of the world.

Starting in 1547, the Jesuits founded schools and university lectureships. Their order became the greatest educationalists for the Church, insisting on the highest standards of leaning. They had to face many opponents in high places, who resented the influence they had on kings and governments. This is not the place to write a history of the Order, but there is no doubt that the beneficial influence of Ignatius, with his compelling personality and ability to make friends, had an incalculable effect on the Roman Catholic Church. That was not all he achieved, because his *Spiritual Exercises* were published in every land and became the means by which men and women from almost every other Church benefited spiritually. Ignatius is famous for this prayer, whose ideals he fulfilled himself: *'Teach us, good Lord, to serve you as you deserve; to give and not to count the cost; to fight and not to heed the wounds; to toil and not to ask for any reward, save that of knowing that we do your will'.*

AUGUST SAINTS

1 Lammas Day
St Ethelwuld
2 Basil the Blessed
5 St Sixtus II
6 Transfiguration; St Dominic
9 St Oswald of Northumberland
10 St Lawrence

St Lawrence

12 St Clare
13 St Hippolytus
15 Assumption of The Blessed Virgin Mary
16 St Roch
20 St Bernard of Clairvaux
22 St Pius X
24 St Symphuria St Bartholemew

25 St Louis of France
26 St Elizabeth Bichier des Ages
27 St Monica
28 St Augustine of Hippo
29 Beheading of John the Baptist
31 St Aidan of Landisfarne

St Louis IX
1207-1270

St Clare

The saints depicted in the decorative heading for the August Calendar are **St Lawrence** (10 August), third-century martyr being grilled alive to reveal the Church's treasure in Rome; **St Clare of Assisi** (11 August), devoted admirer of St Francis, having a vision on the eve of her death and in which she both saw and heard Christ; **King St Louis IX of France** (25 August), the only saint of the Crusades, about to embark at Aigues Mortes in the Camargue for the sixth Crusade in 1248.

ALTAR-PIECE DESIGN FOR ELEVEN AUGUST SAINTS

Shown in the central scene:

The Conversion of **St Augustine of Hippo** (28 August), in a garden in Milan in 387.

In the scenes from top left and round to the right are:

Bartholemew (24 August), like St Thomas he is believed to have evangelised in India; **Pope Sixtus II** (5 August) being martyred by the catacombs on the Appian Way in 257; **Susan** (11 August), martyred in Diocletian's baths in Rome in the third century.

Symphorian (22 August), being flogged to death in c.200 before the statue of Cybele. **Julian of Brioude** (28 August), patron saint of the Auvergne, martyr, evangelising peasants in the hills; **Empress St Helena** (18 August), wife of Constantine I, discovering the true cross in c.320; **Moses the Black** (28 August) being baptised in Egypt.

Caesarius of Arles (27 August) presiding over the Council of Orange in 529; **Basil The Blessed** (2 August) Russian eccentric playing the part of being a 'Fool for God', stealing a pair of shoes to give to a beggar; **Bishop Sidonius Apollinaris** (21 August), defending the walls of Arvernum (Clermont-Ferrand) against the Visigoths in 475.

Design for an altar-piece for eleven August saints

AN ALTAR-PIECE DESIGN FOR TEN AUGUST SAINTS

Shown in the central scene are:

St Dominic (7 August) meeting St Francis of Assisi in 1216 at St Anselm's monastery on the Aurelian Hill, Rome.

In the scenes from top left and round to the right are:

St Aidan of Lindisfarne (31 August) being given his monastery by **King St Oswald of Northumbria** (9 August) in 635. **St Bernard of Clairvaux** (20 August) planning one of the 68 Cistercian monasteries that he founded in the eleventh century; **King St Stephen of Hungary** (16 August) forcing peasants to become Christians in 1001.

Cardinal Cajetan (8 August), founder of the Theatine Order, teaching peasants in Naples after Rome had been sacked in 1527. **Rose of Lima** (23 August) giving presents to her newly baptised Indians in Peru, c.1660.

Alphonsus Liguori (1 August), founder of the Redemptorists, preaching c.1740; **Elizabeth Bichier des Anges** (26 August) leading peasants to her secret place of worship during the French Revolution c.1792; **Emily de Vialar** (24 August), and her home for orphaned children in Languedoc, c.1832.

Altar-piece design for ten August saints

205

AUGUST CALENDAR OF SAINTS' FEAST-DAYS

1st **ALPHONSUS LIGUORI** (1696–1787): Neapolitan lawyer ordained in 1726. Founded Redemptorists to preach to rural poor. Wrote *Moral Theology* which aimed, as did his preaching, at simplicity and gentleness. He held the view that when faced with a moral choice, it is right to choose the milder of the most probable solutions. Canonised in 1839.

ETHELWOLD of WINCHESTER (908–84): Bishop, who began his career as a monk at Glastonbury helping Archbishop St Dunstan in his renewal of the English Church. A tireless reformer who ejected secular clergy from Winchester cathedral and replaced them with monks. Translated St Benedict's 'Rules' into English for those who knew no Latin.

2nd **EUSEBIUS of VECELLI** (283–371): Bishop persecuted by Arian heretics in 355 and driven from his see. He was later restored.

BASIL the BLESSED: Died in 1532. Russian eccentric (see the illustration above). He made himself *'a fool for Christ's sake . . . that he may become wise'* (I Corinthians 3.18). As a shoemaker's apprentice he stole shoes to give to the poor. He got away with this and also even when he criticised Tsar Ivan the Terrible to his face. A church is dedicated to him in the Kremlin in Moscow.

3rd **PETER EYMARD**: Died in 1868. Canonised in 1962. A friend of St Jean-Baptiste Vianney (4 August), who encouraged him to found the Priests of the Blessed Sacrament in Paris for sisters and lay people.

4th **JEAN-BAPTISTE VIANNEY** (known as 'the Curé d'Ars') (1786–1859): Peasant of Lyons, slow to learn, but became parish priest from 1818–59 of the remote village of Ars-en-Dombes. He astonished everyone by becoming a gifted preacher and curer of souls who attracted thousands of pilgrims seeking his advice. He was an outstanding example of the revived post-revolutionary and post-Napoleonic French Church. Canonised in 1925 and made patron saint of parish clergy in 1929. He is remembered for his miraculous supply of grain during a famine.

5th **POPE SIXTUS II**: Martyred in 258 while preaching in the Appian Way catacomb.

AFRA: Martyred in Augsburg in 304 during Diocletian's persecution. She was allegedly a reformed prostitute. A second St Afra or 'Abbre' was the daughter of St Hilary of Poitiers (January 13). Her tomb, c.400, in the cathedral of St Hilaire is decorated with a sculpture of the 'Green Man', the pagan and Christian symbol of death and rebirth.

6th **FEAST of the TRANSFIGURATION.**

7th **VICTRICIUS**: Roman soldier friend of St Martin of Tours (11 November). Like him he refused to serve any more after his conversion. He was then almost flogged to death as a punishment. Made Bishop of Rouen in 385. Sent to Britain in 395 to sort out church problems. He may be the same 'Victricius' whom St Patrick recorded seeing in a dream encouraging him to evangelise in Ireland (see Patrick's life-story in the March Calendar).

CYRIACUS and JULITTA: Martyrs c.303.

HORMIDZ: Persian martyred in 422. Son of a city governor. He was a convert from the official Zoroastrianism.

DOMINIC GUZMAN (1170–1221): Spanish founder of the Dominican Order of teaching friars in 1216 with the blessing of Pope Innocent III. He was inspired to do this through his experiences during the Albigensian Crusade against the Cathars in the South of France and the Pyrenees. He saw the need to convert them from their heresy by good example rather than by a mixture of precept and force. Their Christian heresy was a belief in a dual system in the universe of two first principles, a good God aloof from the world and an evil power in control of all matter, from whom salvation can be obtained through the Holy Spirit. Dominic's method of founding centres of sacred learning with small groups of 'Friars Preachers' were successful in winning over the hearts and minds of the people, which the sieges and brutality of the so-called 'crusade' failed to do. Dominic's order approached their teaching in a more intellectual way than the Franciscan friars and established themselves in the leading European university cities. Their most famous early adherents were St Albert of the Rhine, or 'The Great' (15 November), and St Thomas Aquinas (28 January). From the mid-thirteenth-century onwards the Dominicans were used by the popes to direct the newly-founded Inquisition.

8th **CAJETAN** (1480–1547): Founded the Order of Theatines. Prominent theologian at the Council of Trent of 1545. Not to be confused with the Cardinal who interviewed Luther.

9th **KING OSWALD of NORTHUMBRIA** (602–42): Converted by the monks of Iona, St Columba's foundation, while exiled from his kingdom. He won his kingdom back in 633 and summoned St Aidan (8 October) from Iona to evangelise his people. Killed in battle by the pagan King Penda of Mercia, he died praying for his killers.

10th LAURENCE: Martyred in Rome in 258. As the archivist and treasurer of the Church he was arrested and ordered to hand over the treasure. He produced a crowd of children, sick and old people for whom the Church cared and said: *'This is our treasure'*. In spite of being grilled alive he never gave his secret away.

TIBERTIUS and SUSANNA: Third-century martyrs – he on the Via Lavicana near Rome and Susanna near Diocletian's baths. Sixth-century churches are dedicated to both in Rome. Legend alleges that Susanna refused to marry the Emperor Maximian.

ATTRACTA: Fifth-century Irish nun said to have been given the veil by St Patrick. She founded a hospice for travellers by Lough Gara which survived until King Henry VIII's dissolution of the monasteries destroyed it in 1539.

11th SUSAN or Susannah: Legendary martyr buried near Diocletian's baths, Rome.

CLARE of ASSISI (1194–53): As described in the note on the illustrated heading for this month, she was devoted to Francis of Assisi, who helped her found the enclosed Order of Poor Clares.

THE BLESSED CARDINAL JOHN HENRY NEWMAN (1809–90): Anglican clergyman, leader of the High Church Oxford Movement, poet and theologian who became a Roman Catholic in mid-life (1845). He became head of the Oratorians in England and the most influential Catholic theologian of the nineteenth century. His greatest works, apart from his hymn *'Lead, Kindly Light'* and his poem about a soul going to heaven, *'The Dream of Gerontius'*, were his *Grammar of Assent* on the concept of the Church as a developing faith and his explanation of his conversion to Rome, *Apologia pro Vita Sua*.

Powerful leaders of the Catholic Church in Rome and England mistrusted him, however, and he regarded Pope Pius IX's declaration of papal infallibility as unhistorical and a 'luxury item'. However he was made a cardinal by Pope Leo XIII in 1879. His theology, showing that Christianity is a developing faith, had a profound influence on the Second Vatican Council of 1959–63. He was made one of the 'Blessed' by the late Pope John-Paul II in 1998. His life and works are reviewed in Part VII of this book, 'The Unquenchable Spirit'.

12th MURTAGH: First Bishop of Killala. Either a convert of St Patrick or of St Columba according to rival legends.

JAMBERT: Died in 892. Archbishop of Canterbury who resisted King Offa's demand to make Lichfield in the Danish part of the kingdom the chief see of the Church.

13th POPE PONTIAN and HIPPOLYTUS: Martyred in the Sicilian salt-mines in 235. Previously in Rome, Hippolytus, an able theologian, had had a fierce dispute with Pope Pontian for being too lenient with sinners. They made up their quarrel in the mines.

CASSIAN of IMOLA: Martyr of unknown early date who was allegedly stabbed to death with iron pens by his pupils. Similar legend for St Mark of Arethusa (29 March).

RADEGUND (518–87): Christian victim kidnapped in Thuringia and forced to be Queen of the Frankish King Chlotar I. He killed her brother and she fled to Poitiers. There she founded a nunnery. She was renowned for her charity, self-denial, humility and sweetness.

MAXIMUS the CONFESSOR (580–662): Theologian and abbot. Dedicated supporter of Pope Martin I against the Monothelite Heresy which the Byzantine emperor tried to force upon the Church. Maximus and Pope Martin (13 April) were both martyred cruelly after staged trials in Constantinople. Maximus' life and teaching is described in the text following this Calendar.

FLORENCE NIGHTINGALE (1820–1910): English lady who, at the age of 17, had heard the voice of God call her to serve him. She wanted to become a hospital nurse, but her parents refused to allow her to do so. After years of frustration she was allowed in 1851 to begin two years' training as a nurse with the Protestant deaconesses at Kaiserwerth in Germany. In 1853 she was asked to reorganise the hospital in Harley Street in London for the Institution of Sick and Distressed Gentlewomen.

She succeeded brilliantly and because of this she was invited by her life-long friend Sidney Herbert, Secretary for War, to sort out the terrible conditions in the British military hospitals in the Crimea. She selected 38 nurses to go there with her in 1854 and, famously, went on to create order out of chaos. She revolutionised hospital nursing and the way wounded private soldiers were treated. She devoted the rest of her life to this work and was awarded the Order of Merit in 1907.

14th MAXIMILIAN KOLBE (1894–1941): Polish Franciscan theologian who was martyred in Auschwitz concentration camp, having voluntarily exchanged himself to die in a punishment and starvation cell instead of another prisoner, who was a family man. He was canonised as a martyr for charity in 1982. His statue is one of the ten statues of twentieth-century martyrs from five Christian denominations erected above the door of Westminster Abbey in 1998. These are illustrated in Part VII, where his life-story is also told.

15th FEAST of the ASSUMPTION of the VIRGIN MARY.

16th ARMEL: Died in 552. Abbot in Wales, related to St Samson. He went with him to Brittany and founded monasteries there and in Normandy, Anjou and Touraine.

ROCH (ROCK or 'San Rocco') (1350–80): Son of rich merchant of Montpelier he spent his life as a pilgrim and hermit. In Italy he caught the plague but was cured after being fed by a dog in the woods near Piacenza. Roch then cured many other victims. No one believed him on his return home and he was murdered as an imposter. His story seized popular imagination and he was much venerated in France and Italy by those seeking cures.

KING STEPHEN of HUNGARY (975–1038): Converted by St Adelbert of Prague (23 April), he brought order to Hungary and was crowned King by Pope Sylvester II in 1001. He established monasteries and bishoprics throughout Hungary after widespread forced conversions. He was killed while out hunting.

17th HYACINTH of CRACOW (1185–1257): Dominican friar from Silesia who became the Apostle to pagan Poland, Lithuania and parts of Scandinavia and Russia.

18th FLORUS and LAURUS: Martyred by Licinius in 313 in Dalmatia.

HELENA (255–330): Empress and mother of Constantine I, 'the Great'. Became a Christian in 312. Claimed to have excavated the true cross at Golgotha. This alleged relic became the Eastern Church's most precious possession and splinters of it were put into literally thousands of altar crosses. Her favourite saint was St Lucian (7 January in the West and 15 October in the East). He was the originator of the heresy which his pupil the monk Arius spread and which nearly destroyed the Orthodox Catholic faith from 318 onwards. Lucian recanted his heretical view, but Helena's leaning toward him may account partly for the reason why she and Constantine were so tolerant towards Arius and his followers and restored them after they were exiled at the Council of Nicaea in 325.

19th LOUIS of TOULOUSE (1274–97): Son of the King of Naples and related to King St Louis IX of France (25 August). He renounced his claim to become King of Naples to become a Franciscan. Pope Boniface VIII made him Bishop of Toulouse despite his youth, but he died almost at once. He summed up his 'call' to serve Christ instead of becoming a king by saying these words: *'Jesus Christ is my kingdom. If I possess him alone, I shall have all things. If I have him not, I lose all'*.

JOHN EUDES (1601–80): Jesuit of Caen who worked with St Philip Neri (26 May) in Rome among the sick for 20 years. He founded homes for fallen women and Eudist schools for priests. His preaching was aimed at captivating people's hearts. In this he spread devotion to the Sacred Heart founded by St Margaret Mary Alacoque (17 October).

20th AMADOUR: Hermit of unknown date whose tomb was found in a cave on the steep cliff-side of Rocamadour in central France. He is the legendary founder of the shrine there of Our Lady of Rocamadour, to which pilgrims still flock.

KING OSWIN: Died in 651. St Bede (25 May) describes him as the virtuous Christian cousin of King St Oswald of Northumbria (8 October) and notes that he won the affection of all who met him. Murdered by his cousin and rival King Oswy. He was the devoted friend of St Aidan of Lindisfarne (31 August), the Celtic apostle of Northumberland. Oswin was regarded as a martyr in Northumbria.

PHILIBERT: Died in 684. Influenced by St Ouen (24 August) he built the abbey of Jumieges on land given by Clovis II. He denounced the mayor of the royal palace for his misdeeds, who imprisoned him. After the mayor's death he built more monasteries.

BERNARD of CLAIRVAUX (1090–1153): As a devout 23-year-old noble he became a monk at Citeaux. He was a man of immense energy and great spirituality, devoted to the Virgin Mary and a dedicated supporter of the traditional theology which ignored philosophy and the 'Scholastic' approach of St Anselm (21 April), his older contemporary. He is famous for his quarrel with and ruthless condemnation of the brilliant theologian and monk Peter Abelard. Bernard personally designed or had built literally hundreds of Benedictine monasteries throughout Europe. He had one great failure; with misguided idealism he supported vigorously the launching of the disastrous second Crusade in a campaign all through France and Germany. His teaching and record will be described in the text following this Calendar.

21st POPE PIUS X (1835–1914): He was canonised by Pope Pius XII in 1954. It is difficult to understand the reasons for his exaltation. He was a dedicated opponent of Modernism, the movement in the Church that tried to relate traditional Catholic faith to modern discoveries of science and also to the now widely accepted discoveries of the German schools of higher biblical criticism. He suppressed the biblical research and teaching in France of many scholars like Pere Pouget (see under St Mark in Part II).

SIDONIUS APOLLINARIS (432–82): A Gallic noble who entered the state service of Rome. As the barbarian tribes began to invade the empire he was made bishop of Avernum in Gaul (Clermont-Ferrand) in 470. He struggled to keep his see Christian and Catholic in spite of being made a prisoner by the Arian Visigoths, whose attack on his capital he tried bravely to resist. His published letters, though vain and flowery, give an interesting picture of provincial life in those disturbed times.

ABRAHAM of SMOLENSK: Died in 1221. Learned Russian monk and abbot, sternly conscious that the Day of Judgement awaits us all. His monks resented his severe rule and deposed him on false charges of immorality. Five years later his case was reviewed and he was acquitted. He was canonised by the Russian Church in 1549.

22nd SYMPHORIAN: Third-century martyr at Autun in Gaul, for refusing to worship the goddess Cybele, c.200.

23rd ROSE of LIMA (1586–1617): Spanish Dominican nun born in Peru. First person born in the New World to be made a saint (1671). Her mystical experiences aroused the suspicion of the Spanish Inquisition, but she survived to give great help to the neglected Indians and slaves. She is honoured today as the founder of social services in Peru.

PHILIP BENIZI (1223–85): A Paduan physician and philosopher who became head of the Servite Order in Siena. Sent missionaries to the Tartars. Brought peace in North Italy between the 'Guelfs' and the 'Ghibellines' (the rival papal and imperial parties). He was canonized in 1671.

24th BARTHOLOMEW: Apostle – see Mark 3.14–19. Nothing else is known of him, but he may be the same man as Nathaniel of Cana (John 21.2), who was earlier described in John 1.45–51) by Jesus as *an Israelite in whom is no guile'*. Legends suggest he evangelised in India and was flayed alive in Armenia. Bartholomew was very popular in medieval times as patron of churches and hospitals, for example St Bartholomew's Hospital near Smithfield in the City of London.

OUEN (600–84): A courtier of Frankish King Dagobert who made him and St Eligius – Eloi (1 December) bishops of Rouen and Noyon. Ouen converted pagan tree-worshippers in his diocese and founded monasteries as centres of piety and learning.

EBBE: Died in 683. Daughter of King Ethelfrith of Northumbria. On the advice of St Wilfrid she separated from her husband King Egfrith. She later was made first abbess of Coldingham in Berwickshire, a double monastery for men and women. She was famed for her wisdom and good advice; this even included advice to her ex-husband.

JOAN THORET (1765–1826): Joined St Vincent de Paul's (27 September) Sisters of Charity and ran her own village school during the French Revolution. In 1799 she founded a school for nurses at Besançon in the name of The Sisters of Charity under the protection of St Vincent de Paul. The nursing service spread rapidly in Savoy and also in Switzerland and Italy. She opened a large hospital in Naples in 1810 and worked there until she died. She was canonised in 1951.

EMILY de VIALAR (1797–1856): She used a legacy to buy a chateau in Languedoc as a home for poor children. She opened another in 1835 in Algeria, but was excommunicated by the bishop there, who failed to understand her work. She was vindicated, but she and her community – The Sisters of Joseph of the Apparition (see Matthew 1.18–20) – left Algiers and resettled themselves successfully in France. Determined and shrewd she said that *'Quietly to trust in God is better than trying to save material interests . . . I know that from bitter experience'*. She was canonised in 1951.

25th GENESIUS of ARLES: Martyred at Arles in 250 during Decius' persecution.

KING ST LOUIS IX of FRANCE (1214–70): The only saint of the Crusades and a devout and just king. He became a Franciscan Tertiary and built the Sainte Chapelle on the Ile de la Cité in Paris to house the 'Crown of Thorns' that he bought for a great price. He was captured during the sixth Crusade and ransomed, but died of fever in Tunisia on the seventh Crusade (see the 'Table of the Crusades' at the end of this chapter). An assessment of Saint Louis is given below, together with drawings of the stained glass windows in the Sainte Chappelle, a building which is his greatest legacy to France.

JOSEPH of CALASANZ (1557–1648): After attending three Spanish universities in law and divinity he became a priest and went to Rome. Horrified at the ignorance and moral squalor of the slums, he started a free school in 1597. Other priests joined him and they formed The Clerks Regular of the Religious Schools – The Piarists. He aimed to provide a complete system of primary and secondary schools with a carefully planned curriculum in which children would learn to love goodness. He believed that children instructed in religion and letters would grow up to be happy people. Piarist schools were established in Spain, Bohemia and Poland as well as in Italy. In his last years he suffered from the scheming ambitions of his subordinates. He was canonised in 1767.

26th **NINIAN**: Died c.432. St Bede (25 May) believed that Ninian was a Briton who had become a Christian in Rome and then had been made a missionary bishop to the Picts in Scotland, making his headquarters at 'Candida Casa' or 'The White House' at Whithorn in Galloway. He also seems to have at some early date come under the influence of St Martin of Tours' disciples (11 November) because his main church and several others were dedicated to Martin. Archeological excavations at Whithorn suggest that it was a major site. Ninian's work in Scotland preceded that of St Columba by 230 years.

ELIZABETH BICHIER des ANGES (1773–1838): Born at the Château des Anges near Poitiers. She lived in a village during the Revolution where there was no priest. At considerable personal risk she organised secret meetings for Christian worship. Through this work she met St Andrew Fournet (13 May) who helped her found a community to look after the sick in rural areas. Between 1811 and 1830 she developed this into The Daughters of the Cross with 60 convents in France. Her appeal and rallying cry to helpers was: '*There are ruins to be rebuilt, ignorance to be remedied*'. She became one of the leading restorers of Christian practice in France.

27th **MONICA**: The North African Christian Berber mother of St Augustine of Hippo (see below, 28 August). She was devoted and loyal to him in spite of his rejection of Christianity for Manichaeanism and his licentious life throughout his student days and early manhood. She gave him his Christian conscience and guided him towards his final conversion. Augustine's own *Confessions* record the beautiful mystical experience that they shared at Ostia after his conversion and shortly before her death. Only one other such double-mystical experience has been recorded, that of St Benedict of Nursia (11 July) with his twin sister St Scholastica (10 February).

CAESARIUS of ARLES (470–543): He was one of the many monks of Lerins who became bishops. As Bishop of Arles he resisted the religious interference of the Arian heretic Visigoths and Ostrogoths. As Primate of Gaul he presided over the important Council of Orange in 529, when Pelagianism was finally crushed. It also condemned St Augustine of Hippo's unscriptural innovation of 'Double Predestination' – a philosophical argument that all humans from their birth were destined by God either to salvation or to damnation and that in the latter case no amount of good works would save them.

28th **AUGUSTINE of HIPPO** (354–430): Born of a Berber father and a North African Christian mother, St Monica, at Thegaste in what is now Algeria. Augustine progressed from being a brilliant and licentious student of philosophy at Carthage and was for nine years a devotee of the religion of the Persian Mani (Manichaeanism) to becoming the greatest Christian theologian in the West. His works guided the Church during the centuries of barbaric invasions and dominated Western Church thought for over 1,000 years. However he never got over his obsession with the evils of sex. He also propounded the unscriptural theory of a double predestination, that human beings are from birth either destined for salvation or else to be damned eternally. His life and his two greatest works, his *Confessions* and his *The City of God* are described in the text following this Calendar.

JULIAN of BRIOUDE: Third-century martyr of Brioude in the Auvergne, where his shrine is venerated in a church dating back to the sixth century and where there is a magnificent decorated gallery that was used to house pilgrims. It was there that St Robert of la Chaise-Dieu (17 April) was a canon until he retired to set up his hermit community.

AUGUSTINE of CANTERBURY: Died in 604. As a monk in the monastery of St Andrew on the Celian Hill in Rome, he was chosen by Pope Gregory I to lead a mission of 30 monks to evangelise in Britain. In 587, after a difficult journey because of barbarian raids, he landed in Kent and was well received by Ethelbert, King of Kent, whose queen Bertha was a Christian from Paris. The King was converted and laid the foundations for St Paul's Cathedral in London. Augustine founded the cathedral at Canterbury. The few remaining British bishops, after the Saxon invasions, regarded Augustine as a typical proud and arrogant Roman. He divided England into two provinces – Canterbury and York – for future evangelising, each with 12 suffragen bishops. His was a difficult task, but he laid the foundations for the future, including, with the help of St Theordore (from Tarsus), a school for teaching new clergy.

29th **KING St SEBBI:** Devout seventh-century King of the Saxons in East Anglia who abdicated the throne near the end of his life to become a monk. He gave his wealth to the Church for the poor and was buried in old St Paul's cathedral in London.

MOSES the BLACK (c.330–405): An Ethiopian brigand who became a desert monk in Egypt after a sudden conversion. At his baptism, when he was clad in the customary white garment for the ceremony, the bishop said: *'Now the black man is made white!'* To which Moses replied: *'But God knows I am all black inside'*. He died a martyr, refusing to defend himself against the raiding Berbers.

30th **FELIX and AUDAX:** Early Roman martyrs.

PAMMACHIUS (c.340–410): Roman senator who married the daughter of St Paula (26 January), St Jerome's (30 September) friend and helper in Bethlehem. He knew the prickly Jerome well and wrote to admonish him for the violent language in which he criticised the institution of marriage. He helped St Fabiola (27 December) to establish a hospice for the sick and dying and devoted his wealth to charitable works. He built a church in his house, traces of which have been found in the remains of a villa that can be seen in the crypt of the church of St Giovanni e Paulo on the Caelian Hill in Rome.

Also on 30 August the Anglican Church remembers the great Baptist preacher and author JOHN BUNYAN (1628–88). His life is reviewed in Part VII, 'The Unquenchable Spirit'.

31st **PAULINUS of TRIER:** Died in 358, five years after being banished as a bishop in the West for resisting the Emperor Constantius II's edicts imposing the Arian heresy on the empire.

AIDAN of LINDISFARNE: Died in 651 as first Bishop of Northumbria, a diocese which stretched from the Humber to the Firth of Forth. He is shown by St Bede (25 May) to have played a decisive part in the evangelisation of northern England in the Celtic style of St Patrick's Irish Church, which he had imbibed as a monk in the monastery established by St Columba (9 June) on the island of Iona off Mull in the Hebrides. He first came into prominence when King St Oswald (9 August) of Northumbria invited him to preach the gospel in his kingdom and gave him the sea-girt land of Lindisfarne for a monastery and headquarters. He made it a centre of learning.

St Bede praised Aidan especially for his humility and the way he went on foot or by pony all through his diocese to stay and sup with the humblest members of his flock to teach them the gospel. This was the style brought over from Ireland by St Columba which the learned monk Alcuin pointed out a century later contrasted with the princely clothing of St Wilfrid's mounted escort after he had converted the old Celtic-British church to Rome in 663. It was after this that the gradual alienation of Church leaders from the ordinary people began in Britain and Europe. This produced the dissatisfaction that lasted until the genius of St Francis of Assisi and St Dominic took the gospel into the homes of the people at the beginning of the thirteenth century.

SUMMARY OF AUGUST SAINTS

This August Calendar gives the feast-days of 69 saints, of whom 23 were martyrs and 12 were women. Four of these saints are especially important not only because of their works and achievements, but also because all except one of them made grave errors in judgement through their misguided idealism. Their lives and works will therefore be given special attention in the following pages. Their names are **St Augustine of Hippo, St Maximus the Confessor, St Bernard of Clairvaux** and his dispute with **Peter Abelard** and, finally, **St Louis of France.**

IMPORTANT AUGUST SAINTS

St Augustine of Hippo (354–430), his early life and conversion

Augustine was born at Tagaste in Algeria of a pagan father and a devout Christian mother, St Monica, who were both North African Berbers. He studied rhetoric and philosophy at Carthage, where he led a dissolute youth, as he describes in his famous *Confessions*.

As the outline of St Augustine's early life has already been given in the Calendar for his feast-day on 28 August, it seems best to start here with the most important event of his life, his conversion to Christianity. Augustine described this and the great personal struggle that preceded it in his most popular work, his *Confessions*. Augustine wrote this book after his conversion and when he had become Bishop of Hippo Regis Imperialis, which is now the Algerian seaport of Annaba. It is an important work that is unfortunately often ridiculed by quoting Augustine's prayer to make him chaste. This and his intimate picture of his early life need to be looked at as the humble and frank confession of a bishop on his knees before God.

In his *Confessions* Augustine describes his life as a student of philosophy in Carthage and how he took a mistress at the age of seventeen and became a follower of the Manichaean faith. This doctrine, which denied Christ's humanity and rejected all the Old Testament and much of the New Testament, has already been outlined in Part V. Augustine was a member of the Manichaean Church for nine years, until he realised the shallowness of its beliefs and left Carthage to teach philosophy at Milan. Augustine's *Confessions* tell us how Augustine, after leaving Carthage with his long-time mistress and their son Adeodatus and his devoted Christian mother Monica (see 27

August), was attracted by the sermons of St Ambrose, the learned bishop of Milan. He attended his church services regularly to study his teaching. He soon became won over by the reasonableness and logic of Christianity, but could not bring himself to be baptised, as he knew he would have to give up his sexually indulgent way of life. It was the agony of making his decision over this, which included dismissing his mistress of 14 years, that caused him to pray for God to *'make me pure, but not yet'*.

Writers who mention Augustine often make fun of this remark in his book and make no reference to the painful struggle that he had with his conscience, which he describes in Book VII of his *Confessions*. There he describes how *'my two wills, one old, the other new, one carnal, the other spiritual, were in conflict with one another, and their discord robbed my soul of all concentration'*. This shows the sincerity of his ultimate conversion and the bitterness of the struggle through which he had to go.

Augustine tells how he discussed this problem with his friend Alypius and whether they should both seek baptism. The story of their conversion needs to be told in full; it is not only beautiful, but it shows how even the greatest spiritual experiences may occur in the most unexpected ways, as happened to Augustine, and have a life-changing effect on the individual concerned.

This breakthrough began when Augustine acquired a copy of St Athanasius' *Life of Antony*. It was this book that made Augustine realise the importance of chastity for anyone in God's service. It also made the two friends ask themselves *'What is our aim in life? Can we hope for any higher office in the palace than to be Friends of the*

Emperor? Augustine then realised that "If I wish to become God's Friend, in an instant I may become that now!"' All he had to do was to submit, for he already believed, but he could not quite bring himself to take the plunge.

Augustine postponed the decision from day to day as *'my soul hung back'*. Then the two friends took a villa in the country, which had a garden. One day walking in the garden he tore his hair and struck his forehead in his agony of indecision, saying to himself: *'Let it be now!'* He then heard *'a voice from a nearby house chanting as if it might be a boy or a girl and repeating over and over again, "Tolle, Lege!" – "Pick up and read! Pick up and read!" I began to wonder whether this might be some sort of children's game, but I could not remember having heard one. I then interpreted it solely as a divine command to me to open the book and read the first chapter I could find.'*

He then opened the book he had left on his garden seat – St Paul's Epistle to the Romans, chapter 13. There he read verses 13 and 14: *'"Not in riots and drunken parties, not in eroticism and indecencies, not in strife and rivalry, but put on the Lord Jesus Christ and make no provision for the flesh in its lusts". I neither wished not needed to read further. At once, with the last words of the sentence, it was as if a light of relief from all anxiety flooded into my heart. All the shadows of doubt were dispelled. With a face now at peace I told everything to Alypius. He asked to be shown the text I had been reading and he noticed a passage further on, which said "Receive the person who is weak in faith".'* (Romans 14.1). Both men then committed themselves to become Christians and told Monica, who was filled with joy. They were then baptised, together with Augustine's fifteen-year-old son Adeodatus, on Easter eve by St Ambrose at a ceremony during which Augustine was deeply moved by the music of the sweet chants which Ambrose had introduced into the Church.

St Augustine's teaching and writings

There is space here for only the briefest survey of Augustine's colossal literary output of the 93 books, 1,000 sermons and the vast correspondence and many miscellaneous writings which have been preserved. He was the greatest Christian thinker in antiquity in the West and the most powerful theological influence in the Church right through medieval times and to reformation Protestantism. His great achievement, even though some of his teachings were rejected and have had unfortunate social effects, was to fuse Christianity with Greek philosophical thought and give it a reasoned case as a world-view.

As he wrote in his last great book, *The City of God*, he believed that the true philosophy is the love of God. The only knowledge he ever sought right from his days as a student and as a Manichaean was knowledge of God and the soul. In his *Confessions* he wrote that he had learned from reading the advice of Plotinus that in order to find God one should begin by looking into oneself, because God is imprinted in the human soul. This reasoning led Augustine to develop his own theory of knowledge and of the soul and to produce his unique interpretation of God as Trinity. His studies on these subjects convinced him that in all the nature of creation there is a 'Threeness' which reflected the Threeness of the Trinity of Father, Son and Holy Spirit. Thus of himself he could say *'I am, I know, I will'*. He also put this in different ways as *'Existence, Memory/Mind, Will'* and *'Being, Activity,*

Direction'. He then realised that the human soul is created by him and that unlike the Manichaean teaching of an evil first principle, the principle that bound the Trinity was mutual love. It followed that the soul, in its journey to seek perfection, should respond to the knowledge of God with love of Him and all his works and love of neighbour as of self.

As he reflected on these things in both his great books and in his work *De Trinitate* Augustine constantly reminded his readers of the existence of evil and its cause. Rejecting the Manichaean world-view he saw that '*I cause the evil that I do, through my own free-will*'. Thus we have a choice and evil can be defined as a corruption of good deflected by will from its true self. Alternatively evil can be described as the absence of a perfection that should be present, but which is not present.

In one of his letters on the subject of how we come to faith, Augustine advised from his own experience that '*unless you believe, you will not understand*'. This truth was seen 700 years later by St Anselm (21 April) and immortalised in his prayer: '*I do not seek to understand that I believe, but I believe in order to understand*'. In other words one has first to 'join the club' (or at least have an open mind and be prepared to believe) before one can really hope to begin to see. Augustine admitted how difficult it was to 'join'. He said that in his agony of indecision

he often came so near to doing so in mystical moments, but that these were so brief and fleeting that he made no progress. In retrospect he blamed this on the fact that he was still tied too strongly to the material world and its pleasures to become subject to the influence of the Spirit. It was only at the end of his struggle that he won through to faith, as described above in the story of his conversion. Augustine put that down entirely to God's grace, given freely and unconditionally to him, and which had nothing to do with his own activity. He therefore taught that the Grace of God alone opens the soul to faith, love and charity and shows us the way.

After his conversion Augustine wrote a book on the soul in which he described it as an incorporeal body, a spirit and therefore immortal since it does not have a material life to lose. He then left Milan to return to his home town of Thegaste, where he established a religious community and intended to spend his life in contemplation.

However, the Bishop of Hippo persuaded him to be ordained as a deacon and then become his successor, which he did in 396. Active though he then became in the pastoral care of his diocese and in his campaigns against the heresies of the Manichaeans, Donatists and Pelagians, he always lived in a monastic community together with his cathedral clergy. He imposed on them a strict rule, which was copied in later centuries by other monastic orders.

Our hearts are restless until they rest in you.

Besides his writings against the Manichaeans, Augustine had to deal with the active and often brutal opposition of the Donatist Church in North Africa. This Church was an extreme puritan organisation that was founded by Donatus, Bishop of Numidia, after the third-century persecutions. He and his followers refused to accept anyone back into the Church who had apostasised to save their lives. Later the Donatist church took an extreme view on sin and its followers attacked violently the more liberal-minded followers of the Roman Church. Augustine argued successfully against their bishops and gradually the Donatists were suppressed.

The more difficult heresy that Augustine faced, however, was that of the British monk Pelagius, who had won a substantial following in Rome as a spiritual guide. He taught a revolutionary concept of salvation there from 398 until 410, when he fled from the Visigoth invasion and went to Jerusalem. Pelagius rejected the traditional doctrine that Adam's sin and subsequent 'Fall' had caused all of humankind to be born naturally sinful.

Pelagius believed that God created the human soul to be pure and therefore we are not in need of a further act of divine grace and can reach perfection themselves through exerting their own will to follow the gospel teaching. Augustine pointed out forcefully that the effect of this was to undermine the whole purpose of the Incarnation of Jesus and his sacrifice on the cross. As in most of his criticisms of things that cut across tradition, Augustine carried his argument to extremes. There must be many faithful, who are not learned theologians, and who must wonder what will happen on judgement day, if they admit their faults and give the excuse that nevertheless they tried! Augustine answered this question by saying that it meant that if we did not need divine grace to reach perfection, then there was no point in prayer. St Jerome commented to St Augustine that *'Pelagius suffered from eating too much porridge'*.

The Pelagian heresy was officially condemned at a council in Carthage in 418, when it was agreed that faith and salvation only came through the grace of God, thus the Sovereignty of God, the Almighty's right to save or to condemn, was safeguarded. However this argument led Augustine to develop his defensive argument to an absurd degree and to reach an extreme view on predestination. From the Greek concept that God is omnipotent, he worked out that God knows the result of every act and therefore sees the past, present and future as one. In this sense the final result of an action is predestined. God therefore knows from the very beginning of a life whether someone is predestined for eternal life or for eternal damnation, no matter what he or she may do in their actual lifetime. This meant that some were doomed from the beginning.

This doctrine of Augustine's had a most discouraging effect on believers and Augustine's view was opposed by many, including the learned monks of the Isle of Lerins. It was they who succeeded in having double-predestination declared unscriptural and false a century later at the Council of Orange in 529. However it continued to have its supporters. One of the most notable of these being the sixteenth-century Reformer John Calvin, whose Geneva Church had such a depressing influence on society, since a double-predestination destroys hope and incentive to try and do better. This is therefore an example of how a great theologian may sometimes press his argument through too far and to the point of absurdity.

Augustine condensed the whole body of his teaching into his book *The City of God*, written after Alaric the Visigoth's sacking of Rome in 410. He had been asked to write the book because the fall of Rome had been blamed on the Christians for undermining the ancient Roman virtues. After refuting this argument by showing that Christianity supported those same virtues and that Rome had neglected them, Augustine proceeded to provide a guide to right and wrong and to the duties we have towards God, our neighbours and the state. In doing so, by contrasting the City of God with the unchristian City devoted to self-satisfaction, he brought out the idea of the Church as a dynamic social power, which expounded the Christian doctrine of moral freedom and personal responsibility.

The book had an immense influence on the development of society in the West. Charlemagne had the book read to him regularly and is even said never to have made an important decision without examining it in the light of the *City of God* as well as of the Gospels. The English King Alfred had the book translated into Anglo-Saxon, Sir Thomas Moore, saint and martyr, first came to public notice by giving a series of lectures on the book in London. Queen Elizabeth I of England studied it deeply. Perhaps of all Augustine's works this book has had the greatest influence in instilling ideas of right and wrong behaviour. If his obsessions with evil, especially with sex as an evil and his double-predestination are overlooked, Augustine's writings have much to teach us today. Above all his life and work after his conversion are a monument to all the saintly virtues. His faith and approach to understanding are an outstanding example of what it is to be a Christian pilgrim, even if now and again his great intellect made him stumble. His whole life was a pilgrimage, made in the knowledge as he expressed in one of his prayers that '*We are restless until we rest in Thee*'. Those words were among his last, because the Vandals had invaded North Africa from Spain and as Augustine lay dying in August 430 their army was besieging his city. Fortunately his secretaries managed to save his library when the city was captured and sacked. Otherwise his great faith and learning would not have been passed on to the outside world as the Roman Empire in the West began to collapse.

St Maximus the Confessor (580–662)

It is necessary to introduce the story of St Maximus the Confessor with a brief historical review of the events since St Augustine's death two centuries earlier. In spite of the invasions from the East of the Huns, Goths, Ostrogoths, Burgundians and other tribes from 430 onwards, the orthodox faith was never destroyed. Even though the Vandals swept through Gaul, Spain and across North Africa and destroyed Rome, reducing its population of over 800,000 to 30,000 in the sixth century, a core of clergy and monks survived until the Emperor Justinian (527–65) and his great general Belisarius drove out the Vandals and restored Rome to the Church.

This period proved to be the twilight of Byzantine power over the West. Within two centuries the papacy had succeeded in obtaining the support of the Frankish kings of Gaul, who were victorious over the Lombards and once again the territories around Rome were restored to the Church. The last Byzantine governor in Ravenna simply fled back to Constantinople. A new era then began, which was to lead to the papacy in its own right taking over the governing role that the emperors had exercised in Italy.

The greatest Christian mind in the East and the West at this time was that of the abbot Maximus the Confessor. He was of noble birth, born in Constantinople and after studying theology and law he became secretary to the Emperor Heraclius. He resigned this post when the Emperor, in a vain attempt to unite the Eastern Church in the face of Persian aggression, tried to force it to adopt the Monothelite doctrine of his Patriarch Sergius in Constantinople. This aimed to reconcile the Monophysites of Egypt and Syria with the Orthodox Catholics by proclaiming that in Jesus Christ there is only one divine energy and will.

This, as Maximus pointed out, was inconsistent with the reality of Jesus' human nature. By denying this, the heresy went against the tradition of his being both wholly human and wholly divine. As Maximus taught: *'If there are not two wills in Christ – one divine and one human – then his two natures were not perfect'*. The Emperor and the Patriarch persisted with their heresy and though this doctrine was imposed on the Eastern Church, the policy failed and the schism between the Orthodox and Monophysites continued to disrupt the peace of the Church and Eastern empire.

Heraclius defeated the Persians in 628 and restored the True Cross which they had captured from Jerusalem. However a far greater menace had arisen by then. The Prophet Muhammad had established his monotheist faith of Islam – *'Surrender to God'* – in Arabia and by 629 his troops were raiding into Transjordan. They found the Byzantine armies weakened and exhausted after two and a half centuries of warfare. It is alleged that Muhammad then wrote to Heraclius inviting him to become a Muslim and worship Allah, the supreme God of whom he had proclaimed Jesus Christ was a prophet.

No reply was made by the time the prophet died in 632. However his successors as Caliphs and leaders attacked the Empire relentlessly. By the time Heraclius died in 641, the Byzantines had lost Syria, Palestine, Egypt and Mesopotamia to Islam, and Constantinople itself was about to be besieged.

During this time Maximus had spent some years as abbot of a monastery at Scutari on the Black Sea and had then left to teach in Alexandria. There he wrote his greatest book: *Four Centuries of Charity*. It contains the results of his own experience and studies. In it he showed how spiritual growth in a person occurs when worldly desires are overcome in spiritual combat – the kind that is meant in St Paul's 1st Letter to St Timothy, where he says: *'Go thou my son Timothy and fight thou a good warfare'*. (I Timothy 1.18). In the book Maximus explained that *'the progress of the soul is made perfect when its powers of passion have been completely directed towards God. He rises by divine steps corresponding to those by which God humbled himself out of love for us.'*

Maximus, in a mystical interpretation of the nature and aim of life, taught that this process leads to an ineffable state in which *'the creature is deified and no longer displays energy other than the divine . . . There is no longer any fear of death. Henceforth there is only God, because the person's being enters into the being of the elect'*. The royal road to achieving this is for our soul or spirit to unite itself with God in prayers and love and so to acquire wisdom, goodness, power, beneficence and generosity. In a word, the person then bears the attributes of God for the *'whole aim of faith is the true revelation of its object . . . In sharing the divine light over a long period a person can become full of light themselves'*. Yet at the same time we need to remember that *'Christ is always a mystery, the blessed goal, the point to which God's providence is tending'*.

Maximus did not become involved in the Monothelite controversy until 648, when Heraclius' successor Constans II (642–68) threatened Pope St Martin I with death unless he obeyed his edict that Christ had only one will, the Divine. Maximus went to Rome to speak to the synod of 105 bishops which Pope Martin summoned to debate this issue. They unanimously condemned the heretical edict, declaring that *'In Jesus Christ Our Lord there are two natural wills, the divine and human, and two natural operations, the divine and the human'*. Pope Martin had this published to every part of the Church, to Gaul, the Netherlands, Africa and Constantinople. Constans immediately set about arresting and killing the pope.

After failing at his first attempt to seize Pope Martin in Rome, the Emperor's troops broke into his palace of the Lateran in 653 and dragged him in chains to a ship for Constantinople. He was held in the ship for two years while the Emperor fought off the Muslim attempt to capture the city. Pope Martin and Maximus were given a mockery of a trial, declared guilty of heresy and treason and were flogged mercilessly and exiled. As already described in his story (13 April) Pope St Martin died of starvation in the Crimea in 655. Maximus was retried in 662, when he was blamed for the new pope's refusal to obey the heretical edict. His tongue was cut out, his right hand was cut off and he was sent to the Caucasus where he died of his wounds. Six years later Constans was assassinated in Sicily and his son and successor Constantius IV quietly forgot Monothelitism. The Eastern Empire, except for the part of Asia Minor between the Bosporus and the Syrian border, had been lost for ever and the Monophysites had either become Muslims or else paid taxes to worship as Christians and became known as 'Copts'.

St Bernard of Clairvaux (1090–1153)

As a young man Bernard, after what he was to describe as a *'long process of conversion'*, joined the monastery of Citeaux, high on a lonely site in the Savoy Alps. His abbot was the Englishman St Stephen Harding, third head of the Cistercian Order, who inspired Bernard with his own mystical approach to the faith. Stephen had also drawn up a *Charter for Charity* which defined the spirit and social culture of all Cistercian abbeys for centuries.

The man who promoted this to an astonishing degree of success was Bernard, who succeeded Stephen as head of the order in 1134. In spite of the way one can criticise Bernard for his misguided support of the disastrous second crusade in 1146–49, for his extraordinarily emotional theology of worship, or for his narrow-minded victimisation of the brilliant theologian Peter Abelard, nothing can diminish his achievement in extending the activities of the Cistercian order. He did this on a grand scale to the immense spiritual and economic benefit of France, Flanders, England and Ireland. His achievement can be seen from the fact that when he was made abbot of the impoverished monastery of Clairvaux in 1115 there were only 13 monks in residence, yet when he died 38 years later there were 340 Cistercian abbeys in Europe. Some 68 of these were controlled personally by Bernard and for their construction he introduced the gothic ogival arch for the main buildings. Among his special foundations were the English abbeys of Rievaulx and Fountains, Mellifont in Ireland and Pontigny and Morimond in France. All we have today is their magnificent ruins. However in their prime these abbeys each contained from 500 to 700 monks and many more lay brethren. Their chief occupation, apart from the routine periods of contemplation and worship according to their 'rule', was the large-scale development of sheep-farming, which revolutionised the cloth-producing industry in Europe.

The hallmark of Bernard's mystical system of worship that he imposed on his monasteries was his belief, inherited from St Stephen Harding, that it was more important for the soul to spend time in venerating the mystery of the Trinity than in trying to understand its meaning. This was a deeply spiritual approach that ignored the vigorous reasoned philosophical quest after 'truth' that had been developed in the West by St Anselm, the first of the 'Scholastics' who had only died in 1109. It was inevitable that Bernard would cross swords with Peter Abelard and his philosophical approach in the embryo University of Paris.

Bernard was a preacher of genius. He made Christ the centre of his spirituality but he emphasised also the salutary mediation of the Virgin Mary as being responsible for caring for the Church community. He called her *Domina Caritas*. The cult of Mary is not followed in the Protestant Churches, but her cult in the Roman Catholic Church is inconceivable without Bernard's teaching. Through her he stressed the human element in her son's life as well as in her own. He also pointed out her and Joseph's loving and caring qualities. Bernard's published sermons taught how the Incarnation would have been impossible without Mary's purity, obedience and love. From this he drew the conclusion that Mary had been preserved from original sin. He therefore introduced into his monasteries an annual 'Feast of the Immaculate Conception', a doctrine that became believed widely but was not formally declared a dogma until the reign of Pope Pius IX in 1854. Bernard also saw her as having shared Christ's agony on the cross as she stood at its foot. He therefore regarded her as the 'Queen of Heaven', which ultimately led to Pope Pius XII declaring the dogma of the Assumption in 1950 that she had been bodily assumed into heaven.

Thus it can be seen that, as the late Pope John-Paul II declared, the 'Mariology' of the Roman Church is simply a natural extension of 'Christology'. Mary's power springs from her purity and love. The profound influence of Bernard's Mariology on future generations can be seen in the work of the poet Dante. In his *Divine Comedy* he makes his Beatrice, his heroine and guide, stand aside for the shade of St Bernard so that he can realise his lifetime's wish of seeing Mary standing before the face of God.

Christ was nevertheless the centre of Bernard's spiritual doctrine. He taught that his command to love our neighbours as ourselves was an impossibility in this life. He therefore said that the command was given to prove to us our own weakness, so that we should all cry out humbly *Lord, have mercy on us!* In his work *On Consideration* about the Unity and Trinity of God and of the two natures of 'The Word Incarnate' he referred in a very modern way to the difficult interior experience of Jesus during the 30 years before he began his ministry. He pointed to the misery he must have suffered to learn the mercy which made him willing to suffer all our afflictions, save sin itself, even unto death.

Bernard's interpretation of the religious role of the Cistercian Order was that it should be a contemplative one. He encouraged this contemplation to take a mystical path towards union with God by the imitation of Christ. His mystical approach differed from that of the Greek Fathers or St John Climacus. It was positive, whereas their approach was negative. He described this mystical way in his *Canticle of Canticles*, applying the sexual allegories of Bride and Bridegroom to the ascent of the soul to God through adoration of Christ.

Bernard did this by allegorising the soul's ascent to the 'Word' as that of a kiss. He said that the ascent begins with penance and, in imagination, is a progress towards *'kissing the feet of Christ'*. At that point all sins are forgiven. The progress in the mind then advances to imitation of Christ and to *'kissing his hands'*. Here Christ adorns the penitent soul with the spiritual virtues. Finally a mystical rapture is attained, which Bernard describes as *'kissing the mouth of Christ'*. This is the mystical union which the Greek Fathers also sought to achieve through their method of prayer and rhythmical breathing. Bernard's way of thinking was absorbed into the practice of many mystics in the centuries to come and still attracts practitioners today. Four centuries after Bernard, St Ignatius of Loyola took a similar and positive approach to contemplation, except that instead of aiming at penance he aimed at deepening consciousness and understanding of Christ by immersing himself in his Passion and thus experiencing his suffering in imagination.

St Bernard's dispute with Peter Abelard

If one takes a psychological approach in trying to understand the complex nature of Bernard, one can see from his writings how he subliminated successfully his own innate sexuality. Therefore he was bound to react violently against the free-living approach to theology of his slightly older contemporary, Peter Abelard. Abelard is famous for his love-affair with his pupil Heloise while still a plain lecturer in Paris. Heloise was the orphan of a crusader and ward of Canon Fulbert of Notre Dame. After Abelard was emasculated by Fulbert's thugs, he founded a nunnery, The Paraclete, for Heloise as abbess. Abelard then became a monk and continued the fight he had fought as a lecturer in Paris, seeking to bring about a more modern understanding of the mysteries of faith through reason and philosophy.

Abelard took a dialectical approach to religious studies, one which Bernard abhored. However, arrogant though he was, Abelard's powers of public debate enabled him to destroy the 'Nominalist' arguments on the Trinity of his own teacher, the fashionable Roscelin. He also ruined the reputation of the popular theologian William of Champeaux, forcing him to retire in shame from his post as a university lecturer. These conflicts were basic to the very foundations of Catholic thought at that time. According to Roscelin's extreme 'Nominalist' view, for example, there are no such things as the 'Universal Forms' of Plato, whose teaching St Augustine had fused with that of Christianity seven centuries earlier. In other words universal ideas like 'Good', 'Evil', 'Equality', 'Humanity' and the like are not real, because our experience is always of the individual and of particular characteristics. They are just names, hence the title 'Nominalist' that was given to this line of 'Scholastic' argument.

In refuting Roscelin Abelard was for once on the side of the angels. He tore his reasoning to shreds. The novelist George Moore related this in his book *Heloise and Abelard* (1921) by putting the following words into Abelard's mouth during his description of a public debate on Mont St Genevieve in Paris, where students gathered for discussions: '*So truth and virtue and humanity do not exist at all! You suppose yourself to exist, but you have no means of knowing God. For you therefore God does not exist except as an echo of your own ignorance! Also the Church does not exist except as your concept of certain individuals whom you cannot regard as a unity, and yet who suppose themselves to believe in a Trinity which exists only as a sound or symbol! You had better prepare yourself for the stake!*' As a result of the young Abelard's criticism, Roscelin's work on the Trinity was condemned in 1094.

Abelard's method was to begin a discussion with a selected text, the '*Lectio*'. He then followed this with a debate, the '*Disputio*', in which a different view was expounded and objections were examined and answered. This had a devastating effect on the traditional exposition of biblical texts, including those where the Early Fathers had disagreed. Therefore Abelard's teaching, especially in his greatest book *Sic et Non*, stirred up enormous interest and also violent antagonism. His chief opponent was Bernard of Clairvaux.

In his book Abelard applied his logical system to compare the writings of the Early Fathers. Among the subjects he challenged was their traditional doctrine of Original Sin through Adam. He replaced this with one less hard and emphasised that the consent of the Will is essential in actual sin. He considered there was a major gap in the Church's teaching about Salvation. The Church has in fact never produced a watertight case to prove why Jesus' death and resurrection saved us, treating it entirely as an article of faith. Abelard put forward the suggestion that the supreme value of Jesus' life and death lies in its appeal to love and its example.

More controversially, on the definition of the Trinity Abelard suggested that the Three Persons would be better understood simply as God's Power, Wisdom and Love. He also taught that Jesus was united to God by a moral union. None of these reasonable suggestions suited Bernard, who called Abelard a '*child of perdition*'. He misjudged him, because whenever Abelard reached a point in an argument where a basic tenet of his faith seemed at risk, he would always defer to the Scriptures or to the tradition of the Church. He, like Origen nine centuries earlier, was exploring and suggesting possible answers to mysteries, not creating heresies. He made this clear in a letter to the Abbess Heloise: '*I have no desire to be a philosopher in contradiction to St Paul, nor an Aristotle separated from Christ, for there is no other name under heaven under which I would be saved. The rock on which I have built my knowledge is that on which Christ built the Church.*'

Abelard was following a more modern path than Bernard's. He wanted to guide people to a deeper understanding of their faith by showing how reason and philosophy could be the tools of faith. In the end he became so exasperated at Bernard's refusal even to consider his arguments that he challenged him to a debate at the Council of Soissons in 1140. Bernard accepted the challenge but undermined Abelard's position by distributing extracts to the Council from his works and putting them out of context. He then made the Council refuse to permit Abelard to reply. The Council was therefore forced to condemn Abelard for heresy. Although Abelard announced that he would appeal to the pope, his friends persuaded him that the pope would not listen to him.

Abelard then broke down and was taken into their protection by the monks of Cluny, who opposed Bernard's mystical theology. He died two years later in 1142. His work was however not in vain. His comparative studies of scripture and the Fathers was adopted by Peter Lombard (1100–60) who became Bishop of Paris in the last year of his life. He produced a study, which he called *A Book of Sentences*. In spite of criticism that he had copied Abelard's ideas, it became the grammar for theologians for the next four centuries. Thus through Peter Abelard's pioneering work Peter Lombard became famous and known as 'The Master of the Sentences' and replaced Bernard of Clairvaux's mystical approach to understanding the scriptures by crawling up the aisle to the Cross in imagination.

St Bernard of Clairvaux and the Second Crusade

In the midst of his case against Abelard, this prematurely ageing and always physically weak polymath was suddenly forced into the maelstrom of international politics through his perennial drive to expand the activities of the Cistercians and his own religious writings. He was summoned by Pope Eugenius III, one of his own former monks, in 1145 to rouse Europe to mount a Second Crusade to Palestine. The Saracens had captured Christian-held Edessa on the Syrian border and were threatening Jerusalem and the Holy places.

Eugenius was in a weak position. Rival factions in Rome contested his election and he was forced to live in Viterbo. He was also uncertain about what to do, since on the one hand the Byzantines wanted to take no action and on the other the Armenian bishops wanted him to help them against the Byzantines. He therefore appealed to Louis VII of France to raise an army to save the Holy places. Louis found that his vassals were indifferent to his appeal and that the German King Conrad II was too involved in opposing King Roger II of Sicily. Eugenius therefore turned to Bernard of Clairvaux and asked him to preach for a crusade and to stir up the masses in Europe and raise the Cross once more.

Bernard did not hesitate. The son of a crusader himself, he had long been interested in oriental affairs. He had, for example, drawn up the 'Rule' in 1128 for the Order of the Knights Templar, the guardians of the pilgrim routes to Palestine. He exploited the position of Clairvaux as the most important religious centre in Europe, he issued an encyclical, which only popes were entitled to do, summoning the spiritual and secular rulers and their followers to Vezelay to hear the crusade proclaimed. Bernard's encyclical contained promises from the pope of pardons and privileges. It was also full of comments on the mysteries of salvation, which he twisted round in the manner of a modern Muslim Ayatollah to justify the killing of unbelievers as a way of doing penance to God. It was not the pious and mystical author of the *Canticle of Canticles* speaking, but the self-appointed 'Conscience of Europe'.

Bernard travelled through Burgundy, Lorraine, Flanders and the Rhineland cities preaching the crusade. A vast assembly gathered at Vezelay, where they listened to an impassioned speech from Bernard and roared out *'Give us Crosses!'* For hours afterwards Bernard and his monks were sewing red crosses onto tunics. Meanwhile Bernard had persuaded a reluctant Conrad of Germany to join. He also brought in Louis VII of France by telling him that a crusade was the ideal way of occupying the idle young knights whose way of life was warfare, even if it was only seizing and robbing local towns and villages as was their custom.

The crusade was a shameful disaster. The British contingent decided to have good sport on the way to the East by besieging Muslim-held Lisbon. The two main armies, French and German, wound their ways separately across Europe in May and June 1147, causing havoc on the way and massacring all the Jews they found in the cities along their routes. They reached Constantinople to find the Byzantines totally occupied in dealing with the Armenians in Anatolia. The crusaders were not welcome. Through bad generalship Louis' army was defeated by the Saracens at Laodicea on the Syrian border and Conrad's army was wiped out in an ambush.

The Crusaders blamed Byzantine treachery. The effect of this failure was to teach the Muslims that the crusaders were not invincible and that once the complicated politics of the region were sorted out, they could destroy the Christian Kingdom of Jerusalem. This they finally succeeded in doing under Saladin in 1187. (Note: a table recording the eight crusades is given at the end of this chapter).

Bernard was blamed by the Roman Curia for the disastrous result of the crusade that he had inspired. It was an unhappy end to his life, for he died three years after the remnants of his armies returned. It was also for this reason that Rome opposed his canonisation as a saint for 20 years after his death. No one can deny his greatness as a man and as a spiritual force. His tragedy is the way he abandoned his philosophy of imitating Christ to preach a war which Christ would have loathed.

In this he earned the unenviable reputation of being the first Christian theologian to preach a *Justum Bellum*. This misguided ideal lived on for another two centuries and finally involved another great saint, King St Louis IX of France whose feast-day is also in August. The result of all that misplaced idealism is that it won for us the undying hatred of Islam.

The Visible Legacy of King St Louis IX of France (1214–70)

The life of King Louis and his involvement in the sixth and seventh crusades of 1252 and 1270 has been described briefly in the note in the Calendar for his feast-day (25th August). These were both disastrous; the first ended with Louis' capture by the Saracens and the second ill-planned venture ended with his own and most of his army's deaths from sickness and fever in Tunisia. Louis was not, however, made a saint for his crusading efforts, but because of his personal holiness and for the fact of his Christian attitude to governing his kingdom of France.

Sir Steven Runciman had this to say about St Louis in the third volume of his *History of the Crusades*, *The Kingdom of Acre*: '*Few human beings have ever been so consciously and sincerely virtuous. As king, he felt that he was responsible before God for the welfare of his people; and no prelate, not even the Pope himself, was allowed to come between him and this duty. It was his task to provide a just government . . . This stern devotion won him admiration even from his enemies; and their admiration was enhanced by his personal piety, his humility and his spectacular austerity.*'

We can obtain a glimpse of St Louis by visiting his greatest and most beautiful creation, his Sainte Chapelle on the Île de la Cité in Paris. This supremely beautiful gem of French Gothic art was built in 33 months and dedicated in 1148 to house the Crown of Thorns, which King Louis had bought for a vast sum from the debt-ridden King Baudouin of Jerusalem. It is symbolic of everything that was sacred to St Louis and is the most sublime memorial not only to the saint and king himself, but also to the highest ideals of France as a Christian nation and to her record in that age of faith as the leading example of the true spirit of Christendom.

The Chapelle is built on two floors. The ground floor contains the great pillars that support the second floor and the main chapel. One reaches the second floor by climbing up a winding stone staircase. Then, immediately as one emerges into the open nave of the chapel, especially if one's visit is on a sunny day, one is literally overwhelmed by the stunning beauty, colour and scope of the stained glass windows that form the walls of the chapel and record all the main events and stories in the Bible.

The stained-glass windows, held up by the slender pillars which support the roof, were superbly restored by Viollet-le-Duc after the Revolution. Like the tapestries that illustrate the 'Bible des Pauvres' in the Abbey of St Robert at La Chaise-Dieu, these windows are a monument of medieval art. When the sun shines through the coloured glass windows the effect is dazzling. One can get an idea of this from the sketches of some of the windows on the next page. One can just imagine the effect they must have had when St Louis, clad in his humble robe as a Franciscan Tertiary, carried the Crown of Thorns up the altar steps to its place in the chapel. This monument encapsulates the spirit of those days, the great age of rising faith, when the great cathedrals of France and Germany were being built and when there were four great saints living and communing together in Paris: King St Louis, St Albert the Great, St Thomas Aquinas and St Bonaventure. When so much of value and beauty has been destroyed, we are indeed fortunate to have been given such legacy.

Sainte Chapelle

*Sketches of stained-glass windows
in the Sainte Chapelle*

TABLE 2 – THE CRUSADES (1097–1270)

Introduction: We know from Sir Steven Runciman's masterly *History of the Crusades* that what medieval Europe regarded as devout and chivalrous attempts to recover Jerusalem and the most holy Christian sites, was misguided idealism, cruelly carried out. They need to be outlined here because they did great harm in the name of religion.

The 1st Crusade (1097–99): Bands of Christian pilgrims used to visit the Holy Land fairly freely until after the Seljuk Turks conquered Syria, Iraq and Palestine and invaded Anatolia. After his defeat by them at Manzikert in 1071, the Byzantine Emperor begged the Papacy to launch a Crusade to drive out the Turks, or Saracens as they were called. In 1095 Pope Urban II launched his appeal at Clermont in the Auvergne for a Crusading army to be formed. Its symbol was a red cross on a white background.

Norman, Frankish and Provençal nobles raised several armies which eventually reached and captured Jerusalem in June 1099. They massacred the entire Muslim and Jewish population, an act of wanton cruelty. They then established themselves as kings and princes ruling Palestine and Syria. They also formed the Order of Knights Templar and Hospitallers to defend and tend the pilgrims along the routes.

The 2nd Crusade (1147–48): The Saracens recaptured Edessa in Syria in 1144 and the Holy Places were once again in danger. The crusade failed and the Greeks were blamed, but Jerusalem remained in Christian hands.

The 3rd Crusade (1189–92): Saladin had captured Jerusalem in 1187. Pope Clement III called for a crusade. King Richard of England, Philip Augustus II of France and the Holy Roman Emperor Frederick Barbarossa took part. Acre and the Palestine coastal ports were captured, but the allied forces quarrelled and all that was gained was the right for Christians to visit the Holy Places and Jerusalem.

The 4th Crusade (1199–1204): A collection of French nobles formed an army and, regarding the Greek Orthodox Emperors as enemies, they attacked and captured Constantinople and performed the cruellest and most outrageous acts, plundering and murdering the Byzantine Emperor and his bishops. These nobles, de Joinville, de Villehardouin and others, then made themselves Kings of Athens, Sparta and elsewhere. The chief effect was to ruin the Byzantine Civilisation.

The 5th Crusade (1218–21): Popes Innocent III and Honorius III, hoping to rid Europe of the hundreds of unemployed knights and their followers, blessed this crusade, which sailed to besiege Damietta on the Nile, hoping to exchange it for Jerusalem. St Francis of Assisi accompanied the army, hoping for martyrdom.

The 6th Crusade (1227–29); the 7th Crusade (1248–50); the 8th Crusade in 1270: The Emperor Frederick II (Hohenstauffen) launched his own (6th) crusade, encouraged by Pope Honorius III, who wanted to get him out of Italy. He captured Jerusalem, which the Christians held until 1244.

The loss of Jerusalem decided King Louis IX of France to try again. He failed at Damietta and was captured. After four years as a prisoner he was ransomed for one million gold besants. He took the cross again in 1270 and was persuaded by his brother and heir to invade through Tunis as the Muslim corsairs were dominating the Mediterranean. The King and his army caught fever and dysentry and Louis died.

SEPTEMBER SAINTS

September

1. St Giles
   St Fiacre
2. St Brocard
3. St Gregory the Great
7. St Evurtius
   St Adrian
8. Nativity of the Virgin Mary
9. St Isaac the Great

St Matthew the Tax Collector summoned by Jesus to be a Disciple

21. St Matthew
23. St Linus
26. St Cyprian, Martyrs of North America St Colman of Lann Elo
27. St Vincent de Paul
28. St Wenceslas
29. St Michael St Gabriel
    St Raphael & All Angels
30. St Jerome
    St Honorius of Canterbury St Sophia
    St Otto of Bamberg

13. St John Chrysostom
14. Holy Cross Day
15. St Catherine of Genoa
16. St Edith of Wilton
17. St Lambert of Maastricht
    St Columba of Cordova
19. St Theodore of Canterbury
20. St Eustice

The Archangel St Michael

St John Chrysostom Driven into exile by Empress Eudoxia

The three saints depicted in the heading are **St Matthew** the Apostle and Evangelist (21 September), **The Archangel Michael** (29 September) and **St John Chrysostom** (13 September).

227

ILLUSTRATION OF TWELVE SEPTEMBER SAINTS

This illustration is a design for a tapestry to depict twelve of the saints with feast-days in September. They are depicted in historical order in an imaginary Paradise, about to greet the arrival of new souls, who are being brought in ships as described in Dante's *Divine Comedy*.

The following saints are shown from left to right:

Pope St Linus (23 September), St Peter's successor; **Pope St Cornelius,** (16 September) martyred 253; **St Eustace** (20 September), with the stag he saw carrying the Cross between his horns. **St Jerome – or Hieronymus** (30 September), the translator of the Vulgate; **St Isaac the Great** (9 September), Armenian bishop who died in 438; **St Colman of Llan Elo** (26 September) seventh-century Irish abbot, standing in the water as in his legend; **St Fiacre** (1 September), seventh-century Irish missionary to Gaul, working on his heavenly garden; **'King' St Wenceslas** (28 September) tenth-century Bohemian martyr; **St Hildegarde of Bingen – or 'of the Rhine'** (17 September) eleventh-century abbess with a page of her music; **St Sergius of Radonezh** (25 September), founder of many Russian monasteries; **St Catherine of Genoa** (15 September) fifteenth-century visionary; **St Vincent de Paul** (27 September), important seventeenth-century French priest.

Twelve September saints in an imaginary Paradise

229

ALTAR-PIECE DESIGN FOR NINE SEPTEMBER SAINTS

Shown in the top row are:

St Thecla of Iconium (23 September) escaping into a cave from rapists and being hidden by a fall of rocks; St Cyprian (16 September) being tried for his life; St Sophia, 'Holy Wisdom' (30 September) and her daughters St Faith, St Hope and St Charity.

In the centre row are:

St Peter Clavier (9 September) teaching slaves in the Spanish Indies; St Joseph of Copertino (18 September), 'the Flying Friar'; St Ciaran (9 September) looking at the site of the monastery he founded in the Shannon Valley in Ireland.

In the bottom row are:

St Otto of Bamberg (30 September), missionary bishop to Pomerania; St Deiniol (11 September) seeking a site for his sixth-century monastery on the coast of Anglesey; St Cloud (7 September), grandson of King Clovis who became a hermit by the river Seine.

Design for an altar-piece for nine September saints

231

SEPTEMBER CALENDAR OF SAINTS' FEAST-DAYS

1st FIACRE: Seventh-century Irish missionary to Gaul, who was given land for a hermitage by Bishop St Faro of Meaux (28 October). He was renowned for his herb garden and for his refusal to allow women into his enclosure. A hospice was built nearby and is now the site of St Fiacre-en-Brie. Because the first cabs for hire in Paris (c.1620) were stationed by the Hotel Saint Fiacre, four-wheeler cabs became known as 'Fiacres'.

GILES: Died c.710. He founded a monastery at Saint Gilles in Provençe on land given him by King Wamba. His legend tells that the King was out hunting stags when one of his arrows missed a stag which had taken refuge with Giles (or 'Gilles'). It hit the saint in the leg, wounding him so badly that he became lame for life. He was very popular in medieval times and became patron saint of cripples. His London church is St Giles Cripplegate.

2nd BROCARD: Died in 1231. Frankish Hermit in Palestine. Founded the Carmelites.

3rd POPE GREGORY I ('The Great'): His story has already been told under his original feast-day on 12 March, as it still is in the Anglican prayer-book.

4th ULTAN of ARDBRACCAN: Died in 657. Founded school in Meath, Ireland. He provided illuminated prayer books and fed poor students. Wrote life of St Brigid.

BIRINUS: Died in 650 as Bishop of Dorchester in Oxfordshire. He was sent by Pope Honorius I as a missionary from Lombardy to Britain in about 635. He concentrated on the pagans in Wessex and founded a church in Winchester which became the ecclesiastical centre of the Kingdom of Wessex up to the time of King Alfred.

5th LAURENCE GIUSTINI (1381–1435): Archbishop of Venice. Wrote mystical themes on Eternal Wisdom. Austere but generous to the poor. Canonised in 1690.

6th CAGNOALD: Died in 672. Irish monk who worked with St Columbanus (21 November) at Luxeuil in Burgundy. He became Bishop of Laon. See also St Omer below on 9 September.

7th EVURTIUS: Fourth-century bishop of Orleans.

CLOUD (520–60): Prince and grandson of King Clovis. He became a hermit by the River Seine near the village of Versailles after escaping death at the hands of his uncle who had usurped the throne. See also his mother Queen St Clotilde (3 June).

8th ADRIAN and NATALIA: Husband and wife martyred in Nicomedia in 304.

9th CIARAN of CLONMACNOISE (516–49): Irish monk trained by St Enda (21 March) and St Finnian of Clonard (12 December). Founded monastery of Clonmacnois in the Shannon valley. Very beautiful ruins.

ISAAC ('The Great') (347–438): Leading bishop in Armenia. Opposed the Patriarch Nestorius' alleged heresy that named Mary *Christokos* – 'Mother of Christ' – as it was confusing to call her 'Mother of God'. Driven from his see by Persians, but continued his mission to the Armenians under great difficulty, teaching the gospel in their language.

OMER: Died in 570. Another of St Colombanus' Irish missionary monks to Gaul (See St Cagnoald above). Converted many pagans in the Pas de Calais and was made bishop there. Founded monastery at what is now called St Omer.

BERTRAM: Early eighth-century hermit of Crowland.

JOSEPH of VOLOKOLAMSK (1439–1515): Learned Lithuanian abbot.

PETER CLAVER (1580–1654): Catalan Jesuit missionary to negro slaves in the Spanish Indies. He defended them against rich and powerful colonists.

10th EMPRESS PULCHERIA (399–453): Devout Greek Orthodox Empress, unlike her weak brother Emperor Theodosius II, whom she succeeded after he died in a fall from a horse. He had supported the heretical abbot Eutyches who had wanted to force the dogma on the whole Church that Jesus only had one nature, the divine. Pulcheria, a convinced Orthodox Christian, ordered the case to be submitted to a Church Council at Chalcedon.

In 451 this Council accepted Pope Leo I's 'Tome' or encyclical proclaiming the traditional Church view that Jesus had two natures, human and divine. Sadly, through the posthumous influence of St Cyril of Alexandria (27 June) and in spite of the council's decision, Egypt kept to the Monophysite view of Jesus' nature that Eutyches had also promoted. This caused a lasting schism in the Eastern Church, which was fatal to the Church in Africa and Asia when the Prophet Muhammad rejected Christianity for his Arabs because, as he recorded in the Koran, the Christian sects disagreed over the nature of the God they worshipped.

FINNIAN OF MOVILLE: Died in 579. He was taught the faith in St Ninian's (26 August) monastery in Galloway in Scotland. He was forced to leave because a Pictish girl had fallen in love with him. He went to Rome and was ordained and then sent to Ulster, where he introduced the new Latin text of the Bible – St Jerome's Vulgate. He founded a school at Moville and was made a bishop there. The famous dedication of the Irish Church to Latin scholarship began at about this time as did the production of the gospels in illuminated volumes, of which *The Book of Kells* is such a beautiful example. That is only equalled by the *Lindisfarne Gospels* which were also Celtic-inspired.

AUBERT of AVRANCHES: Died in 725. Bishop of Avranches who established the shrine of the archangel on Mont Saint Michel after having dreamed about him.

NICHOLAS of TOLENTINO (1235–1305): Augustine Friar, tireless pastoral worker and teacher and also a converter of sinners. Many miracles alleged.

11th **PROTUS and HYACINTH:** Martyrs in Rome of unknown date, but with a widespread cult and mentioned in fourth-century martyrologies.

PAPHNUTIUS: A disciple of St Antony of Egypt (17 January) who became bishop of Upper Egypt. He was blinded in Maximus' persecution of 310–12. He opposed the plan at the Council of Nicea in 325 to compel clergy to separate from their wives. St Athanasius (2 May) supported him. Today Greek Orthodox clergy may marry, but not Greek bishops.

DEINIOL: Sixth-century Irish abbot who founded the monastery on the Isle of Anglesey after rowing himself across the Menai Straits. He also founded another on the Welsh River Dee.

12th **GUY of ANDERLECHT** (950–1012): Lay sacristan of Laeken in Belgium. He was sent to Jerusalem and became renowned as a very holy man.

13th **JOHN CHRYSOSTOM** (347–407): Patriarch of Constantinople martyred through imperial interference with the Orthodox Church and rival Egyptian Archbishop's politico-religious ambitions. His story is told in the text following this Calendar.

EULOGIUS of ALEXANDRIA: Died in 608. Bishop who encouraged Pope Gregory I to send St Augustine to evangelise Britain.

NOTBURGA (1265–1313): Servant of Count Henry of the Tyrol. She was sacked by her mistress for giving scraps of food to the poor instead of to the pigs. Recalled to the castle, she starved herself to give food to the poor. She is the patron saint of domestic servants.

15th **ADAM OF CAITHNESS:** Bishop from 1213 to 1222. Cistercian monk appointed bishop by King William of Scotland. His see was in a remote and unruly area dominated by rough Norse earls. Adam tried to enforce the law for the payment of tithes to the Church in cattle. The people revolted and burnt him and his clergy alive in his house.

CATHERINE of GENOA (1447–1510): Had visions all her life, both holy and diabolical. In 1473 she had a 'conversion experience' and she and her husband gave up a life of pleasure to found a hospital and work for the poor and sick. She wrote a popular book describing her experiences: *Dialogue Between the Soul and the Body*. Beatified in 1737 and canonised a few years later. The length taken over her 'cause' shows how much of a pope's time, especially that of the late John-Paul II, is taken up with saint-making.

16th **CORNELIUS:** Made Pope in 251 after Emperor Decius had begun his empire-wide persecutions of Christians. He offended puritanical clergy by pardoning converts who had lapsed during the persecutions and who wanted to rejoin the Church. St Cyprian (see below) supported him. He died in 253 from hardships caused by his exile from Rome, which caused St Cyprian to call him 'Cornelius Martyr'.

CYPRIAN of CARTHAGE: Martyred in 258. He was a lawyer who became a Christian in 246 and was made Bishop of Carthage in 248 during the reign of the first Christian emperor, Philip the Arab. When Decius' persecution began in 250 he ruled his see while in hiding, pardoning those who repented for denying Christ at their trials. In doing so he proclaimed that all bishops had the same powers as the popes in their own dioceses in respect of discipline and teaching. It was during this time that Donatus, Bishop of Numidia, started a separate church (see St Augustine of Hippo, 28 August) with extreme puritan standards and which refused communion or re-baptism to repentant apostates. Eventually Cyprian was arrested, tried and executed towards the end of the greatest persecution until that of Diocletian began 40 years later.

EUPHEMIA: Virgin martyred in Chalcedon in 304.

NINIAN: Died in 432. Hermit of Whithorn in Galloway, whose missionaries taught Christianity to the Celts. Whithorn was popular for pilgrims in the middle ages.

EDITH of WILTON (961–84): Natural daughter of Anglo-Saxon King Edgar. Lived all her life in a nunnery at Wilton near Salisbury. She refused to become abbess, saying she wanted to *'serve her sisters like Martha'*.

LUDMILLA: Died in 921. Wife of the first Czech king to become Christian. Murdered by pagan noble at instigation of her pagan daughter-in-law, the mother of Wenceslas (see 28 September), who was acting as regent for her son. It was Ludmilla who brought Wenceslas up to be a Christian. She and Wenceslas became the subject of popular legends.

17th LAMBERT of MAASTRICHT (635–705): Missionary bishop martyred at Liège by Frankish magnate for rebuking his adultery.

COLUMBA of CORDOBA: Spanish nun martyred by Moors in 853 for protesting that Muhammad was a false prophet.

HILDEGARDE of the RHINE (or of **BINGEN**) (1098–1179): Benedictine Abbess of Bingen. Always in bad health. She had many unusual spiritual experiences, which gave her a reputation as a prophetess. She corresponded with four popes and three emperors. She dictated the warnings of the wrath to come that she received during her visions. They are incomprehensible. She tried to invent a universal language, a mixture of German and Latin, and dictated her equally strange comments on the gospels and the Benedictine rule. Her mystical experiences may have been induced by the hesychastic style of breathing and prayer that was prevalent in the Rhineland among the Jewish community. Her mystical ideas have been compared to those of the English poet William Blake. She is remembered today especially for her beautiful liturgical music.

ROBERT BELLARMINE (1542–1621): Jesuit Archbishop of Capua and classical scholar. As a young priest he had lectured on St Thomas Aquinas' theology in the University of Louvain, where he published his *Disputations on the Controversies of the Christian Faith*. This work was a defence of the Catholic faith and a brilliant examination of the teaching of the Early Fathers. It was so learned that it was banned in protestant England. As Prefect of the Vatican Library from 1605 he was involved in the re-editing of the *Vulgate*. He believed in taking a sympathetic course in controversies, praying for Protestant theologians and recommended caution to Galileo in the way he presented his theories and astronomical discoveries. He was the bishop who recommended the appointment of St Francis de Sales to the bishopric of Geneva (24 January). He also advised Pope Sixtus V to moderate his views on the temporal powers of the papacy. This delayed his cause for canonisation until 1930.

18th JOSEPH of COPERTINO (1603–63): Canonised in 1767. A poor youth from Brindisi who became a Franciscan friar. He experienced remarkable ecstasies and levitations and achieved amazing healings. The Spanish ambassador recorded witnessing one of his levitations, when he flew from the altar to his cell. His levitations were involuntary and his fellow friars complained that they made him grumpy. He bore their complaints humbly as one '*whose conversation was with heaven rather than on earth*'.

19th JANUARIUS: Bishop of Benevento martyred in c.305. Naples cathedral contains a phial of his blood which liquifies at regular intervals as has been recorded for many centuries. A similar liquifaction takes place with the blood of the martyr St Pantaleon (27 July) at Ravello, south of Naples.

THEODORE of CANTERBURY (602–90): A Greek from Tarsus who was made Archbishop of Canterbury by the pope in 672 instead of St Adrian of Canterbury (9th Jan), the black abbot of Monte Cassino, who was too humble to take the office. Theodore only accepted when Adrian agreed to accompany him as an adviser and assistant. The Church organisation in England needed to be improved. It was largely a missionary body run by competing individuals like St Wilfrid (12 October), Archbishop of York. Theodore's solution of the administrative problems included splitting up the Archdiocese of York. This angered Wilfrid, who was deposed and went south to evangelise the pagans along the Sussex coast. Theodore's system enabled the Church to survive many storms until the Reformation.

BREBEUF, Jean de (1593–1649): Jesuit missionary to Canada,. Successful with the Hurons, but martyred by Iroquois after terrible tortures.

EMILY de RODAT (1787–1852): Canonised in 1950. She established the Order of the Holy Family at Villefranche in 1815. This played a prominent part in restoring religion to France after the Revolution.

20th EUSTACE: A popular but probably legendary figure, whose story is similar to that of St Hubert (3 November). He is said to have been one of the Emperor Trajan's generals who saw a vision of Christ's cross between a stag's antlers while out hunting near Tivoli. He became a Christian and was disgraced. Later he was reinstated, won a victory, but refused to give thanks to the Roman gods. He was roasted alive for his refusal. Due to the lack of historical records Eustace was demoted as a universal saint in the 1969 reforms of the calendar and is now only one of the 'Holy Helpers'.

ANDREW KIM, PAUL CHONG HASAN and FRIENDS: Martyred in Korea in 1845. Andrew was bishop of the Christian community in Korea which dates back to the seventeenth-century French missionaries. He and 103 members of The French Missionary Society of Paris were beheaded by the Korean authorities in a persecution of Christians which lasted until 1867.

21st **MATTHEW:** Apostle and Evangelist. See his life story in Part III of this book.

22nd **MAURICE and COMPANIONS:** Martyred in c.287. Maurice commanded the Theban Legion recruited from Christians in Egypt to fight Maximian's campaign against the Gauls. Before a battle on the Gallo-Swiss border at Martigny the army was ordered to pray and offer incense to the imperial gods. Maurice and his legion refused to do so. They also refused to kill the Gauls as they were Christians.

Maximian ordered the legion to parade and to be decimated by the rest of the army. The butchery of Maurice and his 6,000 men continued until they were all dead. After each tenth was killed, the remainder still refused to obey Maximian. The story, like that of St Ursula (21 October) and her companions, may have been embroidered. However the priest of Martigny is convinced that a massacre on these lines did take place there.

23rd **LINUS:** Traditionally believed to have been St Peter's successor. Nothing is known of him, though St Irenaeus of Lyons identified him with the 'Linus' mentioned in St Paul's II Timothy 4.21 as sending greetings from Rome. His martyrdom in about 80 is in doubt since there was no organised persecution at that time.

THECLA of ICONIUM: First-century virgin martyr who hid in a cave behind Myra on the Turkish coast to save herself from being raped and killed by a gang of robbers. Her legend, which St Jerome did not believe, maintains that a fall of rock blocked the entrance to the cave, saving her from her persecutors, but she was never seen again. Her shrine at Myra was referred to in his letters by St Isidore of Pelusium as a popular place for pilgrims. There are 16 other 'Theclas' among the saints, mostly virgins and martyrs in Egypt, Sicily and Italy.

ADOMNAN (627–704): Irish Abbot of Iona, who was converted on Easter eve 688. He recommended that the Irish should adopt the Roman calendar for Easter that had been agreed at the Council of Whitby in 663. He was influential enough to have the Church law of Adomnan accepted, by which women were excused from going into battle with their men and were treated as non-combatants. He wrote the *Life of St Columba* in which he referred to *'Our father Patrick'* – unlike St Bede who never refers to St Patrick in his history, which was about the Anglo-Saxon and not the Irish Church.

24th **GERARD of SAGREDO:** Died in 1046. A Venetian and prior of San Giorgio Maggiore who made a circuitous pilgrimage to Jerusalem travelling via Hungary. King St Stephen of Hungary (16 August) asked him to be his son's tutor. Some time later Gerard was made Bishop of Csanad, in a pagan region of Hungary. On Stephen's death in 1038 Gerard was attacked during an anti-Christian uprising and was transfixed with a lance and thrown into the Danube. In 1333 Venice obtained a share of his relics and placed them on the island of Murano, where he is venerated as Venice's first martyr.

ROBERT of KNARESBOROUGH (1160–1218): Hermit who lived in a cave in Yorkshire. He was evicted several times, allegedly for harbouring robbers among the poor he looked after. King John gave him land in 1216 where he lived until he died.

25th **EUPHROSYNE:** No date. Legendary penitent who probably never existed.

CADOC: Sixth-century abbot of Llancarfan in Wales. Contemporary of St Gildas (29 January) and St Samson (28 July), also widely venerated in Brittany.

SERGIUS of VORONEZH (1314–82): Canonised in Russia in 1549. Aged 20 he and his companions became hermits in the woods north of Moscow and then founded the Monastery of the Holy Trinity and other sister monasteries. His aim was for the monks to live a life of communal poverty and eradicate self-will. He had mystical experiences which he attributed to the Virgin Mary. He had enormous spiritual influence.

Lancelot Andrewes: Bishop who organised the production of King James' English translation of the Bible in 1603.

26th **COSMAS and DAMIAN:** Physicians who treated the poor free and were martyred in Cilicia in c.303.

COLMAN of LANN ELO (555–611): Irish abbot who according to legend was working by a stream, when someone shouted: *'Colman! Get into the water!'*. There were so many monks called Colman in his abbey that twelve 'Colmans' immediately jumped into the stream. There are over 100 early Irish saints of this name.

27th BARRY: Sixth-century hermit disciple of St Cadoc (25 September). Barry island off the Glamorgan coast is named after him.

VINCENT de PAUL (1581–1660): Gascon founder of the Vincentians in France after being court chaplain to King Louis XIV. He was a much-needed missionary to the rich and the nobility at court, but was also devoted to the poor and oppressed. He tried to improve the lot of the galley slaves in the French Mediterranean fleet. In 1633 his order was given the church of St Lazare in Paris and was sometimes called the 'Lazarists'. He helped St Louise de Marillac (15 March) to found the unenclosed order of the Sisters of Charity to work for the poor and nurse the sick. He became a legend in his life-time, opposing the Jansenists of Port Royal, who held extreme views on predestination. He was canonised in 1737. The Society of St Vincent de Paul is active in many lands today.

28th MACHAN: Sixth-century Scottish disciple of St Cadoc. Glasgow Cathedral is built over his tomb.

LIOBA (c.700–80): Abbess of Wessex who led 30 nuns at the request of St Boniface of Crediton (5 June) to help him in Germany. They could all read and write and Lioba's community had great influence around Bischofsheim in Franconia. Hildegarde, one of Charlemagne's future wives (he had three living queens and at least 13 concubines), became a close friend of Lioba.

WENCESLAS (907–29): He became Duke of Bohemia at 15, having been brought up as a Christian by his grandmother St Ludmilla (16 September). He had a pagan mother who conspired to have Ludmilla murdered. Then Wenceslas' pagan brother Boleslav killed him while he was his guest. The martyred Wenceslas became the subject of many Czech legends and as 'Good King Wenceslas' was the subject of the Reverend JM Neale's (died 1866) popular Victorian carol.

LAWRENCE RUIZ and COMPANIONS: Ruiz, a Chinese Dominican missionary from Manila and 15 Japanese converts were martyred at Nagasaki in 1637. They were canonised in 1987. Japanese martyrs include St Paul Miki (6 February) in 1597 and over 100 others who suffered in 1617–1632.

29th THE ARCHANGELS MICHAEL, GABRIEL and RAPHAEL: Gabriel in the Old Testament helped Daniel to understand his dreams. In the New Testament Gabriel appears to Zacharia, the father of John the Baptist and also to the Virgin Mary as the messenger of God. **Michael** was venerated by the Jews (see Daniel 10.13–21) and he appears in the text on the Apocalypse in Revelations 12.7–9 as the commander of the heavenly army of angels against the Dragon and his angels. **Raphael**, whose name means 'God heals', is in the Book of Tobit in the Apocrypha as the travelling companion of Tobias, who is searching for a cure for his father Tobit's blindness. The connection of Raphael with healing and pilgrimages is why he was given a statue at Lourdes.

30th SOPHIA ('Holy Wisdom'): Legendary mother of Saints Faith, Hope and Charity.

JEROME (or HIERONYMUS) (c.341–420): Biblical scholar who had studied under St Gregory of Nazianzus (3 January). As secretary to Pope Damasus he collected a following of devoted ladies in Rome, to whom he acted as spiritual adviser. Pope Damasus asked him to go to Bethlehem to establish a monastery and make an improved Latin translation of the Bible, later called the Vulgate, using as much original material as possible. In 385 Jerome took two of his rich widows with him from Rome, the future St Paula (26 January) and St Marcella (31 January) who financed both the building of the monastery at Bethlehem and Jerome's researches. He was a fierce critic of any early Christian work that he considered unorthodox – hence his condemnation of Origen (see the January Calendar) for his early attempt to define the Trinity. St Augustine of Hippo corresponded with him about his translation, but Jermoe often regarded his comments as being rather condescending.

His emblem of a lion denotes the ferocity of his search for and defence of the truth. He and his helpers were twice attacked and driven from Bethlehem by marauding Isaurian tribesmen. Although he was active at work in Palestine while St John Chrysostom was Patriarch of Constantinople and being harassed by the Empress Eudoxia and the ambitious and scheming Archbishop of Alexandria, Jerome remained aloof.

OTTO of BAMBERG (1062–1139): Swabian priest made Bishop of Bamberg and appointed as his Chancellor by the Emperor Henry IV in 1101. He made a missionary journey to Poland in 1124, establishing churches and making many thousands of converts. He had to return there in 1128 to re-convert the backsliders. Otto Bamber was concerned with the long conflict between the Papacy and the Emperors over their investiture of laymen as bishops, but examined each case on its own merits and never acted in a partisan spirit. He was an excellent pastoral bishop and was canonised 50 years after his death.

SUMMARY OF SEPTEMBER SAINTS

This Calendar gives the feast-days of 71 saints, of whom 12 were martyrs and 13 were women.

Since the life of St Matthew has already been given at length in Part III of this book, the only saint who is not adequately covered in our search for the evidence of the Spirit at work is the life of **St John Chrysostom,** which is given below. His story shows how the Byzantine emperors and empresses tried to control the Greek Orthodox Church to suit their own ambitions and policies and how he became a martyr for resisting the oppression of his country's rulers.

THE TRIALS OF ST JOHN CHRYSOSTOM

This story is told at some length to illustrate the typical intrigues and dangers which confronted Church leaders, not only through the Byzantine Court intrigues in the East, but also in the West. The Church in the East suffered these almost continuously from the time of Constantine's conversion in 312 until the fall of Constantinople in 1453. Similarly in the West, the Church suffered from the interference and military actions of emperors and kings from the time of Charlemagne until Napoleon I, Bismark and Hitler.

In November 397 the Emperor Arcadius and his forceful and ambitious Empress Eudoxia met their chief minister the eunuch Eutropius and a number of bishops to choose a new Patriarch for Constantinople. After rejecting five candidates they chose Abbot John of Antioch in Syria. Eudoxia is said to have exclaimed after the selection of John that: *'There is no dearer wish in my heart than that there should be religious peace in this city'*. She said that Abbot John had all the right qualities to achieve this.

Abbot John was known as 'Chrysostom' or 'golden-tongued' because of his skill as a preacher. His life had been spent mostly in monasteries, but he had acted as coadjutor to the Bishop of Antioch for ten years. The bishop praised his powers of administration and his pastoral work.

John had also written learned books on *The Merits of Virginity* and *The Holy Trinity* and several commentaries on the scriptures. These had inspired the future St Isidore of Pelusium (see 5 February), who may have been his pupil. John Chrysostom was also a man of courage, as he had proved when facing alone and calming down a mob of rioters angered by new taxes. His action avoided the need to bring in imperial troops. While John was being escorted by General Gaias, the commander of the

Emperor's Gothic troops, on the 800-mile journey from Antioch to be enthroned in Constantinople, the Egyptian Archbishop Theophilus attempted to have his own candidate appointed instead of him. The minister Eutropius told him it was too late and that in any case he should warn him that he could inform the Emperor of certain financial irregularities of the archbishop. *'You blackmailing eunuch!'* yelled the Archbishop. Eutropius was forced to give way, but promised to take his revenge.

According to the historian Palladius, the source of these stories, John Chrysostom was a small man with unexpectedly long limbs. This could be seen by the way his emaciated hands and feet protruded from under his humble monk's habit. He wore the hood thrown back over his shoulders to reveal a lofty furrowed brow and a sunburned wizened face and piercing eyes. His only ornament was a plain flat silver cross, shaped in the Eastern style with one longer arm.

John was horrified at the luxurious fittings of his patriarchal palace, so he sold them to raise funds to give to the poor. He also dismissed most of the servants and attendants and lived his customary ascetic life, feeding on soup or gruel. All this at first disappointed the populace who liked to see their patriarch put on a show. The scanty food that he provided for visiting bishops also gave his enemies and rivals a chance to accuse him of inhospitality.

However they were impressed when John began ruthlessly to cleanse the city and entire patriarchy of immoral clergy, the idle and those guilty of heretical practices. He deposed three bishops and two abbots for homicide, simony and consorting with women. He also preached sermons against the vociferous Jewish-Christian sect in the city for their refusal to accept Jesus as Son of God and for protesting that he was only the promised Messiah.

The following three excerpts illustrate the very Christian quality of the sermons John Chryostom preached before the Emperor and Empress and the people of the city. The first is on the duty of loving our neighbour:

'*What the Son has done for you to reconcile you to God, you must do – as far as your human strength allows – by being builders of peace between you and others . . . Also remember that when we come to the moment of sacrifice at the Eucharist, the only commandment of which Jesus reminds us, is to be reconciled with our brother. He who said: "This is my Body" and made it so by his word, is the same who also said: "You saw me hungry and you gave me no food . . . As you did it not to the least of these my brethren, you did it not to me!" Therefore honour Him who wants not golden chalices but golden souls.*'

The second quotation is on the Church as a universal community: '*Christ makes us a single body. Thus those who live in his name look upon Indians as their own members. Is there a union to be compared with that? Christ is the head of all! Men, women, children, deeply divided as to race, nationality, class, work, knowledge, rank, fortune, are all created afresh by the Church in the Spirit. On all alike she impresses a divine form. In the Church no-one is in any way separated from the community. Everyone is, so to speak, merged into everyone else by the invisible power of faith. Christ is everything to everyone.*'

This third quotation tells how God comes down to us through prayer: '*I will speak now on prayer and the incomprehensibility of God. By prayer I mean not that which is only in the mouth, but that which springs from the bottom of the heart. In praying make the mind empty and free of stray thoughts, so as to be able to offer it in a state of readiness when Christ's teachings are taken in. It will then be swept clean for the words of God that it needs to welcome. The inaccessible comes down to us through love. The Son, the visible image of God, makes himself visible in the Incarnation. To see God is to meet Christ in one's neighbour.*'

When John had been Patriarch for a year and was talking to his deacons in the vestry after preaching, he heard a wild shriek of fear coming from the main part of the Basilica. Then in rushed the chief minister Eutropius, bloodstained and in torn robes, begging for sanctuary. He cried out that General Gaias, who was seeking to make himself emperor, had sent his soldiers to kill him and was going to betray his secrets. As he spoke a posse of soldiers burst into the room and rushed at Eutropius. John Chrysostom flung himself in between them and their victim and ordered them to put up their swords: '*Do not desecrate this holy place with murder*'.

Chysostom then agreed to accompany the alleged traitor under guard to the Emperor. He asked Arcadius not to execute Eutropius, who had done much good for the state. He warned him that if, like so many others at the imperial court, Eutropius had taken some state funds for his own use, his execution would cause these others through fear to rush into General Gaias's arms. That would only increase Gaias' power and encourage his ambitions. Arcadius saw the wisdom of this and ordered Eutropius to be sent by ship into exile in Cyprus. No sooner had the ship sailed than Eudoxia had it forced to return and had

Eutropius beheaded. She rejoiced at her coup, for she now only had Gaias and John Chrysostom between her and unimpeded influence over the powerful Arcadius.

Soon afterwards Gaias made his bid for power. He seized three of the imperial ministers and threatened to kill them unless he was made sole Consul. John Chrysostom confronted the general in his headquarters. Gaias called him an interfering priest and demanded he surrender the Church of the Holy Apostles in the city, so that his Arian Christian Gothic troops could have a church of their own. 'Never!' said Chrysostom. 'Never will any misbeliever worship in this city!' Gaias then told him that he had distributed his troops throughout the city and they were already choosing the women they would seize and houses and shops they would loot. Either the Emperor would make him Consul, or he would order the city to be pillaged.

Chrysostom at once told the Emperor to declare Gaias an outlaw and to warn the people of their danger. Arcadius spread the warning. The populace attacked the Goths while they were still scattered through the streets. They killed 7,000 and Gaias perished as he fled towards the Slav territory in the hills beyond the city.

This left Eudoxia with only Chrysostom between her and supreme power. She summoned her ladies Marcia, Castricia and Eugraphia and three dissident bishops – Antiochus of Ptolomais, Acacius and Chrysostom's enemy, Severinus. She reminded her widowed and dissolute ladies of what Chrysotom had said about them: 'They use for the ruin of their souls the property their husbands gained by distortion'. She told the bishops that Chrysostom had taken power from them all. She asked them therefore to seek every means of having him deposed.

Chrysostom soon became aware that Eudoxia and her party were plotting against him, even though she pretended friendliness towards him. However he carried on with his reforms of the Church and left the city in the winter of 400 to discipline erring bishops in Thrace and Ephesus. He deposed them and returned after three months to find that Archbishop Theophilus of Alexandria had joined the conspiracy against him. He had told Arcadius that Chrysostom had sinned by giving the Eucharist to some Egyptian monks whom he had exiled from Alexandria for teaching heretical views about the Trinity.

These Egyptians monks were known as 'The Tall Brethren'. Chrysostom considered them not guilty of heresy. However Theophilus persuaded the Emperor to have the Patriarch tried by a General Council and in order to get learned backing for his case he persuaded the elderly Bishop Epiphamius of Salamis to come to Constantinople and investigate the matter.

Chrysostom realised that Theophilus would pack the General Council with his own bishops and any others he could bribe, using the immensely rich resources of his see of Alexandria. Therefore he decided that it would be wise to warn the people of Constantinople that the secular power was challenging the spiritual authority of the Church. For this purpose he chose a text from the First Book of Kings (18.13) for a sermon in St Sophia:

'Some twelve centuries ago the evil king Ahab ruled over Israel. His wife Jezebel, a worshipper of Baal, had had all the priests of Israel killed except for one, the prophet Elijah. Elijah demanded to see the king. Ahab said to him "Is that you, troubler of Israel?" To which Elijah answered: "I have not troubled Israel; but you have and your *father's house, because you have broken the commandments of the Lord and followed Baal! Now therefore send and gather all Israel to me on Mount Carmel. Bring there also the 450 prophets of Baal and the 400 priests of Asherah, who eat at Jezebel's table."* When they all gathered at Mount Carmel, Elijah came near to the people and said: *"How long will you go limping with two opinions? If the Lord is God, follow him; but if Baal then follow him!"'* Chrysostom then told the well-known story of how Elijah defeated the prophets of Baal and how the people then cried out: *'The Lord, He is God. Seize the prophets of Baal and let not one escape.'*

Chrysostom then broke off his sermon and cried out to the congregation: *'"Now gather to me those base priests who eat at Jezebel's table, that I may say to them, as Elijah did of old: "How long halt ye between two opinions? If Jezebel's table is the table of the Lord, eat at it, eat until you vomit!"'* No-one had the least doubt that Chrysotom was referring to the three bishops in Eudoxia's plot against him. Eudoxia was enraged at the implied insult to her, but kept silent; the plot was not yet ripe.

The people were on Chrysostom's side and a friend told him that *'What those renegade bishops cannot bear and which makes them so hot against you, is that your light shines in their eyes and makes them sore!'* Bishop Epiphanius also took Chrysostom's side. After questioning the 'tall brethren' he found them to be true orthodox Christians. He also examined the three bishops and found them guilty of various offences. He then realised that he had been made a victim of a court intrigue. In a fury he left the city for Salamis, saying: *'I have been on a fool's errand! These 'tall brethren' have perfect faith. They*

were exiled because they had found out some of Theophilus's sins. I leave you the city, the imperial court and all their hypocriscy!' The old man died at sea on his way home.

Archbishop Theophilus then came in person and in great state to the capital. He packed the General Council with 43 bribed bishops, 36 of whom were Egyptian. There were 29 charges against Chrysostom, alleging every crime from heresy and breaking canon law to gormandising in private, refusing to give proper hospitality to bishops and saying treasonable words about the Empress. The Council found Chrysostom guilty of all charges, deposed him as patriarch and applied to Arcadius for further sentencing. On hearing that their beloved patriarch had been deposed, the population rose in his defence. They guarded his house to prevent his arrest. At that moment Chrysostom could have done anything with them, but he wanted no blood shed on his behalf. Steadfast to the principles he had followed all his life, he spoke to the people in the Church of the Holy Apostles. He told them to be calm and that they must await the will of God. Then, to avoid attracting the attention of the populace, Chrysostom was hurried by Eudoxia's soldiers at night through a side door of the imperial palace to the quayside to sail into exile.

As the ship sailed, a terrible earthquake struck the city. Walls and towers collapsed, fires broke out. The superstitious Eudoxia, who had been told of Chrysostom's words about the will of God, begged Arcadius to recall the exile's ship. She cried out: *"It is my fault that God has sent this calamity upon us because of my enmity of his chosen patriarch"*. The ship was recalled and Chrysostom was greeted by a deliriously happy crowd and reinstated as Patriarch.

It was not long before Eudoxia's panic-found faith dissolved. She sought semi-divine honours for herself, such as had been given to Roman emperors. She even had a silver statue of herself placed on a porphyry column and dedicated to her in front of the basilica of St Sophia. This was an open challenge to the Church and Chrysostom was not long in making his views clear about Eudoxia's blasphemous act. He really had no choice. He exposed her by choosing as his text for a sermon the story of how Queen Herodias had St John the Baptist killed. Having told the story, he turned to the congregation and said, so that there should be no doubt about his meaning; '*So, once again Herodias is maddening! Herodias is once more dancing! Once more Herodias is demanding the head of John on a charger*'.

John Chrysostom is sometimes criticised for being tactless and unused to dealing with Eudoxia's ambitious intrigues, but the attacks on him and the Church were too blatant not to be challenged. Once again the Empress called in Archbishop Theophilus of Alexandria. He came up with what he believed to be an unanswerable case against the Patriarch. He sent two of his bishops to charge him with usurping the patriarchy by breaking a law passed in 341. This said that no deposed bishop could be reinstated or allowed to offer the sacrifice of the Eucharist.

However this law had been made by a heretical Arian council. The supporters of John Chrysostom were therefore able to dismiss the charges and the Egyptian bishops departed in confusion. However, Eudoxia assured Arcadius that the law had not been questioned by his orthodox father, the late Emperor Theodosius I. Therefore it must still be good law. Arcadius dithered for two months and then sentenced the patriarch to be deposed and exiled.

By this time it was Holy Week in 403. John Chrysostom was in the basilica of St Sophia and about to baptise 3,000 catechumens before a packed congregation. Arcadius sent his troops to arrest the Patriarch. They stormed into the basilica and used their swords to hack their way through the crowd towards the altar to seize Chrysostom. The crowd panicked, the soldiers tore off the jewels and rich clothing from the ladies. The whole congregation fled to the Baths of Constantine. The patriarch planned to join them there to complete the ceremony.

The soldiers locked the doors of the baths and the people were made prisoners. John Chrysostom surrendered himself to save their lives. He was then sent across the Bosphorous and made to march through the heat from Chalcedon on the long journey to the borders of Armenia. Eudoxia and Arcadius hoped that he would die of exposure on the way. For three years he was left alone by the Empress and was given food and medicine by his friends who had estates in the frontier region. He even continued his studies and managed to carry on a considerable correspondence, so that no important Church appointment was made without his approval.

In 407 Eudoxia died in childbirth but Chrysostom's enemies in the Church did not cease their persecution of him but sent a notorious bully of a Praetorian Guard to march him to a fortress far away in the Caucasus mountains. While this was happening, one of his friends, the deacon John Cassian (future saint, see 29 February), pleaded his case before the Pope in Rome. On the march the ageing John Chrysostom was deliberately starved and suffered from fever and dysentery. Issaurian bandits made repeated attacks and, unable to keep up the fast pace of his guards, John collapsed. He was taken to a church at

Comasus, whose Bishop St Basilicus had been martyred in 312 by Licinius. During the night John Chrysostom dreamed that the Bishop had come to his bedside and said: *'Be of good cheer! Tomorrow we will be together.'* In the morning of 7 September, John Chrysostom died after repeating the doxology: *'Glory be to God in all things'.*

He died a martyr to the Church he had served faithfully and fearlessly all his life. He died as the order for the quashing of his sentence and for his reinstatement came from Rome. It was too late. It was not until 438 that the Emperor Theodoius II, encouraged by his sister the future Empress Pulcheria, attended a service in the Church of the Holy Apostles in Constantinople, when St John Chrysostom's name was inscribed in the list of saints to be remembered and venerated. Only St Cyril of Alexandria, nephew and successor of Archbishop Theophilus, refused to add John's name to the list of saints in Egypt until St Isidore of Pelusium shamed him into giving way.

St John Chrysostom should be remembered along with other heads of the Church who were martyred at the hands of tyrannical rulers and who died for the true faith. These include St Thomas à Becket, (29 December), St Philip of Moscow, (9 January), the Anglican Archbishop Luwum of Uganda and Archbishop Oscar Romero of San Salvador. The stories of the last two of these are told at the end of Part VII, which includes an illustration of their statues that are above the doorway of Westminster Abbey.

St John Chrysostom's best-known memorial today is his own prayer: *'Almighty God, who hast given us grace at this time with one accord to make our common supplications unto thee and dost promise that when two or three are gathered together in thy Name thou wilt grant their requests. Fulfil now, O Lord, the desires and petitions of thy servants, as may be most expedient for them; granting in this world knowledge of thy truth, and in the world to come life everlasting. Amen'.*

OCTOBER SAINTS

1. St Theresa of Lisieux
   St Remi
2. The Guardian Angels
   St Leger
3. St Thomas of Hereford
4. St Francis of Assisi
6. St Bruno (RC) St Faith
9. St Denis of Paris
10. St Paulinus of York Daniel & Companions
12. St Wilfrid
13. St Edward the Confessor

St Luke

St Frumentius
St Simon & St Jude, Demetrius of Rostov
St Bee

14. St Callistus I
15. St Teresa of Avila
16. St Gall
17. St Ethelbert & St Ethelred
    St Ignatius of Antioch
18. St Luke
21. St Ursula St Hilarion
23. St Severinus St Boethius
24. St Antony Claret
25. St Crispin St Isidore the Farm Servant
    Forty Martyrs of England & Wales

Prayer is like a conversation with He who Loves us

St Teresa of Avila 1515–1582

St Francis of Assisi 1181–1226

St Ignatius of Antioch 107 AD   Martyred in Rome

St Luke (18 October) is seen at his desk (top centre) as he writes his Gospel, backed by his spiritual symbol of the winged bull; **St Ignatius of Antioch** (17 October) is shown being killed by a leopard in the Colosseum in Rome (right); **St Francis of Assisi** (4 October), hearing the call from Christ at the church of St Damiano to go and repair his church (bottom, centre); and **St Teresa of Avila** (15 October) is seen to the left, with one of the 16 Reformed Carmelite nunneries that she founded in Spain in the background.

ALTAR-PIECE DESIGN FOR ELEVEN OCTOBER SAINTS

Shown in the top central scene is:

St Severinus Boethius (23 October) writing his book *The Consolation of Philosophy* in prison before his martyrdom in 524.

In the centre are:

St Francis of Assisi (4 October), with Bishop Guido of Assisi. He covers Francis's naked body after he has rejected the world, stripped off his rich clothing and flung it at his father's feet.

On the left side are:

St Remi (1 October) crowning King Clovis of the Franks in 496; St Frumentius (27 October) evangelising in Ethiopia, c.375; St Denis of Paris (9 October) with the church of the Sacré Coeur built 16 centuries after his martyrdom in 258 on Montmartre in Paris; St Simon and St Jude (28 October), martyred in Mesopotamia.

On the right side are:

St Wilfrid (12 October) evangelising in pagan Sussex in c.680; King St Edward the Confessor (13 October) and Westminster Abbey; St Bruno (6 October) and the abbey he founded at La Grand Chartreuse in the mountains above Grenoble; St Demetrius of Rostov (28 October) teaching peasants, c.1705.

Altar-piece design for eleven October saints

OCTOBER CALENDAR OF SAINTS' FEAST-DAYS

1st **GREGORY the ENLIGHTENER** (240–326): Called the 'Enlightener' for bringing the 'Light of Christ' to Armenia. He began by converting the Armenian King Tiridates I, who, according to legend, at first inflicted terrible tortures on Gregory.

REMI (or Remigius) (438–533): Made Bishop of Rheims aged 22. He prepared the Frankish King Clovis for baptism, but the King would only agree to attend the ceremony if he was victorious in battle over the invading Allemani. He defeated them in 496, was baptised by St Remi and then proceeded to support the spread of Christianity throughout his kingdom. It was for this that France is known as the 'First daughter of the Church'.

THERESE of LISIEUX (or 'of the Child Jesus') (1873–99): She wrote her autobiography, *The Story of a Soul*, at the request of the Mother Superior of her Carmelite nunnery at Lisieux to describe what she called her 'Little Way', a simple spiritual guide to a truly holy life. The book was published posthumously after she had died of TB at the age of 25. It was an instant international success. It caused an explosion of religious ardour among thousands who recognised in its pages many of their own desires, failings and wished-for solutions to their own spiritual problems. The book and Therese's life are described in the text after the Calendar. Therese was canonised in 1925. In 1926 she was made the second patroness of France with Joan of Arc.

2nd **LEGER** (616–79): Bishop of Autun who fell foul of the cruel Mayor of the Palace of the decadent Merovingian kings. Because of his criticisms Leger was blinded and then murdered by the Mayor. The 'St Leger Stakes', the first English classic horse-race of the season, was first run on the saint's feast-day in 1776 over 1¾ miles on the flat.

3rd **THOMAS of HEREFORD** (1218–82): Born in Buckingham and trained at the Benedictine monastery in Lisieux, he became Professor of Canon Law and Chancellor of Oxford University. He supported the Barons against Henry III in Simon de Montfort's campaign to insist on the king ruling through regular parliaments. Simon made him Chancellor of England. He advised King Edward I on his succession in 1272 to summon a representative parliament, which the King did. Edward made him Bishop of Hereford in 1275 and he became much loved by the humbler members of his flock. He was a follower of St Thomas Aquinas' theological views and had acrimonious disputes over it with the old-fashioned Archbishop of Canterbury, the former Franciscan monk Peckham. Thomas was canonised in 1320 after many miracles had been witnessed at his tomb.

4th **PERTRONIUS**: Died c.440. Former monk and then Bishop and patron saint of Bologna. Reputed author of lives of the Desert Fathers, *Vitae Patrum*.

FRANCIS of ASSISI (1181–1226): Francis came closer than any saint to living like Christ. He is probably the most popular of all saints because of his intense faith, his humility, his total self-sacrifice for God and his people, his joy both in human relationships and his love of nature and for the way he inspired a spiritual awakening throughout the Western World. His life-story is told in the text after this Calendar, based on the Life written by St Bonaventure, who became Master General of St Francis's Order of Friars Minor in 1257. He quotes the evidence of three of Francis's earliest companions.

5th **MAURUS and PLACID**: Maurus was a sixth-century monk of St Benedict at Monte Cassino. His legend is that he rescued the boy Placid from drowning by walking on water. Placid became a monk and maybe a martyr.

FOY ('Foi' or 'Faith'): Third-century virgin martyr at St Agen in south central Gaul. Her shrine at Conques in her church in a beautiful mountain valley on the borders of the Auvergne attracted the pilgrims on their way to Santiago de Compostella.

BRUNO (1032–1101): He was educated at Rheims and Cologne. Seeking solitude he became a hermit in the desolate Savoy alps, where he attracted a number of companions and began to build a monastery – La Grande Chartreuse. There he founded the Carthusian order with the help of St Robert of Molesme (29 April) and Bishop St Hugh of Grenoble (1 April). He based his order on the style of St Antony of Egypt. It was and is still austere, solitary and silent. One of Bruno's monks became Pope Urban II, who started the Second Crusade and called Bruno to Rome to give him advice.

BLESSED MOTHER MARIE ROSE DUROCHER (1811–49): Born in Quebec in the French part of Canada, she founded The Sisters of the Holy Names of Jesus and Mary to educate the poorest and abandoned children. The work of her order spread to the USA and to Oregon, where she died. Beatified as an American saint in 1982.

6th *On this day in 1536 the **Reverend William Tyndale**, after being kidnapped in Antwerp, was garrotted and burnt by the Inquisition in the Netherlands by order of the Holy Roman Emperor Charles V for publishing his English Bible. More than 80 per cent of the phrases he used are still the basis of the standard English translations today.*

7th JUSTINA: Early martyr, much revered in Padua.

OSYTH: Seventh-century Queen of Sihere, King of the East Saxons in Essex. She founded a nunnery at the village that is called St Osyth after her.

8th PELAGIA the PENITENT: Fifth-century actress and dancing girl of Antioch. She became a Christian after hearing a sermon. She went to live as a hermit on the Mount of Olives, dressed as a man.

SERGIUS and BACCHUS: Martyrs in Syria in c.303.

KEYNE: Sixth-century Welsh Christian woman.

DEMETRIUS: One of the three most popular Greek soldier-saints and third-century martyrs. The other two are St George (23 April) and St Theodore the General (9 November).

9th DENIS and COMPANIONS: He led the expedition of seven bishops and several deacons sent by Pope St Fabian to evangelise Gaul in 250 shortly before the start of the Emperor Decius' severe and empire-wide persecution of the Christians. He is believed to have survived in Paris until 258, when he was executed on the Parisian hill now known as Montmartre. He became the chief patron saint of France.

LOUIS BERTRAND (1526–81): Spanish Dominican friar, missionary to Colombia, Panama and the Lesser Antilles. Canonised in 1671.

10th DANIEL and COMPANIONS: Franciscans martyred in Morocco in 1220 after being sent with St Berard (16 January) by St Francis of Assisi to convert the Muslims.

PAULINUS of YORK: Died in 644 at Rochester, Kent, after evangelising in the North of Britain. He had accompanied St Ethelburga of Kent (8 September) to York to marry King St Edwin (12 October), whom he baptised along with his nobles, as Bede's history describes. Pope Honorius I recognised Paulinus as Archbishop of York, but when Edwin was killed in 632 in battle fighting the Welsh and their Mercian allies, he had to return to the south to protect Ethelburga.

FRANCIS BORGIA (1642–1716): Jesuit rural missionary around Naples. Converted Moorish captives. Canonised in 1839.

11th CANICE (or 'Kenneth'): Seventh-century Irish missionary, perhaps with St Columba (9 June), to Picts in Scotland. Gave his name to the Islet of Inchkenneth and became Abbot of the Irish monastery of Ossory.

12th ETHELBURGA of BARKING: Died in 676. Abbess sister of Bishop St Erconwald (30 April). She is described by Bede (25 May) as a holy miracle-worker.

WILFRID (634–709): Rich noble who became a priest and was for a time Archbishop of York. He visited Rome several times and was deeply attracted to the Roman as opposed to the Celtic style of liturgy and worship in the revived Anglo-Saxon Church. His friend St Benedict Biscop (12 January) accompanied him on one visit to Rome and they both returned loaded with books and sacred relics. At the Council of Whitby in 663–4 he won the Celtic clergy over to the Roman dating of Easter and their style of worship. He obtained large endowments for his churches and several monasteries including Ripon and Oundle. He also adopted the brilliant lifestyle he had seen followed in Rome and by the Frankish Bishops. This involved a complete break with the humble approach of the Celtic Church and of Bishop St Aidan of Lindisfarne (31 August), who had toured his huge see on foot to meet the people 30 years earlier. Wilfred was severely criticised for this and for the splendour of his escort's dress in the eighth-century memoirs of the learned Yorkshire monk Alcuin, who had directed the education of the clergy throughout Charlemagne's empire. Alcuin believed that the increasingly high and mighty style of the bishops was causing them to lose touch with the people and their pastoral duties. This did indeed take place until St Francis of Assisi sent his friars to preach directly to the people all over Europe in 1210.

Wilfrid, in spite of his being an energetic and imaginative apostle of the faith, was proud, ambitious and difficult to manage, as both the King of Northumbria and St Theodore, Archbishop of Canterbury (19 September) found. To Wilfrid's fury in 678 Theodore split Wilfrid's see of York into four for administrative reasons. He appealed to the pope against this in two visits to Rome and in the end his king imprisoned him, only releasing him when he agreed to exile himself from his kingdom. (John of Beverley, meanwhile, was appointed to replace Wilfrid as Archbishop of York.) It was to his great credit that Wilfrid then spent five years evangelising in Sussex and Wessex, where the Saxons had destroyed the churches and paganism was rampant. The fruits of this mission can be seen to this day in the traditions of the churches he and his disciples established along the river valleys that cut through the South Downs. In the end his relations with Archbishop Theodore were restored. He became Bishop of Hexham and died in his monastery of Oundle.

13th FOILLAN: Seventh-century Irish missionary to Gaul along with his brothers St Fursey (16 January) and St Ultan (1 May). He became abbot of a monastery at Nivelles, Belgium.

KING EDWARD the CONFESSOR (1004–66): Saxon King of England. Edward favoured the idea of a Norman succession rather than that of Harold's family. He and his wife Edith were very devout. He founded Westminster Abbey in the marshy land beside the Thames upstream from the City of London. With the object of pleasing his Saxon subjects the Norman King Henry II persuaded Pope Innocent II to canonise Edward in 1161.

Edward's body had been found incorrupt in 1102. St Ailred of Rievaulx (31 August), a Saxon and the most spiritual preacher of the day, preached the sermon in 1163 when Edward's remains were translated to his magnificent shrine in the abbey. The ceremony was a national event and a political success. Saxon pilgrims flocked to venerate their saint and made generous gifts to the abbey treasury.

GERALD of AURILLAC (855–909): The rich Count of Aurillac to the south of Auvergne in France where he founded a monastery. It was taken over by St Odo of Cluny (18 November) who wrote of Gerald's life, making him a spiritually heroic and famous figure in France. 150 years after his death a later member of his family, St Robert (17 April), founded the Abbey of La Chaise-Dieu in the Auvergne in the hills above Brioude which also had a close relationship with the Abbey of Cluny.

14th POPE CALLISTUS I: A former slave who was elected pope in 217. He was attacked by the puritan party in the Church led by St Hyppolitus (13 August) and Tertullian for being too lenient with sinners, especially adulterers. He was martyred by a mob in 222.

15th THECLA of ENGLAND: Died in 790. Benedictine Abbess of Wimborne in Dorset and a cousin of St Lioba (28 September), who took a party of 30 nuns at the request of St Boniface of Crediton to help him evangelise in Germany. Thecla followed her example and became Abbess of Ochsenfurt and Kitzingen.

TERESA of AVILA (1515–82): Teresa's life-story is told after that of St Francis in the text that follows this Calendar. She founded the Reformed Carmelite order in Spain. Her story is one of a life-long internal spiritual development in her search to give perfect service to God. She won through many difficulties. Her books on prayer are still widely read. In 1970 she became the first female saint to be made a Doctor of the Church.

16th LULL (c.710–86): Anglo-Saxon Archbishop of Mainz, cousin of St Boniface of Crediton. Very energetic evangeliser of Germany.

ST GALL: Died in c.630. Irish missionary monk who accompanied St Columbanus (21 October) to Gaul, the Rhine and Switzerland. In 590 he helped found the abbeys of Luxeuil and Annegray in Burgundy, which practised the traditional Celtic extreme austerity. After the Burgundian court objected to the Celtic criticism of their immorality in 620, Gall and the other monks were exiled and followed their leader Columbanus to the Rhine. Gall became the pioneer of Christianity among the Swiss.

HEDWIG (1172–1243): Aunt of St Elisabeth of Hungary (17 November). She married the Duke of Silesia and founded several nunneries, including the Cistercian abbey of Trebnitz north of Breslau (now Wroclaw).

17th MARGARET MARY ALACOQUE (1647–90): As a nun she experienced four visions of Christ at Paray-le-Mondial in Burgundy in 1671. This convinced her of the importance of seeing Jesus's heart as symbolising his love for humankind. Her sister nuns said she was suffering from delusions, but her patience overcame their opposition to her idea. This led to the cult of venerating The Sacred Heart of Jesus.

This approach to faith helped the Church in France to overcome the damage done by the Jansenist's support of the doctrine of Double-Predestination (see St Augustine, 28 August), which had obscured Christ's love of all including sinners. Canonised in 1920.

On this day in 1553 the Reformed English Bishops **Ridley** *and* **Latimer** *were burnt alive in Oxford as heretics by order of the Catholic Queen Mary.*

IGNATIUS of ANTIOCH: Martyred in Rome in c.107–10. As Bishop of Antioch, the headquarters of the Church in the East, he was an important target for the anti-Christian elements in the Roman Empire where, unlike Judaism which was a licensed national religion, the faith was regarded as an illicit superstition. His story and a summary of his important writings are given in the text following this Calendar.

18th LUKE the EVANGELIST: The main article on St Luke has been given in Part III of this book.

JUSTUS of BEAUVAIS: Boy killed by the Romans in c.303 for hiding Christians in the village of St Juste-en-Chausee between Beauvais and Senlis.

19th FRIDESWIDE: Abbess who died in 735. Patron saint of Oxford University. She is believed to have founded her nunnery on the site of Christ Church College.

JOHN of RILA: Died in 946. One of the earliest Bulgarian monks. Founder-abbot of the monastery of Rila in Rhodope. He ruled there for 60 years.

PETER of ALCANTARA (1499–1562): Spanish Franciscan mystic and confessor who gave St Teresa of Avila (15 October) much help, as recorded in the text on her life below.

PAUL of the CROSS (1694–1775): Experienced a spiritual enlightenment while serving as a soldier in the Venetian army in 1720. He left the army to found a congregation of missionaries, The Passionists, whose preaching centred on Christ's Passion. He had many mystical experiences all his life, but never claimed they were from a divine source. One of the later Passionists to work in England was Father Dominic Barberi who received John Henry Newman, the future Cardinal and 'Blessed', into the Roman Catholic Church in 1845.

ISAAC JOGUES and JEAN DE BREBOEUF (1607–46 and 1593–1648): Jesuit missionaries martyred by Iroquois and Huron Indians in Quebec.

20th MARIA BOSCARDINI (1888–1922): Abused by cruel father. Became a Sister of St Dorothy at Vicenzo in 1904. Took menial jobs. Became nurse. Heroic service when hospital at Treviso attacked after defeat at Caparetto 1917. Died of diphtheria after years of nursing patients with the disease.

21st HILARION (291–371): Hermit whose Life was written by St Jerome (30 September). Inspired by St Antony of Egypt (17 January) he went to live in the desert near Gaza. He converted many visitors by his example and teaching. Emperor Julian the Apostate ordered his arrest, but he fled first to Dalmatia and then to Cyprus where he died in his hermitage on the mountain above Kyrenia.

URSULA and COMPANIONS: Legendary virgin martyrs of the early fourth century near Cologne. The legend claims there were over 10,000 of them.

JOHN of BRIDLINGTON: Died in 1379. Canonised 1401. Popular Austin canon regular at whose shrine many miracles were claimed.

22nd PHILIP of HERACLEA: Bishop martyred in Thrace in 304. When the Emperor Diocletian's police closed his church he said: *'God dwells in men's hearts, not within walls'*. He was flogged for this and was then burnt alive for refusing to cast incense before the imperial idols.

DONATUS of FIESOLE: Died in 876. Irish priest and pilgrim to Rome. As he returned home via Fiesole a miraculous event occurred there. This caused the citizens to believe he was chosen by the Holy Spirit to be their bishop.

23rd SEVERINUS BOETHIUS (480–524): Roman scholar, Christian theologian and statesman martyred by Theodoric the Ostrogoth for defending in court a wrongfully accused traitor, whom the tyrant wanted to execute. His greatest work is his *The Consolation of Philosophy*, a brilliant debate on predestination, fate and chance. He wrote it in prison while awaiting his execution. He was a martyr for Justice. See his life and writings in the text after this Calendar.

JOHN of CAPISTRANO (1387–1456): While he was governor of Perugia he felt 'called' to become a Franciscan friar. He played a great part in healing the differences within the Order caused by the fundamentalist 'Spirituals' who wanted the Order to go back to the founder's primitive rule and have no property or possessions. He also campaigned against the Hussites in Bohemia and against the Turks who invaded Hungary after capturing Constantinople in 1453. He carried the cross as he led the Hungarians to victory over the Turks at Belgrade in 1456. It was there that he died of plague.

24th FELIX of THIBIUCA: Martyred bishop of Carthage in 304, executed for refusing to burn the gospels and other Christian literature.

ANTONY CLARET (1807–70): Founded the Claretian Fathers in Catalonia to provide parochial missions and retreats. Queen Isabella II of Spain made him Archbishop of the run-down see of Cuba. He reformed the see in spite of attempts on his life. He also set up scientific and other libraries in Spain. Canonised in 1950.

25th CRISPIN and CRISPINIAN: According to legend, well-born Romans who were martyred at Soissons in France in the third century, during Diocletian's reign. May have been converts of Pope St Fabian's mission to Gaul in 250 that was headed by St Denis.

JOHN of BEVERLEY: Died in 721. Archbishop of York and former pupil of St Adrian of Canterbury (9 January). He ordained the Venerable Bede (25 May). The famous mystic, Dame Julian of Norwich, saw his image in one of her visions as a *'true servant of God and a full saint in heaven'* (see her story in Part IV).

JOHN HOUGHTON and the FORTY MARTYRS of ENGLAND: He was one of the Carthusian monks at the Charterhouse in the City of London who were murdered horribly and slowly by orders of King Henry VIII for resisting his dissolution of the monasteries in 1537. He is remembered along with 40 other Roman Catholics executed in the reigns of Queen Elizabeth and King James I, some for treason and plots against the Crown, others for being active as priests or for assisting them. The number of Catholics executed in those reigns was about 150, compared with the 200 or so protestants burned as heretics by Queen Mary I. Among the Catholic martyrs whose feast-day this is, were the brave Jesuit St Edmund Campion in 1581 and the Franciscan St John Kemble executed in 1679 through Titus Oates' bogus allegations of plots against King Charles II.

26th BEAN: Irish sixth-century hermit of Galway.

27th FRUMENTIUS: Died in c.380. Sent by St Athanasius (2 May) to evangelise Ethiopia.

28th SIMON and JUDE: Apostles believed martyred in Persia (see the end of Part IV).

DEMETRIUS of ROSTOV (1641–1709): A rich Cossack made Bishop of Rostov in 1702. A great preacher who wrote 'A Spiritual Alphabet' on priests' duties to their flocks.

29th COLMAN of KILMACDUAGH: Ascetic Irish hermit, died in 632 on land given by the King of Connaught. Like many Irish saints he had a special affinity with wild animals and birds.

MEREWENNA: Made first Abbess of Romsey in 967 when the Saxon King Edgar refounded it under the Benedictine rule after its destruction by the Danes. Her nuns included a princess of Edgar's Court.

ETHELFLEDA: She used to bathe nude at night in all weathers as a penance. She succeeded Merewenna (see above) as Abbess of Romsey.

30th MARCELLUS the CENTURION: Martyred in Tangier in 298 for discarding his sword and denying his allegiance to Maximian, saying: 'I serve only the eternal King, Jesus Christ'.

ALPHONSO RODRIGUEZ (1531–1617): Became a Jesuit lay brother at 40, working as a hall porter for the Order at Valencia. He was uneducated but had a deep mystical understanding of religion. His job enabled him to meet many people whom he encouraged successfully with his faith. Among these was St Peter Claver (9 September) who often consulted him when he was a student.

31st BEE: Seventh-century Irish nun who came to England and was probably veiled by St Aidan of Lindisfarne (31 August). St Bee's Head on the Cumberland coast is named after her.

FOILLAN: Died in 655. Missionary from Ireland to East Anglia and Gaul with his brothers St Fursey (16 January) and St Ultan (1 May). He succeeded Fursey as abbot in East Anglia until he was driven off by the Mercians and went to Gaul. He was given land for a monastery near Nivelles. He was murdered by robbers while returning there from a visit to St Gertrude of Nivelles (17 March).

QUENTIN: Early martyr, date unknown. Recorded by Sr Gregory of Tours and St Bede as preaching at Amiens, arrested and tortured. Town of St Quentin name after him.

WOLFGANG of REGENSBURG (c.924–94): Great reforming bishop, influenced by St Romuald (19 June). Tutor of Emperor St Henry II (13 July).

SUMMARY OF OCTOBER SAINTS

There are 73 saints in this Calendar; 22 were martyrs and 13 were women. The lives of five of these saints are described more fully below because of their importance and also their relevance to us today – **St Ignatius of Antioch, St Severinus Boethius, St Francis of Assisi, St Teresa of Avila, and St Therese of Lisieux.** Between them their lives illustrate the continuity of the understanding of the faith and its practice over 20 centuries.

IMPORTANT OCTOBER SAINTS

St Ignatius of Antioch (died 107)

Historians are uncertain about the exact age of St Ignatius, Bishop of Antioch in Syria. Judging from the letters he wrote to his churches from Ephesus on his way to be torn to death by wild beasts in the Colisseum in Rome, he must by then have been a mature man. An older man than 60 would have hardly been able to walk 700 miles under guard over the rough mountain tracks from Antioch.

His letters to his churches and the one he wrote to St Polycarp (23 January), Bishop of Ephesus, provide a valuable guide to the tradition and thought of the Church in those early post-apostolic days. For example, he wrote that each local church was a microcosm of the Church as a whole: '*Wherever Jesus is, there is the universal Church*'.

Ignatius warned his churches about the heretical or 'Docetic' view that Jesus's nature was wholly divine, since by denying Jesus's human nature it undermined his saving act for us on the Cross. His letters also shed an interesting light on the early Christian attitude to the Jews. Ignatius said that the Jewish prophets were Christian in spirit. This is why Jesus had said that he had '*not come to destroy the law and the prophets but to fulfil them*' (Matthew 5.7). Ignatius also refuted the gnostic claims that Jesus was not born of woman, but had emerged in some way from the Spirit of God. He showed that the gnostic concept of Jesus was only a shadowy interpretation of salvation. Their doctrine failed to link Jesus's life, death and resurrection as part of God's plan to give a new meaning and purpose for humankind through the '*New Adam, Jesus Christ*'.

Ignatius stressed the importance of Jesus's resurrection, saying that it also meant that for the faithful, our resurrection and therefore our hope. He showed that, contrary to the limited view of the Greek philosophers, God does suffer as he observes our sins. He also taught both the unity of God and the concept of the eternal personality of Christ. He did this more than two centuries before the acrimonious disputes about the Holy Trinity led to bitter turmoil in the Eastern Church. His letters are also interesting as they provide the first record we have that at the Eucharist the bread and wine do become the Body and Blood of Christ after the consecration. He said that otherwise they would not have such a profound spiritual effect on those taking them. St Iranaeus of Lyons, writing over 75 years later, may have read Ignatius' letter on the Eucharist, because he made exactly the same comment about the bread and wine.

Having given his last advice to his churches Ignatius implored them not to try and save him from the terrible fate that awaited him in Rome. He faced this with equanimity, seeing himself as '*the bread-corn of Christ*' which would be '*ground by the teeth of wild beasts so that I may find myself pure bread*'. Finally he advised his readers to be tolerant in discussions with heretics and those whose views differed from the traditional catholic doctrines. His letters therefore have much to teach us today about tolerance and the need to have respect for the faiths of others.

St Severinus Boethius (480–524) and *The Consolation of Philosophy*

Boethius came from an illustrious Christian family during the reign of the tyrant King of Rome, the Arian heretic Theodoric the Ostrogoth. He lived the traditional life of a Roman aristocrat as lawyer, politician, and classical scholar. He also took high official offices, including that of Consul.

He was a Christian theologian of merit who wrote several tracts on the Trinity and against various heresies. Edward Gibbon described him as *'the last of the Romans'*. He translated Pythagoras and Euclid and was a considerable mathematician and scientist. His translations and summaries of the works of Plato and Aristotle were invaluable to future generations since the barbarian invasions had destroyed the great libraries.

His orthodoxy as a Christian cannot be doubted, though some dictionaries of saints imply that his greatest work, and the one for which he is most remembered today, his *Consolation of Philosophy*, is not a Christian work. This view is incorrect and unjust. That it is Christian and an attempt to relate Christian belief with classical philosophy is obvious from his conclusion at the end of the book. He wrote it in prison in Pavia after being tried for alleged treason and condemned to death at the insistence of King Theodoric.

Boethius was a martyr for justice, having vigorously defended two senators who had been accused by Theodoric of corresponding with the enemy on what Boethius showed to be the evidence of forged letters. He wrote his book during a period of the deepest depression at the unfairness of his treatment and fall after a distinguished and honourable career. In his book he aimed to explore certain fundamental philosophical problems and to search the mind of God. The chief question that he examines is why God is justified in rewarding good men and punishing wicked ones if all things are predestined and fore-known to Him.

The book tells how in his imagination Boethius meets *'Dame Philosophy'*. She reminds him that the supreme good in life is happiness, which we all seek. She also warns that *'many roads to happiness are side-tracks. True happiness can only be found in the Supreme God.'* She tells him that in his goodness God has a plan for all creation, this plan is his *'Providence'*, the simple unchanging plan of the mind of God. Parallel with this is *'Fate'* or *'Chance'*, which influences the ever-changing web of events in and through time.

Dame Philosophy then tells Boethius that he must remember *'God is the turning point of the world'*. That is a completely Christian and not a pagan viewpoint. The more a Christian contemplates the mind of God and frees his thoughts from corporeal or temporal things, the closer he will come to the place of divine rest at the centre. Boethius recognises this and, in the single truly Christian phrase in the book, he quotes the *'Lord's Prayer'* – *'Thy will be done on earth as it is in heaven'*. Dame Philosophy then asserts that while God's government does include human affairs he does not interfere directly, but only through the power of love. Once again, that is Christian.

The two debaters then argue about *'Predestination'*. At first Boethius will not accept his opponent's case for it because it interferes with our free will. Dame Philosophy then explains that he has misunderstood what she means. Since God lives in timeless immediacy, *Eternity*, where past, present and future are all one, he can therefore see the end result of everything. Thus in that sense he can see all things as being predestined, but in a different way from how they appear to human beings.

Boethius accepts this argument, but says that surely we can nevertheless always change our minds in action, and it is only if there is room for free will that we can be morally responsible for our actions, good or evil. Dame Philosophy admits that when actions are considered by themselves, they do not lose the absolute freedom of their nature, since to us they concern future events and their outcome from our point of view is uncertain. She also says that although God does have foreknowledge, which he must have if he is omniscient, it is as a spectator of all things from on high. His judgement in dispensing rewards and punishments is then adapted to the future quality of our actions.

Thus we do not place hope in God in vain. If our prayers are right and worthy and in accordance with God's will, they cannot but be efficacious. Our duty therefore is to pray humbly to pursue good, whether we are treated well or ill on earth and even if the wicked prosper. 'God is Love' and that love gives us room to develop and reach toward God's own perfection. The debaters conclude that our 'Consolation' is that we have hope and that through prayer we do have a means of communicating with God.

The relevance to Christianity of this philosophical debate is obvious throughout the book. It is also a subtle exposure of the wrong-headedness of the then-prevailing pagan attitudes of the Stoics and Epicureans. The debate demonstrates also how 'Chance' or 'Fate' interferes with our plans. Therefore we may conclude from it that in his plans for us God takes risks. He may for example even have done so with Jesus Christ, who might not have been obedient unto death, but who rose above temptation.

Many books have been written on this problem and some claim that God cannot take risks with his creation and therefore must predestine the end result. This seems to render life on earth as pointless, but this kind of debate, like that of much theology, cannot be resolved in this finite world. What Boethius provided is a sound basis for faith and a chart for Christians to follow. His book became widely respected as a counter to St Augustine of Hippo's unscriptural 'Double-Predestination' theory, which he had reached by developing his theory of Grace *ad absurdum*. King Alfred of England had the *Consolation* translated into Anglo-Saxon and the poets Dante Alighieri and Geoffrey Chaucer praised Boethius highly.

We may conclude from this debate that Boethius demonstrated that God has not put us into this cosmic play-pen just for his own amusement. Nor would he have given us our free will if he did not want us to create something on our own, unaided by him except for what his *Providence* has given us. The possibilities of this debate are endless. Boethius reached his reasonable and helpful conclusion with elegance and calm courage as he awaited execution, that of being bludgeoned to death in his cell, a fate he suffered in 524, a martyr to the cause of Justice.

St Francis of Assisi (1181–1226) and his 'Friars Minor'

St Francis is the classic example of how great saints and faithful witnesses arise from the most unexpected quarters, especially when the state of the Church and the Faith are at their lowest ebb. Their lives and example bring about great changes and a needed spiritual revival. We may be at such a point now at the start of the twenty first century.

Francis was born in 1181, a time when the Papacy recognised that the Church needed a totally new approach to spreading the faith in Western Europe. Francis' life needs therefore to be shown against the prevailing spiritual background in the Europe of his day. For example, in spite of the support that St Bernard of Clairvaux had won in the early part of the twelfth century for the Second Crusade, there was in France and Italy a growing disillusionment among the mass of the people due to the corruption of senior clergy, their blatant simony, widespread concubinage and great wealth. The ordinary clergy in the villages were ignorant and sometimes illiterate. They were often serfs who had been appointed by their feudal lords to gabble the Mass in dog-Latin to a congregation who understood only the vernacular.

The resulting state of affairs can be judged by the fact that towards the end of his life in 1153 St Bernard had found that the churches were empty in central and southern France. He blamed this on the extraordinary success of the Christian heretics known as the *Cathari* or 'Albigensians'. They had adopted a world-view heresy like that of the Manichaeans, which was outlined in the August Calendar in the life of St Augustine of Hippo.

This heresy was imported from the East after the first crusades. Its supporters could be found in Bulgaria, but chiefly they lived around Albi and Toulouse, and also in Provençe and in the Pyrenees. Bernard sent his Cistercian monks to try to reconvert the heretics, but they failed to make any impression. Something different was needed to bring these sheep back to orthodoxy.

In response to this need various groups of devout laymen attempted a new style of evangelism in the last quarter of the twelfth century. One of these was led by Peter Waldo, a rich citizen of Lyons. Between 1170 and 1176 he began to preach from vernacular translations of the gospels. He taught, as St Antony of Egypt (17 January) had done and as St Francis was to do later in their search for the spiritual perfection,

that his followers should give all their wealth to the poor and imitate Christ. He called his followers '*Pauperes Christi, Pauperes de Laguno*' – 'The Poor of Christ and of Lyons'. He was opposed to the wealth of the worldly clergy, insisting on poverty and the right to abstain from labour and to meditate and live a life of prayer. This was contrary to the feudal system of those days. His followers were what became known sometime later as 'Low Church' and, because of their disregard of certain Church practices, they were considered heretics.

Another group of 'Low Churchmen' in Lombardy had the same objective, following the same ideal of poverty and rejection of a worldly life that had inspired St Antony. They called themselves the *Humiliati*. This group, like the Waldensians and the spiritually-minded Cathari, were attacked by the Church. The Humiliati died out, but The Waldensians evangelised in Provençe, Spain and Savoy and as far away as Bohemia. There they were the predecessors of the martyred John Huss and his Moravian Church. Huss was burnt alive at the Council of Constance in 1415. They were later to be pursued relentlessly in the seventeenth century by King Louis XIV, but communities of them still exist in Savoy.

Pope Innocent III was the reigning pope at the start of the thirteenth century and he was fully aware of the need to deal with these Albigensians. His opportunity to do so came when his envoy, sent to deal with these problems in Toulouse, was murdered in 1208. Innocent therefore summoned the French knights to take up the cross in a crusade to wipe out the heretics.

Francis of Assisi, aged 27, had already embarked by that time on his own spiritual movement in a novel way right outside the traditional

Church way of teaching the faith. He was therefore in danger of being regarded as a heretic, but he had the support of his local bishop. The crusade against the Albigensians, which killed thousands of men, women and children, lasted for nearly 40 years until long after Francis's death. The fact that Francis was able to establish his Order of Friars Minor, itinerant preachers, with Innocent's blessing in 1210 was therefore a miracle. The same applies to Innocent's and his successor Pope Honorius II's acceptance of Dominic Guzman's friars as the first Dominicans six years later.

In spite of their unorthodox approach to evangelism, both Francis and St Dominic (7 August) won the approval for their itinerant preachers because of their obvious simple and profound faith. Francis wanted to appeal directly to the hearts of the mass of people through his wandering friars who lived on charity in their towns, villages and homes. Dominic's method was to appeal to their minds through his well-trained 'Friars Preachers', who established learning centres and were more intellectual than St Francis' simple Friars Minor.

Francis was the son of a rich draper of Assisi called Pietro Bernadone. Although barely five feet tall Francis was a leader of the bright young lads and girls of the city. He had little time for religion or for the family business. He was filled with the romantic ideals of becoming a famous knight at arms and also loved to sing in the style of the troubadours from his French mother's land. When he was 21 he went on a campaign for Assisi against neighbouring Perugia, was captured in battle and imprisoned for over a year. He fell seriously ill and on his release found that his old way of life was inadequate. As we learn from St Bonaventure's life of Francis, he began to feel the call to Christ's service and rode out once again on what he believed was to be a crusade for the faith. When he reached Spoleto he had a dream in which he heard a voice telling him *'Return to your own country and you will be told what to do'*. Francis left the army and went back home.

Then one day in 1207 he heard his call quite clearly while praying before a Byzantine crucifix in the half-ruined Church of San Damiano outside Florence. He heard Christ speaking to him from the cross, saying: *'Go and repair my church which is wholly in ruins'*. The startled Francis, moved to the very core of his being, then committed himself to Christ's service and answered: *'Gladly Lord, I will repair it'*. Immediately he gave all the money he had on him to the priest in charge of the church. Then he went home, took some rich bales of cloth – his father, Pietro Bordone, was away – rode to Foligno and sold the cloth and the horse he had been riding. He walked back to San Damiano and handed the proceeds of his sales to the priest, explaining what he had done. The priest was horrified and put the bag of money on a window-sill, certain that Francis' father would come and claim it. Francis's father returned home and was enraged at his son's theft. He flogged him and chained him in a cellar, demanding the return of the money. Francis's mother released him and he ran off to live like a beggar in doorways and caves.

In due course his father had him summoned before Bishop Guido of Florence to be tried for theft. Francis admitted what he had done. He fore-swore his inheritance as payment for the goods he had taken and, stripping himself naked except for a hair-shirt, flung his clothing at his father's feet saying: *'Until now I have called Pietro Bordone my father, now I give back to him all that I have had of him, desiring only, "Our*

Father, who art in heaven" with whom I have laid up my whole treasure and in whom I trust and hope'.

Bishop Guido, having pity on the young man, threw his cloak over his nakedness. Francis left, proclaiming that we bring nothing into this world and will take nothing out of it excepting only the garment of penitence. As soon as he had left the bishop's palace he exchanged the bishop's rich cloak with the rags of a beggar. His friends gave him a farm-labourer's tunic and a pair of felt boots. He then drew the sign of the cross on the tunic with a piece of chalk and left the city to wander towards Gubbio to make his plans for his future way of life. He then returned to San Damiano to begin his work of restoration.

Francis begged in Assisi for the stones he needed for the church. The citizens gave the stones and friendly peasants helped him to complete the work. He then sought out the local leper colony, which he had avoided until then, horrified by their decayed bodies. He forced himself to embrace and wash them and to tend their sores. He lived at San Damiano, sharing the meagre diet of the priest. Then, having dedicated himself to *'My Lady Poverty'*, he realised that this was not true poverty. So he left to collect scraps of food by begging from door to door in the town and set out to repair two more churches, that of St Peter the Apostle in the town and of St Mary of the Angels, which was in ruins at the foot of the hill below Assisi. He was eventually to name St Mary's the *Portiuncola* – 'The Little Portion', the only possession of his order.

In 1209, when Francis was 28 years old, he heard the priest in the restored St Mary of the Angels saying Mass and using Christ's words at the start of his preaching: *'Lord give thee peace'*. The priest then read the gospel for the day which told the story of how Jesus sent his disciples out to *'preach, saying the kingdom of heaven is at hand. Heal the sick, cleanse the lepers, raise the dead, cast out devils: freely you have received, freely give. Provide neither silver nor brass in your purses, nor scrip for your journey . . . and if a house you come to is worthy, let your peace come upon it . . . but behold, I send you forth as sheep in the midst of wolves.'*

That message inspired Francis to preach the gospel in Assisi. He went to the street corners and always started his little addresses with the priest's words: *'The Lord give thee peace'*. At first he was mocked, but then people began to listen. His words pierced their hearts and soon five disciples, including a rich lawyer and a priest, came to join him. They sold their goods for the poor and eventually established themselves in the Portiuncola, which the Benedictines let them have.

One day Francis gathered his little band of brothers to establish a rule to govern their lives. He opened the gospels at random in three places. First he read from St Matthew Jesus's command: *'If you would be perfect go, sell all that you have and give to the poor and then you will have treasure in heaven, come follow me'*. Then he read from St Luke *'Take nothing for your journey'*. Thirdly from St Matthew he read: *'If any man will come after me, let him deny himself and take up my cross'*. Francis then said: *'This is now our rule'*. With those simple words the Order of Friars Minor, *Fratres Minores*, was born. They were to go out to live and preach the gospel just as the Apostles used to do.

They preached and begged for charity in Assisi and in the neighbouring towns. Their numbers increased to 12. They made such headway with their preaching that Francis decided in 1210 to go to Rome and seek the approval of the Pope. Bishop Guido encouraged him, having at first tried to persuade the brothers to join one of the existing Orders. He then realised that Francis's iron will was determined to follow Christ in a new and unique way, different from that of any other order, sworn to Poverty, Charity and Obedience, symbolised by the three knots in the rope round his waist. Guido gave the brothers his blessing and asked his friend Cardinal Ugolino of Ostia, the future Pope Honorius, to do his best for Francis.

After being at first turned out of the Lateran Palace in Rome, Francis got Cardinal Ugolino to support him and tell the Pope that '*All these men want to do is to live after the principles of the Gospel. To refuse them would be blasphemy.*' The Pope listened, amazed, and then told Francis to return to him when he had increased the numbers of his brethren. He would then approve a 'Rule' for them to follow.

On their return to Assisi Francis found that instead of being mocked in the streets to cries of '*Pazzo! Pazzo!*', he and his friars were welcomed into the houses by a people proud that a son of their city had had his new Religious Order approved by the Pope. Besides, he had already restored three of their churches. Scores of new volunteers joined the brethren and went out to preach in Francis's manner. They, too, nearly always found themselves welcomed because people wanted spiritual guidance and to understand the gospel teaching. The Friars Minor went north into Lombardy and into France, Austria, Hungary and Bohemia. In Germany they met difficulties and even dangers as the Prince Bishops objected to their intrusions and thought them to be heretics. Nevertheless over the next ten years the numbers of the Friars Minor rose to over 5,000. This enabled Francis to obtain a fuller recognition from the Pope and for him to grant new and simple Rule for his Order.

In 1212 a beautiful young woman in Assisi, Clare Offreduccio, the future St Clare (1194–1253), was so taken with Francis that she came and begged him to allow her to join his order and live with the brothers at the Portiuncolo. Francis persuaded her and her companions, including her sister the future St Agnes of Assisi, to live at San Damiano. Then he helped her to found his second Order, the Order of the Poor Ladies of Assisi.

In 1216 Francis was called to Rome for a conference and met St Dominic in the cloister garden of the monastery of St Anselmo, next door to the magnificent Basilica of St Sabina on the Aventine hill with its splendid view over Rome. They discussed their respective missions and agreed to keep in touch, but to go their separate ways, using different styles of evangelising. Dominic set up his learning centres in various cities while Francis's great wave of friars continued to spread and teach in the streets and in private homes all over Europe. By 1217 the administration of such a large order of brethren required the setting up of Provincial Masters. Francis arranged this and then in 1219, relieved of the work of administration, he felt free to fulfil his ambition to go on a crusade. He hoped to die as a martyr, as had five of the missionaries he had sent to convert the Muslims in Morocco.

Francis sailed with the Fifth Crusade and was horrified at the cruelty of the Christian troops that he witnessed at the siege of Damietta in the Nile Delta. He therefore made his way through the lines of combatants and forced himself into the presence of the Sultan to seek peace and to convert him. The Sultan immediately recognised the holiness and sincerity of St Francis, but he could not accept Christianity in place of his faith in Islam. However after an extensive exchange of views he showered Francis with presents and returned him to the crusaders. He also gave him a free pass to visit all the Holy places in Palestine. On his return to Assisi, Francis found that the Order had changed.

The Provincial Masters had bought property so as to carry out their mission more efficiently. They saw that such a large organisation could not continue to exist if it relied solely on charity begged from door to door. Francis was horrified at this breaking of his basic commitment to total poverty, but was persuaded to amend the Rule. His changes were not enough to be practical and with the help of his friend and Patron of the Order, Cardinal Ugolino, he wrote a third set of Rules in 1224. This was the beginning of what was to become a serious split within the Order, between the 'Strict Observers' and the 'Conventual Friars'. Eventually, after Francis's death, the 'Strict Observers' or 'Spirituals' caused such disturbances, that they were forcibly suppressed.

In this way we can see that after the initial explosion of spiritual ardour, the Friars Minor had been forced by their own success to become institutionalised. This is what all religious orders and churches have had to do if they are to survive. However Francis, who was an innovator to the end of his life, overcame this problem by founding a Third Order for lay men and women, 'The Order of Penitence' – 'The Tertiaries'. These were, and are still today, lay people who take a vow of penitence and to practise the faith and help others in many ways while carrying out their ordinary daily lives. This lay order has included kings and royal princesses, starting with King St Louis IX of France and Princess St Elizabeth of Bohemia. Famous men and women including Petrarch, Dante Alighieri and Roger Bacon also joined this Third Order.

By 1224 Francis was nearly a spent force as a result of the austerity of his diet and the exhausting work of founding and maintaining the Order. Leaving the administration to others he now had his own life's pilgrimage to complete. He was helped in this last period of his life by his loyal brother Leo, who led him everywhere on a donkey, as he was too weak to walk. He was often so deep in prayer as he rode through the villages that he never noticed where he was. On one occasion Francis was so overcome with delight at the company of many birds, with their songs and the evidence they gave of the glory of God, that he preached to them. According to Brother Leo they listened to him in silence. His prayers to them and to 'Brother Sun and Sister Moon' express his joy in God's creation and in the wild creatures for whom we should act as stewards. St Bonaventure's *Life* includes stories about his preaching to birds and animals and taming of the wolf of Gubbio.

In the same year there occurred the most dramatic event while Francis was praying on Mount La Vernia in the Appenines, his favourite place for prayer and whose owner had given it to the Order. St Bonaventure records that as Francis fasted there for 40 days in honour of the Archangel Gabriel he *'experienced more abundantly than usual an overflow of the sweetness of heavenly contemplation. He burned with a stronger flame of heavenly desires and he began to experience more fully the gifts of heavenly grace. His unquenchable fire of love for Jesus was fanned into a blaze.'*

This feeling of intense love, like Jesus's own love for humankind, was what Francis had hoped to experience. He also wished to suffer the five wounds that Jesus had received on the cross. He desired this so that he might experience in advance what it was like to be transformed into the

St Francis preaching to the birds

likeness of Christ crucified, '*not by the martyrdom of his flesh, but by the fire of his love consuming his soul*'. As he prayed his wish was granted. A winged Seraph appeared to him in a vision and hovered above him. When it had gone Francis found in his heart '*a marvellous ardour and imprinted in his body the marks of the nails on hands and feet and the wound in his side*'. Francis had received the imprint of the Stigmata, which has occurred since to some 300 others and for which there is no medical explanation. Francis's companions saw the wounds even though he tried to conceal them. When he died they also found that his hands and feet were pierced by thick dark matter, hard as nails

At Christmas in 1225 Francis established a custom which has been followed ever since: he set up a crib in the Portiuncola with models of the babe Jesus, the Holy Family and other figures. After that his health broke down. He was worn out by hardship, austerity and his great efforts. He suffered from terrible pains in one ear and his eyesight failed. Pope Honorius heard of this and made him journey to Rieti, where he was staying, to be attended by his own doctors. There Francis submitted to the most terrible and useless tortures of cauterisation. He then returned as a physical wreck to the Portiuncola, where he died, lying on the ground before the altar, on 4 October 1226.

Pope Honorius canonised St Francis in 1228. The great Basilica of San Francesco was built at the edge of the hill on which Assisi stands and Francis was buried there. The master painter Giotto and others covered the walls and ceilings with frescoes depicting his life. His importance to us and to generations to come is his example of unquenchable and yet simple faith which achieved more in barely ten years of evangelising than any saint since the apostles.

The first 'Franciscan Saint' to be canonised was St Elizabeth of Hungary, whose story is illustrated in the November Calendar. She became a member of St Francis' Third Order, the Tertiaries. Her godfather was Francis' supporter, Cardinal Ugolino, who became Pope Honorius II. When Francis died Honorius sent Elizabeth the saint's cloak, designed by Francis in the form of a cross. She died in 1231 and was canonised in 1235. Her story will be told with the November Saints on the 17th of that month.

In the year 1990 there were 18,000 Franciscan Friars and 16,000 'Poor Clares' world-wide. They continue the work of St Francis and help to bring the gospel tradition to those who seek spiritual guidance.

St Francis being led in deep prayer after receiving the stigmata

St Teresa of Avila (1515–82) and the prayers of a mystic

Theresa was born into the aristocratic family of de Cepeda in Avila in Castile. As a young girl in her 'teens' she was vivacious, fun-loving and witty, but her father disapproved of her taste for romances, fashion and perfume and her social life. He therefore sent her at fourteen to board in an Augustinian convent in the city which provided a 'finishing school' for young ladies. One can think of no more unlikely a start to the career of one who was to found the Reformed Order of Carmelite nuns and 16 convents in Spain, to be imprisoned by the Inquisition, to write two of the greatest books on prayer and to be regarded as a saint in her lifetime.

Her life, spiritual progress and works are intimately linked to make a moving story of the development of a soul and a great leader. Her story also reveals a determined will that drove her forward to win her way through many daunting setbacks. It is a story that reveals her as a role-model for all who find themselves struggling with spiritual problems. It is therefore a story for today.

Most of Teresa's life-story comes from her autobiography. She spent a year and a half at her Augustinian school. A kind nun there influenced her to consider taking the veil, but she was torn between love of her social life and a call to serve Christ. Then she fell ill, perhaps with a nervous breakdown. She left school to live with her uncle Pedro, with whom she read his spiritual books.

These gradually enthused her again with the idea of becoming a nun. By reading St Jerome's letters she found especial consolation for her sense of guilt at her early failure. She learned from them that he was always in ill-health and his experiences seemed like her own.

After a year and a half, and against her father's wishes, Teresa entered the Carmelite Convent of the Incarnation in Avila at the age of 20. She was not completely happy there because the nuns led too free and easy a life. They and their friends, both male and female, were allowed to come and go as they pleased. This conflicted with Teresa's desire for a contemplative life in which she could practice prayer. She did discover however that the humblest convent chores gave her a new freedom, a freedom that she was one day to record as a *'joy so great that it has never failed me and God converted the aridity of my sense into the deepest tenderness'*.

After a year she fell ill again and had to return home to be looked after by her family. At one time she was so ill that she received the Last Rites. She suffered from a semi-paralysis for nearly three years. For much of the time she could scarcely crawl and she was never again in good health. She failed to cure herself with herbal medicines, but she achieved a cure through the system of mental prayer that she had developed and also, she believed, by the help of St Joseph.

She later described her method of helping herself to achieve mental prayer. She always began by thinking of Jesus, not as a physical image, but by trying to imagine his feelings at each stage of his Passion. Her favourite way was to think of him as he prayed in the Garden of Gethsemane before he was betrayed. This helped her to free her mind of worldly thoughts by liberating it to pray, to examine herself, to discover her faults and to receive spiritual inspiration.

She was therefore already at the start of her mystical path, but during her convalescence she felt her spiritual progress was too slow. Then her uncle gave her a book on mystical prayer, *The Third Alphabet* by the Franciscan monk Francis Ossuna. It was the primer of sixteenth-century Spanish mysticism. It showed the sharp division between the *Alembrado* who practised total abandonment of the soul, come what may in spite of the spiritual dangers involved, and the *Recogido* who followed a more controlled way of mental prayer in an active and rational direction. This was the way Teresa was to recommend in her first book on prayer, *The Way to Perfection* (1562).

Through Ossuna's book she also learned about the mystical prayer practised by hesychasts like St John Climacus (30 March) and of its objective of moving through the three stages of 'Purification' and rejecting the world, of 'Illumination' and of achieving 'Union' with God in perfect love, hope and charity. She had no other spiritual guide for the next 20 years, but continued to develop her system of mental prayer. Meanwhile, though her vivacious personality continued to attract too many visitors, she also longed for spiritual protection. She felt that God was calling her to a more contemplative way of life, but her vivacity made it hard for her to give up her social interests.

Sometimes during this inner struggle she went through years-long periods of spiritual apathy and she felt she was failing God yet again. Then one day, when she was 40 years old and had been making some progress with her prayers, she noticed in her oratory a carved image of Jesus that had been borrowed by the convent for a festival. It was a stark image of a haggard and bleeding Christ bound to a column, with Mary Magdalene weeping at his feet. Teresa was suddenly overwhelmed by this physical image and she flung herself down shedding floods of tears, begging Jesus to give her strength so that she would not offend him. *'I believe I told him'*, she wrote later, *'that I would not rise from that spot until he had granted me what I was beseeching of him'*. That was typical Teresa! In that moment she gave herself completely to Him.

That was the great turning point in her life. Her spiritual life quickened and her prayers acquired a new vitality. She continued to read whatever books she could find and was drawn to St Augustine (28 August) after reading his *Confessions*. She was to tell one of her novice nuns that, unlike Augustine, she had never had any sexual temptations, but his sudden conversion in the garden was much like her own experience. The voice in the garden that Augustine had heard *'seemed exactly as if the Lord was speaking to me'*.

She had never found a confessor or spiritual adviser capable of giving her any real help until 1560, when she met the Franciscan and future saint Peter of Alcantara (19 October) in Avila. He guided her subsequently on her mystical journey to the very heights of divine union. By this time she had decided to leave her convent. Taking a few friends with her she left the Incarnation in 1562 and raised funds to buy a small house in the town which she called St Joseph's. She had only 13 nuns, but having obtained a brevet from the Pope, she broke away from the original Carmelites and founded her strict order of Reformed Carmelites or 'Discalced' nuns, so-named because they went barefoot or wore sandals instead of shoes.

This was the first of the 16 convents that she was to found in the next 20 years from Seville to Burgos. The convent of St Joseph's was poor, like all her foundations. The poverty could be seen in the coarse woollen cloth of the nuns' brown habits. It was also evident in the diet which included total abstinence from meat. Besides begging for alms Teresa's nuns followed a strict pattern of prayer, contemplation and working in the garden to produce their vegetables or in the convent spinning and making clothing for sale.

It was also in 1562 that Teresa's confessors, recognising her special qualities, asked her to write a book describing her spiritual life. This book is partly autobiographical but mainly a book on prayer. Having written about the method she had developed she told how this led to her being convinced that Jesus was within her and that she was totally engulfed by him.

She said that her times of deepest prayer sometimes led to a state of mind in which *'the soul is suspended in such a way that it seems outside itself. The will loves, the memory, I think, is lost; while the understanding, though it is not lost, does not reason – but is amazed at the extent of all it can understand.'* This left her filled with tenderness, humility and courage, for she felt her soul had met God. She sometimes seemed to hear an inner voice talking to her. This often frightened her and she wondered if this was the Devil, not God, speaking. Such mystical graces are hard to bear and Teresa had innumerable experiences of them, but she always 'knew' that Christ was at her side. She also realised that the way to Christ must be sought through his humanity in 'friendly intercourse and fragrant conversation with Him who loves us'.

In her *Life* she wrote that her soul was still afraid to engage in prayer without a book to help her. This was why she took to imagining that *'Jesus Christ our God and Lord was present within me – and so I prayed'*. Her confessors encouraged her to concentrate on these mental prayers. She described for her nuns the experience of her growing understanding of prayer as a discovery that *'God, who desires one for his own in order to show us greater favours, held me in his hand . . . God raises the soul wholly to himself, as being his very own and his bride'*.

In her book *The Way of Perfection*, which she began in 1566, she provided a simple guide to prayer and contemplation for her nuns. She wrote that *'I shall speak of nothing of which I have no experience or of which the Lord has not taught me in prayer'*. She told how vocal prayer differed from contemplative or mental prayer, the 'Prayer of the Heart'. She also said that her own and her nuns' aim should be to *'busy ourselves in prayer for those who are defenders of the Church . . . for prayer must be the foundation on which this house is built'*. This required humility and detachment from the world: *'Remember that it is to die for Christ and not to practice self-indulgence that we came here. To conquer the body is a great achievement in the battle of life. We give up our freedom for the love of God.'*

She warned her nuns that although there are many books on orderly prayer that appeal to people with orderly minds and help them to the 'harbour of light', there are others whose minds are like unruly horses not yet broken in. They are like people who are very thirsty, who, seeing water a long way off, strain every nerve to reach it; but always there seems to be someone barring their path. They lose courage and give up even though they are very near the fountain of eternal water of which Our Lord spoke to the Samaritan woman.

In the *Way* she introduces her nuns to the mystical life in her treatment of the 'Pater Noster', so as to bring them into the possession of the 'Kingdom', which for her is God's gift of contemplative prayer. For Teresa 'Our Father' enshrines all prayer and perfection because in it the Lord taught the whole method of prayer and contemplation. She advised that *'Whenever you approach God (in mental prayer) try to think and realise whom you address. He is Supreme Power, Supreme Goodness, Wisdom itself, without beginning and without end, Beauty itself, containing all beauties . . . Some of you have learned this, as I*

have, by experience . . . In contemplation we can do nothing. God does everything, the work is his alone and far transcends human nature. So leave everything to the Lord.'

She told her nuns to remember the words in the Lord's Prayer, *'Thy will be done' . . . 'because our wills are so different from God's will for us. He desires truth, we choose falsehood; he desires the eternal for us, we choose that which passes away . . . I wish to speak of certain things which those who attempt to walk along the way of prayer must of necessity practice. They are: One, Love each other; Two, detachment from created things; Three, true humility. Although humility is put last, it is the most important of the three and embraces the rest . . . The trials given by God to contemplatives are intolerable; they have a heavy cross to bear. If God did not feed them with consolations, they could not be borne . . . His Majesty will strengthen those on whom he wishes to bestow contemplation.'*

Before quoting from Teresa's book *The Interior Castle*, written in 1577, we need to record some of her thoughts and the important events in the 15 years of her life since her founding of St Joseph's in 1562 and also her sufferings and achievements in the last five years before her death. In her *Life*, finished in 1565, she described four stages of mental prayer. For this she used the metaphor of a garden that needed watering and attention. In the first stage, one that she likened to laborious drawing of water in a bucket from a well, the effort is entirely that of the one who prays. The second stage of contemplation is like using a waterwheel to fill the bucket; the wheel does the work, though some personal effort is needed and this is a time of trial for removing idle thoughts, like weeds from a garden. During this stage the inner peace increases. The third stage is when the Lord is active, providing a stream of water through the garden to moisten the soil. At this stage the will is quieter, the soul is free from worries and content to be idle. God is now the supplier and the supply of water is infinite.

This third stage, Teresa said, is when one is in perfect harmony with God, but not yet utterly absorbed in him. This is not complete union, but the faculties are only concerned with the things of God. Finally in the fourth stage, when the garden is watered by rain, the gardener has nothing to do but watch the flowers grow. In this stage the soul should be lost for words. The soul realises it is rejoicing in some good thing in which all good things are there at once. This state rarely lasts for long. Language is not enough to describe it but Teresa wrote that she found that it left her overwhelmed with tenderness, with tears of joy and renewed vigour.

Teresa wrote that from then on God began frequently to grant her the spiritual experiences of prayers of Quiet, leading to Union. She asked herself whether she was deluded in thinking that this came from God and not from the Devil. She asked her confessor. He actually confirmed her worst fears. In her trouble she went to another book, *The Ascent of Sion* by a Franciscan lay-brother, Bernadino da Laredo. He described the union of the soul with God just as she had experienced it.

Then she went to Father Diego de Cagtiona, a Jesuit in Avila. To her relief he was sure that she really was being led by God to some purpose. He advised her not to give up her prayers but to go on as she had been praying. Finally she was visited, much to her surprise, by the Jesuit Father Francis Borgia, once Duke of Gandia and later to be canonised in 1671. After listening to her he said that as long as she listened to the advice she received in prayer, it was not necessary for her to resist any experience that followed. After all, she was unwittingly following the same path that his leader St Ignatius of Loyola had described ten years before in his *Spiritual Exercises*.

After this Teresa began to experience 'locution' – that is to say, hearing voices. Once the Lord, to whom she was praying for help, spoke to her sharply: *'Serve me and don't be idle!'* His voice was loud and clear. Her custom of reading books while preparing herself for these prayers was suddenly brought to an end when both her favourite books, Ossuna's and Bernadino da Laredo's, were placed on the Index of forbidden books. This made her desolate. She had no alternative and, having no Latin, she could not read the New Testament since none was available in Spanish. By order of the Inquisition only the Latin Vulgate version was allowed. However in her distress she heard the voice of the Lord saying *'Be not distressed. I will give you a living book'*.

At first she had no idea what this meant. Then she had a vision while praying. *'I suddenly saw Christ at my side – or rather I was conscious of him, for I saw nothing with my bodily eyes. Ignorant of such things I wept, but He reassured me with a single word'*.

She asked her confessor what this experience meant. She did not know how she knew it was Christ whom she had seen, but that it was quite clear that it was Him. Then she said that his presence was brighter than the sun. Her vision was corroborated by her friend the Franciscan Peter of Alcantara. He defended her against her critics. Her admiration for the ascetic Peter and his spiritual direction was unbounded. For 40 years he ate only three times a week. She wrote of him that *'The world is not in a state to bear such perfection'*.

More mystical experiences flooded over her. She met the great mystic St John of the Cross (14 December), whom she was to persuade to found the male order of Reformed Carmelites in 1568. He discussed these experiences with her and comforted her and he described her in his book *The Living Flame of Love* as having a *'soul of fire'*. During her times of rapture Teresa's body became weightless and her nuns had difficulty in holding her down. This also occurred even when she was taking communion. She said she felt as if a great force was driving her feet up from the ground. Yet she knew that such experiences were by themselves unimportant. Their value was that they led to greater love, obedience, humility and detachment.

Teresa attributed one experience to an actual spiritual betrothal to Christ. She described this and her other experiences in letters to her friends, though she did not boast that this made her any better than others. The stories gradually spread. To her friends and to those who read her books she became a source of admiration and wonder. Her teaching of how to distinguish between good and unhealthy spirituality began to transform the religious life of Spain.

'I suddenly saw Christ at my side.'

Her private visions of Christ were not of a radiance that dazzled, but of a soft whiteness and diffused radiance that did not weary. For Teresa these were experiences of Divine Beauty. On one such occasion Christ took her rosary and it became four large precious stones. It was after this that she experienced her first 'transverberation' in her heart, so passionately did she feel Christ within her. She felt that *'the living flame of love'* cauterised her soul as an angel pierced her with a golden spear with a point of fire. This was followed by a sweet and loving discourse.

As her fame spread, Teresa founded 11 more small nunneries in places where there was a demand for the spiritual example that her nuns provided. She took great care in selecting only intelligent nuns, ones who had sound common sense. *'God save me from stupid nuns!'* she said. She was always frank and outspoken, even in her conversations with the Lord. Once, on the way to set up a new nunnery, and with her nuns and their modest chattels loaded on a donkey cart, Teresa found herself on the wrong side of a flooded river as a storm broke and a bolt of lightening destroyed the bridge ahead of them. It was the only one available to them. She stamped her foot and shouted out to heaven: *'Oh God, if this is what you do to your friends, no wonder nobody loves you!'* Apocryphal perhaps, but typical Teresa.

In 1575 the Inquisition, which mistrusted visionaries and mystics, arrested her. They were encouraged to do so by the envy and jealousies within the old Carmelite Order which resented her 'Reform' and questioned her spirituality. After studying her writings and condemning her mystical experiences as works of the Devil, Teresa and her nuns were declared apostate. She was confined to prison in Toledo for four years. This did not stop her pursuing the path she felt commanded to tread. She immediately began to write her greatest book on prayer, *The Interior Castle*. She waged war with her pen. She appealed to King Philip II of Spain. He mistrusted the monasteries, was anxious for reform and he approved of Teresa, but he had to contend with the power of the Inquisition.

She wrote letters to her friends and to her confessor Don Garcia. Her letters to him fell into the wrong hands and she was accused of having a love-affair with him. This slander was easily refuted and Teresa had the joy of finding that her nuns were still all loyal to her. They refused to accept the new prioress set over them by the unreformed Carmelites. They were interviewed and excommunicated in turn, one by one. This was too much for the King. He had had enough. He ordered that Teresa be brought to see him at the Escorial. When she arrived she, untypically, found herself unable to speak. Perhaps this helped her, because this demonstrated her humility. He considered her appeal was genuine and appointed four assessors to decide between her Order and the claims of the original Carmelites. Meanwhile he ordered the Inquisition's censures on Teresa to be removed, though for the time being she had to remain in Avila. This enabled her to continue her work and to escape the Inquisition, as had also her dear friend John of the Cross. He too had been condemned for his mystical writings. He had been imprisoned in Toledo, but had escaped through the window of his cell.

In May 1579 the king's assessors allowed Teresa to visit her convents again. She found them filled with renewed vigour from their period of trial. She then proceeded with great energy to found five more convents in the last three exhausting years of her life. Her last foundation was to be at Burgos, but she came up against the refusal of the Archbishop.

'Oh God, if this is what you do to your friends, no wonder nobody loves you!'

269

Her inner voice told her: 'Teresa, hold fast!'. She got her way when her many friends and supporters made the archbishop relent.

Before this last immense effort Teresa had broken her arm. It never healed properly and on the way back from Burgos to Avila she fell ill and had to stop. She grew steadily weaker and wrote: 'I hardly care whether I live or die. This is a grace God has given me, and I consider it a great one when I remember how afraid I was of death in the past'. She was almost alone when she died. Her confessor Father Garcia was absent and her friend John of the Cross was far away. She died on 4 October 1582, the feast-day of St Francis. She was canonised in 1622 along with St Ignatius of Loyola and St Francis Xavier. When Pope Paul VI proclaimed her a Doctor of the Church in 1970 he said: 'Her influence has been so great that it is second only to that of the greatest Fathers and Doctors of the Church, if indeed it has been second to them'.

Teresa's Life and books on prayer have been read with benefit ever since her time by clergy and followers of all Christian denominations. All we have done here is to quote a few of her sayings and open some doors for readers to go through on their own. To finish this introductory essay the last words must be Teresa's, taken from her greatest book The Interior Castle. This is her preparation for the mystical life. It built on the foundations laid down in The Way to Perfection. It is the culmination of her spiritual journey.

The book begins with these words: 'The soul seems to me to be like a castle, made of a single diamond or of very clear crystal in which there are many rooms, just as in heaven there are many mansions'. She goes on to describe the importance of learning how to enter the castle. 'This means entering within ourselves . . . and finding out our own faults . . . This is difficult for those souls who have been too busy with outside affairs to practice prayer. They must learn that the door to the castle is meditation and prayer.' Once the soul has entered into itself through prayer 'it is on the way to divine intimacy'.

The castle contains seven mansions. The first three are staging posts of active prayer and self-discipline and lead the soul from too great an occupation with worldly affairs to the fourth or transitional stage. This leads through contemplation to the last three staging posts where mystical prayer is developed. The journey culminates in a spiritual union, which Teresa called 'marriage', and in which the soul enjoys uninterrupted communion with God, the Blessed Trinity.

Her book tells that 'He who dwells in the centre of the Castle is our very good neighbour. He speaks to us through the conversations of good people, through sermons, or reading books; and in many ways He speaks in sickness and trials, and in the truths we learn in prayer. However feeble those prayers may be, God values them highly.'

To reach the fourth mansion we need the help of the Holy Spirit, since this is the staging post where we meet the supernatural. In order to arrive there we must already have spent a long time in the other mansions, so that our soul is no longer troubled with temptations. We should stop all discursive reasoning, though not to suspend understanding, but adopt the Prayer of Quiet to let one's thought fix itself on God. This may cause thoughts to roam about and cause distress, but this must be ignored. One's thought and understanding should simply abandon itself into the arms of divine love. His Majesty will then direct it onward in the light of heaven to the fifth mansion.

In the fifth mansion neither memory, imagination nor understanding are obstacles to the blessings being bestowed. God implants himself in the interior of the soul in such a way that it returns to itself. It cannot then doubt that God has been in it and that it has been in God, though it may take years for this favour to be granted. Our will has no part in this and its faculties sleep. This is the prayer of union in which our souls share something of Christ's suffering in his Passion not only in contemplating the sins of the world, but also some of the joy in doing God's will in suffering to atone it. By loving God and loving our neighbour we do his will and are united with him.

In the sixth mansion the soul, wounded by the fire of love, desires solitude and tries to renounce anything that might disturb it. The soul now desires perfect union, the betrothal. At this stage it is afflicted with the severest spiritual trials. People will mock one for trying to be too holy and suggest that the Devil has taken one over and make all sorts of disparaging suggestions. This kind of trial can last all one's life and is worse than physical trials. One has simply to await the mercy of God, which suddenly lifts the burden and awakens the soul as with a thunderclap. This happens when the soul is often not even ready or even thinking of him. Yet God does not yet reveal himself fully, but lights a spark of yearning, which makes it clear to one that it is He and not the Devil who is leading one.

In the seventh mansion, before the final vision of spiritual union which cannot take place fully in this life, the scales are removed from our eyes and the Most Holy Trinity reveals itself in all three Persons. They are seen in a wonderful way that shows they are one substance, one power, one knowledge and one God alone. Then what we know by faith the soul sees by the eyes as an intellectual vision and knows the truth of Jesus' words that *'If a man loves me, he will keep my word, and my Father will love him, and we will come to him and make our home with him'* (John 14.23). It was this vision which confirmed to Teresa that the Holy Spirit of God was within her and that she was engulfed by God the Trinity.

Teresa is one of the greatest examples of how to combine religious contemplation with an active and efficient career in practical affairs. It took her a lifetime of prayer and contemplation to reach her fullest understanding of the life and purpose of the soul. Her example of holiness is beyond the powers or capabilities of most of us who do not have her training or the length of her experience. Even so her books provide a convincing and invaluable set of circumstantial proofs that prayer can put us in touch with the supernatural. This is of enormous help when we find, as many ordinary people do sometimes after sincere prayer, that a verse in the Scriptures suddenly seems to be speaking to us in a specially meaningful way. At such times we can feel ourselves move on from just 'believing' to a feeling of certainty and 'knowing'. We may not be able to explain it, but it is the way the Holy Spirit does speak to us – through the scriptures – as Jesus promised at the Last Supper with his disciples. We may also find after praying that we get the same conviction as extraordinary coincidences occur, just as they did with Teresa. [1]

(1) Those who have read the account of the French seventeenth-century mystic Mme Guyon in Michel de la Bedoyere's very readable book *The Archbishop and the Lady* (1957), may ask why the Inquisition finally accepted Teresa, while the French Church and Louis XIV sent Mme Guyon to the Bastille. The answer is that Mme Guyon, though her book on inner prayer, *Le moyen court et tres facile de faire l'Oraison ('The short and easy way to pray')*,

271

had been approved by the French bishops, she and her loyal supporter Archbishop Fenelon of Cambrai could not control the over-enthusiastic readers. This led to many people interpreting the book as a private and unorthodox way to salvation, which upset the Church. This, together with the political intrigues at the French court, destroyed Fenelon's career and put Mme Guyon in prison for years, even though she was never accused of being unorthodox as a catholic and most people agreed she had done much good in raising the spiritual standards of her disciples at court. The fact is that the mystical way described by Teresa and Mme Guyon does need to be practised and interpreted with the help of an experienced spiritual guide.

St Therese of Lisieux (1873–97): *The Story of a Soul*

The criterion for calling a saint a 'great' saint may depend on whether one thinks they have brought about great changes in the spiritual life of their day, ones which are also relevant and meaningful to communities and individuals for all times. On this basis the Carmelite nun Therese of Lisieux, who had such a brief life, is in her way as important a saint as her predecessor in her Order, Teresa of Avila. Yet one needs to consider her unique story in the same way that one looks at a masterly miniature portrait. It does not depict the ethereal heights of mystical theology that Teresa of Avila reached, but illustrates the story of what Therese called a '*little soul*', the kind that most of us can identify with and which enlightens the personal and spiritual problems that most people face. She aimed high, but knew her limitations and reached through many personal difficulties of character to the highest degree of holiness and perfection of which she was capable. That is why her book *L'Histoire d'une Ame*, written at the request of her elder sister (who was also her Mother Superior) and published posthumously in 1898, was an instant success world-wide. It is still read with advantage by clergy and lay-people of all Christian denominations.

Pope St Pius X (1835–1914) (21 August) described her as '*the greatest saint of modern times*', 11 years before her canonisation. Pope Benedict XV (1914–22), said that she could not have fulfilled her missions and would have been remembered just as an ordinary unknown nun but for '*the world-wide circulation of* The Story of a Soul'. Pope Pius XI, who canonised her in 1925, said that '*Therese attained to the knowledge of supernatural things in such abundant measure that she was able to point out the sure way of salvation to others*'. Her story, like St Teresa of Avila's and also that of St Francis of Assisi, is a story of relevance for all generations.

Therese was born the third of four sisters in the well-to-do middle-class family of a Lisieux watch-maker. She was devout from her earliest childhood and yet always full of fun. All her sisters became Carmelite nuns and at the age of 15 she wrote '*I want to be a saint*'. This was not done in a vainglorious fashion, but was her simple direct and heroic approach to her life. In her book she tells how her full conversion occurred when she was 14 after a mysterious and debilitating illness. As she looked at a picture of Christ on the Cross, she saw blood coming from his hands. She found herself longing to catch it before it reached the ground. Then, remembering Jesus's words on the cross, '*I am thirsty*', she found herself longing to quench that thirst and, as a result, longing to do so by saving sinners. That was to be her ambition in her short life and for which she tried to perfect her soul.

She became determined to join her eldest sister in the enclosed Carmelite community at Lisieux, even though that was not normally possible until she was 21. First she saw her bishop and impressed him with her faith and then, when her father had taken her on a grand tour of the shrines of most of the great Italian saints, she went to a public audience with the Pope Leo XIII. In spite of being told by her bishop not to speak to him, she boldly begged him to allow her to become a nun immediately. Her wish was soon granted. In 1888 she became the youngest ever Carmelite nun as *'Therese, the child of Jesus'*.

Her book is only 150 pages long. It seems at first to be the musings of a naïve young girl. However, as one reads how she trained herself to develop her own private way of correcting her faults, one soon finds oneself joining her in her little struggles and recognising them as similar to one's own. She called her method *'The Little way of Spiritual Childhood'*. In this she showed how she perceived, even as a girl, how all of us are, compared with Jesus, very small souls. These struggles may seem superficially to be of no consequence to dwellers in the complex world outside a nunnery and a closed order and who are deeply involved in business or political affairs that affect thousands of others. Yet one soon discovers that Therese, like the poet William Blake, had the vision to *'see the world in a grain of sand and beauty in a wild flower'*. She saw all creation in the same way as Blake. She also recognised the need for all creative things to be different, and why a red rose is different from a little violet because only in that way and through the immense diversity of creation can the true glory of God be seen. That realisation and the depth of her devotion to Jesus is why she called herself *'The Little Flower gathered by Jesus'*.

As the many examples in her book show, she explains that what matters is the motive and the resulting action even in the most trivial affairs. Among the examples of the little difficulties, trials and sufferings that she faced in her enclosed world she tells how she failed adequately to dust the cobwebs in the convent cloisters or to weed the garden. She also says how she overcame her sin of pride by forcing herself to be helpful and agreeable to a sister nun whom she disliked. She taught herself to love doing her often-tedious duties, such as folding blankets and her nuns' cloaks properly. Among the lessons these little problems taught her was how God fits our trials to our strength. She discovered that if we listen he increases our strength to face the unknown trials that always lie ahead of us so that we are able to cope with them.

At her entry into the convent her Mother Superior told her that her soul was very simple, but that even so it would become more simple still, because the nearer one gets to God, the simpler one becomes. Therese's story illustrates the truth of this, though she was far from being totally involved in her little problems. She read widely, memorising in particular Thomas à Kempis's *The Imitation of Christ*. She also used the Gospels to help her prayers, which enabled her to know by experience that *'the Kingdom of God is within us'*. She concluded from her studies that *'Jesus had no need of books or Doctors of the Church to guide souls. He, the Doctor of Doctors, can teach without words . . . I know that he is within me. He guides and inspires my every moment of the day, even when I am busy with my daily works and not only during my prayers.'*

The first signs of her fatal illness, tuberculosis, appeared in 1896, yet she was not discouraged because: *'God would not make me wish for something impossible (i.e. to be a saint), and so in spite of my illness I can aim at being a saint . . . so I put up with myself as I am, with all my countless faults'*. This was not boastfulness because in her humility she realised that the difference between herself and the saints *'was as between the summit of a mountain lost in the clouds and a grain of sand trodden underfoot'.*

During the early months of 1897 she woke up to find blood filling her mouth and on her pillow. She knew that her time was nearly over, but wrote that *'the hope of heaven transported me with joy'*. Nevertheless she still hoped that she might be cured and prayed that she could be allowed to achieve her life-long aim of saving souls by being allowed to answer an appeal for volunteers by the Community of Carmelite nuns in Hanoi in Indo-China.

Near the end she wrote what is the crowning message of her *'Little Way'*. She said that the highest grace she had received that year was that of being able to grasp in all its fullness the meaning of Charity. She explained this by saying that until then she had never been able to fathom Our Lord's words: *'The second commandment is like the first: "Thou shalt love thy neighbour as thyself". Now Jesus had made me understand what his will really was by the words he spoke to his apostles at the supper before his arrest and trial: "Love one another AS I HAVE LOVED YOU". They were his friends and brethren for whom he was about to lay down his life.'*

As Therese meditated on those five words, which the present author has put in capital letters, she realised that they summed up the core of Jesus's whole message and of his final act of love as he prepared himself to die. She realised also how imperfect was her own love for her sister nuns, for she knew she did not love them as Jesus loved them. This made her understand two things about Love and Charity. First she saw that true charity lies in putting up with all one's neighbours' faults and weaknesses and also in being inspired by their virtues. °Secondly she realised the importance of the way Jesus stressed the point that we should *'love them as He loved us'*, even unto death.

These thoughts showed her the great difference between the new command 'to love' that Jesus had made, and the old commandment in the Mosaic Law. She found that true love or charity of this kind enlarges the heart.She then quoted St Paul – *'without the spirit of charity we cannot call God our Father'*. She also showed how these thoughts had given her peace of mind by quoting another of her favourite authors, St John of the Cross: *'All good things have come to me since I no longer seek them for myself'*. She told her eldest sister, who had become the Mother Superior of the convent, that she realised Jesus does not command great deeds. All he wants is self-surrender and gratitude, he needs nothing save our love . . . *'Love is the fulfilling of the Law'* (Romans 13.9).

Therese's book is the story of a little soul' – 'little', as is the case with most souls. She triumphed only over little things, but she did so by testing her capacity to the fullest. She also realised that one great important truth about love, which so many more able people have had difficulty in doing, immersed as they are in the world's affairs. With her simple and yet eternal truths Therese's spiritual understanding and example can be compared with those of many great saints, which is why her book is one of the best-loved and most helpful religious works of the past century.

NOVEMBER SAINTS

November

1. All Saints Day
2. All Souls Day
3. St Hubert St Winifred
4. St Charles Borromeo
5. St Zachary & Elizabeth
6. St Leonard
7. St Willbrord
8. St Godfrey of Amiens
9. St Theodore the Recruit
10. St Justus of Canterbury

11. St Martin of Tours
12. St Britius (St Brice)
    St Nicholas
13. St Lawrence O'Toole
14. St Machutus St Albert
    St Leopold of Austria
15. St Margaret of Scotland
16. St Hugh of Lincoln St Gregory of Tours
17. St Elizabeth of Hungary
18. Odo of Cluny

St Martin of Tours   317–397 AD

20. St Edmund
21. St Gelasius
22. St Cecilia
23. St Alexander Nevsky
    St Clement I St Felicity
25. St Catherine of Alexandria
30. St Andrew

2nd–3rd Century AD

St Cecilia

St Andrew

The three saints portrayed in the heading for November are: **St Andrew the Apostle** (30 November) who is shown being crucified on a saltyre-shaped cross; **St Cecilia** (22 November), the early fourth-century virgin martyr who is being stifled to death in a steam bath; **St Martin of Tours** (11 November) who is about to share his military cloak with a half-naked beggar.

ALTAR-PIECE DESIGN FOR THIRTEEN NOVEMBER SAINTS

Shown in the centre is:

St Albert the Great (15 November), the thirteenth-century theologian, scientist and tutor of St Thomas Aquinas.

In the top row are:

St Catherine of Alexandria (25 November) the legendary fourth-century martyr who died on a spiked wheel; **St Gregory of Tours** (17 November) bishop and author of a martyrology; **St Gregory of Sinai** (27 November) fourteenth-century mystic; **Pope St Leo I 'The Great'** (10 November) confronting Attila alone and his invading huns outside Rome in 451.

On the right side are:

St Gregory Palamas (14 November) the fourteenth-century mystic and theologian of Mount Athos, subsequently Bishop of Salonika, receiving his emperor; **Abbess St Hilda of Whitby** (17 November) monastic foundress and defender of the Celtic style of Christian worship.

In the bottom row are:

St Hubert (3 November) bishop who saw the figure of Christ in a stag's antlers; **Bishop St Hugh of Lincoln** (17 November) defending his flock; **Queen St Margaret of Scotland** (16 November), mother of King St David of Scotland. She is shown with **Princess St Elizabeth of Hungary** (17 November) and her miraculous sack of roses.

On the left side are:

Prince Alexander Nevski of Kiev (23 November) saving Russia from the Tartars; **St Gertrude of Helfta** (13 November), the thirteenth-century German visionary.

Altar-piece design for thirteen November saints

277

NOVEMBER CALENDAR OF SAINTS' FEAST-DAYS

1st **ALL SAINTS' DAY**

ROMANUS the MELODIST: Sixth-century Byzantine hymn-writer.

2nd **ALL SOULS' DAY**: Founded in 998 by St Odilo of Cluny to commemorate all the departed souls.

3rd **HUBERT**: Bishop of Maastricht who died in 727. Pioneer evangeliser of the Ardennes who had, like St Eustace (2 November), been converted on seeing the figure of Christ between the antlers of a stag. He died after a boating accident in a flooded forest stream.

WINEFRIDE (Winifred): Legendary Welsh virgin killed by a rapist. A spring spouted from her tomb, since called Holywell. King James II went there to pray for the birth of a son. This was granted and the son later became the Jacobite 'Old Pretender'.

MALACHY (or 'Maedoc' or 'Maol') (1094–1148): Irish Archbishop of Armagh who carried out the Gregorian church reforms in Ireland. He visited the Abbey of Clairvaux to gain advice for this work from Bernard of Clairvaux. He founded the Irish Cistercian monastery of Melfont. He died in Bernard's arms, who called him a saint.

MARTIN of PORRES (1579–1639): Dominican lay-brother, son of a Spanish noble and a freed negress slave of Lima in Peru. Dedicated his life to the poor. He had many visions and ecstasies. Canonised in 1837.

4th **CHARLES BORROMEO** (1538–84): Cardinal Archbishop of Milan, nephew of the Cardinal de Medici who became Pope Pius IV. Pius made him his Secretary of State. He played an important part in the reopening and successful conclusion of the reforming Council of Trent. He wrote liturgical books and was patron of Palestrina's church music. His last years were spent in reorganising the education of the clergy, helped by the Jesuits and the Barnabites. He encouraged St Edmund Campion (25 October) and other clergy on their missions to England, where they were martyred.

Borromeo's influence on the Counter-Reformation was as great as that of St Ignatius of Loyola (31 July) and St Philip Neri (26 May). He died of overwork. Canonised in 1610.

5th **ZACHARY and ELIZABETH**: Parents of St John the Baptist.

6th **ILLTYD**: Early sixth-century Abbot of Llanilltud Fawr on the Gower Peninsular of South Wales. His monastery's earth-covered foundations can still be seen there. His life by St Samson (8 July) says he was a disciple of St Germanus of Auxerre (31 July), St Patrick's friend. He said Illtyd's gifts of prophesy (interpretation) showed he was *the most learned of the Britons in both Testaments and in all kinds of knowledge*.

LEONARD: Sixth-century hermit, traditionally of St Leonard near Limoges in France. One of the Crusaders' most popular saints; they made him patron saint of prisoners of war.

WINNOC: Died c.717. Welsh monk who founded Cornish church of St Winnow and later joined the monastery at St Omer in France. He founded a monastery and a hospital at Dunkirk. His remains were taken to Bergues-St-Winnoc in 899.

7th **WILLIBRORD** (658–731): Yorkshire monk trained by St Wilfrid (12 October). Took mission of 12 disciples to Friesia and visited Rome. Made Bishop of Utrecht until driven out by a pagan king. He returned there in 719 with St Boniface of Crediton (5 June). With Boniface he helped to establish the Church in Thuringia. He also taught in Denmark and Luxemburg. In Utrecht a sacred dance is still performed yearly at his shrine.

8th **WILLEHAD**: Died in 789. Born in Northumbria he devoted his life to being a missionary in Charlemagne's empire. The Emperor sent him to preach to the Saxons, but they massacred his clergy. Willehad escaped and was then made Bishop of Bremen.

GODFREY (or 'Geoffrey') of AMIENS (1065–1115): Vigorous reforming bishop who put down simony, enforced clerical celibacy and organised local government.

9th **THEODORE the RECRUIT**: Early fourth-century martyred Greek soldier. Burnt alive for setting fire to the temple of the mother goddess in Pontus (Asia Minor).

NECTARIUS KEPHALAS (1864–1920): Greatly revered Greek bishop. Canonised by the Greek Orthodox Church in 1961.

10th **POPE LEO I ('The Great')**: Born at Volterra in Tuscany he served several popes on important commissions. With St John Cassian (23 July) he examined and condemned in 429–31 Patriarch Nestorius of Constantinople's explanatory sermons in which he called the Virgin Mary '*The Mother of Christ*' rather than the traditional form of '*Mother of God*' (see under Cyril of Alexandria, 27 June). Elected Pope in 440. His greatest theological achievement was to get the Council of Chalcedon in 451 to condemn the Monophysite heresy which claimed that Christ had only one nature – the divine – and to accept the tradition that he was one person with two natures, human and divine. He confronted Attila and his Huns in 452 and saved Rome. He failed to prevent the Vandals under Genseric in 455 from sacking the city for 14 days. His surviving 96 sermons and over 400 letters written to every part of the Roman Empire show how he formulated Catholic doctrine and asserted the supremacy of Rome. In doing this he laid the foundations for the medieval papacy. On the question of the death penalty for heresy he supported the civil law of his day and did not hesitate to enlist the imperial power to destroy heresy. We have already seen how St Martin of Tours (11 November) and will later see how St Ambrose (7 December) pleaded against the beheading of the Spanish Bishop Priscillian in 383 for unorthodox practices. The death penalty for heresy is not something of which Christ could have approved, but those were difficult times. Leo wrote that such a penalty would act as a warning to others. The Church actively sought the death penalty for the opponents of its traditions for another 750 years. Protestant Churches also relied on their States' laws to follow the same practice.

JUSTUS of CANTERBURY: Died in 627 as the fourth Archbishop of Canterbury. He was one of the second wave of Roman monks sent to Kent.

11th MENAS: Fourth-century Egyptian martyr, patron saint of desert caravans.

MARTIN of TOURS (315–97): Born of pagan parents in Pannonia (Hungary). He was a conscript soldier who became attracted to Christianity and tried to resign from the army. He was flogged as a coward and served out his time. He became a centurion and while still in the army in Gaul he rode through Amiens and saw a half-naked beggar. Taking pity on him he cut his military cloak in half and gave it to him. He became a disciple of St Hilary of Poitiers (13 January). He began his ministry as a hermit in Touraine and founded several monasteries including one at Marmoutiers. These were the first Western monasteries in the style that Hilary had studied in the East. Hilary had him elected Bishop of Tours and encouraged him to evangelise in Northern Gaul where the Celtic pagans worshipped the tree spirits, notably the 'Green Man' who was said to die in the Autumn and to be reborn in the Spring (see details under St Hilary in the January Calendar). It was not too difficult for missionaries to explain that the Green Man was really Christ who died and was resurrected. Martin, together with St Ambrose, Bishop of Milan (7 December), protested against the trial and death penalty imposed in 383 at Trier on the Spanish Bishop Priscillian for unorthodox

practices. Priscillian was the first heretic to be executed as a result of charges made by the Church. His aim however was only to make worship more spiritual. One of Martin's later disciples in the next century was St Ninian (26 August) the first evangeliser of Scotland. He so admired Martin that he named his first church in Galloway after him. Martin became one of the most popular saints in Britain.

12th NILUS of ANCYRA: Died in 430. He was one of the strongest supporters of Patriarch St John Chrysostom (13 September) in his struggle to reform the Eastern Church against the opposition of the Empress Eudoxia. He wrote moral and ascetic treatises.

LEBUIN: English monk of Ripon who founded a church at Deventer in Friesia. He died in 773.

JOSOPHAT of POLOTSK (1580–1623): Abbot of Vilna and Bishop of Polotsk. He took his own and other Kievan sees into communion with Rome. For this he was murdered by a Russian Orthodox mob. Canonised by Rome as a martyr in 1867.

13th BRICE (or Britius): Died in 444 as Bishop of Tours. He was a difficult and independent character which caused him to be exiled from his see for seven years. He was restored later as bishop. He was much influenced by the style of St Martin of Tours (11 November), which may account for his popularity in Britain.

POPE NICHOLAS I ('The Great'): Elected pope in 858 and died in 867. He dealt firmly with the troubled state of the Church during the break-up of Charlemagne's empire. He overcame the interference of the German Emperor Lothair and his bishops. He settled a major theological dispute between Rome and the Patriarch of Constantinople.

DIEGO (1400–63): Franciscan lay-brother who served as door-keeper to the friary of Fuerteventura in the Canary Islands. He worked among the poor and established such a reputation for holiness that he was made Superior of the house.

FRANCIS CABRINI (1750–1817): Italian foundress of The Missionary Sisters of the Sacred Heart in 1780. In 1789 she established this Order in the USA and in 28 years she founded many schools and four large hospitals. She also worked to help the crowds of Italian immigrants. She helped her nuns take the Order to South America, France and England. Her famous cry when faced with difficulties in the work was '*Who is doing this, we or the Lord?*' The work got done. As a naturalised US citizen she was canonised in 1950.

14th DUBRICIUS (or Dyfrig): Sixth-century Welsh bishop who had been a monk on Caldey island off the south coast of Wales with St Illtyd (6 November) and St Samson (28 July). The Welsh sixth-century historian St Gildas (29 January) names him as Bishop of Caerleon, the seat of the legendary King Arthur. From this arose the tradition that he crowned Arthur.

LAWRENCE O'TOOLE (1128–80): Abbot who became Archbishop of Dublin in 1161 at a time when Ireland was rent by tribal warfare. In 1170, when 'Strongbow' Earl of Pembroke landed with his Normans near Dublin, Lawrence became heavily involved in the political negotiations that ended in 1171 with King Henry II being supported by the King of Connacht, Rory O'Brien, in his take-over of Ireland. He did this with the approval of the English Pope Adrian IV. Lawrence later lost favour with Henry and died at Eu in Normandy after visiting him.

GREGORY PALAMAS (1296–1359): Abbot and leading upholder of the silent way of prayer (hesychasm) on Mount Athos. This style of prayer begins with the constant repetition of the 'Jesus Prayer' – 'O Lord Jesus, Son of God, have mercy on me a sinner'. The prayer is said in time with slow rhythmical breathing and leads to total relaxation and freedom from worldly thoughts. It can lead to a sense of illumination through seeing what practitioners believe to be the uncreated light of God, the light that shone from Jesus's face at his Transfiguration. Gregory's monks practised this in opposition to opinion in Constantinople. A fierce debate on the orthodoxy of hesychasm lasted for ten years and ended with Gregory and his monks being excommunicated. In 1347, when John Cantacuzensus seized the imperial throne, he needed the support of the monks of Athos and had the right to communion restored to them. He then made Gregory Bishop of Salonika. This dispute and the successful conclusion for the hesychasts had a remarkable effect on icon painting in Greece and Russia. This can be seen by comparing icons painted before and after 1350. The earlier ones tend to be painted in sombre colours and with gloomy backgrounds. The later ones are filled with light.

15th MALO (or 'Machutus'): Sixth- or seventh-century Welsh missionary to Brittany who founded a church at St Servan near the modern port of St Malo.

ALBERT the GREAT (or 'of the Rhine') (1206–80): A Bavarian who became a Dominican monk at 17. He was a scholar learned in theology, philosophy and in every known science. He became known as 'the wisest man in Europe'. Together with his famous pupil St Thomas Aquinas (28 January) he studied in Paris the newly rediscovered missing works of Aristotle, which Arab scholars had translated in the previous century. These works had caused a major crisis in the Church since they contradicted the traditional view of Plato on the soul, which St Augustine had impressed on the Church's tradition.

Albert supported Thomas Aquinas' lectures on the subject and also his reinterpretation of the soul as the second creative element in the world after that of God. As described in the January Calendar, Thomas and Albert concluded from Aristotle that the human soul existed independently of the body and was therefore the source of a human being's creative ability and moral authority. This view was opposed by the French bishops after Thomas's death in 1274, but was supported successfully by Albert. Albert is so important that his life and works are described in the text after this Calendar.

16th QUEEN MARGARET of SCOTLAND (1046–93): One of the last members of the Anglo-Saxon royal family from before the Norman Conquest. She was beautiful, intelligent, devout and very charitable. After the Conquest she took refuge in Scotland and made a dynastic marriage with the brutal King Malcolm IV. She bore him six sons and gradually and patiently caused him to reform his ways and to support the Church. She herself instigated reforms in the lax Scottish Church and founded several monasteries, churches and hostels for pilgrims. She also restored the ruined abbey on Iona. Her eldest son became King St David of Scotland (14 May). She was canonised in 1250.

EDMUND of ABINGDON (1170–1240): Born in Abingdon and educated at Oxford University. He became Archbishop of Canterbury in 1233. Like his thirteenth-century predecessor St Thomas à Becket (29 December) and his own contemporary St Richard of Chichester (3 April) he had grave disagreements with his King (Henry III) over Church property and rights in Canon Law. He was learned and holy and died in France on his way back from pleading a case for the Church in Rome.

GERTRUDE of HELFTA (1256–1303): Sent as a child to the nunnery at Helfta where she was well-educated and where she lived all her life. At the age of 25 she had a vision of Christ and then devoted her life to contemplation and the study of the Early Church Fathers. She had many remarkable spiritual experiences which she and her visionary friend St Mechtilde (19 November) described in two books, *The Revelations of Gertrude and Mechtilde* and *The Herald of God's Loving Kindness*. The books give a good insight into medieval German mysticism. They include Gertrude's description of her devotion to *'The Sacred Heart of Jesus'*. She was therefore a precurser of St Margaret Alacoque (15 October) in her devotion to this subject, which became widespread among Roman Catholics in the seventeenth century. It is probably for this reason that she is known as 'Gertrude the Great', the only female saint with such a title.

ABBESS HILDA of WHITBY (614–80): Grandniece of King Edwin of Northumbria. She was made the abbess of a nunnery by St Aidan of Lindisfarne (31 August), the great Celtic evangeliser. She was very learned and founded a monastery in the Celtic style at Whitby for both monks and nuns. At the controversial Synod of Whitby in 663 she strongly supported the cause for retaining the Celtic style of worship, liturgy and the dating of Easter. Through the eloquence of the Romish enthusiast St Wilfrid (12 October) she was outvoted and the Roman ways were adopted for the Anglo-Saxon Church. Among her best-known monks were St John of Beverley (7 May) and the former shepherd and poet St Caedmon (11 February).

17th GREGORY the WONDER-WORKER (c.213–c.270): A disciple and close friend of Origen after he had settled at Caesarea, where he became bishop and built a church. He was expert at explaining the gospels and converted large numbers of pagans, using Origen's teaching. He so impresseed St Basil the Great and St Gregory Nyssa's grandmother St Macrina the Elder (14 January) with his teaching that she memorised it and passed it on to her children and grandchildren. This is the origin of Basil's and the Cappadocian Fathers' admiration for Origen. Gregory's funeral oration for Origen, describing his work and importance to the understanding of the faith has already been quoted in the January Calender. Gregory was called 'the wonder-worker' because of the many remarkable miracles attributed to him. These included changing the course of a river and moving a mountain.

HUGH of LINCOLN (1135–1200): A monk of Avalon in Burgundy whom King Henry II made prior of the Cistercian abbey that he had just founded at Witham in Somerset. Hugh was a very upright and determined man and he refused to take office as prior until the king had provided alternative accommodation for the villagers he had ejected to make room for the abbey buildings. He was made Bishop of Lincoln and resisted injustice in every form, whether royal or otherwise. He broke up the persistent riots against the Jews and personally intervened against the cruelty of the king's foresters who assaulted his flock. He took an independent view in politics, outfacing the rage of Henry II with a joke and that of King Richard I with a kiss. He refused to pay taxes to finance Richard's outrageous campaigns in

France. He was renowned for his pets which included a magnificent swan – his emblem.

ELIZABETH of HUNGARY (or of BOHEMIA) (1207–31): Princess, daughter of King Andrew II of Hungary and a direct descendant of King St Stephen of Hungary (16 August), who made his country Christian. At the age of 14, Elizabeth made a dynastic marriage with the Landgrave Ludwig IV of Thuringia. She was very devout and charitable from childhood, but her mother-in-law interfered and she was unhappy until in a miraculous way she succeeded in winning over her husband. Her story and that of her miracle of the roses and of what happened afterwards reads like a fairy tale by the brothers Grimm. She was recognised in Germany by the end of her short life as a saint. Her life is told in the text after the Calendar. Most of the information comes from German sources and histories.

ROSE-PHILIPPINE DUCHESNE (1769–1852): Born in Grenoble, she became a nun. Although she and her sister nuns were expelled during the Revolution, she continued to do good works. In 1805 St Sophie Barat (25 May) made her one of her nuns in her order of The Society of the Sacred Heart. For this Order, see under St Gertrude of Helfta above and St Margaret Alacoque (15 October). In 1818 she went to the USA and set up a school and several nunneries in the Mississippi Valley. Intrigues forced her resignation as abbess in 1840. She then set up a log-cabin school for Indians in Sugar Creek, Missouri. She had to face great poverty there and also the hostility of the white Americans, but lived as a frontier missionary until her death. She was canonised in 1988.

18th MAWES (or Maudez): Fifth-century founder of the Celtic monastery for men and women at St Mawes in the Cornish peninsular of Roseland. Its ruins can still be seen opposite the harbour. He then went to Brittany and became a bishop. He was much revered and retired to the Ile de Modez where he died.

ODO of CLUNY (879–942): He was brought up in the household of William, Duke of Aquitaine. He was made second Abbot of Cluny and increased greatly the number of its monks. Through many visits to Rome he spread the strict principles of the Cluniac observance to many Italian monasteries. He also reformed several French houses on the same lines. Through him and his later successors the Abbey of Cluny became the most influential body in Western Christendom at a time when for two centuries the papacy was in a state of anarchy due to local Roman power bosses and imperial interference.

BAARLAM of ANTIOCH: Priest martyred in Diocletian's persecution, c.304.

MECHTILDE of HELFTA (1251–98): Nun and mystic, colleague of St Gertrude of Helfta (16 November). Her book of spiritual teaching, *The Book of Special Grace*, was published posthumously.

20th KING EDMUND MARTYR (841–69): King of the East Angles who was captured in battle by the invading 'Great Army' of the Danes. He was shot to death with arrows. The Saxons venerated him as a martyr and built his shrine in the Abbey of Bury St Edmunds in Suffolk.

21st POPE GELASIUS: Died in 492. A firm upholder of the supremacy of Rome.

22nd CECILIA: c.Third-century Roman virgin martyr. According to her legend she was affianced by her rich pagan parents to a pagan youth called Valerian. She had vowed herself as a virgin for Christ and told this to her husband on her wedding night. He respected her vow and together with his friend Tiburtius he too became a Christian. Both men were immediately executed. According to the Acts of Cecilia they were recognised as saints and martyrs (14 April). Cecilia was ordered to cast incense at the altar of the imperial gods. She refused and was stifled to death in the steam bath beneath her villa. The foundations of this can still be seen under the church dedicated to her name in the Trastevere district of Rome. She was made patron saint of music because of the legend that her wedding music was played on an organ when she died.

23rd POPE CLEMENT I: Martyred c.100. The fourth pope after St Peter. An important authority on the supremacy of Rome over other Christian centres as explained in his letter to the Corinthian Church, c.96. As an active preacher in Rome he was exiled to the Crimea. He still continued to evangelise until he was allegedly tied to an anchor and drowned. His relics and the remains of his anchor were gathered by St Cyril and St Methodius (11 May) in the ninth century and buried in his church of San Clemente in Rome.

FELICITY of ROME: Martyred in the second century in Rome in the reign of Antoninus Pius. Her sons were also condemned to death as Christians. They may be the seven martyrs revered on 10 July – Saints Felix, Philip, Martial, Vitalis, Alexander, Sylvanus and Januarius. For another St Vitalis of Bologna, see 27 November feast-day.

COLUMBANUS (540–615): Irish monk allowed by St Comgall (11 May), Abbot of Bangor, to take 12 monks as disciples to evangelise in Gaul in c.590. For nearly 20 years he ruled the monasteries he founded in Burgundy at Luxeuil, Annegray and Fontaines. He and his monks were then expelled by the Burgundian court which was offended by their strict moral rules. They avoided being shipped back to Ireland from Nantes and preached in the Rhineland. Columbanus and his disciple St Gall (16 October) then entered Switzerland. St Gall remained there to preach, while Columbanus crossed the Alps and founded a monastery at Bobbio in Lombardy. His monks also went as far south as Sicily. He is still revered as a saint in Bobbio.

PRINCE ALEXANDER NEVSKI (1219–63): Prince of Novgorod, Vladimir and Kiev who saved Russia from the invasions by the Tartars, Lithuanians and Swedes. He succeeded with the Tartars by being patient with them, saying: '*God is not on the side of force, but of truth and justice*'.

24th FLORA and MARY: Martyred by the Muslims in Cordoba in 851.

ANDREW DUNG LOAC and COMPANIONS: Vietnamese priest martyred in 1839 with 116 companions including a Spanish bishop and missionaries of the Paris mission.

25th MERCURY: Soldier martyr in Decius's persecutions, c.250. Many legends.

CATHERINE of ALEXANDRIA: A noble Christian lady who protested to Emperor Maxentius against the enforced worship of idols. Her legend says that she demolished the arguments of 50 pagan philosophers at her trial. Because of their failure they were said to have been executed. While in prison she is said to have converted her prison guards, to have had a vision of Christ and to have been fed by doves. She is believed to have been executed by being crushed on the spikes of a wheel.

Catherine is not mentioned in early martyrologies and she may never have existed, but she had the kind of reputation that attracts legends like iron filings to a magnet. For lack of documentary information about her she was removed from the calendar in the reforms of 1969 and is now venerated only as one of the 'Fourteen Holy Helpers'. St George (23 April) was also treated in this way, but has since been restored to full sainthood.

26th SILVESTER GOZZOLINI (1177–1267): Founder of the Silvestrines, an independent Benedictine congregation that still exists. He did this after rebuking his bishop of Orsino in Italy for his irregular life.

JOHN BERCHMANS (1599–1621): Dutch Jesuit priest of Brabant of exceptional holiness who died young.

27th VITALIS of RAVENNA: Roman martyr and bishop of unknown date to whom the beautiful sixth-century Basilica was built in Ravenna.

VIRGUIL of SALZBURG: Irish eighth-century missionary to Germany who became Bishop of Salzburg. He had theological disputes with St Boniface of Crediton (5 June) and died in 784.

GREGORY of SINAI (1290–1346): He became a monk of St Catherine's monastery at the foot of Mt Sinai after being ransomed from the Turks. He was a mystic and adopted the hesychast or deep-breathing method of prayer developed by St John Climacus (30 March) at Sinai in the seventh century. As a mystic he sought a more suitable place for contemplation first in Crete, then on Mount Athos where he was a contemporary of St Gregory Palamas (14 November) who was also a hesychast. Finally after a Turkish raid he founded a monastery on Mt Paroria on the Black Sea coast and taught his monks the way of silent prayer.

28th STEPHEN the YOUNGER (715–65): Hermit-monk who protested against the iconoclastic laws of the Emperor Constantine V. He was exiled to an island in the Sea of Marmora and then was battered to death for continuing to resist the emperor.

CATHERINE LABOURÉ (1806–76): A Sister of Charity of Paris, the Order founded by St Vincent de Paul (27 September). She nursed the sick and did her duty in an outwardly uneventful life. Inwardly she experienced a 'voice' and had visions of the Virgin Mary. The 'voice' instructed her to have a medal struck with the figures of Mary on one side and of Jesus on the other. In addition the medal was to have 12 stars on it. The European Union flag now contains those same twelve stars. Her holiness of spirit was obvious to all who met her. She was canonised in 1947.

29th BRENDAN of BIRR: Sixth-century Irish monk and contemporary of Abbot St Brendan the Voyager (16 May).

30th ANDREW the APOSTLE: The brother of St Peter and the first disciple to be called by Christ. He is recorded in all the lists of Jesus's disciples in the gospel and was present at the coming of the Holy Spirit at Pentecost. He is believed to have been martyred in Patras in Greece on a saltyre-shaped cross.

SUMMARY OF NOVEMBER SAINTS

This Calendar gives the feast-days of 64 saints, of whom 16 were martyrs and 15 were women. More details are given below about the lives of two of these saints, **St Albert** (15 November) and **St Elizabeth of Bohemia** (17 November).

IMPORTANT NOVEMBER SAINTS

Albert the Great – or 'Albert of the Rhine' (1206–80)

Although he was regarded in Germany as a saint and the most learned man of the whole middle ages, Albert was not canonised and entered into the Roman Calendar until 1931, 650 years after his death. Because of his expertise in every known science Pope Pius XI also made him a Doctor of the Church and said that Albert was the ideal saint for this modern age.

Albert's importance to the Church in his own time was due to his insistence that philosophy and theology are two distinct sciences. It was on this basis that he approached the great crisis caused in the Church in his day by the rediscovery of Aristotle's missing works on the soul. Had there never been a St Thomas Aquinas, his brilliant pupil who profited from his genius, Albert would still have been 'the Great'.

Albert was a Bavarian. He became a Dominican monk at the early age of 17 and then proceeded to master the widest possible range of studies. He began with the study of the natural world in all its aspects. This made him better informed on the world of external reality than any of his predecessors in the Church. This enabled him to attempt what was needed most in his day, which he described in one of his many published volumes as '*to make all things understandable to the Latins*'. He succeeded to such an extent in fulfilling this ambition that his works were immediately used in the universities as essential text-books. His aim was to relate the whole truth about nature known through science, his own experiments and observations, with the truth about God and creation as revealed through the traditional teaching of the Church. He was that rarest of individuals, the complete scientist, philosopher and theologian.

For the next 22 years after being received into the Dominican Order in 1223 he studied and taught in one convent of his order after another, mainly in the Rhineland. Then in 1245 he was made a professor in the young University of Paris. His impact there was astonishing. His combination of so much secular learning and of theology drew thousands of students to his lectures. So many of them came that he had to teach in the open air, in the great space which is now known in Paris as the 'Place Maubert', a corruption of the Place Mâitre Albert.

Albert produced for the first time what the intellectual atmosphere of the middle ages had lacked: a view of knowledge as a whole related to the entire universe of fact and experience. He did so in the spirit and method of Aristotle and in the schools of his day he was ranked as an authority with Aristotle himself. He did not criticise the teaching and errors of others, he simply expounded the truth as he saw it and the errors just disappeared.

Albert's was a vital message at a time when the teaching of the Greek philosophers on metaphysics and above all on the soul and the relation of humanity to God was causing a crisis that threatened the whole basis of Christianity.

More accurately than anyone else, Albert defined and defended the rights of reason in theological studies and analysed its role with regard to mysteries. He taught that reason is not omni-competent because there are things beyond its powers of knowing, or understanding or of proving. The domains of faith and reason are separate. In its own domain reason is free to roam and Aristotle may reign there without any danger to faith. On the other hand, with regard to the possibilities of human knowledge of God in this life, Albert was most reserved, saying that God cannot be directly intelligible save *'through a glass darkly'*. What we can however see is the trace of God through the Scriptures and through experience.

Albert then tackled the critical question of the day that had been raised by Averroes, the translator and commentator on Aristotle and who had threatened the basis of Christian thought as to what was divine in man's own soul and the operation which is its essential characteristic. For Averroes the operation was of a being, God the Ultimate Reality, who so transcended the individual soul, our 'intelligence', that the soul really ceased to be individual. According to Avicenna, a rival commentator on Aristotle's works, this meant that only a special divine intervention made our comprehension of them possible. This was also the Platonic explanation, expounded by St Augustine of Hippo and by its great contemporary supporter in Paris, the Franciscan teacher St Bonaventure. Yet Albert refused to abandon his belief in the individuality of the soul. For him the soul as the principle both of sense life and of vegetable life is united in the body and individualised. As the principle of intellectual life it is separated from the body, for it cannot, as an individual, think in terms of Platonic 'universals', which are really just general descriptive words such as 'man' or 'dog'.

Albert's reward for confronting Averroes was that the Paris Faculty of Arts in 1252 made obligatory the study of Aristotle's 'De Anima'. It should be pointed out here that it was from the study of this with Albert that St Thomas Aquinas developed his own theory of the individual soul, as already described in his 'Life' in the January Calendar. Albert's solution was that the human soul was for each individual a creative intelligence that justified his autonomy and his right as an individual to develop in his own way towards perfection. In this way human beings were indeed entitled to play a part in God's creative work and were not mere cyphers.

By this time Albert had left Paris. In 1248 the Pope had appointed him to organise the Domincan studies in Cologne and then for a short while he was Bishop of Regensburg before returning to Paris in 1262 as Master of Studies at the University. Meanwhile the Averroist faction in Paris, supported by St Bonaventure's Augustinian approach, was causing such rioting among the students that the Pope threatened to close the university. However Thomas Aquinas had saved the day before he left to go to Rome by taking over his master Albert's mantle. He taught what has ultimately become everything that is authoritative in the Catholic Church on these subjects in spite of the fierce opposition by the French bishops after his death in 1274. Thomas' teaching was stoutly defended by Albert and became the accepted authority first in the Dominican Order in the thirteenth century, in the sixteenth by the Jesuits under St Ignatius of Loyola and at the end of the nineteenth century by the orders of Pope Leo XIII.

St Elizabeth of Hungary (1207–31): The Ideal German Woman

The sheer drama of Elizabeth's short life is not always made clear in the English dictionaries of saints, but she became one of the most popular saints in Germany. Her story is one that appeals to every generation on account of her devotion as a wife and mother, her charity and service to others and also for her great heart, determination and fortitude in the face of difficulties and humiliations.

As already described in the Calendar for her feast-day on 16 November, Elizabeth was the daughter of the King of Hungary. She was therefore a royal princess descended directly from King St Stephen. Her family had close links with Rome and her godfather was the Cardinal Ugolino of Sabina, the supporter of St Francis of Assisi and patron of the Franciscan Order. In 1216 he became Pope Honorius III, but continued to keep in touch with his goddaughter.

At the age of 14 Elizabeth made a dynastic marriage with Ludwig IV, Margrave of Thuringia. She went to live in his castle of Wartburg which was surrounded by vast forests. At first her marriage was unhappy because the castle was ruled by her jealous mother-in-law. Nevertheless Elizabeth, who was extremely devout and devoted to charitable work, used to fill sacks with the food thrown away by the castle kitchens and give it to the poor of the district. Her mother-in-law objected strongly to this and made her son order Elizabeth to cease raiding her larders.

However Elizabeth was not one to give in easily. One day her husband, who may have been warned by an informer in the castle, was out riding in the forest and saw his wife carrying a loaded sack. He rode up to her, dismounted and rudely slashed the sack open with his hunting knife. To his astonishment out fell, not the bread and chicken carcasses he had expected to find, but a heap of rose petals. He was convinced that he had witnessed a miracle and was filled with shame. He fell on his knees and begged Elizabeth's forgiveness. He also swore to become a true Christian in future and to help her charitable work.

One is tempted to ask oneself, was it a miracle or was Elizabeth just a very clever wife who knew how to win her husband's love and confidence? Whatever the answer may be, after this happened Elizabeth lived a blissful married life and bore her husband three sons. Ludwig also built a dispensary for her, where she devoted herself to tending the sick and to advising the poor on their personal problems.

Encouraged by her godfather, who had become pope in 1216, she took her vows as a Franciscan Tertiary and wore the cloak of St Francis that he had given her when Francis died in 1226. All went well until Ludwig swore to take up the cross and join the fifth Crusade with his knights. He rode off in 1227 to join a ship at Otranto, but he never sailed because he caught the plague and died.

Elizabeth was distraught with grief, made worse by the fact that as her eldest son was still a boy her brother-in-law Heinrich made himself Regent of Thuringia. He put out a story that Elizabeth was mad and had rushed about the castle screaming. At first he locked her up and then, abetted by his mother, he drove her and her sons out into the forest. It was a typical medieval palace coup. The local peasants took pity on her and led her and her sons to her uncle's castle at Marburg 250 miles away. He was the Margrave of Hesse and he took care of them. Elizabeth, having arranged for her sons to be looked after and educated, then went to live in a nunnery nearby. She resumed her work for the poor, spinning wool and making clothes for them, fishing to provide them with food and tending to their illnesses and wounds in a dispensary that she built.

She was looked upon by the peasants throughout the region as a living saint, but she had to submit to the attentions of a sadistic confessor, Conrad of Marburg. He accused her of acting through false pride. He took away her personal servants and he frequently punished her for her alleged pride, beating her bare back with rods. He also slapped and

Elizabeth and the Miracle of the Roses

struck her in the face. Elizabeth bore all this with patience, retained her good humour, continued with her work and submitted herself to a very meagre diet.

Two years later her husband's knights returned from the crusade and found her at Marburg. They swore to restore her eldest son's right to be Margrave of Thuringia and drove Heinrich from the castle of Wartburg. Elizabeth was by then much weakened by her work and ascetic fare. She continued faithfully to work in her dispensary but soon fell fatally ill and died at the age of 24 in 1231. She was at once acclaimed as a saint throughout Bavaria and in 1235 she was canonised as the ideal wife, mother and model of all that a Christian woman should be.

The Prussian knights of the Teutonic Order then built a cathedral dedicated to her name at Marburg in 1235, the Cathedral of St Elizabeth. It was the first to be built in the Gothic style in Germany. Her shrine there was decorated with a fresco depicting a miracle that her uncle believed he had witnessed. It was almost completely destroyed in 1539 by the Lutherans, but it showed Elizabeth tending a sick beggar whom her uncle saw turn into the body of Christ. Since Elizabeth's death, innumerable hospitals have been named after her.

DECEMBER SAINTS

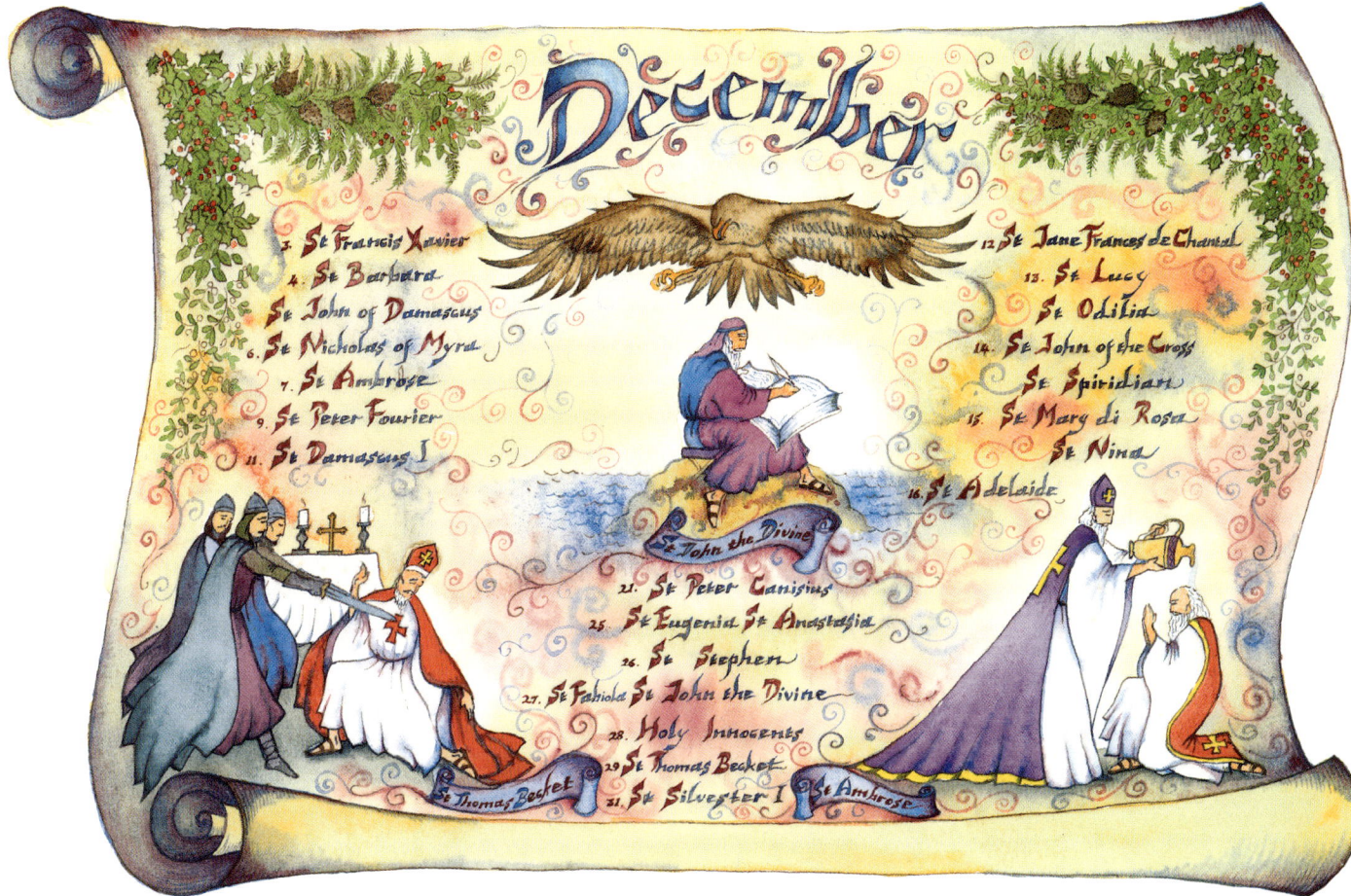

December

3. St Francis Xavier
4. St Barbara
   St John of Damascus
6. St Nicholas of Myra
7. St Ambrose
9. St Peter Fourier
11. St Damasus I

12. St Jane Frances de Chantal
13. St Lucy
    St Odilia
14. St John of the Cross
    St Spiridion
15. St Mary di Rosa
    St Nina
16. St Adelaide

St John the Divine

21. St Peter Canisius
25. St Eugenia St Anastasia
26. St Stephen
27. St Fabiola St John the Divine
28. Holy Innocents
29. St Thomas Becket
31. St Silvester I   St Ambrose

St Thomas Becket

The decorative heading for December portrays three of these saints: **St John the Evangelist** (27 December) with his spiritual symbol of a flying eagle; **St Ambrose, Bishop of Milan** (7 December) baptising St Augustine of Hippo; **Archbishop St Thomas à Becket of Canterbury** (27 December) being murdered by Henry II's barons.

AN ALTAR-PIECE DESIGN FOR ELEVEN DECEMBER SAINTS

Shown in the top row are:

St **Barbara** (16 December) martyred by her father, who is struck by lightning, c.304; St **Eugenia** and St **Eulalia** (25 and 10 December), Roman and Spanish martyrs, c.304; St **Natalia** by her martyred husband, St **Adrian** (both 1 December), 304.

In the centre row are:

St **Sabas** (5 December), founding his 'Laura' or small monastery for hermits near the Dead Sea, c.510; St **Stephen the First Martyr** (26 December) being stoned as 'Saul', the future St Paul, looks on in c.35; St **Lucy** (13 December), Virgin martyr of c.304, whose eyes were torn out.

In the bottom row are:

St **Nicholas of Myra** (6 December), the original 'Santa Claus', fourth-century Greek bishop giving purses of gold to three girls to save them from prostitution. The background is a sketch of the carved tombs and temples in the cliff above Mira on the Turkish coast, where Nicholas had his first hermitage; St **Spiridon** (14 December) fourth-century shepherd bishop of Cyprus; St **Anastasia** (30 December), martyred in Serbia in c.304.

Altar-piece design for eleven December saints

ALTER-PIECE DESIGN FOR NINE DECEMBER SAINTS

Shown in the top row are:

St Eligius or 'Eloi' (1 December) (589–660), Frankish bishop of King Dagobert, famed for his skill as a metal worker. **St Adelaide** (16 December) (931–99), the charitable Burgundian widow of the Emperor Otto I the Great, after being driven from her palace by her sons; **St Thorlac** (23 December) (1133–1193), the evangeliser of Iceland, standing by a salmon river.

In the centre row are:

St Peter Fourier (9 December) (1565–1640), the Augustinian missionary who evangelised Calvinists in Lorraine; **St John of Damascus** (4 December), (657–749), with his great book *The Fountain of Knowledge* after retiring to the monastery of Mar Saba, founded by St Sabas; **St John of Kanti** (23 December), (1390–1473), saintly priest of Cracow in Poland.

In the bottom row are:

St Jane Frances de Chantal (12 December), (1572–1641), at her nunnery by Lake Annecy which she founded with the aid of St Frances de Sales; **St Francis Xavier** (3 December) (1506–1552), famous Jesuit missionary to Goa, Malaya and Japan; **St Peter Canisius** (21 December), (1521–97), Jesuit theologian and missionary to Holland.

Altar-piece design for nine December saints

293

DECEMBER CALENDAR OF SAINTS' FEAST-DAYS

1st: **ADRIAN and NATALIA:** Martyrs in Nicomedia in c.304 (also remembered on 8 September); Adrian, an imperial official, became a Christian because he was so impressed by the fortitude of the persecuted believers. He was imprisoned. Their legend says that Natalia visited him there, dressed as a boy, and witnessed his execution and burning. She then rescued one of his charred hands and escaped. When she died she was buried among the martyrs.

ELOI (or ELIGIUS) (588–660): A Gallo-Roman apprenticed to the Master of the Mint at Limoges. His expertise won him the Mastership of the Mint at Marseilles and he became very rich. He also excelled at engraving. He founded a monastery at Solignac and a nunnery in Paris. King Dagobert of the Franks was so impressed by him that he made him Bishop of Noyon and Tournai. He also became Royal Chancellor, but continued to do missionary work in Frisia and founded more religious houses. Patron saint of metal workers.

2nd **VIVIANA (or VIVIAN):** Roman martyr of unknown early date who had a church dedicated to her on the Esquiline Hill in Rome in the fifth century.

3rd **CASSIAN of ALGIERS:** Martyred with Marcellus (30 October) in 298.

FRANCIS XAVIER (1506–52): Born in Navarre, studied in Paris and became one of the first seven followers of St Ignatius of Loyola (31 July) who dedicated themselves to God on Montmartre in 1534. This was the start of the Society of Jesus, the Jesuits. Under Ignatius' directions they adopted the theology of St Thomas Aquinas (28 January) as written in his *Summa Theologica*. Francis was sent to evangelise in the East in 1541 and succeeded in founding churches in Goa, South India, Malaya and in Japan. He left Japan after two years in 1551 and died on his way to China. Patron saint of missionaries.

4th **BARBARA:** Legendary martyr between 250 and 313. Her story says that she was so beautiful that her father shut her up in a tower to discourage suitors. He then found that she had become a Christian and swore to kill her unless she renounced her faith. She refused, was tortured and executed. As she died her father was struck by lightning. The legend places her variously in Egypt or Tuscany. Because of the lightning she became patron saint of gunners, including the British Royal Artillery. Her emblem is a castle tower.

JOHN of DAMASCUS (675–749): Born and brought up as a Christian in Damascus, where he inherited his father's post as an important official of the Muslim Caliph. He wrote to the Emperor Leo III and protested against his laws against the veneration of icons and was then dismissed from his posts by the Caliph for his diplomatic indiscretion. He retired to the monastery of Mar Saba (founded by St Sabas in c.478, see 5 December) between the Dead Sea and Jerusalem and became a monk and a priest. He then devoted himself to study and writing. His great work is *The Fount of Knowledge* in which he produced a digest of the teaching of the early Greek Fathers and exposed numerous heresies. In particular he examined the teachings of the Koran and described Islam as another extreme Christian heresy, since although his Koran says that God sent his Spirit to the Virgin Mary, Muhammad denied that Jesus was Son of God. He called him a prophet sent as a sign to mankind. The Koran also denies that Jesus died on the cross – 'it was only his image'. Some of his sermons have been preserved, including one on the bodily assumption into heaven of the Virgin Mary after her death. Two of his hymns are included in the English hymnal. In 1890 Pope Leo XIII made him a Doctor of the Church.

5th **CRISPINA:** A distinguished married lady martyred by being beheaded in Nurnidia in 303 for refusing to deny Christ during the persecutions of Diocletian's time. St Augustine (28 October) ranked her with St Agnes (21 January) as a martyr because of her stout defence of Christianity at her trial.

SABAS (439–532): Born at Casaraea in Cappadocia he became a disciple of the hermit St Euthymius the Great (20 January) in Palestine. He set up a 'Laura' for hermits in a rocky gorge leading to the Dead Sea in 478, which later became the monastery of Mar Saba. St John of Damascus (see above, 4 December) retired there to write three centuries later. Sabas was given the rule over all hermitages in Palestine in 493.

BERINUS: Died in c.650. He was sent as a bishop to Briton from Rome in 635 and established his see at Dorchester near Oxford. According to St Bede (25 May) he was *'guided in his duties rather by love than by books'*.

CHRISTINA of MARKYATE (1097–1161): She had a stormy girlhood during which she vowed to remain a virgin for Christ's sake. A bishop attempted to rape her and her parents forced her to marry. A hermit called Edwin helped her to escape from her husband and to have her marriage annulled by Archbishop Ralph of Canterbury in 1122. She became a hermit at Markyate. When many disciples came to her, she established a priory for nuns. She was an expert needle-woman and embroidered the mitres and sandals of the English Pope Adrian IV, who reigned from 1154 to 1159.

6th **NICHOLAS of MYRA:** Fourth-century Bishop of Myra on the East coast of Turkey. He was the original 'Santa Claus' or Father Christmas, whose legend is that he gave a bag of gold to each of three poor girls who were due to be sold into slavery as prostitutes. He also is said to have restored to life three boys who had been chopped up for a stew by a butcher. He became famed for his charity and gifts to needy children. It is therefore wrong to disappoint the very young by telling them that Father Christmas did not exist! He was one of the most popular saints and a patron of churches in many countries. His relics were stolen in 1087 by Italian merchants and translated to Bari – hence his other name, St Nicholas of Bari.

AMBROSE (339–97): A distinguished Roman Governor chosen by the orthodox Christians in Milan by popular acclaim to be their bishop even before he was baptised. He defended his see against the Arian heresy. He rebuked Emperor Theodosius for his slaughter of 7,000 rioters in Salonika, saying that *'the Emperor is of the church but not above it'*. He was more important as a bishop than the pope in his day. He baptised St Augustine. His story is told in full in the text after this Calendar.

8th **THE FEAST of the ASSUMPTION of the VIRGIN MARY.**

BUDOC: Sixth-century saint venerated in Cornwall and Brittany.

9th **NECTAIRE:** One of the deacons sent with seven bishops to evangelise Gaul in 250 by Pope St Fabian (20 January). According to St Gregory of Tours' (17 November) book of martyrs he and the deacons St Baudime and St Auditeur escaped when their Bishop, St Austremoine of Clermont-Ferrand, was martyred. They then evangelised the volcanic mountain region of Monts Dore and the Limagne in the Auvergne, the traditional stronghold of the Gauls in times of danger. Nectaire is believed to have been martyred. He was buried with the other two deacons at Mont Cornadore. Nectaire became revered for many remarkable legendary miracles. In the twelfth century William VII, Count of Auvergne, made a gift to the Abbey of St Robert at La Chaise Dieu to establish a priory and church at Cornadore to house the many pilgrims to the shrine of the saints. The church has a magnificent broad stone gallery that was used to enable the pilgrims to rest, pray and to admire the capitals of the stone pillars that are decorated with the legends of the saint. A village, named after St Nectaire, soon grew around the twelfth-century church which is visited by thousands of tourists and pilgrims. In 1930 the French government named an excellent local cheese St Nectaire to promote the dairy products of the region.

PETER FOURIER (1565–1640): Catholic priest in the Vosges who tackled the problem in that French region caused by the spread of Calvinism from Geneva. He set up a free school for children at his village of Mattincourt, but was driven into exile in 1636 during the war of 1618–48 after a 30 year mission. He was canonised in 1897.

10th **EULALIA:** Spanish virgin martyred aged 12 in c.304.

POPE MILTIADES: African pope who died in 314 as the result of his sufferings under the Emperor Maximian. He survived long enough to witness the triumph of Christianity under the Emperor Constantine the Great and was regarded as a martyr. St Augustine (28 October) praised his moderation and peaceful nature.

11th **POPE DAMASUS I (304–84):** Elected Bishop of Rome in 366 after a terrible scene of sectarian violence between Arians and Catholics in the Basilica of St Maria Maggiore in which 137 combatants were killed. He had to face the widespread imperial support for the Arian heresy until 380, when the orthodox Catholic faith was recognised by the Eastern and Western Emperors Theodosius and Gratian. His reputation as a wily politician was earned as the result of his skill in supporting the orthodox faith in Rome. His other contribution to the Church was his decision to send his secretary St Jerome (30 September) in the last year of his life to Bethlehem to research and produce a reliable translation of the Bible in good Latin, the official Vulgate.

12th **JANE FRANCES de CHANTAL (1572–1641):** Born at Dijon, France. As a devout young widow with four children she was chosen by St Francis de Sales (24 January), her spiritual adviser, to found a nunnery in his diocese of Geneva at Annecy in 1610. This was the start of the Order of the Visitation, established to work for and nurse the sick and needy in their homes. Francis de Sales often visited the nunnery to give spiritual advice to the nuns. St Vincent de Paul (27 September), her younger contemporary, said that she was *'one of the holiest people I have ever met'*.

13th **LUCY:** Virgin martyr of Syracuse, Sicily, in c.304. Her name means Light. She is usually shown holding a dish with her two eyes upon it. Her legend maintains that she was blinded by having them torn out before her execution.

ODILIA (or ODILE): Abbess in the Vosges who was born blind and died in 720. Her shrine in the nunnery she founded at Odilienburg is still a centre for pilgrimages.

14th SPIRIDON: Died in 438. A Cypriot shepherd who became a bishop.

VENANTIUS FORTUNATUS (530–610): Italian who left Ravenna in about 560 to visit the shrine of St Martin of Tours at Marmoutier to give thanks for a cure for his eyes. He remained in Gaul and became a priest and then, in 600, Bishop of Poitiers. He was an accomplished poet and a life-long friend of the ex-queen St Radegund (13 August). He wrote the hymn 'The Royal Banners Forward Go'.

JOHN of the CROSS (1542–91): Great Spanish mystic, poet and theologian. Born in Avila, he became a Carmelite monk and a friend of St Teresa of Avila (15 October) whom he helped with her prayers. She persuaded him to found the Order of Reformed Carmelites for men, a much stricter foundation than the old Carmelite order. Like Teresa he experienced deep mystical ecstasies and miraculous levitations. These and his writings offended the Inquisition and his old Carmelite order. He, like Teresa, was imprisoned in Toledo, but escaped and the persecution died down. He described how his mystical experiences helped him to sustain his faith in his poem 'The Dark Night of the Soul', the experience of disillusionment and feeling deserted by God which Dante had described in the section on Purgatory in his *Divine Comedy*. His other mystical poems include 'The Spiritual Canticle' and 'The Living Flame of Love'.

15th NINO: Died in c.340. A Christian slave-girl in Georgia whose miraculous cures in the name of Christ brought her to the attention of the Queen of Georgia. Her legend goes on to record that the king, Bakur, listened to her story of the gospel and then asked the Emperor Constantine I to send clergy to bring the gospel to his kingdom.

MARY di ROSA (1813–55): At 17 she did social work for girls in factories at Brescia and for the deaf and dumb in hospitals. At 27 she founded the Handmaids of Charity to carry on her work. During the war in Savoy against the Austrian oppressors her order helped those who had lost their homes in the fighting. She died of exhaustion after caring for victims of cholera.

16th ADELAIDE (939–99): Empress of Otto I. She was driven from court by her son Otto II. Advised by St Odilo of Cluny (1 January) and Bishop St Willigis of Mainz (23 February), she founded a nunnery in Alsace and was renowned for her goodness and charity.

17th LAZARUS: Brother of Mary and Martha, raised to life by Jesus.

OLYMPIAS (366–408): Widow and deaconess in Nicomedia who gave large donations to charity. She supported the cause of St John Chrysostom against the charges of the Empress Eudoxia. The Empress accused her of setting fire to a church in Constantinople during the earthquake that occurred when St John was being taken aboard a ship to go on his first exile. Eudoxia had been so frightened by these events that she had at first thought they were a punishment from God. She recalled St John from exile, but attacked Olympias. Olympias had the strength to survive the many indignities heaped on her by Eudoxia and, during St John's second and final exile, she managed to send him succour. He wrote many letters to her from his exile.

BEGGA: Died in 693. Devout sister of St Gertrude of Nivelles (17 March). She married the son of Bishop Arnulf of Metz and so became the ancestress of the Carolingian dynasty.

18th WINEBALD: Died in 761. Anglo-Saxon missionary to Thuringia like his brother St Willibald (7 July) and their sister St Walburga (25 February). They all answered St Boniface of Crediton's (5 June) appeal to sail to Germany and help him to evangelise across the Rhine.

20th DOMINIC of SALOS (c.1000–73): Peasant of Navarre who was made Abbot of the run-down monastery of Silos near Burgos in 1041 by King Ferdinand I of Spain. He made it flourish and he developed a noted scriptorium to copy manuscripts and also a gold and silver workshop. The profits from these activities were given to charity. He was famed for his miracles and his work to free captives from the Moors.

21st PETER CANISIUS (1521–97): Dutch theologian of Nijmegan. Became a Jesuit and head of the order in Bavaria, Bohemia and Austria. He saved Bavaria from the Lutheran reformers, though modern Lutheran theologians regard him as a moderate and faultless man.

23rd THORLAC (1133–93): Dane who studied in Paris and then became the first apostle and Bishop of Iceland.

JOHN of KANTI (390–1473): Polish priest who taught philosophy at Cracow and who opposed the Hussites, but was also moderate in theological debate.

24th CHARBEL MAKHLOUF (1828–98): Son of a Lebanese mule-driver who became a Maronite (i.e. Roman Catholic) monk at the age of 23. He took the name Charbel from a second-century martyr of Antioch. A model monk, he left in 1877 to become a hermit in the ascetic and unworldly style of the Desert Fathers. He look with him Thomas à Kempis' *Imitation of Christ* as his favourite reading. For 23 years many people were attracted to his hermitage by his spiritual advice. After he died a bloody sweat is said to have appeared for many years from his body, as also occurred with St Januarius (19 September). Canonised in 1977.

25th *CHRISTMAS DAY. The Birth of JESUS CHRIST.*

ANASTASIA: Roman matron martyred in Sirmium (Yugoslavia) in 304, but recognised traditionally as a Roman martyr and to whom a church was dedicated in Rome near the Circus Maximus.

EUGENIA (or EUGENIE): A Roman martyr of unknown early date, believed to have been buried in a cemetery on the Via Latina. Her legend says that she left her father's mansion in male dress and became abbot of a monastery in Egypt. She was accused of misconduct, but cleared herself by admitting to her true sex. She returned to Rome and was beheaded for her faith.

26th STEPHEN, The First Christian Martyr: His story is told in Acts, chapters 6 and 7. His vision at his trial in Jerusalem for blasphemy is the classic expression of the Christian image of the Glory of God: *'He, full of the Spirit, gazed into heaven and saw the Glory of God and Jesus standing at the right hand of God'* (Acts 7.15).

It was Stephen's description of this that enraged the Jewish Council and caused him to be stoned to death outside the walls of the city while Saul, the future St Paul, looked on.

27th JOHN the EVANGELIST: Son of Zebedee and brother of James. He is believed to have been the author both of the gospel attributed to him and also of the Revelation of John. His story and that of these two books of the New Testament is given in Part III. His gospel inspired the early Church to believe in the highest form of divinity for Christ – God Incarnate.

29th TROPHIMUS: Sent by Pope St Fabian I (20 January) in 250 as one of the seven bishops to evangelise Gaul. He was Bishop of Arles and a martyr.

THOMAS of CANTERBURY (1118–70): Thomas à Becket was Chancellor and intimate companion of King Henry II. In 1162 the King made him Archbishop of Canterbury. He astonished and angered the King by standing firmly against his seizure of Church property and for ignoring the rights of the ecclesiastical courts to try clergy accused of offences. Most of the bishops, jealous of Thomas, sided with the King. Thomas exiled himself twice to France to escape the King. After his return from his second exile, when Henry and he had made up their quarrel, Henry lost his temper with him again.

On this occasion, four of his knights took Henry's words against Thomas as a command and murdered him in his cathedral. All Europe was horrified and Henry was forced to do penance before Thomas's tomb. Thomas was canonised in 1173. His shrine in Canterbury Cathedral attracted thousands of pilgrims for centuries from all over Europe until it was torn down and robbed of its vast and elaborate treasures by Henry VIII at the Dissolution of the Monasteries. TS Eliot wrote a brilliant play about Thomas and his quarrels with King Henry, *Murder in the Cathedral.*

30th EGWIN: Died in 717. He founded the Benedictine abbey at Worcester after seeing a vision of the Virgin Mary in a field by the river Avon. The vision was also witnessed by a shepherd.

31st POPE SILVESTER I: Pope from 314 to 335. He was an important influence during the reign of Constantine I after the declaration in Milan of freedom of worship throughout the Empire in 313.

SUMMARY OF DECEMBER SAINTS

This Calendar gives the feast-days of 46 saints, of whom 15 were martyrs and 13 were women. The notes in the Calendar outline the lives of the saints adequately for our purpose, but the life of **St Ambrose** below gives some important additional details.

St Ambrose (340–97), Bishop of Milan

Ambrose came from a Christian family. His elder sister became a nun, but he embarked on a career in the law. He became a magistrate and governor famed for his impartial justice. His life was written by his secretary Paulinus at the suggestion of St Augustine of Hippo, whom Ambrose had baptised.

When the moderately Arian Bishop of Milan, Auxentius, died in 374, the devout Catholic congregation of Milan chose the unbaptised Ambrose to be their new bishop. The powerful Arian section of the congregation also accepted Ambrose because of his reputation for fairness. Ambrose felt he was unworthy of such an honour and he fled from the city, which was then the capital of the emperor. Much against his will Ambrose was persuaded to return to Milan, to be prepared for baptism, made a deacon and, at the age of 34, to be installed as Bishop of Milan.

In order to prepare himself thoroughly for his task as bishop, Ambrose immediately began to study many books besides the New Testament writings. The first book that he wrote himself was *De Virginibus*, a tract on the merits of celibacy. His sermons, which St Augustine so admired when he was a professor of philosophy at Milan, were eloquent but rather flowery. Ambrose's second book, *De Fides Resurrectioni*, was written for the boy Emperor of the West, Gratian. It was a guide to the faith and to justify the hope of a future life.

Ambrose resisted the efforts of the Arian community to be given one of the Catholic churches for their own rites. Their pleas were backed by Gratian's mother, the Empress Justina. Ambrose refused, saying that it was not within his power to give away one of God's temples. He was at once threatened with death by Justina's generals unless he submitted to her demand. Ambrose defied him, saying: '*May God grant you to fulfil what you threaten; for then my fate will be that of a bishop and yours that of a eunuch*'.

Ambrose soon found that he not only had to act as a bishop, but also as a politician to resist interference from outside his diocese. When Gratian was killed by the usurping Maximus, who made himself supreme in Gaul, Ambrose went as ambassador to him and persuaded him not to invade Italy. Also in 383 Ambrose made Maximus promise not to execute the Spanish bishop Priscillian at Trier after his condemnation by the Church for what his judges considered heretical practices. They were probably secret attempts to introduce more spiritual elements into worship. Both St Martin of Tours and Ambrose of Milan said that the death penalty for heresy was contrary to the teaching of Christ. Maximus broke his promise and had Priscillian beheaded. That was the first execution of a Christian as the result of a Church judgement. It also marked the start of the Church's practice for the next 1,250 years of handing over heretics to the state to be executed, claiming that such a death was for the benefit of the victim's soul. Also, according to one of his letters written in the next century, even Pope Leo I the Great supported this practice, saying that the death sentence for heresy would discourage others. Those were difficult and dangerous times and heresies often led to sectarian killings, but the question of whether Christ would have approved, which St Martin and Ambrose raised, never seems to have been considered.

Eventually Maximus did invade Italy, but was defeated by the Emperor Theodosius, who was deeply impressed by Ambrose's advice on both political and ecclesiastical matters. He once said *'I know of no bishop but Ambrose'*. That was after Ambrose had taken him severely to task for slaughtering 7,000 people in Salonika as punishment for a sectarian riot. Ambrose excommunicated him and then forced him to repent publicly for his crime, saying to him that *'the Emperor is of, but not above, the Church'*.

Milan was the usual centre of imperial government, and although he was only a bishop Ambrose became more important politically than the pope in Rome. However he always treated the Pope with reverence even when he took him to task for permitting the erection of a statue to Victory in Rome which Ambrose considered to be unsuitable in a Christian city. His respect for the Pope was based on the view that, more than any other figure, he represented the unity of the Church.

Ambrose's attitude to his life can be summed up in his saying: *'Nothing is more dangerous before God or base amongst men than for a priest not to speak out his criticisms freely'*. He held that the Church was the organ of God in the world and that the secular government had the choice of being either hostile to or observant of the divine authority ruling in the Church. He understood what many later popes were to forget to the great cost of the peace of the Christian world, that the world was bound to be ruled by secular leaders and that the Church's task was to lead and inspire them to do it rightly. Yet Ambrose was not just a political bishop; he based his approach to the world on the principle that love and worship must come from the heart.

Ambrose's sermons were admired by St Augustine, who listened to them before he was converted. They were delivered in excellent Latin, which enabled Ambrose to make his points clearly and convincingly. Ambrose was also praised by his other great contemporary, St Jerome. Another of his great contributions to the Church was his introduction of psalm and hymn-singing from the East, though his precise contribution to musical harmony is not clear. He wrote several hymns including the one which begins 'Come Holy Spirit, Light of the Blessed Trinity'. He is also thought to have written the 'Te Deum'.

In his *Confessions* St Augustine described how Ambrose was always busy studying books even while in company with others. As his health failed in the last two years of his life he continued to work for justice for those who were unpopular with the government. He is the perfect example of a Christian bishop with whom to end this Calendar.

PART SEVEN

THE UNQUENCHABLE SPIRIT, 1300–2000

'Lo, I am with you always to the close of the Age'.

THE UNQUENCHABLE SPIRIT

Cardinal John Henry Newman, whose life and works will be examined later in this chapter, wrote that the Spirit, working through the authors of the Gospels, only revealed himself to a certain extent, leaving the apostles and later faithful witnesses to interpret and to make the gospel relevant to new generations born into a rapidly developing world. This is the world that we are going to examine in this part of the book, starting from 1300, when the modern world first began to take shape. The centuries since then have seen massive change, led by the Christian West. These changes have been both to the benefit of mankind, and to our detriment, with the nadir being reached in the two terrible world wars which caused so many to believe that God was failing us.

The object of this account is to seek evidence of the Spirit at work during these last seven centuries. I aim to show the immense strength that so many saints received from the Spirit during this period, without which they could not have acted as they did or achieved so much. I also aim to demonstrate why, in his grant of free will to man, God did not do more to stop all those terrible tortures, cruelty and killings, for God does not seek to interfere directly in our lives, but approaches us to inspire our actions through the Spirit.

It is therefore important to point out in this introduction to the final part of this book, that faith is about the spiritual dimension and that all the religions are only the means by which groups of people come together to worship in the ways that appeal most to them. It is not possible in this book to examine the faiths of non-Christian religions though some important references will be made to them. What matters most is to remember the message that St Basil of Caesarea gave in the fourth century – that 'there is no culture or religion that has not received and does not express a visitation of the Word'. As will be shown further on in the story, Pope John XXIII reminded the Church in 1962 that the 'seed of the Spirit can be seen in all the world's religions'. Therefore we must accept that Muhammad also was called by the Spirit to serve God. He interpreted this in his Koran which, it must be emphasised, is therefore a man's interpretation of his beliefs, much of which are based on and include the same origins as the beliefs of both Jews and Christians.

THE CHURCH AND THE FAITH FROM 1300 TO THE REFORMATION

History is never tidy. 'The Age of Faith', the thirteenth century, which began with St Francis of Assisi and culminated with St Albert the Great and St Thomas Aquinas, might have been expected to launch a new era for Christendom. Instead it ended in disaster after King Philip of France tried to murder the profligate Pope Boniface VIII. This was followed by the flight of the popes from Rome to Avignon in 1305. Then began two centuries of warfare between the 'Guelphs', the Italian city-states and princes who supported the popes, and the 'Ghibelines' who supported the emperors. After 1300 there were no more great saints, except for St Catherine of Siena, until the sixteenth century.

I am therefore going to begin this study of the 700 years from 1300 until modern times by examining the work of the great Christian humanist and charismatic poet, Dante Alighieri (1265–1321), who began to write his *Divine Comedy* in 1310. This poem of 30 long cantos shows how a great and spiritual mind saw the problems of the Church at the beginning of the fourteenth century, when the power of the universal Church in international affairs began to fade. At that time Dante was living with the La Scala family in Verona, after being unjustly exiled as a Ghibelline supporter from his native Florence. His poem describes an imaginary journey of the soul through Hades, Purgatory and Paradise to the Empyrium, the seat of God. It is an allegory aimed at interpreting the whole of Christian experience, revealing the corruption in the Church and Empire and the inward corruption in the human heart.

This poem has for centuries been more popular than any other Christian work of imagination and inspiration, including the works of the blind English Puritan poet John Milton and the Baptist minister and preacher John Bunyan. The poem also broke new ground by being the first literary work to be written for the general public in Italian, thus helping to create that beautiful and musical language. It was an immediate success in Italy and internationally. In every century since then the *Comedy* has been illustrated by great artists including Botticelli, William Blake and Delacroix and it inspired Michaelangelo's 'Last Judgement' fresco in the Sistine Chapel.

Before writing his poem Dante Alighieri had described in his *De Monarchia* the relationship that should exist between the Empire and the Church, between the spiritual and the secular. He wrote that ideally the secular order should be founded on reason, while the Church would be left free in the spiritual sphere based on revelation. Through this partnership Dante hoped that the ideal society would be achieved, aiming at earthly perfection and happiness and, through the Church, looking forward to eternal beatitude in the life to come.

It is only possible here to give the briefest outline of the *Divine Comedy*, which describes Dante's experience in a dream. He tells how in his dream he was accompanied by Virgil through Hades and then by his childhood love Beatrice through Purgatory and the nine heavens of Paradise. The journey begins with Dante's vision of the gates of Hell, above which there is an inscription which warns that *'Through me is the road to the City of Desolation, the road among the Lost Creation. Abandon hope, you who enter here.'*

On passing through the gates Dante describes how he sees the figures of the traitors Brutus and Judas Iscariot in the very mouth of Satan. For Dante the worst of human crimes was that of betrayal. Soon after this

Dante and Beatrice meet the souls of Thomas Aquinas, Albert of the Rhine and Bonaventure in the Seventh Heaven

Dante sees the shade of the man he regarded as the latest enemy of the faith, Pope Boniface VIII, who died in 1303 after being attacked by the troops of his enemies the Colonna cardinals and the French agent sent by the king of France, Philip IV. Boniface was guilty of many things – simony, nepotism, gross extravagance and of forcing the abdication of his predecessor Pope St Celestine V and imprisoning him. Boniface was also charged with ruining the Church's relationship with the Holy Roman Empire.

Dante continues his story after leaving Hades, and he describes how Beatrice, symbolic of the Virgin Mary, leads him up the Mountain of Purgatory. There he looks down and sees the souls of some of his late friends arriving by ship to be purified before advancing to Paradise. He also listens to the experiences of some of the other penitents. They described how they had had to suffer what they called *'The Dark Night of the Soul'* in which they found themselves apparently deserted by God. This is the earliest literary use of this phrase, which describes the experience of extreme aridity and loss of faith that was to be immortalised in a poem of that name by the mystic sixteenth-century Spanish poet St John of the Cross (14 December).

After climbing the Mountain of Purgatory, Beatrice leads Dante through the nine heavens of Paradise. In the seventh Heaven of the Sun the two travellers find themselves surrounded by dozens of flickering lights dancing in chains and communicating with each other in musical harmonies. They discover that these lights are the souls of the Hebrew prophets and the great Christian theologians from the beginning of the Church's history. They include Thomas Aquinas, his philosophical rival the Franciscan Bonaventure and Thomas's tutor, Albert of the Rhine.

These three thirteenth-century divines were Dante's favourite theologians. At the time he wrote, none of them had yet been canonised. Thomas was not canonised until 1323, two years after Dante's death. Bonaventure was made a saint in 1482 and Albert was only included in the Roman Calendar in 1931. In his poem Dante shrewdly described them laughing at the unimportant differences that had once divided them on earth.

In the eighth heaven Dante and Beatrice meet St Benedict of Nursia (11 July), the founder of the monastic movement in Western Europe. They also met St Peter Damian (21 February), the eleventh-century supporter of the Gregorian Reforms in the Church. Then, as they reach the Empyrean, the celestial goal of their journey, Beatrice points out to Dante the vacant seat that awaits the shade of his hero, Henry of Luxemburg. Henry became Emperor in 1308 and died in 1313, perhaps of poison, before he could achieve his great hopes for a perfect relationship between the Empire and the Papacy. Henry had indicated his ideal aim by declaring on his election that his duty as Emperor was not just to any single nation but to his *'Brother Man'*.

Thus Dante takes the whole theme of his allegorical work up to the beginning of the fourteenth century, showing that the ideal for the papacy was still to be looked for in the future. He ends his poem after seeing the glory of the Three Persons of the Trinity in one brilliant blinding moment, as they rotated in three concentric spheres. Then, as further powers of representation fail him, Dante writes that he realises that, in his poem, his will and desire have been guided all along by the spirit of Love – *'the Love that moves the sun and the other stars'*. In finishing his work in this way Dante emphasises what had been most lacking in the Church – Love and Charity.

THE FIRST MOVEMENTS TOWARDS CHURCH REFORM

When Dante wrote his poem the Holy Roman Empire was already dying on its feet in the face of the growing independence of national governments. His ideal was to safeguard the Church through a recreation of the old Roman Empire in such a way that would free it from worldly cares and so be enabled to act spiritually and without political interference. This ideal plan was premature, since there was no universal organisation capable of making it work. This did not happen until the papal lands were absorbed into the Kingdom of Italy in 1870, when the Vatican City became protected by the state. This freed the papacy from having to raise armies, engage in wars and even to compromise spiritually with its enemies. This, together with the modern means of instant global communication, made it possible for twentieth-century popes to be recognised at last as important world moral and spiritual leaders.

The miracle of the papacy's survival can be judged by the fact that between the fourteenth and sixteenth centuries Rome was besieged and sacked six times. There were also other developments that distracted the attention of European society from religion. During the Renaissance there was a growing interest in the old classical ideals, in philosophy, the arts and in humanist intellectual pursuits. This began the process that changed the Western world's attitude to religion, making man the centre of interest rather than God. The general public were already losing faith in the Church's teaching and there was an urgent need for radical reforms

The earliest of the reformers in the Church in England was Bishop John Wycliffe (1330–84). He saw the need, against the contrary ruling of the papacy, for an English translation of the Bible and was the first to support a plan to have one made and published. He was also critical of some of the practices of the Church, arguing against the mystery of Transubstantiation at the Eucharist, preferring to regard the presence of the Lord in the sacraments as a purely spiritual one. These ideas spread and influenced the priest and theologian John Huss in Prague. He was burned alive as a heretic in 1415 at the fourth Lateran Council in Constance in spite of his having an imperial passport granting him safe-conduct.

For reasons which can readily be understood from the unstable political conditions of those centuries, the papacy was always on the defensive theologically. As a result it forgot that one cannot suppress the Spirit, especially when questions were raised about the interpretation of Christ's words. Also in England and Germany there were strong objections to the way the Roman Curia demanded a full year's worth of the income from any newly appointed bishop or abbot. The reformers also wanted to free the Church from the interminable daily 'offices' for the worship of a long succession of saints, many of whom seemed to have no spiritual relevance. The traditionalists opposed vernacular translations of the Bible; Bishop St John Fisher, a few years before he was martyred in 1535, even warned that to give a vernacular bible to the people *was as dangerous as giving a sharp knife to a baby*.

The reforming movement within the Roman Church was ignored. Even the decision to submit the election of future popes to a 'General Council', which had been agreed at the Council of Constance that ended the dual papacy in 1417, was quietly shelved by Pope Martin V and forgotten by Rome. There were, however, thoughtful men who encouraged the Church to take a more spiritual approach in religion.

Foremost among these was the Dutch monk Gerard de Groote (1340–80) who founded the order of The Brotherhood of the Common Life. By the end of the fifteenth century the Brotherhood had founded 80 communities in Flanders and Germany, all aiming at achieving a spiritual revival.

As the Roman Catholic historian Philip Hughes described in his *History of the Church*, De Groote tackled the problem of *'the dangerous humbug into which the way of the interior life of the Church had deteriorated'*. His spiritual approach was one of the means by which dissatisfaction with the decaying monastic system spread amongst the Catholic scholars like Erasmus of Rotterdam (1466–1536). He was for a while a member of the Brotherhood and wrote his influential book *In Praise of Folly* in 1509. In that book he criticised the wasteful life in the monasteries, which had by then almost outlasted their usefulness. Erasmus also mocked the practices of the popes. In one hilarious scene in his book Erasmus described an imaginary conversation at the gate of heaven between St Peter and the shade of Pope Julius II. The subject was papal marriage. In the course of the argument Julius agreed that popes should not marry, but then cheekily asked *'but what about them having children?'*, as so many recent popes had done.

The most successful exponent of the new spiritual approach to the faith was another member of the Brotherhood, the skilled calligrapher Thomas à Kempis (1380–1471). His book *The Imitation of Christ*, which probably borrowed heavily from Gerard de Groote's sermons, was copied and printed all over Europe. It was exactly the spiritual guide that the rising merchant classes were seeking. The book encouraged people to think for themselves about the true purpose of the Gospel. It thus broke new ground and provided a system of private meditation which the Church and the lax monasteries failed to do.

The author of the book challenged the traditional attitude of the Church by asking the reader: *'What doth it benefit thee to discuss the deep mystery of the Trinity, if thou art from lack of humility displeasing to the Trinity? I would rather choose free compunction than to know the definition.'* The book then went on to teach that goodness matters more than learning and it made men realise how far short of the Christian ideal were the Church's practices.

Erasmus's criticisms of the Church and the monasteries became particularly relevant in England where King Henry VIII's Chancellor, Cardinal Wolsey, instead of using the funds of his rich abbey of St Albans for charitable works, spent them on building his vast palace at Hampton Court. It was acts like this and the lessons of Erasmus that led Henry VIII to dissolve the monasteries from 1534–7 and use the proceeds to bolster his plans to preserve the Tudor dynasty and to win the support of his courtiers.

Erasmus was the close friend of another of Henry's chancellors, the former speaker of the House of Commons and future martyr, Sir Thomas More. More was a traditionalist in his view of the Church. In his picture of the ideal Christian society in his *Utopia* his solution was for a society that was controlled by a strong theocracy of the kind condemned by Dante in his *De Monarchia*. It was not unlike the style of the totalitarian Islamic State created by the Ayatollah Kohmeini in Iran in 1979, when he forced the Shah into exile.

In the midst of these debates the dam that had shored up the Church against the rising tide of demands for reform was shattered by the Augustinian friar Father Martin Luther (1483–1546). Luther, who had been much influenced by the Brotherhood of the Common Life and by Erasmus, was professor of theology at the Saxon university in Wittenberg. He had already been shocked in 1510 by the laxity and levity of the Italian clergy he had met during a visit to Rome. Instead of being enlightened on spiritual matters by his visit, as he had sincerely hoped, he was forced to return home and to rely on his own resources to solve the problem which gave him most concern. This was the question of his personal salvation and his chances for a future life. He toiled for several years in search of a solution, devoting his studies to St Paul's Letters. At last, in about 1514–15, while preparing a set of university lectures, he found his solution.

In St Paul's Letter to the Romans Luther read the words *we hold that a man is justified by faith apart from works'* (Romans 3.28). These words struck Luther like a thunderbolt. They showed him to his great relief that works were not necessary for salvation, though he later explained that to a true believer works were expected to follow faith, just as fruit followed blossoms on a tree. In an autobiographical fragment written towards the end of his life he described this experience as *'feeling myself to have been born again and to have entered through the open gates of Paradise'*.

In the years from 1510 to 1516 Luther was not remotely concerned with Church reform, but with interpreting St Paul's Letters. Within two years this changed dramatically. Far away from Luther's university in Saxony the Medici Pope Leo X was facing serious financial, as opposed to spiritual, problems. The papacy was bankrupt through artistic extravagance and the excessive cost of the wars to preserve the independence of the Church lands in the face of French and Imperial opposition and rebellious Italian city-states. Leo had decided nevertheless to embark on a vast scheme – the building of a huge new basilica of St Peter to replace the old, crumbling sixth-century building.

In order to raise the necessary finance for this he encouraged the sale of allegedly holy relics in which a large and profitable trade had developed. Many German princes and bishops had already engaged in this traffic. Leo hoped that increasing profits from the trade would enable them to subscribe to the new St Peter's. This trade in relics had been mocked a century before by the English poet Geoffrey Chaucer (1340–1400). In one of his *Canterbury Tales* Chaucer tells how the Pardoner persuaded his clients to seek pardons by confessing their sins over alleged saints' relics which he knew were only *'piggies' bones'*. They paid up, got their pardons, and so believed they were excused from having to spend many years in Purgatory.

Leo's solution to his financial problems was to sell pardons or indulgences on a grander scale than had ever been attempted before. He offered indulgences for sins for considerable sums to raise funds for St Peter's. He published his prospectus for this all over Europe. He also included one unique promise in the sale, that the purchaser would be indemnified for future as well as for past sins. Never before had so fraudulent a prospectus been issued. When the prospectus reached Wittenberg in 1517, Martin Luther was horrified. Having struggled for years to solve the problem of his own and other believers' chances of salvation, he now read that forgiveness for sins could be obtained for cash. Faith was not required!

The controversy that Luther was to arouse over this began very quietly in a correct academic manner. Having thought the matter over, he posted a notice of a forthcoming university debate on the door of Wittenberg church. This was the customary place for advertising public and university matters. In his notice he listed 95 theses to be discussed in a public debate. He introduced his subjects modestly with these words: '*Out of love for the faith and a desire to bring it to light, the following propositions will be discussed under the chairmanship of the Reverend Father Martin Luther, Master of Arts and Sacred Theology*'.

Among the 95 theses was one that questioned the right of a pope to sell indulgences. Luther did not question the right of a pope to absolve penitents, quoting the 'power of the keys' from St Matthew's Gospel and Christ's message to St Peter. However it seemed to him that peddling pardons like Colosseum souvenirs trivialised sin by debasing true contrition. Also Luther questioned something that Rome could not ignore. This was the contention that a pope's 'keys to heaven' reached beyond the grave. Since Pope Leo had promised that future sins would be pardoned, this was bound to include sins that would be committed probably long after the pope's death! Surely that was beyond his powers. How, Luther asked, could indulgences sold for cash to unremorseful sinners free them from the agonies of Purgatory even for

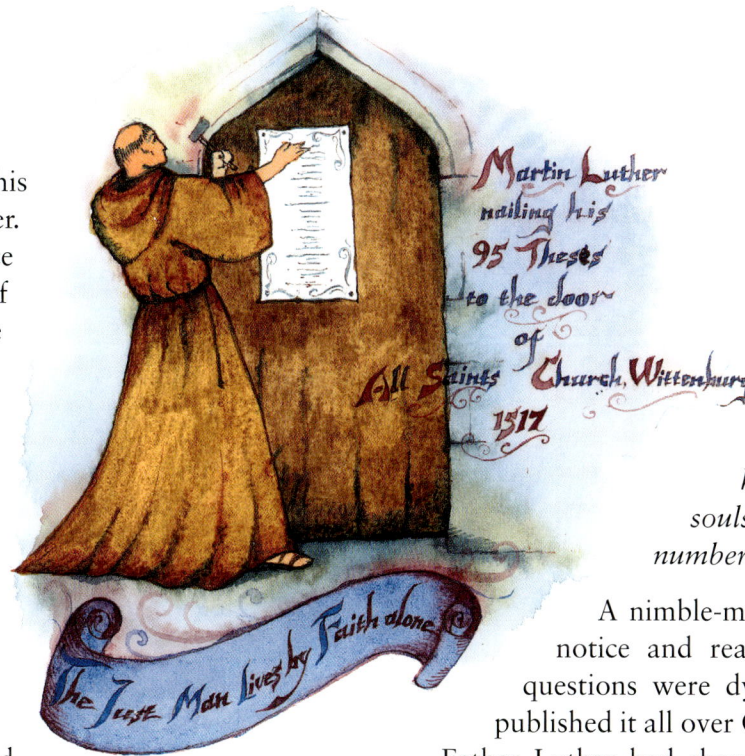

future sins? He then added that '*the unbridled preaching of pardon makes it no easy matter, even for learned men, to rescue the reverence due to the Pope from the shrewd questions of the laity, to wit: "Why does the Pope empty Purgatory for the sake of holy love and for the dire need of the souls that are there, if he redeems a number of souls for miserable money?"*'

A nimble-minded printer and publicist read the notice and realised that these peaceful academic questions were dynamite. He copied the notice and published it all over Germany, revealing that the scholarly Father Luther had shown up the Pope and discredited the entire practice of pardons being sold for cash.

Immediately the sale of indulgences plunged like the shares in a stock-market swindle. Pope Leo was horrified at the damage this caused to his fund-raising plan. He appealed to Frederick the Wise, Elector of Saxony, to restrain Luther, but Frederick rather liked his controversial friar Martin Luther and ignored the Pope's plea.

Therefore in 1518 Leo ordered the eminent theologian Thomasso de Vio, Cardinal Catejan, Master General of the Dominicans and head of the Inquisition, to interview Luther at Augsburg and correct him. Their meeting is illustrated on the next page. The meeting was barren of

Martin Luther nailing his 95 Theses to the door of All Saints Church, Wittenburg 1517

The Just Man lives by Faith alone

Martin Luther and Cardinal Catejan meet at Augsburg in 1518

results. Each side represented completely different points of view. Catejan's was the traditional view of the Church that, as Christ's chosen representative on earth, the Pope was infallible. Luther took a more humanist and forward-looking view and wanted his questions answered because they raised issues that had disturbed the ordinary laity as well as scholars. However Catejan refused to listen to this questioning of the pope's plan from a member of the lower clergy. Luther therefore asked him for advice over his own personal questions about salvation. Catejan simply told him to go away and read the Bible. He then dismissed Luther, who managed to escape almost certain arrest through a side door of the castle.

Luther came away from Augsburg a changed man. He now knew that the Pope's and the Church's official view utterly ignored the prime question of human salvation through Christ's self-sacrifice. This was a shameful disgrace and Luther was hurt to the very depths of his soul. He resolved that the papacy had to be challenged strongly and publicly. Although no official record was made of his interview with Catejan, Luther sent an account of it to a friend which was then published all over Germany. The extreme view to which he had come is clear from these words: *'You may see whether or not I am right in supposing that, according to St Paul, the real Antichrist holds sway over the Roman court'*.

Luther's language became increasingly violent. He refused to compromise. By breaking the dam of medieval discipline, which had already been weakened by the events of the past two centuries, Luther set open rebellion in motion. He translated the Bible into German, thus creating the backbone for a great literary language. As accounts of the Gospels began to circulate in Luther's vernacular Bibles, the German peasantry learned for the first time that the sympathies of Christ and his apostles had lain with the poor and oppressed like them and not with the princes of the Church and State who presumed to speak in his name. Luther's challenge to ecclesiastical prestige encouraged the peasants to rebel. They were eager for a greater share in an increasingly prosperous Germany. To encourage this Luther published his pamphlet *Karsthaus* or *Pitchfork John*, in which he pledged to protect the peasantry and made himself their champion.

Various universities condemned the 95 theses, but Luther responded with a tract called *Indulgence and Grace* to further his cause. His increasingly rebellious tone was now very obvious as he wrote: *'If I am called a heretic by those who suffer from my truth, I care not for their brawling; for only those say this whose dark understanding has never known the bible'*. The Pope was now advised to abandon the sale of indulgences. Luther was summoned to Rome, but declined the invitation. The Pope sent him a bull of excommunication which Luther burned.

Others now took up the challenge to the papacy. The evangelists Melancthon, John Calvin and Zwingli did so in Geneva. Another evangelical was Martin Bucer. From his base in Strasburg he was to have great influence on the English Archbishop Cranmer as he tried to find a compromise over the definition of the bread and wine at the Eucharist. Bucer's chief aim was to achieve a spiritual reform of the whole of society. Meanwhile Erasmus kept quiet. He had kept in touch with Luther in the early stages, but in 1525 Luther broke off relations with him. Erasmus had nothing more to add to the reforms of the monasteries that he had already suggested. He did not want a complete break with tradition.

Meanwhile Luther had published his famous open letter entitled 'To the Christian nobility of the German nation, concerning Rome and the reform of the Christian Estate'. He demanded an end to papal extortion in taxes and payments for benefices. He wanted the papal legates expelled from the land. He also demanded that the German clergy should renounce their loyalty to the Vatican. In going as far as this, Luther showed the extent to which he was being influenced by the German princes. What had begun as an academic debate now became a demand for a revolution – the Reformation.

At an Imperial Diet at Worms in 1521 the Emperor Charles V had Luther tried for heresy, only to discover that only three of the electoral princes supported the charge and that the great body of the German nobility applauded Luther's actions. Luther refused to retract a word of his writings and is alleged to have said: 'Hier stehe Ich, Ich kann nicht anders' – 'Here I take my stand, I can do no other'.

The progress of the Lutheran reformers was rapid in Germany after the Diet of Worms. Instead of making room for a quiet and constructive debate on what might have been seen as a forgivable error on the part of the financially hard-pressed Pope Leo, the German princes forced forward their own nationalist aims rather than their religious affections. The Roman Church was equally guilty, as Cardinal Catejan's reply to Luther's questions revealed, in regarding itself and its bigoted attitude as infallible and not subject to question. Luther's propaganda for reform was so successful that at the Diet of Speyer in 1526 the

Emperor Charles V was forced to concede that each prince of the Empire could decide for his own state between the Roman Church and the Reform. The motion agreeing to this said that in making his decision each prince 'must behave as he could answer to God and the Emperor'.

This freedom of choice was somewhat reduced in scope at the Second Diet of Speyer in 1529, but most of the princes who were there and their followers rejected its restrictions so violently that they became known as the 'Protesters' or 'Protestants'. The old German word for Protestant was Eigenot, from which the French name for the Reformers, Hugenot, was derived.

The Protestants, however, soon became divided over many issues and definitions. Calvin had his own severe style in Geneva, where he influenced the visiting Scottish reformer John Knox to adopt St Augustine of Hippo's unscriptural doctrine of a double-predestination. On the Eucharist they also differed from Luther's reformed Church. The long-term effect, especially after Cranmer brought Bucer over to England in 1550 to lecture in Cambridge and to help him with his Prayer Book, was to cause some distortion and loss to the early style of the Church.

The conflict between the reformers and traditionalists in France has already been mentioned briefly in the life of St Francis de Sales in the January Calendar. At first King Francis I gave mild support to the reform movement and encouraged the production of a vernacular Bible. Then the contest ceased to be purely religious and led to eight mainly dynastic civil wars taking place in France over the course of the next 70 years.

The voice of the Holy Spirit could hardly be heard in Europe during this time. The full tragedy of the religious wars which followed in Europe for the next century and which caused such a schism in the universal Church, was summed up by Bishop Simon Barrington-Ward in a letter to me. He wrote that they were *'the product not only of the courage and integrity of reformers on either side, but also of the worldliness of the Church which had departed everywhere from Christ's central teaching about forgiveness and loving our enemies, and looking at our own errors and not just at those of others. The result was a loss of truth and obedience to God in Christ for which we all need to repent. Yet the Holy Spirit continued to be active on both sides and to produce saintly Protestants and Puritans and saintly Anglican divines, who tried in the sixteenth and seventeenth centuries to reach across the divide, like Richard Hooker, Lancelot Andrewes and Richard Baxter, and also the Catholic St John of the Cross, St Ignatius of Loyola, St Francis de Sales and Archbishop Fenelon.*

THE ENGLISH REFORMATION

The Reform in England, which began in 1527 in the reign of King Henry VIII, was not fully achieved until 1558, after the death of the Roman Catholic Queen Mary and the succession of Queen Elizabeth. The English Reformation was the result of dynastic rather than religious reasons. It began because King Henry wanted to preserve his Tudor dynasty by a male heir, but his Queen of 21 years, Catherine of Aragon, had not provided him with a son.

From 1527 to 1533 Henry's chancellor, Cardinal Wolsey, sent Thomas Cranmer (1489–1555), on diplomatic missions to the Emperor Charles V, to the European universities and to Spain to seek advice on what he called *the King's great matter*. Cranmer sought advice on the validity of Henry's plea that his marriage to Catherine should be annulled because he had sinned, according to the Book of Leviticus, by marrying his brother Arthur's widow.

In the course of his travels Cranmer discussed a whole range of other religious matters with the reformers of Geneva and Strasburg and became converted to their case against the principle of the pope ruling the national Churches. By 1533 Cranmer had not only won the confidence of the King, but was also a firm ally of the family of Anne Boleyn, the King's mistress and future wife and queen and an ardent Lutheran. In quick succession King Henry made Cranmer Archbishop of Canterbury, divorced Catherine, married Anne Boleyn, disestablished the monasteries and used the rich proceeds of their lands for himself and to secure the support of his courtiers. Then, finding that his bishops supported Pope Clement VII rather than himself, he denounced the papacy and made himself Supreme Governor of the English Catholic Church.

In spite of these actions Henry still regarded himself as a Catholic and forced through laws to protect the traditional teaching of the Church. He suppressed all opposition to his determination to govern the Church. In 1535 he beheaded Bishop John Fisher and his former chancellor Sir Thomas More for treason in not recognising his supremacy in the Church.

It is interesting to note that although Cranmer had obtained papal approval for his appointment as archbishop, he swore a significant oath at his consecration. In this he promised *'to prosecute and reform matters wherever they seem to me to be necessary for the reform of the English Church'*. Nevertheless he had to proceed slowly, only going so far as the King would permit. The King did however order that an English translation of the Bible should be chained to the pews in every church.

That Bible, known as 'The Bishop's Bible' was a poor translation in indifferent English. There was in fact another English translation of the Bible available. It had been produced by a great scholar, the Revd William Tyndale (1494–1536). He was a Gloucestershire vicar who had embarked on his translation determined, as he said, *'so that every ploughman in England should be able to read and understand the Gospels'*. His bishop refused to permit his translation to be published. Tyndale therefore had his translated Gospels printed in Germany and smuggled into England. He then began to complete his translation of the Old Testament in Antwerp, where he found diplomatic sanctuary in 'The English House', the headquarters of the English cloth trade. However, an English Catholic spy deceived him into making a visit outside his sanctuary, which enabled the Emperor's men to seize him.

Tyndale was declared a heretic for his translation work and was garrotted and burnt at the stake. King Henry was too involved in a diplomatic negotiation with the Emperor to intervene.

Cranmer's chance to further the cause of reform in England came when Henry's son Edward, by his third wife Queen Jane Seymour, became King in 1548 as Edward VI. He had been brought up to support reform and during his short reign Cranmer was able to transform the English Church of England to an evangelical faith. His foremost achievement in this was his preparation of the 1552 *Book of Common Prayer* and its 42 Articles of Faith for use in all parish churches. He was not left entirely free in this, because he had to work in conjunction with the Scottish theologian John Knox (1513–72), who had been appointed one of the five royal chaplains. Knox was later to reform the Scottish Church to a Calvinistic style of Presbyterianism, which did not have any bishops.

King Edward died of tuberculosis after a reign of only five years. On his death-bed and in order to preserve the Reformed English Church, he and his ministers appointed Lady Jane Grey, a distant Tudor cousin, as the rightful heiress to the throne instead of Henry's allegedly illegitimate daughters the Catholic Mary and the Protestant Elizabeth. Cranmer, fully realising the risk he was taking, agreed reluctantly to sign the document favouring Jane as the heir to the

throne. There was too much at stake in the reformed English Church for him to do otherwise in view of Mary's known passionate adherence to Rome.

Jane's reign lasted nine days before her supporters brought Mary from exile at Framlingham Castle to the Tower of London to be proclaimed Queen in Cheapside in the City on 19 July 1553. In August the first arrests of the reforming bishops began and Cranmer was sent to the Tower. He was tried for treason in November, found guilty and condemned to death. In December by Act of Parliament church observances throughout England were restored to those in force at the end of the reign of Henry VIII. Bishops Ridley and Latimer were burned alive as heretics in St Giles, Oxford in October 1555. '*Be of comfort Master Ridley*' said Latimer as he was tied to the stake opposite St John's College, '*and play the man; we shall this day light a candle by God's grace in England as I trust shall never be put out*'.

For Cranmer the Queen also reserved a show trial for heresy in the form of a debate in Oxford University's church of St Mary's. She wanted him to be publicly humiliated together with the whole of his reformed church. At first and in private Cranmer obliged by recanting his views and accepting the doctrine of Transubstantiation. He agonised over this decision for weeks, hoping to be reprieved from his sentence to be burned alive. However, as the inevitable death by burning approached, he decided on

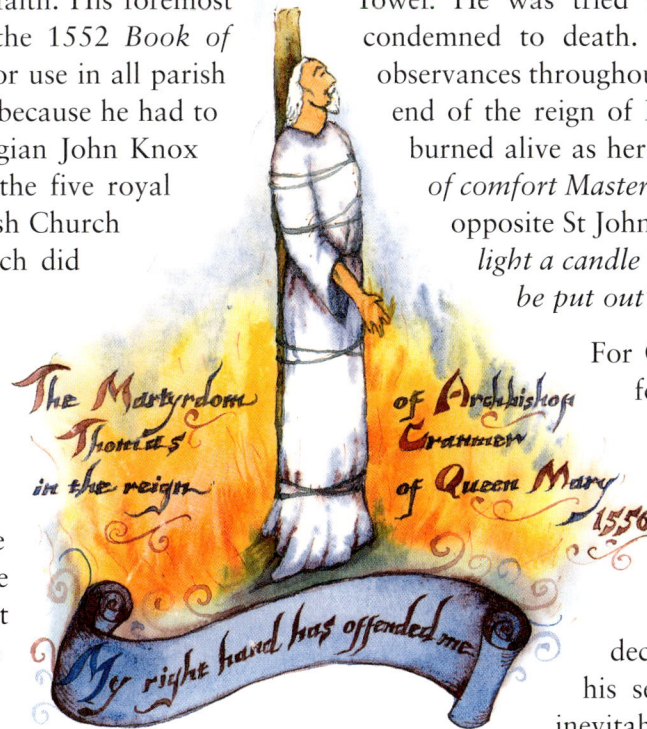

The Martyrdom of Archbishop Thomas Cranmer in the reign of Queen Mary 1556

My right hand has offended me

315

one last valiant act. Instead of the humiliating scene that had been planned for him in St Mary's church and which was to contain his full public confession, he entered the pulpit and ended his speech by saying: '*I signed my belief in Transubstantiation for fear of death, but not in my heart. As for the Pope I refuse him as Christ's enemy and Antichrist with all his false doctrine.*' He was dragged down from the pulpit and hurried away to the stake. As the flames took hold he thrust his hand into the fire, saying '*This is the hand that hath offended*'. He died a martyr for his cause.

In spite of the burnings of about 300 protestants during Mary's reign, Cranmer's English Church endured and was restored after Mary's death by her sister Queen Elizabeth. Elizabeth wanted neither extreme Catholic tradition nor excessive Protestant zeal. Cranmer's prayer book was reintroduced in 1559. In this version the 42 Articles (later reduced to the present 39) included the statement that '*the body of Christ is given, taken and eaten in the supper only after an heavenly and spiritual manner; and the means whereby the body of Christ is received and eaten as faith*'. This was due to John Knox.

The history of what followed and the attempt by the Spanish armada to invade England in 1588 and destroy the English Church, is too well known to be described here. The subsequent executions of some 150 Catholics as traitors or agents sent to murder the Queen, were the understandable consequence of the Spanish threat to the nation. Those were hard and dangerous times. The tragedy is that such titanic waves of religious dispute and killing do not die down quickly; they can and do continue for centuries. This is why, for example, we still suffer from the effects of the persecution of Catholics in Ireland by Protestant settlers sent there by King James I and from the memory of Cromwell's brutal and bloody campaigns in Ireland and the penal laws against Catholics that followed.

THE RESULTS OF THE REFORMATION IN EUROPE

By 1550 about 40 per cent of Europe, including the Scandinavian countries and Iceland, had turned Protestant. This was reduced to about 25 per cent of Europe by the Roman Catholic Counter-Reformation wars and the Thirty Years' War of 1618–48. Meanwhile in France, although King Francis had at first been sympathetic to the reformers and welcomed the translation of the Bible into French, he soon despaired of the Protestants' extremism. France descended into a series of eight civil wars, partly religious, but mainly dynastic. These lasted until the protestant King Henry of Navarre became a Roman Catholic and inherited the French throne as King Henry IV.

Meanwhile the reform movement within the Roman Catholic Church made some headway through the debates in the Council of Trent (1545–63), which was convoked after pressure from the Emperor Charles V. He had hoped that it could bring about a reconciliation between Catholics and Protestants. Although it failed in this, it did bring about some important ecclesiastical reforms in the Roman Curia, in providing for better education for the clergy and, most important of all, it produced a new Missal to replace the multitude of medieval offices.

The first long-term benefit of the Reformation to the faith was the intellectual freedom that made critical study of the Bible possible. This began with the revolutionary expositions of the German philosopher Hermann Reimarius (1694–1768). It has continued right to our own time at Tubingen and Heidelberg in Germany and through Protestant theologians like Karl Barth (1886–1968), whom Pope Pius XII declared to be the greatest theologian since St Thomas Aquinas. It can therefore be seen that the work of the Spirit continued even though at a terrible initial cost.

The studies of these theologians, freed from the obstruction of the Roman Curia, have revolutionised our understanding of the Scriptures. This would not have been possible without the freedom from obstruction from the papal Curia. Nevertheless the Vatican still declared that the innovative scholar Hans Kung, Pope John's official theological adviser to the Second Vatican Council in 1960–3, was no longer to function as a teacher. Fortunately the German government provided Hans Kung immediately with a professorial chair at Tubingen. The Spirit will not be suppressed!

THE REFORM AND THE FUTURE AMERICAN STATES

A second fortuitous benefit resulting from the Protestant revolution of the sixteenth and seventeenth centuries, was the way English Puritans migrated to form settlements on the East Coast of America. These all sought freedom from religious oppression in Europe. It was they who founded the 13 colonies along the whole Eastern seaboard of what was to become the United States of America in 1776, a land where there was and is complete religious freedom. Later generations called these first settlers 'The Pilgrim Fathers'.

One of these settlements was established in 1634 by the Roman Catholic courtier of King Charles I, Lord Baltimore. He named his property Maryland after Charles' French Roman Catholic Queen Henrietta Maria. Like the other emigrants, they too sought freedom from political and religious restrictions, as did the founders of the last of the 13 colonies to be established. This was Pennsylvania, founded in 1681 with the blessing of King Charles II by the Quaker William Penn. Penn was much admired by the French philosopher and historian Voltaire (1694–1778) in his *Lettres Philosophiques,* which were published in 1734. These were written after Voltaire had spent two years in England studying English government, churches and society.

The Quakers or The Society of Friends, founded by George Fox (1624–91), were unorthodox but devout Christians. They had no clergy and were anti-clerical because they considered the churches had distorted the original gospel. They also rejected baptism because they said Christ never baptised. They were called Quakers after one of their number explained at his trial in court for being a dissenter, that *'men should tremble at the name of the Lord'.* They refuse to fight in war, but serve willingly in the field with the medical and ambulance services. They also devote themselves to charitable works (e.g. the Cadbury and Fry families) and to fulfilling Christ's commands. One fine example of this is in the 'Great Law' of William Penn's first Assembly in Philadelphia on 7 December 1681. This proclaimed that no human being born in Pennnsylvania could be made a slave. Thus slavery was automatically extinguished there in one generation. Finally the lasting achievement of these protestant settlers has been to produce in the USA a nation in which over 50 per cent of the population attend the churches. This is a higher figure than in any European nation today.

ANGLICANS AND PURITANS

The title 'Anglican' is derived from the title *Anglicana Ecclesia*, which was first used in Magna Carta in 1215 to differentiate the 'English Church' from the Church elsewhere in Europe. It was also used in King Henry VIII's Act of Supremacy in 1534 to describe the Church which he exclusively had the power to rule over and reform. Then, in the reign of Queen Elizabeth I, the Church of England became *'both Catholic and Reformed'*, thus preserving its continuity with the Old Catholics though not in communion with the Roman Catholic Church.

The name 'Puritan' was first used in the 1560s for those members of the Church of England who were dissatisfied with the Elizabethan Settlement of Religion. These included people who had returned from exile during Queen Mary's reign and pressed vigorously for the purification of the Church. These also included those who, like the Scottish theologian John Knox, refused to recognise bishops. The Puritans, most of whom were influenced by Calvin's Geneva Church, attacked what they regarded as unscriptural practices, such as the wearing of vestments and using the sign of the cross at baptism. They also advocated a Presbyterian form of church government rather than through bishops. They were strongly opposed by Archbishop John Whitgift, who got an Act against Seditious Sectaries passed by Parliament in 1593.

The two men who did most, after Thomas Cranmer, to shape the Church of England as we know it today, were Canon Richard Hooker (1554–1603) and Bishop Lancelot Andrewes (1555–1625).

In his book *Of the Laws of Ecclesiastical Polity* (1593–1603), Canon Hooker placed the ideal of the Church in a mid-way position between Roman Catholicism and the Geneva-inspired Puritans. Bishop Andrewes and his council of theologians set up by King James I provided it in 1611 with the Authorised Version of the Bible, over 80 per cent of which was taken directly from the martyred William Tyndale's version of 1524–35.

Hooker's great single contribution was to define the Anglican tradition as a threefold cord – Bible, Church, Reason. He avoided extremes by giving Scripture absolute authority where it spoke plainly, but where it was silent or ambiguous he said that wisdom should consult tradition in an interpretative way and be clarified through reason. His views on this were therefore the same as those of that earliest of Christian theologians Origen in the early third century. On relations between church and state, Hooker sought unity. In his view the Puritans adopted an impossible position, claiming loyalty to the Queen but rejecting her Church. However Hooker conceded that since scripture prescribes no particular form of church government, reason permits that in any land *'the public society of God'* is free to choose its own rites, because the church is an organic institution in which the Holy Spirit still leads men into further truth by the light of reasoning.

Hooker therefore wisely expected further progress in religion and in reform to be made in the light of future new knowledge and changing circumstances. In this he was taking the often-ignored stance of the fifth-century St Vincent of Lerins, that Christianity is a developing faith, which is what Cardinal John Henry Newman was to teach the Roman Catholic Church 250 years later. Thus the basic tenets and ideals of the English or Anglican Church are soundly traditional and as orthodox as the earliest primitive church before Rome claimed the supreme ecclesiastical authority.

THE BAPTISTS

The Baptists John Smyth and John Bunyan were true Friends of God. Smyth's founding of what is now the Baptist World Alliance and Bunyan's classic story *The Pilgrim's Progress* illustrate how much seekers after spiritual truths can achieve when freed from unscriptural and doctrinal restraints.

John Smyth (1554–1612)

Smyth was the leader of an extreme puritan group who dissented from the concepts that led to the unity of the Anglican Church and state. He took his followers to Holland and there developed the theory that led to the formation of the Baptist Church. He taught that the only true Christians were those mature individuals who were baptised by total submersion in the name of Jesus Christ. Their reception of the Holy Spirit followed this automatically, as it betokened a convert's repentance and belief in Christ. He based this on St Paul's teaching that baptism denoted the believer's union with Christ in his death, burial and resurrection, which is the sign of incorporation into the 'body of Christ' into which we all die from our old ways.

Some of Smyth's followers returned to England after his death and were amongst the first English emigrants to America in 1620. From these small beginnings various independent sects of Baptists developed and ultimately formed the Baptist World Alliance of independently ruled communities. Their members now number more than 40 million and form one of the largest churches in America. There are now also over a million adherents in India through the work of the devout and popular William Carey (1761–1834). He began his mission there in 1793. When praised for his work, he replied '*Oh, I simply plod on*'.

John Bunyan (1628–88)

John Bunyan was the greatest literary genius produced by the Puritan movement in England. He was born to a poor Bedfordshire yeoman family and was the son of a travelling brazier and tinker. In 1644 at the age of 16 he was conscripted into the Cromwellian army. He saw little fighting, but during his three years' service he met many extreme left-wing members of that intensely argumentative and religious army, the Levellers, Quakers, Ranters and the Seekers.

On his release and return to Bedford Bunyan went through a painful process of conversion, from 1650–55. He began by attending the local Anglican church, but was dissatisfied with it and became influenced powerfully by Calvinism. As a result he suffered all the terrors of one who believed that he was not destined to be saved. Then he joined a group of Baptists and soon proved himself to be a powerful preacher.

In his autobiography, written in 1666 while he was in prison as a 'Dissenter', he described one of his sermons in which he said: '*I sent myself in chains to preach to those in chains and carried such fire in my own conscience that I persuaded them*'.

In 1660 Bunyan was again sent to prison under an old Elizabethan law for conducting a 'conventicle', a meeting of Dissenters. He was not released until 1672 when King Charles II published his Declaration of Indulgence. Finding that his old Baptist community had appointed another leader, he obtained a licence to preach and became the leading light in a group of Congregationalists. After another short term in prison he published his greatest work in 1678, *The Pilgrim's Progress*, which he had begun to write during his first imprisonment.

The book is an allegory of Bunyan's own experience of conversion, doubt, persecution and eventual survival as a seeker after truth. Its hero, 'Christian', is Bunyan, who begins his pilgrimage loaded with the burden on his back containing his sins. The story is like a traditional folk tale. Christian leaves the 'City of Destruction' by a gate, symbolic of Christ's way. He goes through the Slough of Despond and the Valley of the Shadow of Death. He is joined by several unreliable characters, Interpreter, Talkative and Ignorance and he exposes them. After passing through the Delectable Mountains he comes to the River of Life. There before the Cross he finds that his burden of sin tumbles from his back as he receives the free pardon of Christ and is numbered amongst the elect. He also receives white garments and a sealed roll which he is to hand in at the Celestial Gate.

Yet all the crises of the past are not over. This initiation of grace in the soul is not the end, but the beginning of the final drama in which Christian is joined by two more companions, Faithful and Hopeful. All three are now fixed on the path of salvation in spite of the horrors of the temptations they now have to undergo.

These three are plunged into the worldliness of Vanity Fair. Here Bunyan illustrates the persecution that he had suffered himself and likens it to that which the saints of God had to endure. However the bright hope of assured salvation is dimmed again as Christian and Hopeful are imprisoned in The Dungeon of Despair. He finds the key called Promise, the assurance given by the gospels, which unlocks the door and he is freed. His problems are still not over. Christian, like Bunyan the physician of the soul, still has to meet and deal with the sceptic Mr Worldly-Wise. However they negotiate their way past Doubting Castle, whose owner is Giant Despair. Nothing stops Christian, who arrives finally at the Celestial Gate where the trumpets sound for him. Success at last after a story whose happy ending has always been in doubt.

Bunyan turned his pilgrim theme into a famous hymn, now in the English Hymnal, which is sung regularly in churches: *'He who would valiant be 'gainst all disaster, let him in constancy follow the Master. There's no discouragement shall make him once relent his first avowed intent to be a pilgrim'.*

Bunyan's book was praised in the eighteenth century by Dr Samuel Johnson and Dean Jonathan Swift. It found its way into most English homes, where Bunyan was regarded as a literary genius alongside Homer. His book has been translated into many languages and yet loses none of its moving drama, which describes the pilgrimage to faith of so many.

THE SPIRIT UNDER PRESSURE IN THE AGE OF REASON AND DURING THE ENLIGHTENMENT

The seventeenth and eighteenth centuries were times of wars and civil strife, but they were also a period of conflict in Western thought between reason and faith, which completed the break with medieval traditions. This movement of thought and belief, in what we now call the 'Age of Reason' and the 'Enlightenment', developed in Europe as philosophers examined the interrelated conceptions of God, Reason, Nature and Faith. They undermined existing systems of government and religious beliefs. They also led to the downfall of the French Ancien Regime and to the birth of the United States of America. Together with the Industrial Revolution of the eighteenth century these laid the foundations of the modern world.

This modern world of ours, with all the achievements of the Industrial Revolution, would not have been possible without the discoveries of two great and devout French mathematicians and physicists and of one English scientist of genius. These were Renée Descartes, Blaise Pascal and Sir Isaac Newton, who were all motivated by a deep spiritual and religious sense and a desire to fathom the mighty works of God. The stories of their lives and works and also of two great evangelists, the American Jonathan Edwards and the English clergyman John Wesley, which are given below, will illustrate the profound changes in thought that took place in this period. After these lives I include that of the nineteenth-century scientist, Michael Faraday, who was also motivated by his religious zeal.

Renée Descartes (1596–1650)

This great French philosopher and mathematician began his career as a military engineer. He then concentrated on his mathematical researches in Germany. There he discovered the chain relationship that linked algebra, geometry and all physics and science. Then in 1629 he went to live in Holland, preferring its atmosphere of intellectual freedom to that of France. He stayed there for 20 years, apart from three short visits to France. In 1637 he produced his epoch-making work *Discourse on the Method of Properly Guiding the Reason in Search of Truth and Science.* He followed this in 1642 with his *Meditations on First Philosophy, in which the Existence of God and then Distinction between Mind and Body are Demonstrated.* In 1644 he published his *Principles of Philosophy* and in 1649 *The Passions of the Soul.* Descartes dedicated this last work to Queen Christina of Sweden. She invited him to Stockholm, where he died a month later.

Descartes was a deeply religious man. His *Discourse on Method* sought the philosophical basis for certainty. He started from a position of doubt, doubting everything, in order to seek something that was beyond doubt. In this process he came to define all knowledge as coming from sense-perception. His method of reasoning has influenced French thought ever since. He concluded empirically that there was a difference between body and soul and between matter and spirit. Having decided that this was beyond doubt, he made it the basis of his philosophy and reached his famous conclusion '*Cogito ergo sum*' – 'I think, therefore I am' and that *Deus est* – 'God exists and is existence itself', just as Moses had defined God in the words coming from the burning bush in Exodus.

To demonstrate the existence of God, Descartes followed St Anselm's argument that he must be the most perfect being conceivable and he must exist, otherwise it would be possible to imagine an even greater being. That is impossible without implying that God is less than perfect, which would be a self-contradiction.

Descartes wrote that *'the soul is always thinking'*. He affirmed that this soul, this 'self', is incapable of annihilation because it is independent of all other substances.

However, Descartes admitted that the question of whether this 'self' survives the body eternally can only be answered categorically if one had knowledge of God's future decisions, something we do not possess. Even so we can say that if God does not annihilate the soul, then the 'self' will continue to exist in spite of its body's death. St Thomas Aquinas would have agreed with Descartes.

In the field of advanced mathematics and physics Descartes opened the path that Sir Isaac Newton was to follow and then reach some revolutionary conclusions. Voltaire summed up the importance of these two mathematicians at the end of his essay on them in his *Lettres Philosophiques* in 1733–4. He wrote of these two that *'Descartes gave sight to the blind and saw the faults of antiquity and his own age. The range that he has opened has, since his time, become infinite. Today the universities of Europe have found that that system is a vast abyss. Now it remains to be discovered what Newton has dug up at the bottom of this precipice.'*

That was written only six years after Newton's death, a man whom Voltaire admired greatly. The brilliant sequent to Voltaire's prophecy will be described briefly in the essay on Newton's life, which follows the account below of another great French mathematical genius and religious thinker, Blaise Pascal.

Blaise Pascal (1623–62)

Pascal was born in Clermont-Ferrand in the Auvergne. He proved himself a brilliant mathematician and physicist before he concentrated on spiritual and religious matters. He is one of the most profound of French thinkers. His genius as a theologian gives him a unique eminence among thinkers not only in his own age but also in modern times.

Pascal's earliest religious works were his letters known as *Les Provinciales*. They were written in 1656–7 in defence of the Jansenist community of Port Royale, where his sister was a member and which had come under attack from the Jesuits, the French Church and the French Court. The letters are a highly valued monument of French literature and were an immediate success both in France and England on account of Pascal's brilliant attack on the casuist doctrine of the Jesuits. He showed that these always led to a lax form of morality, inconsistent with Christian doctrine.

In opposition to the Jesuits, Pascal emphasised the soul's union with the mystical body of Christ through love and charity. He believed the ideal of evangelical perfection to be inseparable from a Christian life and that is to be 'Christ-like'. Pascal's letters had a posthumous success in 1678, when the saintly Pope, the Blessed Innocent XI, condemned half the Jesuit propositions that Pascal had already denounced.

Pascal's immortal but unfinished work is his great 'Apology' or explanation that he planned to write to justify the Christian faith. This was only in note form when he died, but it was published posthumously as his *Pensées*. Pascal's *Pensées* reveal that he aimed to prove that man's natural desire was for happiness through God. It is not possible here to do more than quote a few of the more memorable thoughts that Pascal had noted down. He began by stressing the need to know our true selves: '*Nous sommes des êtres finis, transfigurés par une cause qui nous dépasse et atteint l'absolu et l'infini*' . . . ('We are finite beings, transfigured by a prime cause that goes far beyond us and reaches to the absolute and infinite') and he concluded: '*Quelle chimère*'.

One of the most moving things that Pascal wrote down was his own treasured personal *Memorial*. This summed up a profound spiritual experience of enlightenment and conversion that came to him in 1654. The words that expressed this for him meant so much to him that he sewed the paper containing them onto his coat: '*FEU*' – '*Dieu d'Abraham, Dieu d'Isaac, Dieu de Jacob et non des philosophes et savants. Certitude, sensation, joix, paix, le Dieu de Jesus Christ*'. . . *Lundi 23ième Novembre 1654, jour de St Clement, pape et martyr*'.

These thoughts had come to him in one blinding flash in which he saw the true God and dismissed the arguments of the Deists and the rationalisations of the other philosophers and savants of his day. Pascal concluded from his reflections on his life and faith that without God man lacks even the deep consciousness of his wretched state and his need for grace, which he said is obtained through the living faith in Christ our saviour. Therefore '*all those who seek God outside Jesus Christ and who stop at nature, fall either into atheism or deism, which are two things abhorrent to Christianity*'.

Pascal described the feelings that accompanied what was for him a second conversion, that of being 'born again', by comparing them with those described by St Teresa of Avila in her autobiography. '*I cannot explain this simultaneous pain and pleasure that the suffering body and the joy of the spirit can be compatible. It was a spiritual pain so excessive, joined to a happiness so delicious that it was for me quite sublime. The soul knows what grace God has given it in making proof and how that pain is legitimate.*'

Having described his pictures of the happiness of man without and also with divine grace, Pascal then described man as an incomprehensible mixture of greatness and abjectness. He is lost in the universe, incapable of reaching the supreme good to which his nature aspires. He then asks: '*Qu'est que l'homme dans l'infini? Misérable sans Dieu.*' Our misery compels us to seek him, so that man can go beyond himself. Happiness is to be found outside ourselves and God helps us to see ourselves clearly.

One of Pascal's most provocative ideas is his challenge to the sceptics, his famous argument of '*le Pari*', 'the Wager'. He advised doubters and unbelievers to make a bet that God exists. He argued that if there is no God, they would lose nothing; but if there is a God, they would win everything and eternal life. So why not make the bet? At first sight this seems a sleight of hand or even blasphemous, but Pascal's notes explain that the bet is to be made through adopting the discipline of faith, which requires humility of soul. Thus his argument for the bet was exactly what the many doubting Thomases of the Age of Reason needed to jolt them out of the attractive but empty rationality of the philosophers.

In his plan for his apology for Christianity, Pascal allowed only a limited role for reason and philosophy. He wrote that '*Reason's last step is the recognition that there are an infinite number of things which are beyond its powers. It is merely feeble if it does not go so far as to admit that the heart has reasons of which reason knows nothing.'*

Pascal then explained that it is impossible to know God without first knowing Christ through the Gospels, because *'knowing Jesus Christ strikes the balance, since he shows us both God and our own wretchedness'*. In contrast to this Pascal then considered the greatness of man with God and showed that with God man is more than just man – *'l'homme est plus que l'homme'*. He then wrote that although man is nothing but a reed, he is a thinking reed – *'un Roseau, le plus faible dans la nature; mais c'est un Roseau pensant'*. Thus if the universe crushes him, he alone will know why, while the universe will know nothing of it. Man is made for the infinite. Nothing that is finite can satisfy him. It is the heart that senses God, not reason. That is what faith is, but to know God without loving him is not to know him. Therefore Pascal prayed to God to grant him grace to love him, without which he believed he would be lost for ever. Thus this mathematical genius, who discovered advanced calculus and created the world's first calculating machine, saw God as the pole to which humanity is pointed.

Sir Isaac Newton (1642–1727)

Newton is known as the greatest figure in the entire history of science. He laid the cornerstone for the future understanding of dynamics and mechanics which, within a century, made possible the machinery for the Industrial Revolution. The whole of modern science began with his great book *Principia Mathematica*, which he published in 1687. This explained for the first time the way in which a single mechanical law, gravity, could account for the phenomenon of the heavens, the tides, the motion of the planets and also of objects on the earth. It was the key to the science of engineering and much else besides.

Less well-known is Newton's devout religious motivation. This inspired him from his student days at Trinity College, Cambridge and later as Lucasian Professor of Mathematics to make his researches to seek out the secrets that lay behind God's creation of the universe. Without these being understood, the forces of nature cannot be harnessed for any machinery or engineering process; but this is what the Industrial Revolution achieved through Newton's work.

All his life he was profoundly interested in religion. He studied the works of the early Church Fathers and sought evidence for his own principles of faith. This led him to accept that Jesus was indeed the Messiah sent by God.

As a mathematician Newton could not accept the fourth-century defensive arguments for defining God as a Trinity of Three Persons in One Being, but this did not discourage his faith. The doctrine of the Trinity is not written, but only implied in the scriptures. Newton is a classical example of a man achieving greatness through the inspiration of the Spirit.

Jonathan Edwards (1703–58)

Edwards was the heir to a distinguished family of Congregational and Calvinist clergymen. In the parishes along the Connecticut River he became the leader and inspirer of the First Great American Revival in 1734 and again in 1740. Through this he changed the whole future development of religion in what was to become the United States. It was through him that the pious bigotry of the early Pilgrim Fathers was overcome. These early settlers had established a fanatical approach to faith which had eventually led to such crimes as the unjust conviction and hanging of 19 alleged witches in Salem in 1692 and later to the hanging of 15-year-old Mary Dyer because she refused to give up being a Quaker. (Though a later generation in Boston erected a statue in memory of her.)

Edwards was born in Connecticut, where his father was a pastor. His family were pious Puritans. They sent him to Yale to study divinity and he was ordained into the Congregationalist ministry, becoming pastor at Northampton in Massachusetts in 1727. The town was the most important in the colony after Boston. While at Yale he had studied Newton's *Principia Mathematica* and discovered the immensity of the universe Newton had revealed and which was far more complex than the Babylonian style of astronomy that Jonathan had learned from the Book of Genesis.

It took Edwards many years to adjust his ideas about God and his relationship to that vast universe, but in the end he was able to expound a theology that fused fully with the new science that Newton had revealed. Jonathan also steeped himself in John Locke's *Essay Concerning Human Understanding* (1690), and his treatises on government and the works of the Reformation divines. He then interpreted these in the light of the contemporary philosophy he had studied. He thus provided himself with a sound basis from which to preach his own expanded faith in terms that the Protestant settlers would understand.

In a sermon published in 1731 on 'God glorified in the Work of Redemption', Edwards blamed New England's moral ills on its self-satisfied conviction of its own religious excellence. What the settlers missed in his view, was that faith, which abases man and exalts God, must be insisted on as the only means of salvation. In other words mere 'works' were not enough. This and other sermons were followed by a great religious revival in Northampton, during which hundreds professed their faith in public. Edwards then wrote a book describing the many types of conversion experience that he had witnessed, called *Faithful Narrative of the Surprising Work of God*. The book had a profound effect in America and in England. Suddenly Jonathan Edwards became an international figure.

In 1740–41 Edwards and his disciples went outside Massachusetts to the other colonies. Through their preaching of a simple and fundamental faith they attracted vast crowds, whose emotional reactions produced mass public conversions. This was the start of the second part of the Great Awakening in which Edwards' method of driving his points through to the crowds often involved the preaching about the terror of Hellfire that would punish sinners and deliberate unbelievers.

Because of this emphasis on the awful fate awaiting sinners, Edwards is sometimes said to have established the tradition of the 'Hellfire and Brimstone' preachers in the frontier regions as the United States expanded to the West. Jonathan did more than that. His theology went much deeper. As a convinced follower of Newton's theories and yet also following his theological predecessors' premise that God was the creator and sustainer of reality, Edwards applied that premise to the vastly expanded Newtonian universe.

Edward's congregation was typical of those in most early New England parishes, brought up in the original 'Protest' style of the Pilgrim Fathers. They regarded themselves as entitled to set themselves up as authorities on every aspect of religion. They were highly emotional, arrogant and hidebound, constantly making and unmaking their pastors and arguing in cabals amongst themselves; they were far too self-centred and daily questioned whether they had been 'saved'.

The myth that these Puritans had escaped from European authoritarianism to live a life of religious toleration in America wears rather thin when one considers the pharisaical way they and their descendants behaved. Jonathan's congregations were still like this at heart and Jonathan Edwards became the victim of the citizens of Massachusetts at the very moment when he became seriously evangelical in the light of his understanding of the Newtonian Universe. They could not accept his criticisms of their shallowness and they turned on him and in 1750 he had to leave his parish.

Nevertheless it was this fusing of the meaning of Newtonian and traditional Christianity which makes Jonathan Edwards so important a figure in American religious history. The fact that he was on the right track was realised by the scholars at the fledgling university of Princeton, who elected him to be their President in 1758. He looked forward to a promising career there, but this was suddenly cut short one month after his taking office, when he died from the effect of an inoculation against small-pox.

In assessing Edwards' immediate affect in New England, it is clear that his two 'Awakenings' changed people's lives. His legacy for the future lay in his books: *The Distinguishing Marks of a Work of the Spirit of God* (1741), *Thoughts on Revival* (1742), his *Treatise Concerning Religious Affections* (1746) and *Original Sin* (1758). Jonathan Edwards has been described as America's greatest theologian. He certainly took traditional theology a great step forward by fusing its understanding of God and our relationship to him in the light of the immense potential of the Newtonian universe.

John Wesley (1703–91)

The son of an Anglican clergyman, John went to Christ Church, Oxford in 1720. He was ordained in 1725 and became a Fellow of Lincoln College, Oxford. In 1729 he became the leader of a bible-study group started by his undergraduate younger brother Charles (1707–88). This 'Holy Club' became known in the university as the 'Bible-Moths' or 'Methodists', the name that John was to give to the religious societies that he formed later. The group extended their activities to social work in the prisons and workhouses, helping the inmates to read and with their debts, providing medicines and finding them work. This philanthropic activity was to become a major feature of the Methodist Societies.

In 1736 John accepted the invitation of General Oglethorpe, the governor of the new Crown Colony of Georgia, to go and preach to the Indians and to oversee the spiritual life of the settlers. This colony had been established by the government in 1734 to protect Virginia and Maryland from the Spaniards to the south in Florida. The mission failed. Utterly disillusioned and having lost faith in himself, John returned to England in December 1737. He wrote in his journal that '*I went to America to convert the Indians, but alas who shall convert me?*'

On his return to England John was helped and influenced by a group of Moravians, members of a reformed central European church. He described his 'second conversion' in his journal. This occurred while attending a Moravian meeting in the City of London at Aldersgate, during which there was a reading from the preface to Luther's commentary on St Paul's Letter to the Romans. John recorded that '*at a quarter to nine, while he (Luther) was describing the change which God works in the heart through faith in Jesus Christ, I felt my heart strangely warmed. I felt I did trust in Christ, Christ alone for my salvation; and an assurance was given me that he had taken away my sins, even mine, and saved me from the law of sin and death.*'

The immediate result of this experience was that John felt called powerfully to go out and share his new-found gift by spreading the good news of salvation by faith. He decided to set out to do this preferably through recalling the Church of England to its spiritual mission. Failing that, he was determined to do so by whatever other means were available. He began by getting himself invited to many Anglican pulpits. He soon found that he was denied access to them because of his enthusiasm and claim to be inspired by the Spirit, a claim the clergy found shocking and indecent. John therefore began to

John Wesley 1703–91
& Charles Wesley 1707

Soldiers of Christ Arise

concentrate on forming societies of fellow-thinkers in Bristol and London and preaching elsewhere in market places, lanes and even in the open fields.

In 1739 Wesley attracted a gathering in Bristol of over 3,000 people and made many converts, changing their lives. He did not preach violently and dramatically like Jonathan Edwards and his followers in America, but quietly, logically and convincingly. He gathered his converts into local societies for fellowship and spiritual growth. He explained to them that Christianity is essentially a social religion; to turn it into a solitary one is to destroy it and fail in its purpose.

The societies were quite separate from the Established English Church. John wrote rules for them and began to attract some ordained clergy as well as gifted laymen to run the local branches. John travelled some 8,000 miles a year on this work through England and covered some 250,000 miles on horseback in 30 years. He still met considerable opposition from the regular clergy. Step by step he was compelled to create what was in effect a separate Church organisation, with annual conferences aided by his printed tracts and a monthly magazine. He preached a truly Pauline doctrine and against the more extreme Calvinist elements in his congregations. These believed that God eternally predestined men either to salvation or to damnation. Instead he proclaimed the possibility of universal redemption by faith alone and emphasised the added privilege of the Christians of the divine assurance of salvation and the gift of God's

Holy Spirit within them and that they were children of God. That was pure Pauline teaching. In this way he constantly called his followers to pursue good, holiness of life and perfect love.

In 1760 'Methodism' began to spread in America, but the War of Independence from 1776–83 drove most English preachers back home. This led to John Wesley trying to persuade the Bishop of London to ordain clergy especially to go out and preach in America. He did so in vain, as the Bishop refused to oblige him.

Therefore John was compelled to make up for the shortage of trained preachers by ordaining his own candidates. He ordained 27 of them and the work continued. By this time he had built up a huge following in England and by the time he died at the age of 88 he had over 300 Methodist preachers and more than half a million members of his societies.

Throughout his life John and his brother Charles regarded themselves as members of the Anglican Church, though Charles deplored the independent ordination of preachers in America. Charles's major contribution to the Anglican Church and to the Methodist Societies was his astonishing production of 5,500 stirring hymns. These included the popular hymns sung so often in churches today, 'Hark, the Herald Angels Sing, Glory to the New-born King', 'Soldiers of Christ Arise and Put Your Armour On' and 'Love Divine, All Love Excelling', which is a favourite today at wedding services. John and Charles Wesley's contribution to Christianity in England and elsewhere has been immensely important especially in the way Methodists have contributed to charity and to the social services.

Michael Faraday (1791–1867)

Faraday was a child of the eighteenth century. His achievements and inventions in the fields of electricity and electrolysis, however, properly belong to the nineteenth century. His life is described here because, as a Christian and scientist, he illustrates how the faith and physics of men like spiritual achievers such as Descartes and Newton enabled their successors to create the essential foundations of modern industries. He was born in Surrey in England and left his primary school at the age of 14 after being apprenticed to a bookbinder. This was not much of a start for the scientific pioneer that he became and whose portrait once appeared on British £20 notes and the bicentenary of whose birth was commemorated by the Royal Mail in a special postage stamp.

The key to Michel's motivation in his life was his Christian faith and his desire to serve God according to the talents he had been given. He was a devout member of a small and little-known Christian sect, the Sandemanian Church. This demanded total faith and total commitment and Faraday, like all its members, organised his life through a literal interpretation of the Bible.

Even as an apprentice bookbinder Faraday interested himself in the developments in physics and chemistry that were then going on in the scientific world. He went to every public lecture on these subjects that he could. After attending some lectures by the famous chemist Humphrey Davy, he sent him a copy of the notes he had made on the series. These so impressed Davy that he appointed Faraday to be an assistant in his laboratory at the Royal Institution in London. Faraday was then 21 years old.

His initial scientific work was directed towards solving chemical problems. He succeeded in liquefying chlorine and other gases and isolated benzene. In 1825 he was made a director of the laboratory. He also developed further the experiments in electrolysis begun by Davy. In 1834 this enabled him to produce what are now known as Faraday's Laws of Electrolysis. He was led towards this research and into that of electricity by his belief that electricity is one of the many manifestations of the unified forces of nature and therefore of God's creative activity.

In pursuing this line of research Faraday came to believe that since an electric current could cause a magnetic field, a magnetic field should be able to produce an electric current. His research in this field enabled him in 1831 to demonstrate how what he termed the principle of induction produced an electric current. This made it possible for him to design a dynamo and generator to produce electricity by mechanical means.

This was only the start of Faraday's inventive achievement. In spite of being disbelieved by European physicists, Faraday was able to demonstrate the entire phenomenon of electromagnetism. He wrote up his work on this and many other matters in the three volumes of *Experimental Researches in Electricity* between 1839 and 1855. Amongst his achievements was the elucidation of molecular structure which has given important information about galactic magnetic fields. He also showed that the electrical phenomena exhibited by lightning, electric eels and voltaic cells are all related.

Faraday's scientific world-view was derived from the message of the Bible. He believed in the unity of forces in nature and this guided all his research and experiments since he saw that this linked up with his belief in the unity of God.

His religious understanding showed him that the universe is sustained by the power of God and that its behaviour is orderly and dependable, because God is faithful. Therefore for Faraday, just as there are moral laws to govern our lives before God and fellow men, so also in creation there are physical and chemical laws which govern the material world.

Faraday ceased his research work in 1855, but he continued to lecture. In 1861 he published six of his lectures to children in what has become a classic of science literature, *The Chemical History of a Candle*. Faraday was a very humble man. In his youth he used to carry *The Improvement of the Mind* by Isaac Watts in his pocket; besides its wise council on self-help, this urged readers to be watchful over their hearts and minds in case they should deceive themselves by becoming too proud.

Faraday's experience in life taught him the values of this advice. Therefore when high honours were offered him, including election to the Royal Society, he always refused. In his answer refusing the invitation from the Royal Society, he said that if he accepted it, he would '*not answer for the integrity of my intellect for a single year*'. It can therefore be said of him that he was inspired by his faith to seek spiritual truths as a scientist.

THE SPIRIT AT WORK IN THE NINETEENTH CENTURY

It would take many books to record how the work of the Spirit inspired Christian works of scores of men and women in the nineteenth century. They broke new ground by founding Christian institutions for charity, they changed the laws to allay many social wrongs like slavery, the need for prison reform and shorter working hours for children in the mines and women's rights and much else besides. Among these were some Roman Catholics who became saints, as did the village priest Jean-Marie Baptiste Vianney (the Curé d'Ars, see the Calendar for 4 August). He was one of the many priests who helped to restore the Church and faith in France after the attacks during the Enlightenment and the French Revolution.

Because of the lack of space here, I am only going to mention a handful of these Friends of God before looking at the lives of the three most outstanding Christian heroes of the century. First therefore, among the many others that could be mentioned, are the names of the Quaker and prison reformer Elizabeth Fry (1780–1845) and of William Wilberforce (1759–1833). He was the member of the English parliament who fought all his career to abolish slavery and finally achieved his ambition in the last years of his life. To these must be added Anthony Ashley Cooper, 7th Earl of Shaftesbury (1801–85), the English politician and philanthropist who wrote of his life's work that *'By God's blessing my first effort has been for the advancement of human happiness'*. His work for factory reforms, and for improving public health and housing, is well known. He was one of the chief founders of the Young Men's Christian Association and he established free 'Ragged Schools' for destitute children. He was also the leader of the evangelical group within the Church of England.

These three are just a sample of the many in Britain, France, the United States and elsewhere, who helped to change society by their charitable and Christian endeavours. To do justice to them all would require a full book. Instead I am going to concentrate on the lives of the three of those whose influence and works live on most strongly today. These are John Henry Newman, the Anglican clergymen who became a convert to Rome and the greatest Christian theologian of the century; Jean Henri Dunant, the Swiss Calvinist who founded the International Red Cross; and finally William Booth, the English Methodist minister who founded the world-wide Salvation Army.

John Henry Newman (1801–1890)

Newman was the son of a minor banker in the City of London. At a very young age he was strongly influenced by the evangelical Protestants of the Clapham Sect, of which William Wilberforce was a leading member. It was through them that he underwent a conversion experience which, as he later described in his autobiography *Apologia Pro Vita Sua*, took place at the age of 15 between 1 and 21 August 1816.

This was the start of a life-long pilgrimage of thought, study and spiritual conviction which was to take him into the Roman Catholic Church. In defence of this spiritual journey he wrote that *'to live is to change'*. Quite early on in his youth Newman began to drift away from the semi-calvinism of the Clapham Sect and towards Lutheranism. It was at this time that he acquired his love of the Athanasian Creed, which he described as the war-cry of Christianity. He then entered Trinity College, Oxford, where Church revivalism was strong. He studied for a degree in Classics, or *Literae Humanores*. He was appreciated in the university as a brilliant student, but he was a poor examinee. In spite of only getting a third-class degree he was elected as a Fellow of Oriel College in 1822. He was ordained into the Church of England in 1824.

At Oriel he became a friend of John Keble, who would gain fame as a poet and hymn-writer and in whose name Keble College was later founded at Oxford. Keble and Newman became the leaders of what became known as the Oxford Movement. This group set out in 1833 to revitalise the Anglican Church through its 'Tracts for the Times'. Before this movement began, Newman became a serious student of Church history. This led him to move away from the ideas of the extreme evangelists. He explained this in his *Apologia* in 1866 in which he described how he had been carried away by the broad philosophy of Clement of Alexandria and Origen. He wrote that: '*Some portions of their teaching came as music to my ears. I understood these passages to mean that the exterior world, physical and historical, was but a manifestation to our senses of realities greater than itself. Nature was a parable; Scripture an allegory; pagan literature, philosophy and mythology, properly understood, were but a preparation for the gospel.*'

As he reviewed the past, he saw that from the first direct divine dispensation granted to the Jews, the process of change was slow. Also he saw that even in his time and as past experience indicated, we could anticipate further and deeper disclosures of truths still to be unveiled. No other passage in his autobiography is more significant in revealing Newman's genius as an 'ideas man' than the one in which he described these thoughts. They were eventually to be the basis of the lesson of a

John Henry Newman, Cardinal~
1801–90

Lead Kindly Light!

'Developing Faith' that he took with him to the Roman Catholic Church and which led to his spiritual domination of the Second Vatican Council in 1959–63.

In 1833 Newman took a long holiday around the Mediterranean while recovering from a severe illness. During this trip and while his ship was becalmed off Sicily, Newman wrote his famous hymn which begins: *'Lead Kindly Light, amid the encircling gloom, lead Thou me on'.* It ends with these words: *'The night is gone; and with the morn angel faces smile, which I have loved long since, and lost awhile'.* The hymn summons up the image of Newman as a lonely pilgrim, facing the elements, but with the light of battle in his eyes. It also suggests the shadow of a struggle, as yet undefined, that was going on deep inside his mind.

The actual start of the Oxford Movement was dated by the Oratorian and Newman scholar Henry Hastings as the day, 22 January 1832, when Newman gave his University sermon as the Vicar of St Mary's church. Newman gave this title to his sermon as 'Personal Influence, the Means of Propagating the Truth'. In it he gave the example of the Apostles to show that *'a few highly endowed men will rescue the world for centuries to come'.* This objective was the inspiration of the movement.

In 1833 the Oxford Movement published the first of a series of 'Tracts for the Times'. It was a challenge to the Anglican Church and was written by Newman, who had already written to a friend that the *'Clergy are dead!'* His Tract No.1 was entitled 'Thoughts on the Ministerial Commission: Respectfully Addressed to the Clergy'.

It was a four-page summons to battle to oppose the 'world' and act on the authority of *'our Apostolic Descent . . . Choose your side! Abstinence is impossible in these troublous times: He that is not with me is against me'.*

The subsequent tracts covered various subjects of debate that were going on in the country and the Church, such as interference with Church property, the shallowness of liberal criticism of *The Book of Common Prayer,* the dictatorial influence of worldly men in politics and other subjects. The tracts brought scores of letters from sympathetic clerics from all over England.

One of the tracts attacked the 'Dissenting Churches' for separating themselves from *'the only Church in this realm which has the right to be quite sure that she has the Lord's Body to give to the people'.* Yet even by December 1833 some conservative clergy already began to scent what they called 'popery' in the tracts and parted company with the movement. They refused to accept Newman's doctrine of the Apostolic Succession and the Real Presence at the Eucharist.

Newman was seeking a *via media* in his preaching. The Oxford High Tory and High Churchman and future Prime Minister, William Ewart Gladstone, wrote at the height of Newman's popularity that *'There has been nothing like his influence in Oxford since Abelard lectured in Paris!'* However Newman did not seek popularity. He went on to preach non-controversially on self-denial and hunger for holiness and on the all-consuming love of God for humankind. His tracts 38 and 41 defined the glory of the English Church as occupying, as the Elizabethan Settlement had intended, a middle way between popery and Puritanism. However he also suggested controversially that its aim should be to undo the great historic drift from Catholicism in a 'Second Reformation'. This led to Newman having difficulties over the 39 Articles, to which all Anglican clergy had to swear. They were to be the Achilles heel of his *via media* and also for him as a non-Catholic.

The confrontation that proved fatal to his membership of the English Church came about with Newman's 'Tract 90' in 1840. Even though he still rejected the Catholic claim for the infallibility of the Roman Church as being only supported by tradition and not by scripture, he attempted in this tract to prove that the 39 Articles were not incompatible with the Roman Church's tenets. This caused a guerilla warfare to break out between High and Low churchmen in Oxford. It was also at this moment when, as Newman described in his *Apologia*, he felt his position in the Church of England was at its height, that he himself began to have his first inner doubts about his place in that Church.

These doubts began as he steadily mastered the subject of the 'teething troubles' of the fifth-century Greek Church concerning the nature of Christ. It is not clear how long this problem worried him, but he was also much affected by another ancient problem. This was the fifth-century schism and judgement on the African Donatist Church. He saw that this Church had, like the English Church, been cut off from the body of the universal Church. This shook his confidence to the core that the Apostolic Succession applied to the English Church and he had increasingly serious doubts. He had therefore reached a point in his pilgrimage of faith beyond which he could not see, though he still believed that both Rome and England were equally Churches and equally defective and that Rome had corrupted the ancient Primitive Church.

The heads of the Oxford colleges asked Newman to cease publishing his tracts. He offered to resign as Vicar of St Mary's. The Hebdominal Board of the University declared that six extracts from 'Tract 90' were inconsistent with the 39 Articles. By this time Newman was almost at the parting of the ways. All he wanted to do before resigning his fellowship of Oriel and going over to Rome, was to finish writing his 'Essay on the Development of Christian Doctrine'. The Essay was essentially conservative, but it eventually taught the Roman Catholic Church a lesson that it never forgot.

Newman left Oxford to a retreat in the monastic sanctuary and church that he had built in nearby Littlemore and on 8 October 1845 he was received into the Catholic Church. The publication of his 'Development' was delayed until 1847, while Newman went to theological school in Rome to study to be a priest. He had broken with his old world and friends. His relationship with Keble ceased in 1846. In 1847, after his ordination as a Catholic priest, he was granted his wish to become an Oratorian and in 1848, with Cardinal Wiseman's help, he and five others established their Oratory in Birmingham.

The essential part of Newman's pilgrimage of faith had now been fulfilled, though three of his most memorable works were still to be written – *A Grammar of Assent, Apologia pro Vita Sua* and his poem *The Dream of Gerontius*. He was also mistrusted by some leading Roman Catholics, notably his fellow convert Cardinal Manning and others in Rome. They still regarded him as a heretic·

He therefore had to overcome much opposition and suffer many disappointments in his work.

Much of Newman's *A Grammar of Assent*, which he began in 1866, was an argument against Victorian doubt, asking the question 'How can religious belief be justified?' In it he argued from basic principles that with regard to the Trinity the believer grasps the definition from the principles that make it up. That is to say, not from the doctrine itself, but from the scriptural facts from which it is derived. He also considered 'probability' to be the very guide of life and is sufficient certitude in helping us make our assent to doctrine. In this Newman was basing his thought on his own life's experience. He also drew attention to that other certitude, that growth in truth is a personal growth through present suffering.

Newman's *Apologia* was written in a few intense weeks in 1864. It was in response to a challenge by The Revd Charles Kingsley that Newman's desertion to the Roman Church *'was unmanly'*. The book explained his spiritual journey, which has already been covered here in earlier paragraphs. The book made Newman a national figure.

In 1877 Newman produced a new version of his 'Essay on Development' which was to make its mark in the Roman Church over the next 80 years. In 1879, encouraged by an appeal from the Duke of Norfolk, the senior Roman Catholic in England, and eventually supported by Cardinal Manning, Pope Leo XIII made Newman a Cardinal. Manning paid this tribute to him: *'the singular and unequalled services rendered by Dr Newman to the Catholic faith . . . His submission to the Church alone has done much to awaken the mind*

of Englishmen to the Catholic religion . . . The veneration of his powers, his learning and life of singular piety and integrity is almost as deeply felt by the non-Catholic population of this country as by members of the Catholic Church.' His elevation was acclaimed throughout the country.

Newman's third great work after his conversion to Rome was his poem *The Dream of Gerontius*. He wrote this in memory of Father John Gordon, the first of his Birmingham Oratorians to die. It was written and published in 1865. It contains two hymns which are still popular today and were set to music like the rest of the poem by Sir Edward Elgar as an Oratorio: 'Firmly I believe and Truly . . . ' and 'Praise to the Holiest in the Height'. The subject of the poem is a soul's journey to heaven and ends with the triumphant words: *'Go, in the name of Angels and Archangels; in the name of Thrones and Dominations; in the name of Princedoms and Powers; and in the names of Cherabin and Seraphin; go forth'.* When sung by a full choir and accompanied by a full orchestra in a candlelit cathedral, the oratorio is sublime. It is also an enduring obituary to Newman himself, faithful witness and Friend of God, who died on 11 August 1890 and was beatified in 1990. He was one of the most passionate and profound of religious pilgrims.

Jean Henri Dunant (1828–1910)

The picture on the next page shows Jean Henri Dunant starting his private rescue operation for the 40,000 unattended wounded that he discovered on the battlefield of Solferino in Lombardy. The battle had been fought on 24 June 1859, two days before Jean had arrived from Algiers after completing some loan arrangements for his Geneva-based

Jean Henri Dunant on the battlefield of Solferino in 1859

family bank. He was actually on his way to meet the French Emperor Napoleon III to explain his ideas for France's North African colonies.

He was still dressed in his white tropical suit when he arrived at the battlefield. The French and Savoy armies, aided by a contingent of Garibaldi's volunteers, had defeated the Austrians in a bloody battle, but almost nothing had been done for the 40,000 wounded soldiers. There were only a few French canteen girls and a few score of army doctors. Thousands of French, Italian and Austrian wounded were lying down in the open fields, in the shelter of ruined churches and barns, or else crawling about seeking help. They had had no water, food or medical attention.

Jean-Henri immediately assembled convoys of wagons driven by local people from nearby Castiglione. These took water, soup, linen bandages, clothing, food and tobacco to the wounded on the battlefield. He paid for this through his family bank. He also obtained the approval of the French army commander Marshal Macmahon to allow captured Austrian doctors and medical orderlies to tend the wounded of both sides.

Jean Henri's rescue work saved the lives of thousands of wounded men and he went through the most exhausting and terrible experience of his life. As he made his way back home through Italy, he was asked to stay and rest in many Italian family castles and villas. In all these places he told the story of Solferino and of the appalling lack of doctors, nurses and medical facilities. This had one remarkable effect on his hostesses and women listeners. They were unanimous in their suggestions that a voluntary nursing organisation should be set up immediately in every

city and be ready to go into action in case of war. Jean Henri seized upon their idea and added to it his own plan for making doctors and medical staff neutral on a field of battle. He set to work at once to find a means of implementing these humanitarian plans in every country, using all his connections with European royalty and bankers.

Jean Henri was an idealist and humanitarian. He was so inspired by his Christian beliefs that he applied its principles to all his activities. As a young man he was one of the founders of the World's Young Men's Christian Association, the YMCA, whose hostels are so well known today in many countries. In his business affairs in the French North African colonies he had devoted himself to devising grand schemes for development to end the privation of the native inhabitants. The same humanitarian urge drove him to undertake the mighty task of awakening Europe to the needs of those wounded in battle and also for prisoners of war. He began his campaign in 1862 by publishing his book on the battle, *Souvenirs de Solferino*. This proposed the establishment of societies in peacetime to prepare for the relief of the wounded in any conflict. It also made a strong case for the adoption of a Convention to protect wounded soldiers and medical staff on a field of battle.

These ideas were developed further and were ably lobbied by Dunant in Paris, Turin, Brussels, Berlin and Geneva and attracted widespread support. In February 1863 a Swiss charitable association, the Geneva Society for Public Welfare, set up a five-member commission to consider Dunant's ideas. This commission included Dunant. By the end of the month they had formed 'The International Committee for the Relief of Wounded in Time of War'. This later, at Dunant's suggestion, became the 'The International Committee of the Red Cross'. The Swiss emblem of a red cross on a white background was also adopted as its emblem. The creation of national voluntary Red Cross Societies was agreed by 16 European states in 1864. At the same time they agreed a modern international humanitarian law to govern the whole system under a Geneva Convention. Britain joined the Red Cross in 1867.

In the same year a disastrous business crisis ruined Dunant. The loans he had made in Algeria for his bank were supposed to have been secured against the deeds of large freehold properties, but when the crisis struck the country, it was found that the relevant documents, unknown to Dunant, were not in order. Dunant's substantial loan was therefore uncovered. In those days before companies could have limited liability, all debts had to be paid by the directors. Dunant was made bankrupt and was deprived of his Geneva citizenship. He was penniless and had to be supported by friends, sometimes in Paris and eventually in a hotel garret in Basle.

For anyone else this would have been the end of their career, but Dunant never wavered in his efforts, in spite of the ignominy that overshadowed him, to achieve his other great humanitarian ambition. This was that of achieving an International Convention to give rights to prisoners of war. While working for this cause he maintained a correspondence with his royal supporters, especially the Queen of the Belgians, the Queen of Prussia, the Saxon royal family and also the Tsar of Russia. The popular author and publicist Charles Dickens also took up the cause to raise public support through his writings. So did a Swiss lawyer friend in Geneva. The task took Jean Henri many years, but

gradually his message got across. It became clear that something had to be done for prisoners of war, who had absolutely no human rights, either for pay, for aid, for correspondence home or for anything else. They just rotted in prison camps, or were forced to do road-work.

All attempts at reaching an international agreement failed until a young Swiss journalist discovered Dunant's humble retreat. He published an account of his lifetime of dedicated work to the Red Cross and the prisoners of war. The article about him and the need for an international agreement was given world-wide publicity. Dunant was immediately given a number of annuities to help him financially. Finally in 1901 he was awarded the first Nobel Peace Prize. At last in 1907 the Hague Convention on the Treatment of Prisoners of War was signed. Everyone knew who was responsible for it: Jean Henri Dunant. He had been through the 'Valley of Despond' and suffered like many of the saints before winning through to his goal. It is through him that the International Red Cross is today one of the two largest Christian charities, the other one being the Salvation Army, whose origins will be described next.

Those countries which signed the Convention guaranteed to pay prisoners of war and to permit them to send and receive letters from home. They were also allowed parcels of clothing and food and certain approved living conditions and medical care. Rights of repatriation were granted to non-combatants like padres and doctors and the totally disabled. Regular visits from representatives of the overseeing power, Switzerland, were also insisted upon. These representatives had considerable powers, as some of my friends who were British prisoners of war in Germany discovered even as the German armies were being driven back to Berlin in 1945. Few men have achieved more good than Dunant, a true Friend of God.

William Booth (1829–1912)

Booth began life in Nottingham as an apprentice to a pawnbroker. This gave him a first-hand experience of poverty and the depths to which many unfortunates were driven. This led to his experiencing a powerful religious conversion in a Wesleyan chapel. In 1846, inspired by the preaching of the American evangelist James Caughey who was touring England, Booth became a Methodist 'local preacher' at the age of 18.

In 1848 Booth moved to London and was employed as a pawnbroker in Walworth. His religious zeal was as strong as ever. In his spare time he began holding open-air evangelical meetings. He married his wife Catherine Mumford in 1855, who was also a Methodist. His own Methodist minister objected to his open-air meetings. Booth therefore joined the Methodist New Connection and was ordained as a minister in 1858. He then conducted evangelical campaigns in various parts of the country, developing the methods that he would later employ to great effect in his Salvation Army. He also had a profound spiritual experience when he saw a vision of Jesus Christ and knew instinctively that he was called to do special work for God.

In spite of his success as a regular minister William resigned in 1861, though he continued his open-air preaching. In 1865 he was invited to lead open-air and tented meetings in the impoverished East End of London. He then formed The Whitechapel Christian Mission to enable him to reach the unchurched masses in the district, most of whom came from families dependent on ill-paid casual labour in the docks. William Booth was an enthusiast for stirring tunes and hymns and used these to attract the crowds before he preached to them.

In 1878 he changed the style of the Whitechapel mission, renaming it 'The Salvation Army'. The 'Army' was given a military uniform, bands led by drums and tambourines, flags and military ranks. William Booth became the first 'General' of the Army. Units of the Army were established in many industrial cities and the Army became a truly religious organisation with trained preachers, male and female. Besides preaching the gospel, the Salvation Army differed from all other Churches except the Quakers, since it ignored the sacraments and refused to have ordained ministers.

William's wife Catherine was the chief influence in the Army's avoiding giving the sacrament of Holy Communion because of her own aversion to wine or alcohol of any kind. This aversion arose from the horrific scenes of drunkenness from cheap drink she had witnessed in the East End of London's public houses, which led to widespread wife-beating, abuse of children and general moral and physical depravity.

Over the next ten years the work of the Army spread and England was stirred by its success. Evangelising alone however was not to become its sole activity. William and Catherine Booth's experience in the slums and amongst the down-and-outs of the East End compelled them to answer another great call. They established their first rescue homes for abused women and prostitutes and established dormitories for men who otherwise slept rough and never washed. Salvationists, even today, often joke that for these unwashed rejects of society *'every bath is a baptism'*.

This charitable work required substantial sums of money. This was raised from the Booth's rich supporters, but a great deal of money was also collected in the streets by the roving Army bands. These bands raised a serious problem, because one of the chief aims of the preachers, was to campaign against the widespread drunkenness in the poorest parts of the cities. This made them extremely unpopular with the publicans and brewers, because the 'Salvationists' preached outside their public houses. The publicans hired teams of roughs to assault the Salvation bands and drive them away. They then summoned the police to charge the Army band for causing a public disturbance, which they themselves had caused.

In 1882 a total of 669 Salvationists, including 250 women, were brutally assaulted by the hired henchmen of the publicans. The publicans used then to summon the police, but it was the Salvationists, not the hired ruffians, who were charged in court with disturbing the peace. The local magistrates were mostly brewers or themselves owners of public houses and so they had no difficulty in finding the battered bandsmen and Salvationist girls guilty. Thus in 1884 over 600 Salvationists were sent to prison.

In the same year saboteurs burned down 56 Salvation Army homes for the needy. The injustices and this wanton destruction were so blatant that the newspapers campaigned against this abuse of the law. Like the blood of the martyrs 18 centuries before, which brought support for the Church, so did this publicity win widespread acclaim for the Salvation Army and support for their work.

Before then, in 1879, William Booth had begun to spread his Army's activities in the USA. He had also taken it to Australia in 1880 and sent his daughter Catherine in 1881 to introduce the Army to France. She was soon popular there and became known as 'La Maréchale'. In 1890 the Army was established in most European countries and in Canada, India, South Africa and South America. In each country the Salvationists carried on the work of looking after the homeless, the deprived, the unchurched and those who were so far depraved that no other charity could cope with their needs. The degree to which the Army was appreciated and trusted abroad can be judged from the fact that in Berlin during World War II even the Nazis allowed the Salvationists to continue to operate their vans with soup and food for those who had been bombed out of their homes in the RAF raids.

William Booth was active in writing pamphlets and books to publicise the need to support his Army's efforts. The most effective of these books was his *In Darkest England, and the Way Out* (1890). He was helped in writing this by WT Stead, the greatest of Victorian journalists. The book contained well-thought out proposals for relieving pauperism and attacking vice. It also proposed legal aid for the poor, the system through which the Exchequer now provides all legal support for those who would otherwise not be able to seek justice. In addition the book also recommended the establishment of rescue homes for women and girls in moral danger, homes for released prisoners and aid for alcoholics. There was enormous public support for these proposals and they were gradually put into effect by new laws and many new charities.Catherine Booth, William's wife and greatest supporter and most helpful critic, died in 1890. She had become an ardent Methodist and was an outstanding preacher for the Army. She played an

A Salvation Army band being attacked in the East End in 1882

important part in the campaign that led to the passing of the Criminal Law Ammendment Act in 1885. This was designed to protect young girls from abuse. She had studied the scriptures deeply and they were the basis for all her views and activities and her conviction that the sacraments were not necessary for salvation.

After Catherine's death William Booth travelled widely abroad and became an international as well as a national figure. He even opened a session of the United States' Senate with prayer. King Edward VII invited him to his coronation, but William refused to accept any of the high honours that were pressed upon him. He continued to work and preach until the end of his life, in spite of increasing blindness. His funeral procession in 1912 attracted vast crowds as it wound through the City and East End of London, where he had done so much good.

Today the Salvation Army numbers more than one million members world-wide and continues to carry on the same work that William and Catherine Booth began. A century after William began his work, the saintly Mother Teresa of Calcutta (1910–97) emulated him by working among the poorest and most neglected rejects of Indian society.

Mother Teresa also founded an order of nuns to carry on this work in other countries and established 80 nunneries before she died. Teresa was canonised by the late Pope John-Paul II on 20 October 2003. No such honour is planned for William Booth, but there is still room for his statue to be erected in Trafalgar Square on the one empty plinth beside those that have statues of our other nineteenth-century military heroes.

THE SPIRIT AT WORK IN THE TWENTIETH CENTURY

Introduction

The twentieth century was dominated by the two World Wars and their aftermath. More people were killed in battle or for their faith or race or politics than the total number of deaths in all previous conflicts. It was a century in which there were unprecedented advances in every field of human activity and thought. It was also a time of revolutionary political change.

I will therefore begin by giving brief details of the lives of ten representative twentieth-century martyrs whose statues were erected above the entrance to Westminster Abbey in 1998. They honour heroes and heroines of five different Christian denominations who gave their lives for the faith. In this way they remind us of the one great spiritual achievement of all Christian Churches in that century, the combined effort initiated by Pope John XXIII in 1961 to foster the ecumenical movement aimed at bringing all Christian denominations closer together. The statues are carved in white Portland stone, but in the illustration overleaf they are portrayed in colour and as they might have appeared in their lifetimes:

St Maximilian Kolbe (1894–1941): This Polish Franciscan priest and theologian gave his life voluntarily in the place of another prisoner and was starved to death in a punishment cell in Auschwitz concentration camp. He was canonised in 1981 by Pope John Paul II.

Manche Masemola (1903–28): Born in the Transvaal, she defied her parents to become a Christian and joined the Anglican Community of the Resurrection. Her parents murdered her for refusing to change her faith back to Islam. Her mother was baptised in 1969.

Archbishop Janani Luwum (died 1976): He was a schoolteacher who converted to the charismatic christianity of the East African Revival in 1948. His Anglican Church worked closely with the Roman Catholics and Muslims in Uganda to try and mitigate the results of the tyrannical policies of the usurper President Colonel Idi Amin. On 12 February 1976 Archbishop Luwum delivered a protest to Amin against his acts of violence. He was summoned with his bishops to Kampala. His bishops were told to leave. As they left, Archbishop Luwum said: *'They are going to kill me, but I am not afraid'*. He was never seen again.

Princess St Elizabeth of Russia (1864–1917): A German princess who married a son of Tsar Alexander II. Her husband was assassinated in 1905. She then devoted her life as a nun to charity and the care of women, but was murdered by the Bolsheviks in 1917. The Russian Orthodox Church canonised her after the collapse of the Soviet Union.

Martin Luther King (1929–1968): A Baptist minister in Georgia, USA. For many years he led a non-violent campaign for the Civil Rights movement to abolish the segregation laws against coloured people. He was imprisoned but succeeded in having the laws abolished. In 1967 he was awarded the Nobel peace prize. He knew the dangers that he ran and said: *'If physical death is the price I must pay to free my brothers and sisters from permanent death of the spirit, then nothing can be more redemptive'*. He was assassinated in Memphis on 4 April 1968.

Archbishop Oscar Romero (1917–80): He was born in San Salvador and was made Archbishop in 1977. At that time the right-wing government oppressed the peasants ruthlessly. Romero identified himself with the peasants and in 1979 he delivered in person a dossier to the Vatican

Ten Twentieth-century Martyrs

filled with evidence of the government's murders and injustices. He spoke in public against the cruelty of the regime and, knowing the risks, said: *'I must tell you as a Christian, I do not believe in death without resurrection. If I am killed I shall rise again in the Salvadorean people.'* He was shot dead by government agents on 24 March 1980 as he celebrated mass. Although he died a martyr, his cause for sainthood has not progressed far in Rome due to the Church's dislike of the Liberation Theology and its Marxist tendencies among the peasants in Latin America. Nevertheless the people of San Salvador honour him as a saint, hero and martyr for justice.

Dietrich Bonhoeffer (1906–45): Lutheran minister and theologian. For him *'the Church is the Church only when it exists for others'*. In 1933 the Nazis closed his by then illegal seminary called the Confessing Church. He saw that Adolf Hitler's National Socialism was a counter-religion and a danger to Christianity. Since he believed that true discipleship demanded political resistance against a criminal state, he began to work with groups that were committed to overthrowing Hitler. He was arrested in 1943 and was hanged by the Gestapo on 29 April 1945. As he was led out to his death he told his fellow prisoners: *'This is the end, but for me the beginning of life'*.

Esther John (1929–60): She was born into a Muslim family in India and went to a Christian school and became converted. She refused her parents' demand to marry a Muslim. She changed her name to Esther John and worked in an orphanage. Later she worked as an evangelist for American presbyterian missionaries in the Punjab. For this she was brutally murdered in bed in Chichawatni. A chapel was built there as a memorial to her. Her mother was baptised as a Christian in 1963.

Lucian Tapiedi (1921–42): The son of a sorcerer in Papua, Tapiedi was educated at Christian mission schools. He became a teacher and an evangelist. He remained at his post during the Japanese invasion in 1942 and was speared to death for hiding some European missionaries whom the Japanese wanted to behead.

Wang Zhiming (1903–73): Born in Yunnan in China and educated at a mission school where he later taught. Under communist rule he remained loyal to the state, but refused to cooperate with the Red Guards during the Cultural Revolution of Mao Tse Tung. He and his wife were arrested in 1969. In 1973 he was executed before a crowd of 10,000 people.

In 1980, when the policy to destroy religion was seen to have failed, his wife and two remaining sons were released from prison and Wang was rehabilitated posthumously by Communist Party officials. The number of Christians in Yunnan has increased tenfold to 30,000 since the 1960s and Wang is remembered with reverence.

The Spirit at work in two great twentieth-century popes

If the poet Dante Alighieri were writing his *Divine Comedy* today, I am sure that he would reserve two more seats in the Ninth Heaven for Pope John XXIII and Pope John Paul II alongside the one he described as awaiting the soul of Prince Henry of Luxemburg. Like Prince Henry, who said on his election as Holy Roman Emperor that his duty lay *'not to any single nation but to his Brother Man'*, these two popes have fulfilled Dante's finest ideals as moral and spiritual leaders. Pope John XXIII, by the resolutions of his Second Vatican Council, brought the Roman Catholic Church up to date and in a better state to face the modern world. Pope John Paul II (who died in 2005), by his spiritual and practical support for the opponents of Communist rule in Eastern Europe, helped to bring about the extinction of the tyrannical and atheist forms of government that had dominated that region and threatened the world for over 70 years. Between them these two great spiritual and yet conservative leaders changed the course of European history and gave the world new hope, as the following texts explain.

Pope John XXIII's *Aggiornamento* brings the Roman Catholic Church up to date

Pope John XXIII (1881–1963), was Patriarch of Venice when, at the age of 77, he was elected to succeed Pope Pius XII in October 1958. In view of his age he was regarded at first as a genial and conservative stop-gap pope. Within three months, on 25 January 1959, he shook the whole Roman Catholic Church by announcing that a Second Vatican Council would open in St Peter's in October 1962 and that its purpose was to produce an *aggiornamento* or 'bringing up to date' to modernise the Church and to work for the reunion of Christians. This announcement was entirely Pope John's idea. The Curia in Rome received it with hesitation and only got the preparations for the council under way rather slowly.

Pope John forged on ahead alone, determined to break with the exclusive and anti-Protestant model of the Church that had been inherited from the decisions of the Council of Trent (1545–63) 400 years before. He disavowed the anti-semitisim of that Council and

worked for rapprochements with the Protestant and Orthodox Churches. He appointed the leading modern theologian, the Swiss priest Hans Kung, as the official theologian to the Council. He made provision for greater freedom of administration in each of the Catholic Provinces. He backed up his own plans for the Roman Catholic Church by commissioning Hans Kung to publish a book, *The Council and Reform*. This summed up the ideas which the Pope wanted to be discussed in the forthcoming debates in the Council and was distributed widely.

In order to express his thoughts on what he hoped would be achieved in the Council Pope John issued two encylicals, *Mater et Magistra* in 1961 and *Pacem in Terris* in 1963. In these he stressed the rights of conscience and freedom of worship and emphasised the need for the Roman Catholic Church to recognise the importance of women in public affairs. In this way he transformed the image of papal authority even in Protestant eyes and to the despair of the conservatives in the Curia. He enlarged the acceptable frontiers of Roman Catholic theologians and established a public dialogue between Roman Catholics and other Churches, which he hoped would revolutionise the old attitude of the Church to other Christian denominations and to other faiths. He then went even further by announcing that *'the seed of the Spirit can be seen in all the world's great faiths today'*. This marked a complete U-turn from the doctrines that had lasted since the days of the Crusades and reminded the Roman Catholic Church at last, after 15 centuries, of the announcement by St Basil of Caesarea that *'There is no culture or religion that has not received and does not express a Visitation of the Word'*. If only the Roman Catholic and the Reformed

Churches had not failed to study the life of this great saint, how much unhappiness and how many wars might have been avoided!

In these ways Pope John, far from being a stop-gap pope, transformed the relationship between Rome and all other Churches and marked the launching of a long-term ecumenical debate between them in a search for unity. Pope John only lived long enough to preside over the first session of the Second Vatican Council. His inspired plan to modernise the Church was so firmly established with the great majority of the 2,100 delegates in St Peter's, that the pedestrian documents prepared by the Curia were rejected. They were then rewritten according to Pope John's ideals and were agreed in the three sessions that followed under the guidance of his successor, Pope Paul VI. The pace of change has been slowed down by the more conservative approach of the Curia and Pope Paul VI and Pope John Paul II, but the Roman Catholic Church is now well-placed to face the twenty-first century.

Finally, one more of Pope John's statements in his encyclicals needs to be recorded here: *'In this age which boasts of its atomic power, it no longer makes sense to maintain that war is in fact an instrument with which to repair the violation of justice'*. With this statement he introduced another aspect to the age-old question of what is a Just War. Pope John XXIII was beatified in 1998.

Pope John Paul II makes history

The first thing that Pope John-Paul II did after his election, was to pay a state visit to his native land of Poland in June 1979. In his first meeting with the Communist leaders and also in his first broadcast sermon to the Polish people, he demanded respect for human rights as well as for Catholic values. Nothing like this had been said in public in Poland by such a charismatic figure since the end of World War II. His sermon and pictures of the gigantic crowds of Poles listening to it in the streets were broadcast world-wide. During his visit Pope John Paul met the workers in the Nowa Huta district where he had been made to labour in the quarries during the war. From there he thundered out another message, that workers must not be abused and treated merely as a means of production.

A year later, when the Polish economy was in ruins, a strike was called at the Lenin Shipyards in Gdansk by the labour leader Lech Walensa. Pope John Paul watched the scene of the strike on his television set. What he saw made him immediately send his secretary, Monsignor Stanislaw Dziwisz, to Poland on what was described as a rest cure. In reality he was to be the Pope's eyes and ears, since the pontiff was convinced that great events were about to take place. Photographs of the Pope and the famous Black Madonna of Czestochowa were put up on the gates of the shipyard. The workers there gathered in front of them on their knees to pray as the strike spread. Meanwhile Pope John Paul kept silent until the strike movement began to paralyse the country in August. Then, as if he had met them by chance, the Pope said two brief prayers to a group of Polish pilgrims in St Peter's Square. He then said to them: *'These two prayers show that all of us here in Rome are united with our compatriots in Poland, with the Church in particular, whose problems are so close to our heart'*.

With these words he publicly blessed the strike. He then sent a letter to the Roman Catholic Primate of Poland saying: *'I pray with my heart that the Polish Episcopate may again help the people in their difficult struggle for daily bread and social justice and for the protection of their inalienable rights to life and development'.* The letter was broadcast throughout Poland. That night the Polish government gave way and, after discussions with the Workers' Committee, the first independent union behind the Iron Curtain, 'Solidarity', was formed and Lech Walensa signed the resulting agreement with a souvenir pen decorated with a picture of the Pope. He then went to visit the Pope in Rome in May, where the Pontiff held a private mass for him and all his Solidarity delegates.

In January 1981 Ronald Reagan took office as President of the USA. His Polish-born national security adviser, Zbigniew Brezinski, showed the Pope satellite photos of the tents and equipment the Russians were assembling along the Polish border, probably ready for an invasion. Shortly afterwards the Russians backed off. Reagan then sent aid to Solidarity and gave the Vatican information from satellites in space and US intelligence agents.

In March 1981 the President was shot and severely wounded by a gunman and only survived by a miracle. Six weeks later on 13 May the Pope was shot in St Peter's Square by a Turk who was a Bulgarian agent. No vital organ was hit, but John-Paul II needed a five-hour operation to remove the bullet. A defecting Bulgarian attaché from the Bulgarian embassy in Paris told the French that the plot to kill the Pope had been instigated by the Kremlin. More US satellite photos were then given to the Pope. These showed the advance of yet more military vehicles to the Polish border

In October the USSR forced the Polish Government to appoint the communist General Jarulzelski to rule Poland and to control the increasingly rebellious workers' unions. What they feared most was the possible effect of Solidarity's first national congress, when it intended to call upon the other European workers to set up independent trade unions. General Jaruzelski also feared that the USSR would actually invade, so he declared a state of martial law and arrested hundreds of suspected dissidents.

At the news of these events Pope John Paul II decided on a strategy to ensure that the Solidarity movement should be preserved, even if it had to go underground. The first step would be to make a dramatic return visit to his homeland. The announcement of the planned visit made President Reagan enter the fray by imposing economic and diplomatic sanctions against the USSR and the Communist government in Poland. Six months later Reagan went to meet the Pope in Rome. Between them, the Pope and the President agreed a strategy of moral pressure to bring about the collapse of the Soviet empire. Reagan announced that he would not withdraw his sanctions until martial law ceased in Poland, political prisoners were released and the dialogue between the government, the Church and Solidarity was resumed.

Then in June 1983 the Pope returned once more to Poland. He went immediately to interview a very nervous Jarulzelski, who implored him to restrain at least the more extreme elements in Solidarity. The Pope replied that *'I am anxious to reach a certain state of normality as soon as possible; then Poland will be regarded differently by other countries'.* By this he meant the ending of martial law. He then paid a visit to Lech Walensa, whose Solidarity movement was no longer just an outlawed trade union, but had become a symbol of resistance to communism throughout Poland.

After a further 90-minute talk with Jarulzelski, in which he was outspoken and persuasive, the Pope returned to Rome. Shortly afterwards martial law was lifted. Three years later in 1986, the regime in Poland announced a broad amnesty and released 225 political prisoners. In 1990 democracy was restored and Lech Walensa was elected President of Poland.

Two Visions of the Virgin Mary

There have been several accounts of visions of the Virgin Mary in the twentieth century. The first of these to be accepted as miraculous by the Roman Catholic Church was the Virgin's appearance at Fatima in Portugal in 1917. Three very young peasant children saw her when they were walking in the countryside. They gave their parents such a convincing account of this that shortly afterwards a vast crowd gathered at the scene. The Virgin Mary then appeared again. After examining many of these witnesses the Vatican was convinced that a miracle had occurred. It also accepted the children's story that they had been given three secret messages by the Virgin. Two messages, which were revealed later, were rather banal, typical of what one might expect to be given to young children, but the last message prophesied the wounding or murder of a pope or bishop dressed in white. Two of these children died after World War II. The last one to survive as an elderly nun was visited by Pope John Paul II, when he went to Fatima to beatify the two children who had died. The Pope had been convinced that he himself was the white-clad figure whose attempted murder had been prophesied at Fatima and that the Virgin herself had saved his life.

There is no rational or watertight explanation for the Fatima appearances. Nor is there one for the repeated appearances of the Virgin Mary to six young children and teenagers during the summer of 1981 in the rocky mountain behind the village of Medjugorje in Croatia. The children saw them daily, usually in the evening, and continued to do so for several years. They questioned the Virgin and received similar messages as the ones at Fatima about the need to seek peace between neighbours, a much-needed message in the Balkans. The children went into ecstasies when the virgin was with them. These so convinced the local people and their Franciscan clergy that they have now attracted many pilgrims to the mountain to listen to mass in the open. One of our friends who went there said that her visit was an unforgettable experience for both her and her sister. The Roman Catholic Church has not yet accepted the visions as genuine. Perhaps the acceptance of healings and of the three original witnesses, who still claim to experience the Virgin at Medjugorje, will eventually convince the authorities in Rome of their genuineness.

Meanwhile more new causes for beatifications and canonisation are being examined in Rome to add to the 1,000 or more new saints whom Pope John Paul II canonised in his 25-year reign, or 40 new saints a year. The best-known of these is **St Josemaria Escriva (1919–94)**, the founder of the strict order of Opus Dei, through which he established scores of university colleges and schools in Spain and in other Spanish-speaking countries. This order now has 80,000 members, all from rich families or business people, whose priests compel them to give a substantial part of their income to the Order. It undoubtedly did much good for the faith in Spain after the Civil War, during which Escriva himself worked bravely and in secret against the communist government in Madrid. He was however a determined opponent of all Protestant churches.

Three other new saints canonised since 1990 must also be mentioned. One is the first Australian saint, the popular evangeliser **St Mary Mackillop**, a Sister of the Cross who was born in Melbourne in 1842. Another is 'Poland's Becket', the martyr **Father Jeray Pupielusko**, the champion of Solidarity, the banned trade union movement, whose spirit he kept alive until the communist government's thugs murdered him in 1984. Finally Pope John Paul beatified the gypsy trader known as '**El Pele**', who was shot in 1936 by General Franco's anti-clerical militia. Besides these we can expect one day that the cause of Brother Roger, the German-Swiss who founded the Ecumenical community at Taize in Burgundy just before World War II, will be recognised for the way Brother John still attracts thousands of pilgrims annually to Taize. One of these pilgrimages by over 1,000 young people was led there by Archbishop Dr George Carey in 1992.

All these were or are faithful witnesses to the faith, yet no non-Roman Catholic hero or heroine who has devoted his or her life to advancing the Kingdom of God on Earth has ever been considered for the Pope's attention or recognition. Until this situation is rectified in some acceptable way in which Catholics and Protestants both honour each other's heroes and heroines, the ecumenical movement to bring all the Churches closer together will be bogged down by out-of-date Vatican prejudices. Though I regret to say this, it must be said.

Jesus Christ appears to two future bishops in 1934 and 1936

Some people tend to think that events such as the appearances to individuals of the Virgin Mary or of Christ only happen in Bible stories, as when St Paul was converted before the gates of Damascus. But here are two records of Christ appearing in the twentieth century, which are both convincing and quite inexplicable.

The account of the first vision was given in the obituary in *The Daily Telegraph* on 6 August 2003 for Metropolitan Anthony of Sourozh (1914–2003). Anthony was the senior Russian Orthodox archbishop in Western Europe and the best-known Russian Orthodox priest in Britain. He was born as Andre Bloom in Lausanne, where his father was a Russian diplomat. The family escaped from the Russian revolution and settled in Paris. As a student Andre was an unbeliever, but he was persuaded in 1934 to attend a lecture by an Orthodox priest. The claims that the priest made so affronted him, that he decided to check them by reading the Gospel of St Mark.

As the obituary described it, '*It was while reading this that he suddenly became aware of someone standing opposite him, and realised that this was Christ. The resulting certainty never left him.*'

Andre had begun to study medicine at the Sorbonne and then served as a medical orderly in the French Army in 1939, before joining the Resistance. He secretly became a monk in 1943, and made his vows in the Orthodox Church as Anthony of Sourozh. He was ordained priest in 1948 and became a vicar in 1953 of a Russian Orthodox church in London. Anthony became a popular preacher and BBC broadcaster to Russia and wrote several popular books on religion, including the bestseller *Living Prayer*, which was translated into ten languages. In a series of broadcast discussions with the atheist Margharita Laski he said that *'I know that God exists, and I am puzzled to know how you can manage not to know'*. After all, he had seen him!

The second future bishop to tell how he became a Christian after seeing a vision of Jesus Christ, was The Right Reverend Hugh Montefiore, who won wide respect as Bishop of Birmingham and who died in 2005. In his autobiography *Oh God, What Next?* he tells how he, a Jewish boy, had a vision of Jesus at Rugby School in 1936. He gave me permission to quote his account of this, after I had explained that I would like to include it in this book: *'I was enjoying an hour or so of adolescent melancholy in my study, when I suddenly became aware of a figure in white, whom I clearly saw in my mind's eye. I use this expression because I am pretty sure that a photograph would have shown nothing special in it. I heard the words "Follow me". Instinctively I knew this was Jesus – heaven knows how, I knew nothing about him. Put like that it sounds bare; in fact it was an indescribably rich event that filled me afterwards with overpowering joy. I could do no other than follow his instructions'.*

Hugh Montefiore had himself baptised as a Christian in the school chapel. World War II broke out three years later and he served as an officer in the Royal Artillery at the siege of Kohima in Assam in March 1944. After the war Hugh Montefiore was ordained as a priest in the Church of England. He became a well-known Bishop and was the author of several very readable and popular books including one, *The Paranormal* (2003), in which he made a convincing case for the many forms of extra-sensual perception.

The Spirit of God and the problem of what is a 'Just War'

'Thou shalt not kill' says the Law of Moses, which is common to the Jewish, Christian and Muslim faiths. Yet to war we all went in self-defence against a barbarous enemy, Nazi Germany. In the case of my aircrew and I, though we set out to kill, we prayed to God to bring us home safely from our missions. It was not long before we learned that there is no glory in war, but what made our tasks seem so worthwhile was our belief that they might shorten the ghastly conflict by a day or even by an hour. It was such simple thoughts as these that helped us to face the enemy metal in the right frame of mind.

The most helpful contribution that I have found to the question of what is the right approach to war as a Christian, was made by Archbishop Robert Runcie (1921–99) in his address in St Paul's Cathedral in 1982 at the memorial service for the dead in the Falklands War. He praised our armed forces for their bravery and lack of rancour against the enemy, but he asked the congregation also to remember the Argentinian dead and to pray for their families and parents. Then he said this about war and patriotism: *'War springs from the love and loyalty which should be offered to God being applied to some God-substitute, one of the most dangerous being nationalism'.*

These words upset the triumphalist members of the congregation, but I believe they have helped to change the nation's attitude to war, provided it is told the whole truth by its leaders. I believe also that the Archbishop was inspired to say them as the result of his own experiences in battle in World War II, during which he won a Military Cross for a particularly gallant action while he was a tank commander in the Scots Guards. I learned this from his friend the late Tony Tremlett, former Bishop of Dover. He told me that in the evening after that action Robert Runcie had come to see him in great distress. He had just been to see the charred bodies of the young Germans he had killed and was in despair as he believed that his murderous deed meant that he could no longer seek to be ordained in the Church after the war. Tony, who was padre to a battalion of Grenadier Guards, knew Robert well and calmed him down, but he knew that for years afterwards Robert Runcie was haunted by that memory and feeling of guilt.

Tony Tremlett's account reminded me of another very moving contribution to the way Christians should look at war. This was made by Nurse Edith Cavell, who had been condemned by the Germans to be shot in Brussels in 1915 for helping allied prisoners of war to escape. As she was leaving her prison cell after taking Holy Communion and was walking out to be executed, she said to the padre accompanying her: *'Patriotism is not enough. I must bear no ill-feelings towards anyone'*. Those words are now inscribed beneath her statute opposite the church of St Martin's-in-the-Field in Trafalgar Square in London.

An experience in the hands of Providence

In March 1945 I and my aircrew were caught in a cyclone on our way back from dropping supplies to secret agents near Singapore. After flying in thick clouds for four hours and being thrown all over the sky by immensely powerful air currents, we had no means of finding how far off course we had been blown. We were beyond the reach of any radio-direction beams and could not even estimate the wind speed and direction in the darkness. We had already been flying for 19 hours, having taken off from Ceylon (Sri Lanka). Our supply drop had been made an hour before we flew into the storm. This meant that the cyclonic winds of around 100 knots could have blown us hundreds of miles off our course for our landing strip on the Cocos-Keeling Islands. These lay 13 degrees to the south of the equator, half-way between Ceylon and Australia. Our only hope for estimating our position was if a gap in the clouds enabled us to use our sextant on the stars. We had only enough petrol lcft to last us for four more hours' flying time.

I prayed for the stars to come out and asked the navigator to prepare a graph of the altitude over the Cocos for the next few hours of the star Rigelkent in the Southern Cross. We could then use it to do what my Advanced Navigation course had taught me, which was to 'home on a star position line'. Meanwhile we had to fight violent air currents that made it very hard to control the aircraft. We were flung from one mountainous and seething cumulus cloud to another, which were being lit up by lightning like vast electric bulbs for what seemed to be several minutes at a time.

At last, with only 80 minutes' worth of petrol left, we broke out through the clouds into a brilliant starlit sky. The navigator quickly took sights on three stars and used them to plot our position on his chart. We could only hope that it was reasonably accurate, as the air was very bumpy and made the sextant's artificial horizon unreliable. I then asked for a course to a point on the star position line of Rigelkent that we had drawn on the chart and which went through the Cocos. In particular I asked that this position should be 50 nautical miles upwind of the estimated position of the islands. I thought that this would allow for errors in our star shots due to the bumpy conditions. I altered course for this position and after flying towards it for the necessary number of minutes, the navigator gave me a new course which, if our star-sights were accurate, should take us directly over the islands. However, when we had flown the estimated time to the Cocos from that position, we could not see any sign of the islands. I then told the crew that we now had to make a square search for the islands. This meant flying the first ten-mile leg of a square before turning at right angles and then going on increasing each leg of the square by another ten miles until we found the islands or ran out of petrol and had to ditch in the sea. They did not need me to spell out that this was the moment of truth for all of us.

We turned our aircraft, an American B-24 Mark 5 'Liberator', 90 degrees to port and then flew for three minutes before turning 90 degrees to starboard on the next leg of the square. We had been on this course for about three minutes when my mid-upper gunner called out: '*Light flashing on the starboard beam, probably 12–15 miles.*' We flew towards it. The light flashed 'CK', the Cocos call-sign. The stars had brought us home! I was too overcome with emotion and relief to answer the joyful shouting of my crew. I thanked God for bringing us home after we had flown for 23 hours and 40 minutes.

I then slept for ten hours and then sunned myself on the white coral sand and listened to the roar of the great ocean rollers as they crashed onto the reef a few hundred yards away. I felt spiritually uplifted and filled with awe, as I remembered how the light from the stars had guided us safely back home. That light had left the stars countless light-years ago, which made me realise more clearly than ever before that God's providence, in creating an orderly universe, had done so because

he had a purpose in his creation. I felt as though God himself had literally placed that star position line in my hand. All I had to do to get home safely to the Cocos was to have faith, keep my head and go by the book. Truly, as the seventeenth-century cartoon on our navigation manuals of a man using a sextant showed, '*Man is not lost!*'

I once told this story to a friend of ours in Sussex, Vice-Admiral Peter Dingemans, CB DSO, whom I knew had distinguished himself fighting his great ship HMS *Intrepid* in the Falklands War in 1982. His experiences there were in far more dangerous circumstances than mine on that flight to the Cocos in 1945. During our conversation he told me that he too had found strength through his faith during that war. He kindly gave me permission to quote his words about this in a letter. He wrote that '*on the first day of the landing 72 aircraft attacked the Amphibious Force in San Carlos Bay, and I could not have come through that time without my faith in God and my belief in the power of prayer*'.

The whole of life as a spiritual battle

Life is a spiritual battle because we are always being faced with demanding choices between what is right and what is wrong. This choice was made bravely by the Reverend David Wild, MBE MC, padre to the Oxford and Buckinghamshire Light Infantry, whose soldiers were made prisoners of war after using up all their ammunition defending the perimeter of Dunkirk in June 1940. I knew David well, as he had prepared me for my Confirmation. As a non-combatant he was entitled under the Hague Convention to be repatriated after his capture. He and his wife of only one year, Mary, had talked over this possibility before he had embarked for France. They had decided that his duty as padre was to stay with his men. As a result he spent four years in a prison camp in Poland. His main occupation there, apart from attending to the welfare of the Other Rank POWs, was to confront the German camp commanders whenever he found them breaking the Geneva Convention on the rights of prisoners of war. He did this with great success and at great personal risk and suffering.

After the war David's work in the camps was recognised by the award of an MBE and his bravery in tending the wounded in action before Dunkirk had won him a Military Cross. He returned to Eton as a housemaster and chaplain in 1946. On his retirement he wrote a book about his wartime experiences, using the notes he had made while he was a prisoner. This was still only a draft when in 1991 I sent him a copy of my first book. In his reply to this he sent me a copy of his manuscript and asked me if I could suggest a suitable title for it, because he felt that his own idea of *Memoir of an Army Padre in Prison* could be misinterpreted.

I read the manuscript with great pleasure and was convinced that it should be published. I wrote back and suggested that since the one great thing he had given his companions was hope, he might call his book *Prisoner of Hope*. This was a quotation from the Book of the Prophet Zechariah, who had encouraged the Israelite prisoners in Babylon by addressing them as '*Ye Prisoners of Hope*'. David and his publisher were delighted with my suggestion and the book went through at least two editions.

I happened to mention David's name when my wife Penelope and I were staying with friends in Dorset and met The Reverend and Mrs Colin Fox. Colin told me that he knew David's book well and that he himself had been an army chaplain. He then said that his own father had also been a padre during the war and had, unknown to everybody, kept a diary from the day his regiment landed in Normandy until the end of the war. Colin discovered it among his father's papers after his death. He was so moved by it that he had it printed for private circulation. He then sent me a copy and gave me permission to quote from it in this book:

The War Diary of an Army Padre in 1944–5

The Reverend George Fox, MC, was the Regimental Chaplain of the 8th Northumberland Fusiliers, which fought from Normandy to Germany as the 3rd Reconnaissance Regiment. Padre George began his diary on 16 June 1944:

'*5/6/44. Services were held in various areas and all of them very well attended, no longer is coercion needed, men come and find in things spiritual a consolation, even their wildest dreams in peace time could have told them that to the Church they would have to go.*

23/7/44. I had some very realistic services, we knelt and prayed at the altar, we left refreshed to face the world.

2/8/44. Three cars knocked out on Vire-Tichebrai Road, two killed, but too near enemy lines to get them; after three days the MO managed to reach them, one was burned beyond recognition, half out of the AFV and the other one, Trooper Opie, our star footballer, crushed on to the wheel – it was most difficult and unpleasant but we extracted their remains – as we undertook this task, the thought of a young life and futility of war impressed itself upon both of us – this method is wrong, these lives are needed to build the world. We shall be worse off after this show economically, morally and spiritually.

29/9/44. I took services with 'C' Squadron, a Holy Communion with their HQ, and short prayers with the troops guarding the canal – all these services are most impressive – if only the enthusiasm that is being shown now can be brought back to England, and men's energies centred around their Church. What a difference it could make to the Church and Country at large. For the first time many of these men have experienced something of Christ – religion is no longer something ethereal, but a reality, which plays such a great part in the happenings of daily life.

23/10/44. The last few days of life have been very hectic in contacting all my units. Yesterday I had perhaps one of the most impressive evening services I have ever held, this one was held in a barn with straw on either side, the men fixed an electric light in one corner, and from the candles on the altar we all worshipped God – God was there and refreshed we went away.

January 1945. I had to conduct three funerals, their bodies had been retrieved from the minefield, one man was in small pieces, and when wrapped in a blanket, one man could carry it . . . I was impressed by the RE officer who helped me with the bodies, the one who was in pieces he wanted to carry himself and place in the grave, he said "He is one of my men and I want to carry him, Padre" – such humaneness exists amongst all these men, they are in the midst of death throughout the day in lifting mines.

March 1945. After supper casualties came in, one man had been killed, a Sgt Rasworthy, he will be a great loss as he was one of my most ardent communicants, always willing to help. I buried him in the darkness at about midnight. As I stood over the trench with two sergeants from HQ I felt an amazing feeling of the Divine presence; across the road an ammunition dump was going up, tracer bullets soaring into the air, shells exploding, but yet Christ was near for a short time.

April 1st. Easter Sunday, what a wonderful day to spend in killing or being killed . . . It made me feel so depressed, the first time I had missed a service on that day. I went round the troops who were in the line and just reminded them of the day, they all reminisced about the good old days, what Church they used to attend etc.

On the morning of 4th May cease-fire came to the armies in North West Europe.'

Padre Fox was awarded the Military Cross for his work in the field and for his contribution to the morale of the regiment. Sadly his hopes for the future of the Church were not realised. The numbers in the congregations of the Anglican and Catholic Churches in England and elsewhere have been falling steadily. This is partly due to the way social life has changed.

In England fewer parents are introducing their children to the Bible or even having them baptised. The public education system is making a mess of what it calls 'RE'. Meanwhile increased wealth and the availability of a far greater variety of leisure activities have caused football, golf, TV and other such activities to take the place of an hour's church at week-ends.

Do the falling numbers in their congregations mean that the Churches have failed?

This question was put to Robert Runcie by the journalist Bernard Levin during an interview that was reported in *The Times* newspaper on 30 March 1987. This interview has not been mentioned in any of the biographies about Robert, which is a pity because, as usual, the Archbishop gave a most helpful and understanding reply. He told Bernard Levin that *'It depends from where you look at the Church, when you say it has failed. Saints have been nurtured in the parishes; it isn't the public debates in Church synods or about the ordination of women or even about the social and political implications of the Gospel that really advance the Kingdom of God. Far more people than you may imagine in comparison with the numbers in the pews, are motivated by Christian values as they support the nursing services, or the Welfare State, or create Amnesty International or Oxfam'.*

It can be seen from this last sentence that the Archbishop was drawing attention to the astonishing multitude of charitable schemes in this country and elsewhere which are a witness of how the Christian spirit is now in action. That is far more important than regular attendance at church. It demonstrates the fact that over the centuries Christian values have been absorbed into our Western way of life, like the successive strata in the formation of solid rock. Christian values have therefore become deeply ingrained in the whole structure of Western society regardless of whether people believe in God or not. Even so, this humanist approach could achieve so much more through the added strength that comes through faith and the Spirit.

Science and the Faith today

The absurd war fought by the Roman Catholic Church and traditionalists against the great scientific discoveries from the sixteenth century ended in 1958 when Pope Pius XII, in the last year of his life, declared that the 'Big Bang' theory of creation is in accord with the description in Genesis 1.3, when God said *'Let there be Light . . . and there was Light'.* That light was the Big Bang, when the new creation filled the void that had existed before and when only the Spirit of God moved above the waters.

Astro-physicists are still investigating the origins of the Universe and are reaching astonishing conclusions on the source of the planets and the basic star-dust that contained the essential elements for the creation of life.

Many more revolutionary discoveries will be made in this field in the twenty first century which the churches will be called upon to relate to the Scriptures and to show how they are relevant to God's spiritual plan for humankind. It was for this reason that Pope Pius XII's predecessor, Pius XI, at last declared that St Albert the Great, who died in 1280, *'had that rare and divine gift, scientific instinct, in the highest degree . . . he is exactly the saint whose example ought to inspire the present age'.*

In 1998 Pope John Paul II declared that the evidence of a host of scientific researches suggested that *Homo Sapiens,* who appeared about 100,000 years ago, may have originated from earlier forms of life. This suggestion, if confirmed by the Church, will require some adjustment in the age-old doctrine of Original Sin from Adam's disobedience.

How else could humankind be but sinful by nature, since the first living creatures from which we come were literally brought up in the primordial gutters of the earth? That was why God needed to send us his Son to transform so much that was imperfect in us and to give us the strength that can only come through faith and the Spirit of God.

It took nearly 140 years from the publication of Charles Darwin's *The Origin of Species* in 1859 for the evolutionary process to be acceptable to followers of most Churches, though scientists are far from being unanimous on how it happens. However there are still some teachers who refuse to accept the fossil evidence of forms of life millions of years ago or that the light from the stars has taken up to several millions of years to reach us. There are still some states in the USA where it is illegal to teach the subject of evolution in schools or universities.

The future of the world-wide Anglican Church

The Anglican Church represents about 70 millions, half of whom belong to African sees which are increasing rapidly in numbers. In Britain the task for the Anglican Church from 2003 under the new Archbishop of Canterbury, the scholarly, patient and wise Dr Rowan Williams, is to promote the spiritual understanding of the faith. The Archbishop is rightly making the debate on homosexuality subordinate to a broader goal of enlightenment and, with the aid of an understanding media, he may succeed in treating this subject as more of a social than a religious matter. Even so, there remains a danger that the Episcopalian Church in the USA, the independent American Province of the Anglican Communion, may decide to cut loose from the Anglican Church.

The great African sees of the Anglican Communion, especially the huge Nigerian one, may also eventually decide to go their own way. This would not be a disaster, but be more akin to the offspring of a family growing up and going out into the world, yet hopefully retaining a close spiritual relationship with the rest of the family. The African Churches in this family are perfectly capable of building an African style of worship that looks back to their own innate spirituality before the Christian missionaries came to them. These African provinces of the Anglican Communion already have their own heroes and heroines, like the Uganda martyrs of 1887 and Archbishop Janani Luwum in 1974. They can look up to the achievements of great African Christians such as the two Nobel Peace Prize winners, Archbishop Tutu and Nelson Mandela, while theirs are the fastest-growing churches in Africa.

Hope for the future in the New Churches!

Evidence of the existence of the innate desire for spiritual guidance and expression is found in the way the Pentecostal Churches are spreading and in the growing popularity of the Charismatics and their style of worshipping since the 1960s.

The Pentecostal Churches are made up of groups of Christians who emphasise the descent of the Holy Spirit at Pentecost and the continuing work of the Spirit. The movement, most prominent amongst the Afro-Asian communities in the USA, in the West Indies, in Africa and amongst West Indian and African immigrants to Britain, originated in the ministry in the USA of Charles Parker (1878–1925). He linked baptism to 'speaking in tongues' and he taught that the revival of the Spirit in his churches reflected a restoration of the gifts promised by

Christ. The worship in these churches is participatory in form. It involves vigorous music and chanting, hand-clapping and dancing, and raising of arms. There are many varieties of this Church, each one with its own individual style. The first Pentecostal World Conference was held in 1947 and the second one was held in Paris in 1949.

The Charismatic Movement first took shape in the Episcopal Church in the USA, growing out of the Pentecostals. The movement, which has spread to other Churches, aims to produce a new understanding of the Person and work of the Holy Spirit, leading to the 'baptism of the Spirit' and to 'being born anew'. This is what Jesus taught Nicodemus according to St John the Evangelist (see John 3.3–8).

Those working for this charismatic revival are especially successful in Africa, where their spiritual style matches the natural spiritual emotions aroused by the existing African religions. Thus by emphasising that the heart and the emotions should be as much engaged in worship as the head and the intellect, the missionaries win through to the souls of those they seek to convert, who are mostly illiterate. I have seen this work impressively with a very large congregation in a new church in the Kikuyu Reserve near Nairobi in Kenya.

It is difficult to define the membership of the Charismatic movement. It varies in degree from church to church but it is widespread all over the world and probably now covers about 350 millions, compared with an estimated 300 million in 1980. Their charismatic style and music has spread to both Protestant and Roman Catholic churches. It was praised by Pope Paul VI who in 1973 even celebrated a mass in the charismatic style in St Peter's in Rome.

The Ecumenical Movement or 'Churches Together'

There has been another spiritual revolution since World War II. Compared with the fear of 'Popery' and the disregard of the Roman Church that was taught to many an Anglican child between the two great wars, the relationship today is one of mutual attempts at cooperation and understanding. For example, in my own parish of Steyning in Sussex, as in most English parishes, a covenant has been signed by the clergy of the Anglican, Roman Catholic, Methodist, Baptist Churches and the embryo 'House Church', promising *'to do nothing separately that we could do together'*.

The ecumenical ideal has transformed attitudes and the whole approach to evangelism and relations between the Churches. There are still important differences between them, especially over what happens to the sacraments after their dedication at the Eucharist or Holy Communion. However one day, through the work of ARCIC, the Anglo-Catholic International Committee, it may even become possible for Catholics and Protestants to take the sacraments together, as it is already possible to do at funeral masses and weddings.

This ecumenical work seems temporarily to have reached a road-block over the Anglican and Methodist decisions to ordain women as priests. Archbishop Runcie met this in Rome on his last visit to Pope John-Paul in November 1989. However, in an unreported late-night interview on Independent Television on his return, he said that there was great hope for the future for achieving eventually *'a unity in all its rich diversity'*. It is significant therefore that Pope John Paul II used these same words during his visits to Poland and also to Paris when he apologised for the way the Catholic Church had persecuted the Lutherans in Poland and the Huguenots in France in the sixteenth and seventeenth centuries.

A complete union between all the Churches might be impossible, but a closer relationship moving towards a unity of purpose and a unity rich in all its diversity, might give the Churches just the stimulation they need. Whatever is done – and some advance will be made – it will involve some sacrifice, as an elderly Canon of the Roman Catholic cathedral in Arundel pointed out in a combined Churches service in Steyning a few years ago. He said that in order to move towards unity *'we would all have to give up some things that we hold most dear'*. Cardinal John Henry Newman would have relished this, because the lesson that he taught his Church was that to live is to change.

The Miracle of 'Alpha International' at Holy Trinity, Brompton

There has been one other remarkable positive development in bringing the Anglican and Roman Catholic Churches closer together through the support given to the 'Alpha Courses' by the Archbishop of Canterbury and Cardinal Murphy O'Connor, the Archbishop of Westminster. The Alpha courses, now run by Alpha International, were started in 1992 by the Revd Sandy Millar at the church of Holy Trinity, Brompton in London and they have been developed there by him and through the charismatic and popular publicist the Revd Nicky Gumbel. The evening courses, spread out over three weeks or so, are designed to attract young people after their working day. They have a social atmosphere and involve planned study with discussions afterwards. The discussions are wide-ranging. Their appeal to those seeking renewal of their faith or for sorting out doubts can be judged by the fact that whereas there were only five registered courses in 1992, more than 1,750,000 young people attended the courses in Britain and abroad in 2001. Each course helps many to find their faith.

In January 2002 more than 450 French church leaders, most of them Roman Catholics, attended the first French Alpha course in Paris with the full blessing of the French Catholic bishops. This took place in Paris at the church of St Honoré d'Eylau and included delegates from Belgium as well as France. More than 50 French parishes sent groups of six or more people. As well as the Roman Catholics there were also delegates from the Salvation Army, Baptist, Mennonite, Orthodox and Lutheran Churches.

The Alpha movement is now international and explains its educational and spiritual purpose in the most up-to-date style of literature, video films and pamphlets. This whole brilliant enterprise could be as significant for the future of evangelisation as was the equally devout approach of John and Charles Wesley's 'Bible Moths' and their first Methodist Societies. The numbers attending the Alpha courses are increasing each year and is spreading to many countries as a result of their popularity and their video films. This proves how much can be achieved by the work and spiritual inspiration of the clergy in one English parish. Some people may criticise Alpha for producing too rigid and limited an approach to belief, but this is to assume that the word of God always falls on stony ground. Instead, those who really benefit from Alpha are those who realise that it is only a beginning. As St Anselm taught 900 years ago, our spiritual journey lasts the whole of our lives.

A modern Saint in all but name – The Reverend 'Tubby' Clayton, CH MC DD (1895–1972)

The Revd Philip Bayard Clayton, CH, MC, DD, known to all affectionately as 'Tubby', founded 'Toc H' or 'Talbot House' in Poperinghe behind the trenches in Flanders in 1915. Toc H was a rest house that Tubby acquired for his soldiers so that they could have rest and a Christian atmosphere after being released for a few days from the fighting. He was filled with spiritual energy and love and had a charisma that inspired everyone he met with Christian charity and zeal. He not only inspired people with a strong Christian spirit, but in so-doing he also chose them to go out and help him to get many good works done.

We have seen in the Illustrated Calendar in Part VI of this book that many popular saints founded holy Orders of men and women to go out into the world. Tubby also did just that. He began to do this after 1918 by getting the friends he had made from all over the world at Poperinghe to set up Toc H clubs throughout the Commonwealth. Through these they enjoyed the comradeship they had found in the war and they supported innumerable charities whose activities ranged from one-day events to ones that established lasting good works. Wherever he saw a need for this kind of help, Tubby went into action.

One example of this is the way he set up Toc H units to serve seamen, a much-neglected set of men in those days. For this he needed to raise large sums of money. Tubby had a genius for doing this. For his seamen he went to the bosses of the shipping companies and the owners of the oil-tankers and simply told them his needs. They then gave him what he wanted and the material means to carry it out.

Tubby was not the sort of clergyman who could easily be fitted into a normal parish. He was himself a complete Christian organisation, faithful to the Church of England, but too independent a spirit to be made a bishop. As he was a popular national figure, they made him Vicar of All Hallows by the Tower, one of Sir Christopher Wren's most beautiful churches. On one side of him, therefore, Tubby had easy access to the financial resources of the City, while on the other, London's East End, he faced all the problems that widespread poverty and vice bring. *'Sin is advancing from the East'*, Tubby announced at one of his luncheons at 3 Trinity Square, to which a friend had invited me. We all stopped talking to listen to the appeal he was obviously going to make.

He wanted us to help him acquire a large ruined bomb-site and to turn it into a floodlit play-ground and games pitch for the youth of the area, who had nowhere to go in the evenings. I joined the others in offering my help and so became a regular guest at his lunches. We bought the site and got planning permission from the City Planning Department. That left us with the task of funding the work and managing the playing ground. By then Tubby, who had been doing another dozen or so charitable tasks, came and said he had got Princess Alexandra to be the playground's Patron and that with her support it would be easy for us to raise the funds we needed. Tubby then left us to it and went on working at his other schemes.

That was how Tubby worked, choosing his workers and giving them tasks and thus freeing himself for his nationwide and sometimes world-wide tasks. None of his schemes, here or in the USA or the Commonwealth, ever failed. Tubby was far too good a judge of men for that to happen. Also when he really was pressed for money and support, he just went to the top and contacted members of the Royal Family, the US Ambassador in London or the Pilgrim Trust and top people everywhere. For all this work King George V made him a Companion of Honour in 1936.

The most visible of Tubby's achievements now is the beautiful church of All Hallows, which had been completely destroyed by bombs in the war. His greatest problem there was how to replace Wren's beautiful and intricately designed tower and steeple. Tubby went to America through the Pilgrim Trust for this and in due course the whole structure, made of aluminium and a perfect replica of the original, was built in the US and installed by crane on All Hallows on Tower Hill.

The last time I saw Tubby was when he held a memorial service for a popular City Solicitor, Hugh Francis, CBE of Herbert Smith. Hugh was a very devout Christian and did his best to apply the gospel teaching to all the cases that were brought before him for his advice. Tubby ended his address for Hugh by saying: *'I suggest that you should all try and remember Hugh by thinking like him of the Gospel teaching whenever you are faced with a serious problem, or when perhaps you may be about to sack someone. Before you commit yourself therefore, take a walk round the block or come and pray here or withdraw yourself from the immediate pressures and prejudices of the world. Then ask God for advice.'*

Not long afterwards I had to interview a young clerk whom my office manager had reported as having broken one of our more important rules. Before having him up before me I asked myself what Tubby would have done with him in my place.

The young clerk had been bouncing very large cheques through his bank in an attempt to make money by stagging popular new issues of stock very heavily. The bank manager had complained. When I interviewed the lad I found out that he was genuinely ashamed. I also realised that he was very ambitious and was obviously in the wrong job as a clerk in the general office. So I decided to take a calculated risk and I asked him if he would swear never to break the rules again and would like to leave his no-future clerking job and move into one of the investment departments, where he could learn more about the business of making money. He jumped at the offer and having given me his word not to offend in that way ever again, I gave him the new job. He was an immediate success. I think that Tubby would have approved; one has to take risks as a leader (after all, Christ took a risk over us!).

Many years after I had retired, I learned that that young man had become a senior director of a very successful finance company. I laughed to think that he would never know that but for Tubby's words, his City career would have been blighted at the start.

The miracle of the survival and recovery of the Russian Orthodox Church

The recovery of the Russian Orthodox Church from the oblivion into which it was sent by the communists in 1927, is a miracle and a prime example that even total tyranny cannot suppress the Spirit. The Russian Church has always been more an arm of the state than has been the case elsewhere, but its prominence in public affairs, the size of its congregations today and the unashamed support by the younger generation, proves that persecution stimulates the faith and keeps it alive.

Christianity and the other World Faiths

In their publication *We Believe in God* in 1987, the Doctrine Commission of the Church of England stated that: *'The persistence of worship, prayer and lives of service and dedication in so many communities of faith, despite the powerful pressures and ideologies ranged against them, makes the debate about God still the most important question confronting humankind today'*.

This expresses an awareness and a willingness to enter into dialogue with other faiths that simply did not exist 60 years ago, when I first came face to face with the problems involved. This happened to me on a most unforgettable occasion, when my RAF squadron in India entertained the fighter pilots of Number One Royal Indian Air Force Squadron, who had been escorting and defending us as we dropped supplies of food, water and ammunition to the isolated garrison of Kohima in March 1944. Without the bravery and skill of those Hindu, Muslim and Sikh pilots, our casualties would have been very high.

The party took place at Alipore near Calcutta, where both our squadrons were being re-equipped after the battle. Towards the end of the evening, when we were discussing our personal experiences during the month-long battle, I summoned up enough courage to ask a Hindu pilot a question that had always intrigued me. I asked if he would tell me whether he or his friends used to pray before taking off to attack the enemy. He was not in the least offended and said: *'"I always prayed to Brahma, the Creator and also sometimes to his other identity, Vishnu the Preserver"'*. The Muslim squadron leader who was next to us then joined in the conversation. *'"I too always prayed and asked Allah, the creator and the merciful to bring me back"'*. A Sikh pilot with a magnificent pale blue Air Force turban then said that he always prayed to *'"Nam, the name of the Lord"'* and asked me to whom I prayed. I said that *'"I too prayed to the Lord, and asked him to bring me back, but not in the place of anyone else including any of you lot"'*.

My remark caused some laughter and then the Indian squadron leader leant forward and said: *'"What we have just discussed means that we all pray to the same God or to his Spirit, even if we do so under different names"'*. I then thanked them for being so frank and said: *'"This also means to me that, although we are all kept apart on earth by high walls which keep us away from each other's temples or churches, those walls do not reach three miles up into the sky where you boys risked your lives for us over Kohima!"'*. *'"Exactly"'* said the Muslim, *'"and that makes us all true brothers in arms, regardless of our faiths!"'*

This brief encounter can hardly be called a dialogue, but it changed completely my outlook on religion, and because of it I realised that the approach of our Churches was far too exclusive. These Indian pilots all believed that the Spirit of God had touched their faiths, as St Basil of Caesarea had taught over 1,600 years ago, a lesson which had been ignored or forgotten by the Church. This made me uncomfortable about my own faith for years until at last in 1962 Pope John XXIII announced at the Second Vatican Council that the seeds of the Spirit could be seen in all the world's faiths. There was therefore a way through the Spirit for all faiths to meet. This filled me with joy and I felt relieved of a terrible burden of doubt.

This enlightened approach to other faiths in the 1960s brought us hope. Since then the attitudes of Western Society to those of other faiths and other races seemed to be improving until the surge of ruthless politically minded Imams began to preach a doctrine of hating the West in their *Madrasas*. This teaching is quite alien to the Muslim faith, but it appeals to an impoverished and unemployed generation of youths seeking a purpose in life. In the debate about God the greatest question therefore is how can we break this chain of hate, to solve the dichotomy of contrasting faiths, symbolised opposite in the picture of Hagia Sophia, one of the earliest and greatest of Christian churches, and subsequently a mosque.

Hagia Sophia

Rearmament then taught them of the need to build a bridge over the gap between their peoples and cultures. By coming together in a truce this group of former enemies learned how like each other they were. Through that a mutual respect developed and peace came at least to part of the Lebanon.

They were not alone in their new-found way of thinking, as I knew from my own experience with my Hindu, Muslim and Sikh fighter pilots after the Battle of Kohima. It is because of this and great events like the collapse of the Communist regimes in Eastern Europe, that I am convinced that sometime in this new century the tide will turn against the terrorism backed by fanatics and evil-minded politicians posing as religious leaders. I believe in this victory of right over wrong and of faith over sinfulness and of a progressive society over the narrow vision of a fanatical terrorist culture.

'Breaking the Chain of Hate' is in fact the title of a pamphlet issued by what was at first called the 'Oxford Movement' and then as 'Moral Rearmament', based in Caux above Lake Geneva. It is now developing a mission aimed at 'Initiatives of Change' for moral and spiritual renewal. The pamphlet was issued to announce the mission of four men from the Lebanon, two Muslims and two Christians. They came to London to tell large public meetings how and why they, who had been ardent fighters for their respective Christian and Muslim militias, had at last realised the error of their ways. They now realised they worshipped the same God and that their cultures did not teach them to go out and kill, as they had been doing in the terrible war in the Lebanon for the past 20 years and more. A visit to Caux and Moral

We know that in Britain today practising Christians, Jews, Muslims, Sikhs and Hindus alike are all minorities. Yet we have far more in common in our social aims and religious beliefs than we have that divides us. This should enable us to build a multi-faith society to which all faiths are able to contribute. This is a worthy and essential spiritual objective that lies behind that famous saying of the Prince of Wales, that

Eternal Father, source of Life and Light whose Love extends to all people, all creatures, all things: grant us that Reverence for Life which becomes those who believe in you, lest we despise it, degrade it, or come callously to destroy it. Father let us save it, secure it and sanctify it after the example of your Son Jesus Christ Our Lord. Robert Runcie.

'Grant us reverence for life'.

if he is called upon to reign, he would welcome a change in the title given to our sovereigns in the reign of King Henry VIII which would make him *'Defender of all faiths'* rather than just the Christian faith.

'Grant us reverence for life'

Another saying of the Prince of Wales also points out the spiritual effort that all people of good will and of all faiths need to share. In a speech to the American Architects' Association in February 1990 he expressed his hope that *'we might strive for an age of reverence – reverence for what gave us life and for the fragile world we live in'*.

I first came across these words *'Grant us reverence for life'* when I read them in the autobiography of the great medical missionary, organist and theologian Albert Schweitzer (1875–1965). He described how they came into his mind as he was being paddled in a canoe up the Ogowe river in Gabon to tend a sick patient. He said that the words came to him unsought as he thought about Christ's teaching about love, while at the same time gazing at the beautiful primordial scene of forest and animal and bird-life on both banks of the river. This suddenly made him realise that to the Creator, all life is sacred and should be revered.

This thought and that phrase helped him to sum up for himself his own observations of life and to find how close they were to his religious convictions. Thus for Schweitzer 'reverence for life' became a way of life – love in action on a cosmic scale. Albert Schweitzer's words may have given Archbishop Robert Runcie the inspiration for the prayer that he gave me permission to print and illustrate in my first book, *The Way to the Kingdom*:

'Eternal Father, source of life and light, whose love extends to all people, all creatures, all things; Grant us that Reverence for Life which comes to those who believe in you, lest we despise it, degrade it or come callously to destroy it. Rather let us save it, cure it, sanctify it after the example of your Son Jesus Christ, Our Lord'.

CONCLUSIONS

As the stories of *The Friends of God* show, the Spirit of God is always with us. Therefore frequent and often wilful historical misinterpretation does not destroy my conviction that God has a purpose for his creation. Humanity can and will question the reasons for this but they will never discover a finite answer. We can only accept his wonderful grace and believe in God.

We saw in the Calendar that saints and faithful witnesses will always come forward, so we do not need to be afraid or abandon hope if a Christian asks *'How long have we got?'* The answer is that we are now living a mere 70 generations after the time of Christ and 1,000 generations from the arrival of Homo Sapiens. If our physicists and astronomers are right, our World still has three or four billion years to exist. That means that some 100 million generations of our race are still to pass by. We are therefore even now probably still only at the very beginning of true religious understanding. We need to remember this with humility whenever we are tempted to pass judgement on any new discovery or development in the universal Church which differs from traditional ways.

Thus it is worth remembering how near we are to the time when Christ walked among us and also how far from the end of Earth's existence as we seek a sensible perspective for our lives and our theological debates. That is why I do not fear for the future of our faith, even though there will be many upheavals over the centuries to come that will change the World completely, as seas rise, mountains wear away, and the great tectonic forces cause continents to drift and new mountain ranges to arise. As Jesus himself said: *'Heaven and Earth may pass away, but my words will not pass away'*.

There is, in fact, much in recent books on the faith to support this optimism. Professor Rcvd Keith Ward, recently retired as the Regius Professor of Divinity at Oxford University, has written in his book *The Case for Religion* (2004): *'God is known as a transforming power throughout the world, but in varying degrees and in different ways.'* In an interview with Mary Wakefield, which was published in *The Spectator* on 11 September 2004, he said that *'the most hopeful sign for the future is that religious experience is more common than we realised. Everybody admits to having had a religious experience of some sort . . . and I've never met a world-class physicist who doesn't think there's more to the universe than just atoms bumping together; something mind-like is at work, some intelligence.'* As suggested in the introduction to the Holy Spirit at the start of this book this is a truth that was at work in the caves even before history began. The Spirit of God is not going to leave us now particularly since, as Pope John XXIII proclaimed at the Second Vatican Council, *'the seed of the Spirit can be seen at work in all faiths today'*.

There is increasing evidence of converging spirituality between the world's religions. They all share some fundamental beliefs. Jews, Christians and Muslims, for example, all trace their faith back to Abraham. Christians and Muslims revere the Virgin Mary. The Koran quotes God as saying of the Virgin that *'we sent our spirit into her womb'* and that Jesus was born as a sign to the world. There are therefore solid grounds for each of the world's great faiths to enter into constructive dialogues with each other.

This also means that the Friends of God, the faithful witnesses in the future, may come from all faiths. However long it may take, however patient we must be, the Kingdom of God on earth will one day be achieved, and Jesus' prophesy will be fulfilled: *'there shall be one flock and one Shepherd'* (John 10.16). It will however need to be a faith that, while being rich in its diversity, will also be contained in a glorious unity, one in which clergy, scientists, artists and others will be inspired by the Spirit of God to build together a new and perfect creation. So let us 'give thanks to God' for all his gifts.

Give thanks to God

BIBLIOGRAPHY

ENCYCLOPAEDIAS & DICTIONARIES

The Cambridge Companion to Christian Doctrine.
Cambridge University Press, 1995.

Encyclopedia Britannica. Encylopedia Britannica Corporation, 2003.

Fox's Book of Martyrs. Zondervan, 1978.

The Oxford Companion to Christian Thought.
Oxford University Press, 2000.

The Oxford Dictionary of Saints. Oxford University Press, 2004.

The Oxford History of Islam. Oxford University Press, 2000.

The Penguin Dictionary of Saints. Penguin, 1996.

EARLY CHRISTIAN WRITINGS

Smith, Dr William and Wace, Dr Henry, *The Dictionary of Christian Biography, Volumes 1–4.* John Murray, 1877, 1880, 1882, 1887.

PUBLICATIONS OF THE DOCTRINE COMMISSION OF THE CHURCH OF ENGLAND

The Nature of Christian Belief (A statement by the House of Bishops of the General Synod of the Church of England, 1986.)

We Believe in God. Church House Publishing, 1987.

We Believe in the Holy Spirit. Church House Publishing, 1991.

THE MAKING OF SAINTS, MYSTICISM AND THE PARANORMAL

Armstrong, Kazren, *The English Mystics of the Fourteenth Century.*
Kyle Cathie, 1991.

Beevers, John, *Autobiography of St Theresa of Lisieux.* Doubleday, 1989.

Clement, Olivier, *The Roots of Christian Mysticism.* New City Press, 1993.

Duffy, Eamon, *Saints and Sinners: a History of the Popes.*
Yale University Press, 1997.

Maddocks, Morris, *The Vision of Dorothy Kerin.*
Hodder & Stoughton, 1991.

Montefiore, Bishop Hugh, *The Paranormal.* Upfront Publishing, 2002.

Obbard, Elizabeth Ruth (ed.), *Medieval Women Mystics.*
New City Press, 1995.

St Teresa of Avila, *The Interior Castle.* E. J. Dwyer, 1980.

St Teresa of Avila, *The Way of Perfection.* E. J. Dwyer, 1984.

Taylor, John V. (Bishop of Winchester), *The Go-Between God: The Holy Spirit and the Christian Mission.* SCM, 1972.

Woodward, Kenneth L., *Making Saints.* Chatto and Windus, 1991.

HISTORIES

Fletcher, Richard, *The Conversion of Europe, from Paganism to Christianity, 321–1386.* Harper Collins, 1997

Julius, John, *Byzantium*. Penguin, 1988.

Mundy, John H., *Europe in the Middle Ages, 1150–1309*. Longman, 1973.

Runciman, Sir Steven, *History of the Crusades, Volumes 1–3*. Cambridge University Press, 1951–54.

St Gregory of Tours, *History of the Francs*.

Sordi, Marta, *The Christians and the Roman Empire*. Routledge, 1988.

Ward, Philip, *The History of the Church, Volumes 1–3*. Shead and Ward, 1952.

THEOLOGY

Barton, Stephen and Stanton, Graham (eds), *Resurrection*. SCM Press, 1994.

Carmignac, Jean, *La Naissance des Évangiles Synoptiques*. Éditions Francois Xavier de Guibert, 1995.

Guitton, Jean, *Portrait de Monsieur Pouget*. Gallimard, 1941.

Holroyd, Stuart, *Gnosticism*. Element Books, 1996.

Kung, Hans, *Credo*. SCM Press, 1993.

Nicholl, Donald, *Holiness*. Darton, Longman and Todd, 1981.

Paget, Elaine, *The Gnostic Gospels*. Weidenfeld and Nicolson, 1979.

Pope John Paul II, *Crossing the Threshold of Hope*. Knopf, 1994.

Strange, Roderick, *The Catholic Faith*. Oxford University Press, 1986.

Thiede, Professor Revd Carsten Peter and D'Ancona, Matthew, *The Jesus Papyrus*. Weidenfeld and Nicolson, 1996.

Tresmontant, Claude, *Enquête sur L'Apocalypse*. Éditions Francois Xavier de Guibert, 1995.

Tresmontant, Claude, *Problèmes de Notre Temps*. Éditions Francois Xavier de Guibert, 1991.

Wiles, Professor Maurice, *God's Action in the World*. Xpress Reprints, 1993.

Wiles, Professor Maurice, *Remaking of Christian Doctrine*. Xpress Reprints, 1994.

Wilson, A.N., *Jesus*. Sinclair-Stevenson, 1992.

Wilson, A.N., *Paul: The Mind of the Apostle*. Sinclair-Stevenson, 1997.

Wright, N.T., *The New Testament and the People of God*. SPCK, 1992.

Wright, N.T., *Jesus and the Victory of God*. SPCK, 1996.

Wright, N.T., *What Saint Paul Really Said*. SPCK, 2000.

CHRISTIAN ART

Borchegrave, Helen de, *A Journey into Christian Art*. Lion, 1999.

Talbot-Rice, D., *The Beginnings of Christian Art*. Hodder & Stoughton, 1957.

Temple, Richard, *Icons and the Mystical Origins of Christianity*. Element Books, 1990.

BOOKS WHICH CONTRIBUTED MOST TO PART VII

Barrington-Ward, Bishop Simon, *Why God?* Lion, 1997.

Barrington-Ward, Bishop Simon, *The Jesus Prayer*.
Bible Reading Fellowship, 1996.

Carey, Dr George, *The Gate of Glory*. Hodder & Stoughton, 1992.

Carey, Dr George, *Spiritual Journey*. Continuum, 1994.

Cupitt, Revd Don, *After God*. Weidenfeld and Nicolson, 1997.

Cupitt, Revd Don, *The Sea of Faith*. SCM Press, 1984.

Dante Alighieri, *The Divine Comedy, Volumes 1–3*.
(Translated and with a commentary by Dorothy Sayers.) Penguin, 1995.

Gumbel, Nicky, *A Life Worth Living*. Kingsway Publications, 1994.

Hart, Ellen, *Man Born to Live: The Life and Work of Jean Henri Dunant, Founder of the Red Cross*. Gollancz, 1953.

Montefiore, Bishop Hugh, *O God, What Next?* Hodder & Stoughton, 1995.

Pascal, Blaise, *Pensées*. Penguin, 1995.

Sachs, Jonathan, *Faith in the Future*. Darton, Longman and Todd, 1995.

Schweitzer, Albert, *Out of my Life and Thought*. Allen and Unwin, 1964.

Seaver, George, *Albert Schweitzer: The Man and His Mind*.
A & C Black, 1948.

Ward, Professor Keith, *A Vision to Pursue: Beyond the Crisis in Christianity*.
SCM Press, 1991.

Ward, Professor Keith, *The Case for Religion*. One World Publications, 2004.

USEFUL BIOGRAPHIES WRITTEN SINCE 1989

Ackroyd, Peter, *The Life of Thomas More*. Vintage, 1999.

Boulay, Shirley du, *Teresa of Avila*. Hodder & Stoughton, 1992.

Clark, Mary T., *Augustine*. Geoffrey Chapman, 1994.

Copleston, F. C., *Aquinas*. Penguin, 1991.

Daniel, David, *William Tyndale*. Yale University Press, 1994.

Evans, G. R., *St Anselm*. Geoffrey Chapman, 1989.

Gilley, Sheridan, *Newman and his Age*. Darton, Longman and Todd, 1990.

Hastings, Adrian, *Robert Runcie*. Mowbray, 1991.

Hattersley, Roy, *Blood and Fire: William and Catherine Booth and their Salvation Army*. Little, Brown, 1999.

Hurn, Adrian, *Francis of Assisi*. Chatto and Windus, 2000.

MacCulloch, Diarmid, *Thomas Cranmer*. Yale University Press, 1996.

Marsden, George M., *Jonathan Edwards: A Life*. Yale University Press, 2003.

Spink, Kathryn, *Mother Teresa*. Harper Collins, 1997.

Wills, Garry, *St Augustine*. Weidenfeld and Nicolson, 1999.

INDEX

B

C

D

E

F

G

WILLIBRORD, *St:* 7 November
WILLIGIS, *St:* 23 February
WINEBALD, *St:* 18 December
WINEFRIDE, *St:* 3 November
WINNOC, *St:* 6 November
WINWALOE, *St:* 3 March
WITHBURGA, *St:* 17 March
WOLFGANG *of REGENSBURG, St:* 31 October
WOLSEY, Thomas (Cardinal and Chancellor): 307, 314
WULFSTAN, *St:* 19 January
WYCLIFFE, John (Bishop, reformer and translator of the
   Bible into English): 306

X, Y, Z

XAVIER, *Francis, St:* 3 December

YVES, *St: See under Ives, St*

ZACHARIAS *(Pope), St:* 22 March
ZACHARY *and ELIZABETH, Sts:* 5 November
ZADONSK, *St: See under Tikhon of Zadonsk, St*
ZENO, *St:* 12 April
ZWINGLI (reformer): 311

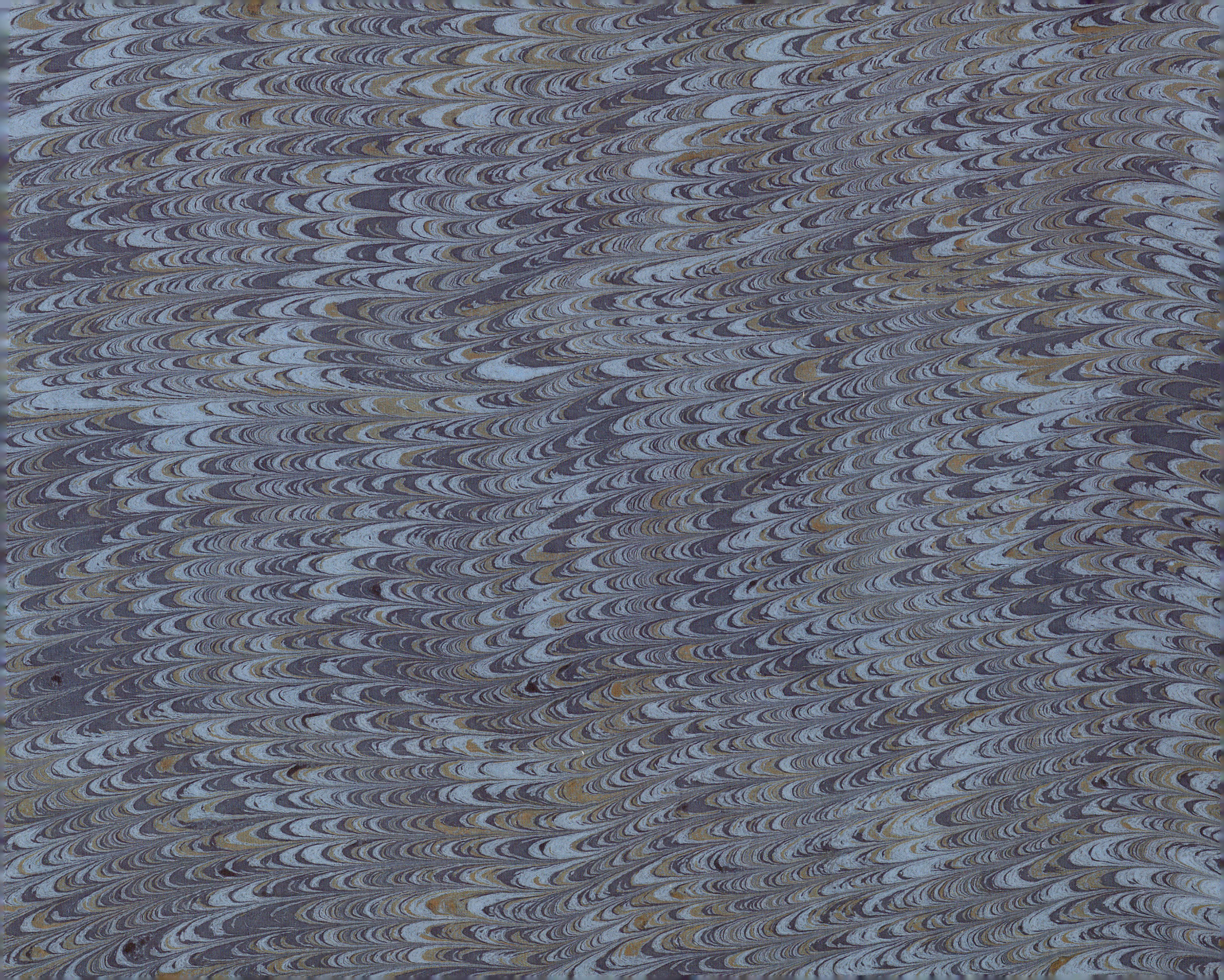

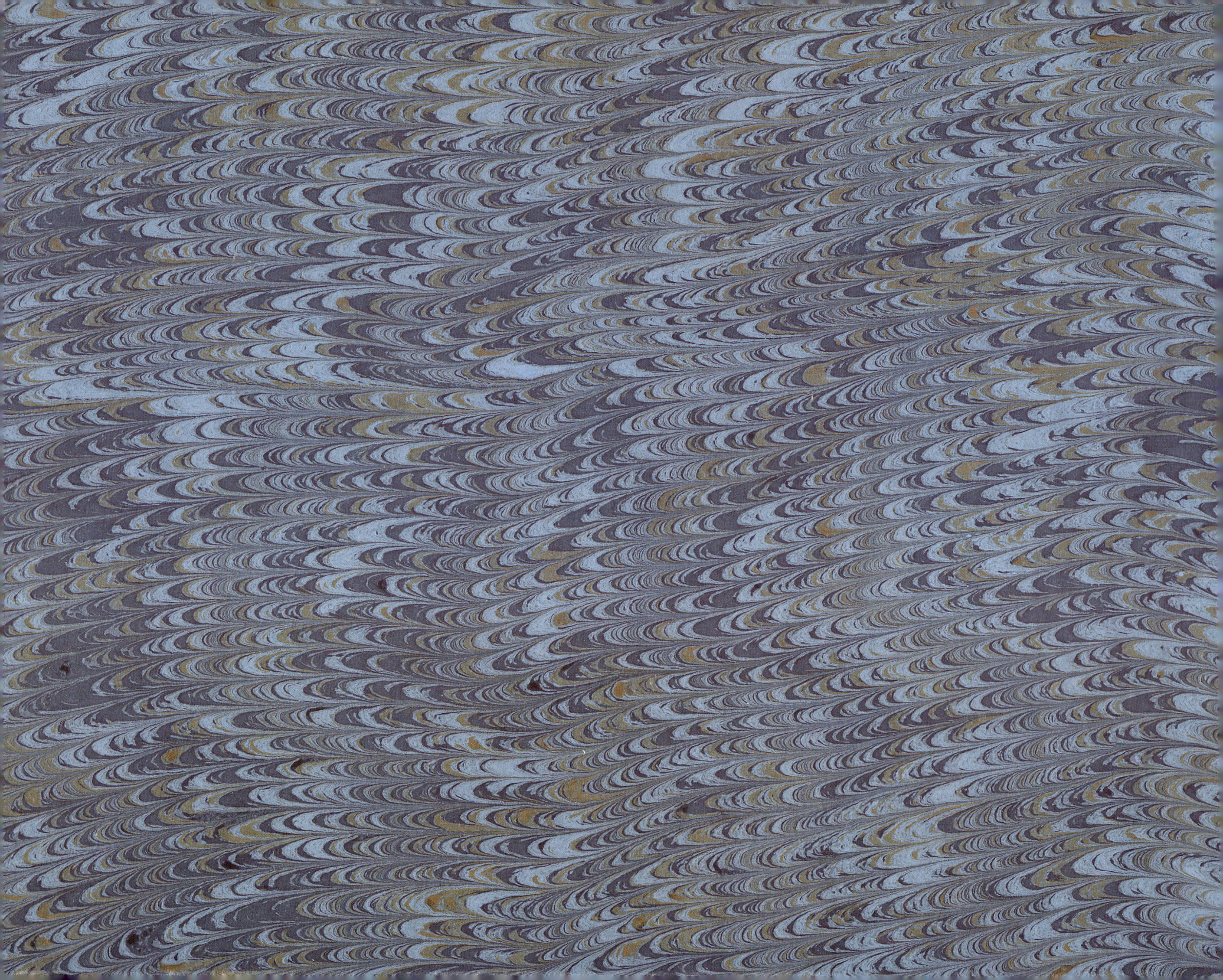